OCR
Psychology

Alan Bainbridge | William Collier | Sandra Latham | Sarah Middleton | Bryan Saunders | Series Editor: Fiona Lintern

Official Publisher Partnership

Heinemann is an imprint of Pearson Education Limited, a company incorporated in England and Wales, having its registered office at Edinburgh Gate, Harlow, Essex, CM20 2JE. Registered company number: 872828

www.heinemann.co.uk

Heinemann is a registered trademark of Pearson Education Limited

Text © Alan Bainbridge, William Collier, Sandra Latham, Sarah Middleton, Bryan Saunders and Fiona Lintern

First published 2008

12 11 10

10 9 8 7 6 5 4

British Library Cataloguing in Publication Data is available from the British Library on request.

ISBN 978 0 435806 93 4

Edited by Jane Anson
Designed by Hicks Design
Typeset by Phoenix Photosetting
Original illustrations © Pearson Education Limited 2008
Illustrated by Asa Andersson, Graham White & Phoenix Photosetting
Picture research by Zooid Pictures
Printed in China (SWTC/04)

Contents

Websites

There are links to relevant websites in this book. In order to ensure that the links are up to date, that the links work, and that the sites are not inadvertently linked to sites that could be considered offensive, we have made the links available on the Heinemann website at www.heinemann.co.uk/hotlinks. When you access the site, the express code is 6934.

Acknowledgements

The authors and publisher would like to thank the following individuals and organisations for permission to reproduce material in the book.

Photographs

Page 6 67photo/Alamy; Page 13 Hulton-Deutsch Collection/CORB/Corbis UK Ltd.; Page 20 Mark Harmel/Alamy; Page 25 David Fisher/Rex Features; Page 26 Associated Press/PA Photos; Page 27 Charlie Frowd/ABM/www.evofit.co.uk; Page 64 Moodboard/Corbis UK Ltd.; Kristy-Anne Glubish/Design Pic/Corbis UK Ltd.; Page 70 Photolibrary Group; Page 77 JUPITERIMAGES/Creatas/Alamy; Page 86 Department for Transport; Page 92 Funhaler/Clinical Cell Culture; Page 100 JUPITERIMAGES/Comstock Images/Alamy; Page 103 Charlie Newham/Alamy; Page 109 Science Museum/Science & Society Picture Library; Page 127 Digital Vision; Page 158 Steve Coleman/Stone/Getty Images; Page 163 Lew Merrim/Science Photo Library; Page 185 Marc Atkins/Ama/Corbis UK Ltd.; Page 196 Jonathan Goldberg/Alamy; Page 210 Eric Lalmand/Epa/Corbis UK Ltd.; Page 234 Brigitte Sporrer/Zefa/Corbis UK Ltd.; Page 237 Bubbles Photolibrary/Alamy; Page 248 JUPITERIMAGES/BananaStock/Alamy; Page 260 Tom Grill/Corbis UK Ltd.; Page 264 Gideon Mendel/Corbis UK Ltd.

Artwork and text

Page 10 Table showing age of first conviction Farrington et.al. Home Office findings no. 281 (2006) *Criminal Careers and Life Success*, available at http://www.homeoffice.gov.uk/rds/pdfs06/r281.pdf Crown Copyright material is reproduced with the permission of the Controller Office of Public Sector Information (OPSI). Page 11 Principles of Theory of Differential Association E. H. Sutherland (1947) *Principles of Criminology*, PA: Lippincott, Williams & Wilkins, pp.75–77. Page 52 Statistics on majority influence W. F. Abbott and J. Batt (1999) *A Handbook of Jury Research*, PA: Ali-Aba. Page 56 Statistics on reoffending Prison Reform Trust. Page 56 Statistics on depression/suicide risk in prisons Howard League for Penal Reform. Page 64 Ethnicity of defendants and victims Death Penalty Information Center. Page 86 Statistics on drink-driving *Alcohol Misuse 2006: Campaign Evaluation*, chapter 3, available at http://www.scotland.gov.uk/Publications/2007/08/03114725/5 Crown Copyright material is reproduced with the permission of the Controller Office of Public Sector Information (OPSI). Page 94 Statistics on stress Health and Safety Commission, *Health and Safety Statistics 2005/06*, available at http://www.hse.gov.uk/statistics/overall/hssh0506.pdf Crown Copyright material is reproduced with the permission of the Controller Office of Public Sector Information (OPSI). Page 94 Statistics on working days lost due to stress Health and Safety Executive, *Revitalising Health and Safety*, available at http://www.hse.gov.uk/costs/ill_health_costs/ill_health_costs_intro.asp Crown Copyright material is reproduced with the permission of the Controller Office of Public Sector Information (OPSI). Page 97 Extract from Hassles and Uplift Scale A. D. Kanner, J. Coyne, C. Schaefer and R. Lazarus (1981) 'Comparison of two modes of stress measurement', *Journal of Behavioural Medicine* 4(1). Page 101 Social Readjustment Rating Scale Published in *Journal of Psychosomatic Research* vol. 11 T. H. Homes and R. H. Rahe The Social Readjustment Rating Scale pp.213–18. Copyright Elsevier 1967. Page 123 Statistics for neurotic disorders National Statistics, *Mental Health*, available at http://www.statistics.gov.uk/cci/nugget.asp?id=1333. Crown Copyright material is reproduced with the permission of the Controller Office of Public Sector Information (OPSI). Pages 123–6 *DSM-IV* classifications American Psychiatric Association and *ICD-10* classifications World Health Organisation. Page 150 Definition of sport Australian Sports Commission. Page 155 Eysenck's Personality Dimensions Published in *Personality and Individual Differences: A Natural Science Approach*, Plenum, New York 1985 H. J. Eysenck and M. W. Eysenck. With kind permission of Springer Science and Business Media. Page 165 Sport Orientation Questionnaire D. L. Gill and T. E. Deeter (1988) 'Development of the Sport Orientation Questionnaire', *Research Quarterly for Exercise and Sport*, 59(3), 196–202. Page 167 Apparatus for the 'dancing mice' study and Partial copy of graph showing results of study R. M. Yerkes J. D. Dodson (1908) 'The relationship of strength of stimulus to rapidity of habit formation', *Journal of Comparative Neurology and Psychology*, 18, 459–82. Reprinted with permission of Wiley-Liss, Inc. a subsidiary of John Wiley & Sons, Inc. Pages 174–5 Sport Competition Anxiety Test (SCAT) and Analysis R. Martens (1977) *Sport Competition Anxiety Test*, Champaign, IL: Human Kinetics. Page 176 Competitive State Anxiety Inventory-2 (CSAI-2) R. Martens, D. Burton, R. S. Vealey, L. A. Bump and D. Smith (1990) 'Development and validation of the competitive state anxiety inventory – 2', in R. Martens, R. S. Vealey and D. Burton (Eds) *Competitive Anxiety in Sport*, Champaign, IL: Human Kinetics Books. Page 180 Diagram showing sport-specific self-confidence R. S. Vealey (1986) 'Conceptualisation of sport-confidence and comptitive orientation', *Journal of Sport and Exercise Psychology* 8(3), 221–46. Page187 Cohesiveness in sport groups A. V. Carron (1982) 'Cohesiveness in sports groups: interpretations and considerations', *Journal of Sport and Exercise Psychology*, 4, 123–38. Page 189 Graph to show level of response in the alone, mere presence and audience conditions N. B. Cottrell, D. L. Wack, G. J. Sekerak and R. H. Rittle, 'Social facilitation of dominant responses by presence of others', *Journal of Personality and Social Psychology*, 9, 245–50, 1968. American Psychological Association, reprinted with permission. Page 190 Diagram showing layout of 'cockroach run' R. B. Zajonc, A. Heingartner and E. M. Herman, 'Social enhancement and impairment of performance in the cockroach', *Journal of Personality and Social Psychology*, 13(2), 83–92, 1969. American Psychological Association, reprinted with permission. Page 191 Percentage of games won by home teams B. Schwartz and S. F. Barsky (1977) 'The home advantage', *Social Forces* 55(3), 641–61. Copyright © 1977 by the University of North Carolina Press. Used by permission of the publisher www.uncpress.unc.edu. Page 204 Profile of mood states W. P. Morgan (1979) 'Prediction of performance in athletics', in P. Klavora and J. V. Daniel (eds) *Coach, Athlete and the Sport Psychologist*, Toronto: University of Toronto, pp.173–86/F. J. Nagle, W. P. Morgan, R. O. Hellickson, R. C. Serfass and J. F. Alexander (1975) 'Spotting success traits in Olympic contenders', *Physician Sportsmed*, 3, 31–34. Page 207 Social Physique Anxiety Scale E. A. Hart, M. R. Leary and W. J. Rejeski (1989) 'The measurement of social physique anxiety', *Journal of Sport and Exercise Psychology*, 11, 94–104. Page 209 Changes from baseline on three competition lifts C. Maganaris, D. Collins and M. Sharp (2000) 'Expectancy effects and strength training: do steroids make a difference?', *The Sport Psychologist*, 14(3), 272–8.

Introduction

OCR A2 Psychology focuses on applied psychology and on approaches and research methods in psychology.

The first A2 unit is *Options in Applied Psychology* (G543) and is concerned with the application of psychological theories and research to aspects of the real world. The four areas of applied psychology covered in the OCR specification are as follows.

Forensic Psychology

This option begins by examining some of the influences that psychologists have used to explain criminal behaviour, such as family and other learning influences and the role of biological factors. The option continues by examining how psychology can inform the investigative process, methods of interviewing, factors influencing witnesses, detecting lies and creating an offender profile. You will also study how psychology can inform behaviour in the courtroom by helping us to understand the numerous influences on the jury's decision-making process. Finally, this option will examine the ways in which psychology can inform the penal system by studying research into the effects of imprisonment, alternatives to imprisonment and a variety of treatment programmes.

Health and Clinical Psychology

This option begins by examining the factors that influence our lifestyles. This includes a study of theories of health belief, research into health promotion and reasons for non-adherence to medical regimes. Secondly this option examines the topic of stress: the causes of stress, ways of measuring stress and techniques for managing stress. This option then focuses on clinical psychology. Dysfunctional behaviour is difficult to define and this section examines the ways in which mental-health problems have been defined and diagnosed. There is also an examination of three major theoretical approaches to explaining and treating dysfunctional behaviour and these are the biological,

behavioural and cognitive approaches. Finally you will study the characteristics of some mental-health disorders. You will need to know about one of these disorders in detail and be able to describe how this disorder has been explained and how it can be treated.

Sport and Exercise Psychology

This option begins with an examination of individual factors relevant to the study of sport. These include personality factors, aggression and motivation. The option then examines the key issues of arousal, anxiety and self-confidence within a sporting context. You will also study social psychological factors that can be applied to sport, such as group cohesion, audience effects, leadership and coaching. Finally this option examines exercise psychology, and this section looks at the relationship between exercise and physical disorders and the relationship between exercise and mental health. There is also an examination of key issues with the topic of exercise sport, including burnout and withdrawal, body image in sport and drug abuse in sport.

Psychology of Education

This option begins by looking at the key theories relevant to teaching and learning, including stage theories such as that of Piaget, and behaviourist models. You will also examine personal approaches to learning, such as different learning strategies and differences in cognitive style. There is then an examination of ways in which appropriate educational behaviours can be encouraged. This includes the study of motivation, techniques for encouraging educational engagement and student beliefs and expectations. The third section of this option focuses on the social world of teaching and learning, and examines the importance of social and personal development as well as student–student social interactions and student–teacher social interactions. The final section looks at dealing with diversity and concentrates on how students can reach their educational potential. Here you will study how to deal with additional needs (remedial support, gifted and talented pupils) as well as considering issues around enabling minority ethnic groups.

You will study two of these areas and will then sit a 1.5-hour examination on these options. There is plenty of support through the Exam Café sections of the book, which show you exactly what the examiners are looking for. However, as you are studying these areas you should remember the skills that you learned at AS. It is important to read critically and to evaluate the theories and research that you have studied. At AS level you did this for individual studies. At A2 level it is still important to do this, but you should also try to consider the whole body of research in relation to the applied topic area.

The specification suggests studies and research relevant to each of the subsections in the options. In most cases we have described and discussed the suggested studies. However, in a few cases we have also included additional research or have replaced the suggested study with a more appropriate or more up-to-date piece of research. Where a substitution has been made an explanation has been given.

The second A2 unit is called *Approaches and Research Methods in Psychology* (G544) and is divided into two sections.

The first section is the research methods section, and in the examination you will be asked to design a piece of research. You will be given a short passage setting the context and the topic for the research and will then be asked specific questions relating to the way you would conduct this research. You will have covered a great deal of research methodology in the AS course and it is important to draw on this and to consider methodological issues throughout the A2 course. The more practical experience you have of designing research and collecting and analysing data, the better.

The second section covers approaches, perspectives, methods, issues and debates. Again, some of these areas will be familiar to you from the AS course, although some are new. In this section you are expected to consider approaches etc. that arise throughout the AS and A2 courses and these will continue to be important should you choose to continue your study of psychology to degree level. For example, you

should have a good understanding of the different approaches and perspectives in psychology, as well as issues such as ethics, ecological validity and qualitative and quantitative data. The themes identified in the specification include determinism and free will, reductionism and holism, nature–nurture and psychology as a science. It is important to consider these issues and debates throughout the whole A2 course. The more you are able to discuss these issues and debates with your fellow students, the more you will come to understand them. Remember that psychology is about theories and that it attempts to explain human behaviour. Always ask yourself whether the explanations are supported by the evidence – be critical, ask questions and above all, think about the material that you are reading.

We hope that you will enjoy the A2 course and that you will find this book interesting and thought-provoking.

Exam Café

In our unique Exam Café you'll find lots of ideas to help prepare for your exams. You'll see an Exam Café at the end of each option and at the end of the research methods and approaches sections. You can Relax because there's handy revision advice from fellow students, Refresh your memory with summaries and checklists of the key ideas you need to revise and Get the result through practising exam-style questions, accompanied by hints and tips on getting the very best grades.

FREE! Exam Café CD-ROM

You'll find a free Exam Café CD-ROM in the back of the book. This contains a wealth of exam preparation material: interactive multiple-choice questions, revision flashcards, exam-style questions with model answers and examiner feedback and much more!

Fiona Lintern

Fiona Lintern
Series Editor
September 2008

Forensic Psychology

Contents

Studies used in the Forensic Psychology option

Turning to crime

Making a case

Reaching a verdict

After a guilty verdict

Full references for the studies can be found in the References section on page 330

Introduction

The word 'forensic' comes from the Latin *forensis*, 'pertaining to a forum'. In ancient Rome the forum was a marketplace where people gathered not just to buy things but also to conduct all kinds of business, including public affairs and legal disputes. The word later came to be restricted to refer to the courts of law.

The word 'forensic' has been used in English since 1659 and now indicates the application of a particular area of scientific knowledge to legal problems and legal proceedings, for example in forensic anthropology, where anthropological knowledge is applied to identify human remains found at a crime scene.

Forensic psychologists apply psychological knowledge to help them understand the behaviour of criminals, the police, judges, barristers, witnesses and the jury in the courtroom and in the preparation of cases for legal proceedings.

What can you do as a forensic psychologist?

There are increasing numbers of careers opening for forensic psychologists in prisons and in the clinical settings of hospitals.

The biggest employer is the prison service. Within a prison the psychologist would be involved with psychometric assessment of risk, administering treatment programmes and ongoing research programmes as the service continues to discover what works in reducing crime. They would also be trying to reduce stress in the prison and applying their expertise to understanding the motivation behind any one individual's criminal acts; either to provide evidence when the case comes to trial, or to work with the offender so that when the case comes up for parole they can offer an informed opinion of whether this person can safely be set free. The job is varied and demanding, with very good earning potential as a fully chartered forensic psychologist.

Below is an example of a day in the life of a prison psychologist in a UK prison, which gives a flavour of prison life.

'There are always meetings scheduled, but a lot of work gets diverted into whatever the crisis might be that day. This may come from the people who are at the highest risk of suicide and self-harm, who are first-timers in custody, and also from those who are detoxing. People are very frightened when they first come to a prison because of its reputation. We try to see the individual as someone who is dealing with the impact of incarceration; it is a distressing time for them.

'There are also learning and development programmes, where high-risk prisoners get intensive therapy. For example, a prisoner might be anxious because he has a court hearing coming up. He might be categorised as high risk because he is an impulsive character. He may find it difficult not to react when he gets news. If he is able to convey to officers that he is anxious, he can be moved to a safe cell so he cannot harm himself.'

To become a prison psychologist, you must first gain at least an upper second class accredited degree in psychology and then a forensic science masters degree followed by two years' experience under the supervision of a Chartered Forensic Psychologist where you must obtain specific competencies.

Weblinks

If your school has access, full details of careers as a psychologist can be obtained from the British Psychological Society website (see Contents page).

A full job specification for a prison psychologist can be viewed on the prison service website (see Contents page).

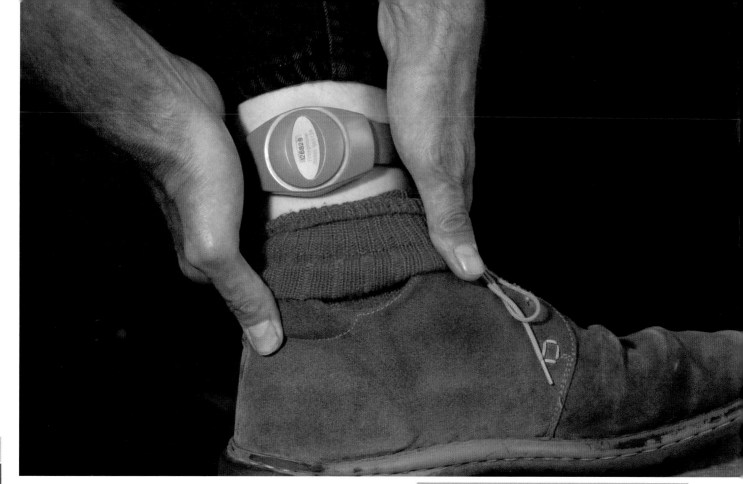

Figure 1.1 A tag can be seen as a 'badge of honour'

The other main area where forensic psychologists work is in the clinical setting. The skills used in risk assessment and treatment programmes with offenders are also valuable in a clinical hospital setting with the mentally ill and people who have been diagnosed with borderline personality disorders and substance abuse.

A third career path would be in research: remaining as an academic and driving progress in the field with attachments to prisons, police forces or hospitals as appropriate. The same educational credentials would apply.

Other careers are within the police force, perhaps as an antisocial behaviour coordinator, or within the probation service, providing treatment programmes for those not given custodial sentences. Despite its glamorous image, there are only a handful of profilers and for most, this is usually not a full-time role; it is something a psychologist does alongside other work.

New pathways are opening up for crime analysts who look for patterns in crimes and crime scenes. They may work for the police and fire services, the armed forces or the security services. The job involves a lot of data analysis using computers, so an ability to use spreadsheets and databases would be a key part of the role. It is possible to progress to senior levels with competitive salaries.

The Forensic Psychology option is designed to follow a rational progression through the criminal justice system, applying psychological understanding to four parts of the criminal justice experience:

- Turning to crime
- Making a case
- Reaching a verdict
- After a guilty verdict.

Turning to crime

This area looks at three influences that have been used to explain how people become criminal: upbringing, cognition and biology. It is important to point out straight away that it would be extremely unrealistic to see these influences as mutually exclusive. Instead we must accept that in reality many factors may work together to make a person turn to crime. However, as students of the topic of forensic psychology it is useful to tease these influences apart in order to examine them in detail and assess their individual contributions to explaining crime.

If we look at the typical profile of an average criminal, we find many common features. They often have very poor literacy and numeracy skills, having left education early after a pattern of truanting and disaffection with school and its rules. At home they will often have a dysfunctional family where they lack atttention, guidance and support that would help them stay at school. Using drugs becomes a way of passing time and making money, and this increases the risk of a criminal conviction. Their first court appearance is often in their teens and any punishment may be seen as a risk worth taking, or even a badge of honour in the case of tags.

Making a case

This area examines how psychologists' research into the effectiveness of interviews and interrogation techniques has lead to increased knowledge and awareness of the problems of leading witnesses and accuracy of testimony. This research has prompted new guidelines for the conduct of police interviews and trials, which have helped to ensure a fairer outcome for defendants.

One of the most controversial areas of research is offender profiling, which has developed over the last 15–20 years. The basic idea is that the scene of a crime can reveal clues about the behaviour of the perpetrator and these can aid the police in their search for suspects.

Reaching a verdict

This area looks at how psychologists have contributed to understanding the influences on jurors as they watch a trial unfold, and their discussions and group behaviours in coming to their verdict. Psychologists have had a major ethical and practical problem to overcome in order to create meaningful findings: it is illegal to interview jurors to find out about their deliberations since they swear an oath to keep them secret, even after the trial is over. Psychologists have therefore been obliged to use mock and shadow juries, often with samples of undergraduates to

conduct their research. Nevertheless, a considerable body of knowledge now exists which can inform court procedures.

After a guilty verdict

The final area looks at the work of forensic psychologists in the prison system, who are trying to turn criminals away from crime by educating them and changing their way of thinking towards a more pro-social orientation. Prison only works as a deterrent for about 35–40 per cent of offenders; the rest re-offend. It seems that despite the treatments and punishments, age has the greatest effect, with young men growing out of a criminal lifestyle as they reach their mid- to late twenties.

From time to time people want stiffer penalties and demand the return of the death penalty. The evidence for this is disturbing as it seems ineffective as a deterrent, and there is evidence from the USA that it is applied with discrimination towards black offenders, particularly when there has been a white victim.

Ever hopeful of positive change, psychologists who are motivated to help people work with offenders to try many treatments. They would probably argue that even though the results are often disappointing statistically, behind the statistics are individuals who have been turned around to the benefit of their own futures and those of their families.

Key terms

mock jury a jury made up of a sample of particpants who are shown a video or transcript of a court case and have to come to a verdict in a laboratory situation

shadow jury a jury made up of participants who sit in a courtroom watching events unfold and then discuss the case as a jury with the researchers observing them. In this way they are exposed to the same witnesses, emotions, etc. of the real courtroom, without the ethical difficulties of secrecy being broken

Turning to crime

Pause for thought

◆ Is it true that crime runs in families?

◆ Do criminals think differently from other people?

◆ Is there any evidence that criminal behaviour has a biological cause?

This area will consider how a person might turn to a life of crime by looking at three influences:

◆ upbringing

◆ cognition

◆ biology.

Introduction

Upbringing

When we talk about the influence of upbringing, we mean influences from families, friends, teachers, and general life experiences, such as where a person has been brought up.

It is a statistical fact that crime is higher in some areas of towns and cities than others. It is also a statistical fact that males are more likely than females to appear in the crime figures. However, even in crime 'hot spots', not all young men commit criminal acts, so as questioning individuals we have to ask why some people commit crimes and others do not.

It is unlikely that we will find a single factor that will explain this, but we can try to build a picture of effects that come together as potential triggers of criminal behaviour.

Cognition

Cognition is a word psychologists use to describe the thinking process.

Where do our thoughts come from? Why do people think differently about the same things? What shapes our opinions and beliefs? This complex and fascinating area is still to be truly investigated. At present,

neuroscience can tell us which parts of our brains become active when we are engaged in some thinking activity, but the only way of accessing thoughts is to ask the person thinking them to tell us. Why should they tell the truth? Can they describe what they are thinking? It is difficult to put thoughts into words, and writing out a stream of consciousness makes very little sense.

Psychologists believe that criminals have different thought processes, allowing them to view their criminal behaviour as logical and attractive, and that the guilt and remorse/conscience that prevents law-abiding people from acting criminally is absent. We have to ask why this should be, and come up with an explanation. Research involves interviews and inventories or questionnaires and sometimes discourse analysis. These methods all have problems which will be expanded upon later.

Biology

A biological explanation of crime has huge appeal. We have made great strides in understanding all aspects of human functioning through medical advances and technology that allows us to see inside our bodies and analyse ourselves right down to molecular level. If we could do the same for the causes of crime in criminals, we could potentially 'cure' them. Psychologists have looked at genetic, neurological, neurochemical, gender and evolutionary explanations of crime.

So far, a complete biological explanation evades us, but the interaction of some biological predispositions with environmental influences can explain the individual differences we see where only some 'at risk' individuals take the step into criminal behaviour while their peers stop short.

Themes and perspectives

This part of the specification is an excellent area in which to develop knowledge of the issues around nature and nurture.

Psychologists no longer advocate the importance of one or other of these possible influences; instead, the emphasis is now on the interaction between nature and nurture. The following activity, applying some critical thinking to the nature–nurture debate, can bring this to life and is an excellent preparation for an essay.

Try this ...

Find some accounts of street crime in your local paper or on the internet.

Divide into three groups. Each group should start with a different premise (opening statement of an argument), for example:

- that criminal behaviour is the result of upbringing
- that it is the result of criminal thinking (cognition)
- that it is biologically based.

Each group should come up with two arguments in support of their premise, with evidence and an intermediate conclusion.

Finally, the class must reach an overall conclusion based on the strongest evidence. If you imagine this as a continuum with nature at one end and nurture at the other, where did you end up?

1 Upbringing

The three studies we will consider in this section are suggested as an evidence base for the influence of upbringing on criminality; they are not the only studies available, but they provide a starting point for discussion. In considering these studies, we must be aware that it is not possible to separate out influences. For example, biology will always underlie human behaviour, leading to individual differences that are exceptions to a common pattern of behaviour.

In the first study Farrington offers us a complex picture of the development of a group of boys through their lives into adulthood and parenthood in order to investigate the influence of the family on the tendency to become involved in crime.

1.1 Disrupted families

Key study
Farrington et al., The Cambridge Study in Delinquent Development

Aims

1. To document the start, duration and end of offending behaviour from childhood to adulthood in families.

2. To investigate the influence of life events; the risk and protective factors predicting offending and antisocial behaviour; the intergenerational transmission of offending and antisocial behaviour, and the influence of family background.

Design A prospective longitudinal survey. In the latest report on the group, data were gathered from interviews at age 48 and searches of criminal records.

Participants The study was based on 411 boys aged 8 and 9 who were born in 1953/4, from the registers of 6 state schools in East London. The boys were predominantly white working class. 397 different families were involved and there were 14 pairs of brothers and 5 pairs of twins in the sample. At age 48, of the 394 males still alive, 365 were interviewed (93 per cent).

Selected results

- At age 48, of 404 individuals searched in the criminal records, 161 had convictions.

- The number of offences and offenders peaked at age 17, closely followed by age 18. There were 11 offenders and 17 offences per 100 males at age 17.

- Those who started criminal careers at age 10–13 were nearly all reconvicted at least once (91 per cent) and committed 9 crimes on average compared with an average of 6 crimes if they started at 14–16. These two groups committed 77 per cent of all the crimes in the study (620 out of 808).

- Self-reported crimes not covered by official statistics indicate that 93 per cent admitted to committing one type of offence at some stage in their lives.

- A small proportion of the males in the study (7 per cent) were defined as 'chronic offenders' because they accounted for about half of all officially recorded offences in this study. On average, their conviction careers lasted from age 14 to age 35.

Most of these chronic offenders shared common childhood characteristics: Farrington describes them as 'persisters' (convicted before and after their 21st birthday) and compared to those with no convictions they are more likely to have: a convicted parent, high daring, a delinquent sibling, a young mother, low popularity, disrupted family, and a large family size. A similar pattern emerges for desisters (those who commit crime only up to age 20).

The proportion of men leading successful lives (successful on at least 6 of the 9 criteria of life success) increased from 78 per cent at age 32 to 88 per cent at age 48. Even persisters improved their life success to 65 per cent between age 32 and 48. The most important finding was that the desisters were no different in life success from the unconvicted.

Conclusion Farrington concludes that offenders tend to be deviant in many aspects of their lives. Early prevention that reduces offending could have wide-ranging benefits in reducing problems with accommodation, relationships, employment, alcohol, drugs and aggressive behaviour. The most important risk factors are criminalty in the family, poverty, impulsiveness, poor child-rearing and poor school performance. Hence, there is scope for significant cost savings from effective early-intervention programmes targeted on under-10s.

Key terms

intergenerational transmission the occurrence of (criminal) behaviour through successive generations of the same family

risk factors those factors that make it more likely that criminal behaviour will occur

protective factors those factors that will prevent criminal behaviour

criteria of life success a set of nine criteria that are used to judge whether someone has succesfully turned away from crime. They include: no drug use in the last 5 years, no self-reported offence (of 6 specified) in the last 5 years, satisfactory mental health and no convictions in the last 5 years

Check your understanding

1   Is this a valid piece of research? If so, what gives it validity?

2   Can it be generalised? If not, why not?

3   Give one strength and one weakness of longitudinal research.

4   Most importantly, what can we conclude from this research?

Take it further

1   Why should we be cautious when drawing conclusions from correlational data?

2   This study is longitudinal in design. What problems are associated with such designs?

3   This study collects both qualitative and quantitative data. What are the advantages and disadvantages of this?

Age at first conviction	No. of offenders	Percentage reconvicted	Total no. of convictions	Average no. of convictions	Career duration (years)*
10–13	35	91	316	9	14
14–16	51	84	304	6	15.5
17–20	43	65	113	2.6	9.9
21–30	19	37	38	2	10.2
31–50	19	42	37	1.9	6.6

* Excluding offenders with one conviction.

Table 1.1 Age of first conviction, by criminal career measures. (Source: Farrington et.al., 2006)

1.2 Learning from others

The second piece of evidence, the theory of differential association, was intended as a comprehensive explanation of criminal and some non-criminal behaviour.

The final version of differential association theory was presented by Sutherland in the form of nine principles, which can be found in his textbook *Principles of Criminology* (1947, pages 75–77). These are as follows.

1   **Criminal behaviour is learned.**

Sutherland believed that criminal behaviour was not inherited or a result of any other biological condition. In other words the individual, without prior influence from others, is incapable of inventing criminal behaviour.

2   **Criminal behaviour is learned in interaction with other persons in a process of communication.**

Sutherland believed that such communication usually involved verbal interaction, however it could also involve the use of gestures without words. This point supports the first by once again claiming that individuals cannot become criminal by themselves.

3   **The principal part of the learning of criminal behaviour occurs within intimate personal groups.**

Sutherland felt that intimate personal groups provided the largest influence on the learning of criminal behaviour. He felt that impersonal agencies of communication such as newspapers and films (media) played a relatively unimportant role in the 'birth' of criminal behaviour. (Contrast this with modern theories of media influence.)

4   **When criminal behaviour is learned, the learning includes the techniques of committing the crime, which are sometimes very complicated, sometimes very simple and the specific direction of motives, drives, rationalisations, and attitudes.**

A criminal has to learn the techniques of the trade from someone, he also learns the attitudes taken and excuses made for behaving in a criminal fashion.

5   **The specific direction of motives and drives is learned from definitions of the legal codes as favourable or unfavourable.**

Groups of people may see certain laws as pointless or discriminatory and therefore feel they can flaunt them or that it is right to break them, for example underage drinking laws.

6   **A person becomes delinquent because of an excess of definitions favourable to violation of law over definitions unfavourable to violation of law.**

This is the principle of differential association. Individuals become criminal due to repeated contacts with criminal activity and a lack of contact with non-criminal activity.

7   **Differential associations (number of contacts with criminals over non-criminals) may vary in frequency, duration, priority, and intensity.**

According to Sutherland, a precise description of a person's criminal behaviour would be possible in quantitative form by analysing the number of contacts with criminals, which would lead to a mathematical ratio being reached. Unfortunately, as he pointed out, an appropriate formula had yet to be developed due to the sheer difficulty involved!

8   **The process of learning criminal behaviour by association with criminal and anti-criminal patterns involves all of the mechanisms that are involved in any other learning.**

Really, so your name is Ethel and you were born in 1927?

Yes, I just look young for my age.

Can I have a Malibu and Coke?

Figure 1.2 Are there any laws that you think are worth breaking?

In this point, Sutherland claims that criminal behaviour is learned just like every other behaviour. In other words, he felt there was nothing 'special' or 'abnormal' about criminal behaviour, or criminals for that matter, thus going against the claims of biological and pathological theorists.

9 **While criminal behaviour is an expression of general needs and values, it is not explained by those general needs and values, since non-criminal behaviour is an expression of the same needs and values.**

A thief generally steals in order to obtain money. However, such an action is no different from the work of an honest labourer, so this need in itself cannot explain theft.

Summary Sutherland's theory is based on two core assumptions:

1 Deviance occurs when people define a certain human situation as an appropriate occasion for violating social norms or criminal laws.

2 Definitions of the situation are acquired through an individual's history of past experience.

The theory emphasises the social–psychological processes by which people produce subjective definitions of whether an action is criminal. Sutherland argued that it is necessary to examine the normal learning process whereby a person comes to define a particular situation as more or less appropriate for deviant behaviour. This is what happens in the peer group and the street gang as a young person moves away from parental influence. It seems a powerful explanation for certain types of violence, but falls short when applied to crimes commited by individuals acting alone.

Check your understanding

1 This is a theory that considers behaviour from the social–psychological perspective. What does this mean?

2 What are the strengths of the theory?

3 What are the weaknesses of this theory? (Hint: look at principle 7 on page 11.)

1.3 Poverty and disadvantaged neighbourhoods

Thirdly, we can consider a study on the effects of poverty or disadvantage, which are often suggested as a reason for turning to crime. Government figures show that the most disadvantaged 5 per cent in society are 100 times more likely to have multiple problems than the most advantaged 50 per cent, including conduct disorders, police contact, cannabis use, mood disorders and alcohol abuse. The Peterborough Youth Study, one of the 'Study of the Social Contexts of Pathways into Crime' (SCoPiC) studies, set out to test these factors and others to see which in fact were the most significant predictors of criminal behaviour.

Key study
Wikström, The Peterborough Youth Study

Design A cross-sectional study.

Sample Nearly 2000 Year 10 (14- to 15-year-old) students.

Methodology Interview and data collection.

Take it further

Think about the following questions, then discuss the questions in pairs, and finally share your thoughts with the class.

1 Could it be true that there would be no crime if no one ever had ever seen a crime being committed?

2 Being totally honest, what laws in our society do you think are worth breaking?

3 Have you ever broken those laws because you have learned to from your friends?

4 How have you defined a situation to feel it is worth breaking those rules? Give an example.

5 According to Sutherland, you will become delinquent when more of your associations (friendships) are more deviant than law abiding. Is this true?

6 He did not feel that the media had a part to play. Do you agree?

Figure 1.3 Would growing up here make you more likely to commit a crime? A school playground in the 1950s

- family social position (social class, ethnicity and family composition)
- individual characteristics (dispositions, self-control and morality, social situation, family and school bonds, parental monitoring and truancy)
- social situation (family and school bonds, parental monitoring and opportunity for truancy)
- lifestyles and routine activities
- community contexts (neighbourhood disadvantage and school attended).

Of these, the most important was the youths' individual characteristics and the way they lived their lives, which strongly affected their involvement in crime.

Youths with many individual risk factors offend frequently, while youths with many individual protective factors rarely offend. Key risk factors are weak family and school bonds, poor parental monitoring and truancy, weak morality (antisocial values and low levels of shame) and poor self-control. Surprisingly, social disadvantage was *not* a strong predictor of delinquency in comparison to lifestyle factors, but those from a lower social class did have more risk factors than those from a more comfortable background.

Conclusions The findings suggest the presence of three groups of adolescent offenders:

1 **Propensity-induced**

These youths have an enduring propensity to offend; it is a personality or individual characteristic. This is only a small group, but is responsible for a high number of different and more serious offences. They also tend to have a wide range of high-risk factors, such as weak family and school bonds, low levels of

Selected key findings

- 44.8 per cent of the males and 30.6 per cent of the females have committed at least one of the studied crimes (violence, vandalism, shoplifting, burglary and theft of and from cars) during the year 2000.
- 9.8 per cent of the males and 3.8 per cent of the females have committed a serious crime of theft (i.e. robbery, burglary or theft from or of a car).
- High-frequency offenders tend to commit a wide range of different crimes.
- One in eight offenders were reported to or caught by the police for their last committed crime.
- Offenders are more often victimised than non-offenders and violent offenders are particularly more likely to be victims of violence.
- Offenders are more often drunk and more often use drugs than other youths.

Explanatory factors The study covers a wide range of factors that may predispose to criminal activity:

Figure 1.4 How much do other people's ideas influence our values?

self-control, antisocial values and low levels of shame interacting with a high-risk lifestyle. The offending by this group may be interpreted as being more about their individual characteristics (an enduring propensity to offend) than about situational risks.

2   **Lifestyle-dependent**
This is a group of youths who are average in terms of individual social adjustment. Offending by this group appears to be highly dependent on lifestyle. Those with a low-risk lifestyle rarely offend, while those with a high-risk lifestyle frequently offend. A high-risk lifestyle is defined by spending a large amount of time on peer-centred activities in public settings, especially if socialising with delinquent peers and using alcohol or drugs.

3   **Situationally-limited**
These are individually well-adjusted youths who may occasionally offend if their lifestyle exposes them to high levels of situational risk. Substance abuse seems to be of particular importance in explaining their occasional offending. There is little to suggest that this group will develop serious problems of criminality.

This study is currently being followed up with more investigation of the influencing factors.

Check your understanding

1   What is a cross-sectional study?

2   Why are offenders often also the victims of crime?

3   What does this study suggest is the key characteristic that makes offending more likely?

2 Cognition

A second influence that can explain why an individual turns to crime is the way they think. Psychologists apply the term 'cognition' to the mental processes that determine our actions, feelings and beliefs. The basic assumption is that there must be a difference between the way a law-abiding person thinks and the way a criminal thinks.

This has important implications for the philosophical debate about free will versus determinism in relation to criminal responsibility. In seeking an explanation for criminal behaviour we are looking for the biological, cognitive or social drivers of criminal behaviour. This is by definition being determinist. We are then left to decide how far these determining factors are under conscious control and hence whether indidivuals can override them if they want to avoid committing criminal acts. For the most part, the law takes the view that we are fully responsible for our actions at all times. An exception to this is a plea of diminished responsibility. When this happens, the offender may have admitted guilt but the jury then has to decide whether any allowance should be made for the effect of a mental illness or extreme provocation or other extreme circumstance which led to the offence and whether the individual is fit for trial. This happened in 1981, in the case of Peter Sutcliffe, the Yorkshire Ripper, when the jury were faced with deciding whether his defence of paranoid schizophrenia as the reason he killed women was justified or whether he was responsible for his acts. They decided on the latter, but Sutcliffe only spent a few months in prison before being sent to Broadmoor (a psychiatric prison) because prison staff and doctors decided that his original plea was clearly genuine.

Section summary

- In considering the influence of upbringing, we have looked at how families are clearly influential in a person's chances of becoming criminal. It seems clear that disrupted families with criminal parents give any individual a high risk of following them into crime.

- We can also assume that early intervention programs may mitigate the risk.

- If the young person belongs to a deviant peer group the risk factors increase as criminal acts become norms of behaviour. Each group will make their own definition of the rules they will adopt and those they will ignore.

- If the family lives in an area of poverty or disadvantage, the risks increase as they feel alienated from the mainstream of society and its values of an honest work ethic based on a good education leading to a job or career.

- There may be individuals with characteristically high-risk behaviours who adopt a permanently criminal lifestyle while others are more influenced by situational factors and therefore are potentially easier to rehabilitiate.

The rules that a court uses to decide whether to uphold a plea of diminished responsibility are the McNaghten Rules (1843). If the plea is upheld, the outcome is usually indefinite imprisonment. The argument runs that if a person is insane they will not be deterred from committing other criminal acts, and so treatment and incarceration make more sense than punishment.

Actus reus is the Latin term used to refer to the 'guilty act', which in combination with the *mens rea*, the 'guilty mind', produces criminal responsibility according to UK law. Both must be present together. If a person is judged as having diminished responsibility, they cannot have the *mens rea* and therefore cannot be found guilty.

Cognitive psychological research has been directed at moral development, patterns of thinking and the sorts of attributions criminals make about their actions. In the specification this is covered by the following terms.

- criminal thinking patterns
- moral development and crime
- social cognition.

2.1 Criminal thinking patterns

Here we return to the assumption that criminals think differently from non-criminals. In an attempt to decide whether this is correct, researchers have somehow to find out how people think. A moment's thought will instantly throw up a problem with this: how can we ever know what someone is thinking? Cognitive psychologists believe that it is possible to discover a thought process just by interviewing a person and asking them what they are thinking in a particular situation. Alternatively, researchers can ask for written answers by means of questionnaires or can look at diaries, letters or, more recently, blogs to find out what people are thinking. If we accept for a moment that it is possible to find out someone's thought processes in this way, what questions might we ask them?

The evidence base for criminal thinking patterns has been heavily influenced by the work of two doctors working with criminals in a mental hospital. Their project spanned 14 years and has been published in stages in a series of books.

Aims

1 To understand the make-up of the criminal personality.

2 To establish techniques that could be used to alter the personality disorders that produce crime.

3 To encourage an understanding of legal responsibility.

4 To establish techniques that can be effective in preventing criminal behaviour.

Participants The study was based on 255 male participants from various backgrounds: black, white, those from the inner city, those from the suburbs, wealthy, poor, etc. were all evaluated. The population

U3

1

of studied offenders was composed of those confined to the hospital who had been found guilty but because of their insanity were considered more suited to indefinite secure treatment, as well as a roughly equal number of convicted criminals who were not confined to the institution and had not made that plea. If they are found not guilty by reason of insanity, the prisoners are not sent to prison but instead to a secure mental hospital, as is the case in the UK. They are considered incapable of guilt because they do not meet the criteria for *mens rea*, even though they have committed a criminal act. The other criminals did not use the plea. There was no control group of non-criminals to see if they also had these thought patterns.

Methodology A series of interviews was conducted with the participants over a period of several years.

Selected findings According to Yochelson and Samenow, criminals …

- are restless, dissatisfied and irritable
- while at school, considered requests from their teachers and parents as impositions
- continually set themselves apart from others
- want to live a life of excitement, at any cost
- are habitually angry as a way of life
- are lacking empathy
- feel under no obligation to anyone or anything except their own interests
- are poor at responsible decision-making, having pre-judged situations.

Of the 255 participants, most dropped out of the study; 30 completed the programme of interviews, but only nine genuinely changed as a result, by the standards established at the start of the programme. The programme consisted of Freudian-based therapy that attempted to find the root cause of their criminality in their past lives. By discovering this and facing it, the criminals were then expected to improve their behaviour by stopping their lying, drug and alcohol abuse and theft of hospital supplies.

Yochelson and Samenow acknowledge that the patients lied and gave the answers they thought would help their situations improve when the doctors began the study. As a result, Yochelson and Samenow changed their emphasis from finding a cause of criminal behaviour to examining the thinking process. Many of the thinking errors they found would be part of a modern-day diagnosis of antisocial personality disorder, which is generally considered to be exceptionally difficult to treat.

Conclusion In all, 52 thinking patterns were distinguishable in the criminal personality. These were considered to be 'errors' in thinking. Although not unique to criminals, they were thought to be displayed more by criminals. As there was not a control group, it is not possible to be certain about this as non-criminals may be just as likely to display these errors as far as we know. The lack of a control group may well be because this research evolved out of clinical practice with a group of patients, rather than being set up from scratch.

Check your understanding

1   Why was the sample a problem?

2   The other great weakness of this research is the lack of a control group. Why does this matter?

3   Design an ideal control group for this study.

2.2 Moral development and crime

Typically, moral development has been studied in normal children and other researchers have then applied the findings to criminals. When we talk about moral development we mean how a set of values has been learnt by children during their upbringing, usually from parents or carers. These values become inbuilt and determine our sense of right and wrong. It is believed in the UK that by the age of 10, children clearly know the difference between right and wrong and therefore the criminal justice system sets the age of criminal responsibility at this point. This means that a child of 10 or over can be sentenced to imprisonment in a young offenders' institution. The murder of James Bulger in 1993 was one such example. Jon Venables and Robert Thompson were asked directly during their trial whether they knew it was wrong to take away the child, hurt or kill him (this was to establish a *mens rea* or 'guilty mind') and they were found guilty at the age of 11. Other European countries take a different view on the age of culpability: it is 18 in Germany and 8 in Scotland. Bearing this in mind, we will consider a study of moral development.

Key study
Kohlberg, Moral development in children

Kohlberg was fascinated by Piaget's work on the moral development of children. His doctoral thesis (Kohlberg, 1963) has become the foundation for a major theory in psychology where he outlines six stages of moral development (see Table 1.2).

Aim To find evidence in support of a progression through stages of moral development.

Participants The study took place in 1963 and was based on 58 boys from Chicago, of working and middle class, aged 7, 10, 13 and 16.

Methodology Each boy was given a 2-hour interview with ten dilemmas that they had to solve. (The most famous of these was the **Heinz dilemma**.) Some of the boys were followed up at 3-yearly intervals up to age 30–36, making this a longitudinal study.

In 1969, Kohlberg also studied children in the UK, Mexico, Taiwan, Turkey, the USA and Yucatan.

Results Younger boys tended to perform at stages 1 and 2, with older boys at stages 3 and 4 suggesting support for development through stages. These patterns were consistent in the cross-cultural studies, although progression was slower in the non-industrialised societies. No support was found for stage 6 in this sample and in 1978 Kohlberg revised his view and agreed there might not be a separate stage 6.

Conclusions There does seem to be support across cultures for the stage theory. The methodology has been heavily criticised, but more recent replications (Thornton and Reid, 1982) with criminal samples have suggested that criminals committing crime for financial gain show more immature reasoning than those committing violent crimes, suggesting that Kohlberg's stages can be applied to types of criminality.

Heinz dilemma Heinz's wife was suffering from terminal cancer. In an effort to save her he went to a chemist who had developed a cure which might help her. Unfortunately, the chemist wanted much more money for his cure than Heinz could afford and refused to sell it for less. Even when Heinz borrowed enough money for half the cost of the drug, the chemist still refused to sell it to him. Having no other means of getting the drug, Heinz broke into the chemist's laboratory and stole it.

- Should he have broken into the laboratory? Why?
- Should the chemist insist on the inflated price for his invention? Does he have the right?
- What should happen to Heinz?
- What if Heinz did not love his wife – does that change anything?
- What if the dying person was a stranger? Should Heinz have stolen the drug anyway?

Check your understanding

1 How appropriate is the use of moral dilemmas as a means of discovering someone's moral behaviour?
2 What is the problem with the all-male sample?
3 Give two strengths of Kohlberg's research.

Level 1 Pre-morality	**Stage 1 Punishment and obedience orientation.** Doing what is right because of fear of punishment. **Stage 2 Hedonistic orientation.** Doing what is right for personal gain, perhaps a reward.
Level 2 Conventional morality	**Stage 3 Interpersonal concordance orientation.** Doing what is right according to the majority to be a good boy/girl. **Stage 4 Law and order orientation.** Doing what is right because it is your duty and helps society. Laws must be obeyed for the common good.
Level 3 Post-conventional morality	**Stage 5 Social contract or legalistic orientation.** Doing what is morally right even if it is against the law because the law is too restrictive. **Stage 6 Universal ethical principles orientation.** Doing what is right because of our inner conscience which has absorbed the principles of justice, equality and sacredness of human life.

Table 1.2 A summary of Kohlberg's stages (1963; 1978)

Weblink

You might be interested to read the full judgement for Thompson v the United Kingdom (see Contents page).

2.3 Social cognition

Social cognition refers to the way our thoughts are influenced by the people we mix with, but also, to look at it the other way around, how we can understand social phenomena by looking at an individual's cognitions. In particular this subsection will look at the perception of the social situation, the judgement of the individual and their memory for social stimuli. This should help us to understand intrapersonal, interpersonal, and intergroup processes.

In the context of the criminal and crime, the social context is the criminal act, so it is thought to be helpful to try and find out what a criminal is thinking when they commit the crime. By this means, in theory, it should ultimately be possible to treat any 'faulty' cognitions and put someone back on the road to a crime-free life.

What the criminal is thinking will differ depending on whether the crime is being committed individually (intrapersonal) or within a group or gang (interpersonal/intergroup). Another potential benefit of gaining understanding of the criminal thought process is for crime prevention. Knowing how a potential burglar weighs up the costs and benefits of breaking and entering your property could reduce crime because you could then ensure that the costs looked too great for the opportunist burglar to take their chance. Similarly, potential victims of assaults would benefit from knowing how they might be singled out as a target.

One of the main researchers who has looked at the relationship between type of offence and the attributions offenders make about their criminal acts is Gudjohnsson, in a series of studies in the 1990s.

Key terms

intrapersonal within oneself

interpersonal between one person and another

intergroup between one group and another

attributions explanations an individual gives for another person's behaviour

pathology the study and diagnosis of disease by looking at blood and tissue samples under a microscope

Gudjohnsson identifies two important types of attributions. First there are 'internal' versus 'external' attributions. Internal attribution is where a person attributes the cause of behaviour within themselves. External attribution refers to social and environmental factors, which include provocation and social pressures. The second type of atttribution is what he calls the mental element. 'I killed John because I was depressed and lost control of myself' would be a mental-element attribution. Guilt is the third dimension and is the offender's remorse about the offence.

Key study

Gudjohnsson and Bownes, The attribution of blame and type of crime committed

Aim To examine the relationship between the type of offence and the attributions offenders make about their criminal act and then cross-validate earlier findings on an English sample.

Methodology To use the Gudjohnsson and Singh (1989) 42-item 'Blame Attribution Inventory' (GBAI) to measure the offender's type of offence and attribution of blame on the three dimensions: internal/external, mental element and guilt.

Participants 80 criminals who were serving sentences in Northern Ireland. They were divided into groups. The first group of 20 subjects had committed violent offences including homicide and grievous bodily harm (GBH). Their mean age was 29. The second group of 40 sex offenders included rapists, paedophiles and those who had committed sexual assault. Their mean ages varied from 41 for the paedophiles down to 28 for the other offenders. The final group of 20 had committed property offences including theft and burglary. Their mean age was 29.

Results

Type of offence	Guilt	Mental element	External
Violence	8.1	5.3	5.8
Sexual	12.7	5.7	2.4
Property	5.5	4.0	3.0
Total	9.8	5.1	3.4

Table 1.3 Mean scores on the GBAI for violent, sexual and property offenders

As expected, those who had committed sexual offences showed the most remorse about their behaviour; this was followed by those who had committed violent acts against the person.

Very little difference was found in the mental element scores for all offenders. With regard to external attribution, the highest scores were found for violent offenders and the lowest for sex offenders.

When comparing the English findings with the findings from this study, violent Irish prisoners showed lower mental element, lower guilt and higher external attribution scores.

Conclusion The findings show strong consistency with earlier findings across the offender groups, which suggests that there is a strong consistency in the way offenders attribute blame for their crimes across the two countries. The only real difference was in the violent prisoners, which may be a result of the violence prevalent in Northern Ireland at the time of the 'troubles' of the 1980s and early 1990s.

Check your understanding

1. Why do we need to know how offenders attribute blame?

2. What is the difference between an 'internal' and an 'external' attribution of blame?

3. Why would we need to be cautious about the findings of an inventory?

Section summary

- Research by Yochelson and others has suggested that criminals think differently from law-abiding people. They have certain biases in their thinking which means they see themselves existing apart from the mainstream of society without obligation to others, lacking empathy and seeking excitement. Their decision-making is poor and they lie habitually.

- A criminal's moral development is restricted to the lower levels of Kohlberg's hierarchy, reflecting the biases found by Yochelson. In stage one and stage two of Kohlberg's theory a person does what is right to avoid getting into trouble or for a reward or personal gain. A criminal may believe that because the chances of getting into trouble are quite slim and the rewards for crime are quite substantial then there is little moral pressure on them to behave within the law.

- Criminals make attributions about their crimes which allow them to reduce any feelings of guilt they may have. Gudjohnsson has found that they attribute blame differently for different types of crimes, with sexual crimes creating the most guilt. It was also found that attributions are affected by the social context and social pressures surrounding the criminal.

- Understanding how criminals think offers potentially the greatest opportunity to change faulty thinking and reduce reoffending.

3 Biology

A third influence that may affect an individual's likelihood of turning to crime is biology. When considering this influence we would include genes, hormones, neurology, gender, pathology, and evolutionary explanations. Research into the search for a genetic explanation of crime, which is very much an active and ongoing field, is discussed on pages 21–22. Genetic variation may be responsible for causing differences in an individual's levels of aggression which may lead to violent crime; however it is unlikely that we would find biological explanations for fraud, theft, drug-dealing etc. There are many other areas of biological explanation which are outside the scope of this specification, such as the effects of taking steroids associated with 'roid' rage and addiction. Cases have been reported where a brain tumour has been implicated in changing the personality

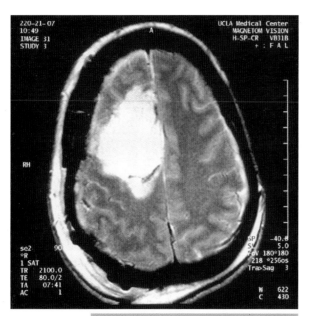

Figure 1.5 MRI scan of a brain tumour

Raine has also been conducting longitudinal research to look at early risk and protective factors for violent behaviour. He has found that low physiological arousal, birth complications, fearlessness and increased body size are early markers for later aggressive behaviour. Notice how these factors complement the work of Farrington described on pages 9–10, giving us a more complete picture of why some individuals turn to crime.

Aim To take a multi-factorial approach to understanding antisocial and aggressive behaviour in children with a biological focus.

Methodology A review article.

Procedure To review and summarise the findings from a selection of articles covering neuropsychological, neurological and brain-imaging studies and report the findings as they relate to antisocial behaviour through a child's development.

Results In summary, Raine draws together many different threads. He believes that a low resting heart rate is a good predictor of an individual who will seek excitement to raise their arousal level, creating a fearless temperament.

In addition, there is much new research suggesting that the adolescent brain is still forming its final connections in the pre-frontal lobes right up to the early twenties (Blakemore and Choudhury, 2006; Sowell et al., 1999). Activity in the pre-frontal lobes has been shown to be lower in impulsive individuals who are likely to be antisocial and aggressive (Raine, 2002). This may explain why offending peaks during adolescence. Birth complications and poor parenting with physical abuse and malnutrition, smoking and drinking during pregnancy all add to the risk.

Conclusion Raine concludes that early intervention and prevention may be an effective way of reversing biological deficits that predispose to antisocial and aggressive behaviour.

of an individual from a well-behaved, caring person to a violent and uncontrolled individual. Such was the case of Charles Whitman, who after his death was found to have a cancerous tumour called a glioma in the hypothalamus and near the amygdala, which is associated with experience of emotion.

In another type of brain damage, a railway worker called Phineas Gage suffered catastrophic damage to his prefrontal lobes when a bolt was blown through his cheek and up through his eye into his brain (Harlow, 1848). Following this injury he recovered well physically but psychologically he became a different person, going from a sober, quiet family man to a violent drunk. This was one of the earliest cases that suggested that the pre-frontal lobes are involved in the moderation of our aggressive or violent behaviour.

3.1 Brain dysfunction

Adrian Raine is Professor of Psychology at the University of Southern California. He is often asked to stand as an expert witness in trials involving criminals who have committed murderous acts without premeditation, because of his belief that such individuals may show abnormal differences in metabolic activity in parts of the brain.

He has conducted much research using PET scanning technology to provide an evidence base for this belief.

Weblink

There are details of Raine's ongoing research on the home page of his website (see Contents page).

Check your understanding

1 What is a review article?

2 Why is lower activity in the pre-frontal lobes an indicator of impulsive aggression?

3 What are birth complications?

1 Raine is looking for mainly biological factors to explain criminal behaviour, but he is not being reductionist. Explain why.

2 Raine's more recent work has led him to believe that biological predispositions are 'switched on' by environmental conditions. If these environmental conditions do not exist, then the child is much less likely to turn towards crime. What does this suggest about crime prevention?

3 A major concern about all biological explanations is the 'labelling effect', leading to certain expectations and a self-fulfilling prophecy that someone's biological make-up will predispose them to crime. How can this be resolved ethically so that the researcher's knowledge is used for the benefit of society?

3.2 Genes and serotonin

In the 1960s it was proposed that males with an extra Y chromosome (males should have one X and one Y chromosome) were predisposed to be violent criminals (Price et al., 1966). This genetic abnormality became known as 'the supermale syndrome'; individuals who had it were above average height and below average intelligence. The XYY theory offered the prospect of a genetic explanation, which carried with it the weight of scientific knowledge and potentially offered possibilities of screening people before they had committed a crime, cutting the risk to the population at a stroke. However, later research failed to find more than low correlational support for the original findings. The over-representation of XYY individuals in prison populations may have had more to do with their lower intelligence, making them more likely to get caught and to have suffered poor educational performance, which in itself is a risk factor for becoming criminal.

Despite this early setback, researchers have continued to search for genetic explanations for criminality, looking at how crime often runs in families and conducting twin and adoption studies for evidence. Christiansen (1977) looked at 3586 twin pairs in Denmark and found a 52 per cent concordance rate for criminality in monozygotic twins and a 22 per cent concordance for dizygotic twins. There have been many criticisms of this work, however, in that, first, the identifying of the twins as mono- or dizygotic was done before genetic testing became a reliable and recognised method. Some of the twins in the early research will have looked similar but actually not been genetically identical. Secondly, when monozygotic twins are reared together they share the same environment and experiences, so how can we be sure their behaviour has a genetic cause? Thirdly, the correlation only holds strong for property crimes, not other crimes. More recently, a meta-analysis of the gene–crime relationship correcting for these factors has shown much lower concordance (Walters, 1992).

Key terms

PET scanning technology use radioactivity to show and record glucose metabolism in the active part of the brain. Glucose is mixed with a radioactive tracer and injected into the person, who then completes a task while being scanned. The brain needs the glucose for its activity and draws it to the active area which then shows as red/yellow

reductionism an approach that reduces a complex phenomenon such as human behaviour to the simplest explanation possible. Often this means looking for a biological basis for behaviour. The advantage of a reductionist approach is that it can give a greater understanding of something by revealing evidence for a cause of behaviour. The disadvantage is that humans and their environments are so complex that the reductionist explanation falls short of giving the whole explanation of the behaviour

monozygotic twins identical twins

dizygotic twins non-identical twins

Adoption studies have been fraught with similar problems. People who adopt are generally of a higher socio-economic status: while not necessarily wealthy, they will have been confirmed as financially sound as part of the adoption process. This may account for the better outcome of the children, because they are able to provide a richer, more supportive home environment and are able to invest more time in their children. In 1993, Brunner et al. reported on a study of a family with a genetic abnormality, some of whose members were violent and criminal. This case study is unable to explain criminality in general, but it does illustrate the continuing appeal of a reductionist genetic explanation.

Key study

Brunner et al., A study of violence in a family with genetic abnormality

Aim Brunner and his colleagues wanted to explain the behaviour of a large family in the Netherlands where the males are affected by a syndrome of borderline mental retardation and abnormal violent behaviour. These included impulsive aggression, arson, attempted rape and exhibitionism.

Participants The study was based on five affected males from the family.

Methodology Data were collected from analysis of urine samples over a 24-hour period.

Results The tests showed disturbed monoamine metabolism associated with a deficit of the enzyme monoamine oxidase A (MAOA). In each of the five males a point mutation was identified in the X chromosome of the gene responsible for production of MAOA.

Conclusion MAOA is involved in serotonin metabolism. The defect in the gene leading to impaired serotonin metabolism is likely to be responsible for the mental retardation in the family and this in turn may account for the violent behaviour. Brunner concluded that the MAOA deficiency in this family was associated with a recognisable behavioural phenotype that accounted for their inability to regulate their aggression. However, not all the males in the family were affected by the violent behaviour, even when they suffered the mental retardation. In addition, this is an extremely rare condition and even if it were responsible for the criminal behaviour, it is not yet possible to generalise this very far.

Key terms

point mutation a single point mutation occurs when a single nucleotide is replaced with a different one, in this case on the X chromosome

nucleotide one of the structural components, or building blocks, of DNA and RNA. A nucleotide consists of a base (one of four chemicals: adenine, thymine, guanine, and cytosine) plus a molecule of sugar and one of phosphoric acid

phenotype the observable traits or characteristics of an organism, for example hair colour, weight, or the presence or absence of a disease

serotonin a neurotransmitter that is believed to play an important role in the regulation of anger and aggression: lower than normal levels can lead to depression. It is sometimes called the 'feel-good' chemical

Check your understanding

1 Why might this study be labelled as reductionist and determinist ?

2 Why is the problem metabolising serotonin important in explaining the findings of this study?

3 This could be considered a case study of a family. What difficulties does this create when we try to generalise from it?

3.3 Gender

The last part of this section will look at an evolutionary psychological explanation for criminal behaviour. This combines current theory and knowledge of evolutionary biology with psychological factors to explain behaviour.

Both Farrington's and Raine's works refer to risk taking and impulsiveness in offenders. In the following study, evolutionary psychologists look for an explanation of why males exhibit this trait more than females. This fact is reflected in the far higher number of males involved in violent criminal behaviour. The age–crime curve in Figure 1.6 shows this clearly and is a robust finding in all cultures where crime is a problem. However, in the UK in 2008 we are seeing the rise of girl gangs and increased violence between girls, which also needs an explanation.

What is the evolutionary advantage of being a risk taker? Why have males specialised to be more competitive? Demographers call *external* causes of death accident, suicide or homicide; *internal* causes are disease and illness. Young males are far more likely to appear in the statistics for the former, which are all affected by attitude to risk. For example, young male drivers underestimate objective risks and overestimate their own ability in comparison with older drivers (Brown and Groeger, 1988). In addition, young men are most likely to try drugs and least likely to seek medical help for injury or illness. In summary, males will exhibit risk-taking behaviour whenever there is a chance that other males and females will see them. Evolutionists believe that this is because of the pressure of mate selection for continuance of the human species. Males have to 'win' a female from other males. Once in a partnership, their risk-taking behaviour becomes moderated unless they become single again, for example through divorce.

Another feature of Daly and Wilson's 2001 study (described below) is the 'short time horizon' they notice with young male offenders. This means that these individuals want instant gratification and not long-term delayed pleasures. This would be in line with their short lifespan expectation from their risky behaviour. It would have had

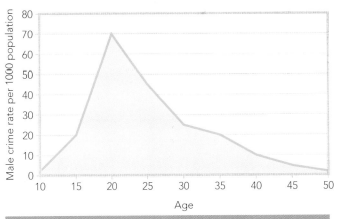

an evolutionary advantage when at risk from predators or dependent on sources of foraging in our distant past, but logically should apply to both sexes on that basis. However, in the case of females, it would seem that once a female has been 'won' it is likely that she will become pregnant to pass on the genes of the successful male.

Key study
Daly and Wilson, Investigation of gender-related life expectancy

Aim To find out if homicide rates would vary as a function of local life expectancy in Chicago, a city divided into 77 longstanding community areas or neighbourhoods with relatively stable boundaries and social and economic characteristics.

Methodology A correlational study using survey data from police records, school records and local demographic records collected by population census.

Procedure The study examined local communities in Chicago which had lower than average male life expectancies, varying from 54.3 to 77.4 years, and plotted various correlations between the data collected.

Results Life expectancy proved to be the best predictor of neighbourhood-specific homicide rates, which ranged from 1.3 to 156 homicides per 100,000 persons per annum (the correlation was strongly negative at –0.88). Daly and Wilson asked if it was really possible that young men in these neighbourhoods actually discounted the future and expected to live shorter lives, thereby escalating the likelihood that they would increase their risk taking for short-term rewards. Another key finding was that the neighbourhood-specific rate of absenteeism from school was also negatively correlated with life expectancy.

This could also explain why these young men see little point in investing effort in school performance. Daly and Wilson examined truancy rates and found strong correlations with life expectancy (primary school truancy $r = -0.50$, $n = 77$, $p = 0.001$; high-school truancy $r = -0.32$, $n = 77$, $p = 0.001$). One possible explanation they suggest is that parents are unwilling to invest in their child's education by enforcing attendance because they are also operating on a short time horizon.

In the case of females, Wilson and Daly (1997) hypothesise that reproduction will occur earlier in the life span as one moves from high to low life expectancy neighbourhoods. The median age of new mothers was 22.6 years in the ten Chicago neighbourhoods with the shortest life expectancies, compared with 27.3 years in the ten neighbourhoods with the longest life expectancies. This is their active choice.

Daly and Wilson believe that young adults are still driven by ancient adaptive traits, such as risk taking and early reproduction, which is a rational response to the unique local circumstances that these young people grow up in, leading males into crime.

Check your understanding

1. Are negative correlations any weaker than positive correlations?

2. What would a perfect positive correlation look like?

3. The research above quotes a 0.001 level of significance: normally we would use the 0.05 level. What does significance mean and which is the stronger level?

4. Can we legitimately use evolutionary explanations based on ancient behaviour patterns to explain modern behaviour?

Section summary

- The biological explanation of criminality covers many different areas, leading to a tendency to be reductionist. However, reviews such as Raine's are drawing together several variables to make it more coherent.

- It is unlikely ever to be possible to find a single biological cause of criminal behaviour, because crime exists in many forms.

- The attraction of a biological explanation is that it offers the possibility of screening for the future.

- Against this is the danger of labelling individuals before a crime has been committed and ignoring the possibility of free will being able to override any predisposition to criminal behaviour.

U3

1

Making a case

Pause for thought

◆ Have you ever wondered about how a crime comes to court?

◆ Are the police any good at detecting liars?

◆ Does profiling a suspect really work?

This area will consider how psychology can inform the investigative process.

Introduction

After a crime has been committed, the police have to create a case that will stand up in court. It is their role to gather evidence from witnesses, alibis, suspects and forensic teams working at the crime scene.

Once a suspect has been found and arrested, under normal circumstances the police have 24 hours in which to release them or charge them with an offence (there are different rules for suspected terrorists). When the arrest occurs, the suspect is taken to the police station 'on suspicion' and the clock is started as the custody sergeant books the suspect in. The clock can be stopped at any time and then restarted if the police release a suspect on bail to gather more evidence or to check alibis. The police are bound by the Police and Criminal Evidence Act (PACE) to conduct their interviews without undue force and respecting the rights of an individual who is 'innocent until proven guilty' by a court. Assuming they have enough evidence, the case is handed to the Crown Prosecution Service (CPS) to decide if the case is strong enough to take further. If so, the suspect is normally bailed to appear in front of the magistrates who will either deal with the case themselves or pass it up to the Crown Court. This decision is usually based on whether the sentencing powers of a magistrate are sufficient to match the severity of the crime. However, it is anyone's right to be tried by jury, and some suspects demand this right, and so the case goes to the Crown Court.

It is called the Crown Court because anyone who commits a crime in the UK is actually breaking the law, which is represented by the Crown (the Queen or Regina in Latin). Criminal trials are therefore set up as Regina v Fred Bloggs, for example.

The Crown Prosecution Service is independent of the police, but works alongside them, reviewing cases constantly. They may agree with the police that some crimes are serious enough to keep the suspect in custody, in which case they are remanded to a prison to await trial.

Weblinks

You can visit the Criminal Justice website for interactive walkthroughs in all the roles of a court case (see Contents page).

Try this ...

Ask your local community police officer if you can visit a custody suite (police cell block) or invite him or her to talk to you about what happens during an arrest or interview.

In this area we will be looking at the interviewing process, which is very different for witnesses and suspects, and also at the role of profilers, who have had a significant influence on police practice in recent years. Profiling techniques are now part of police training for detective work, and are another tool in their investigative armoury. Profiling has taken off because of the development of more sophisticated computer databases and the controversial holding of biometric data on more and more individuals.

1 Interviewing witnesses

Key to any crime is the interviewing of the witnesses, who may have vital evidence to give. However, psychologists have shown through much earlier work that what a witness sees and remembers is influenced by many factors, making it far from a literal recall of events. In the AS course, you saw how Loftus and Palmer (1974) examined the way in which leading questions affected the accuracy of recall. It is well known that memory is reconstructive, using cues and schemas to create a narrative of events. In witnessing a crime a witness may experience strong emotions or get a partial view of events which may be over in seconds. In addition, the complexity of the legal process means that many months will pass before the witness testifies in court, and days may elapse before the first interview by the police when the witness will be asked to make their first statement.

For obvious reasons, recollection needs to be as accurate as possible. Several psychologists have investigated ways to encourage accuracy. In addition, they consider factors that will affect the testimony of the witness, and which the police and courts need to be aware of. Three influences will be examined in this section:

- recognising faces
- weapon focus
- the cognitive interview.

1.1 Recognising faces

In her book *Recognising Faces* (1988), Bruce cites the case of George Ince, who was tried for murder in a case that rested almost entirely on identification evidence. The witnesses were the husband and daughter of a murdered woman, who saw the attacker for at least 20 minutes. The daughter identified Ince from an ID parade, but it later transpired that she had earlier been shown his picture, contravening 1969 regulations for the conduct of ID parades. Ince was later discharged, because he was able to produce an alibi. This case highlights issues that arise with the investigative process and opens up some areas for investigation by psychologists.

Bruce and other researchers in the field have shown that there is a clear difference between recognising familiar faces, which we are competent at, and unfamiliar faces, which are quite a different problem.

Sinha et al. (2006) summarised 19 results of face recognition research from a meta-analysis of papers on the subject. Of these points, eight are relevant to witnesses trying to recreate a stranger's face by reconstruction.

Key terms

biometric data data about people that are recorded and kept; they include biological features such as fingerprints, iris scans and DNA samples

schema a mental structure containing information that we hold about something which in turn connects to other schemas, creating a representation of the world or what we call 'knowledge'

reconstructive memory when we recall something, it does not happen literally like a tape recorder; using a schema we fit together likely events to make a story, some of which may be highly accurate and some very inaccurate

cue anything that will jog our memory and help us to recall something; it could be a taste, a smell, a sound or an image

meta-analysis a study of studies. It gathers second-hand data but allows a researcher access to a huge variety of samples and procedures which taken together may be more meaningful than a single piece of research

Figure 1.7 This highly pixellated image of Madonna is still recognisable. Try holding it at a distance to 'lose' some of the pixellations

1 Humans can recognise familiar faces in very low-resolution images. (Hence poor quality CCTV images are still recognised.)

2 This effect increases with the familiarity of the person. (The *Crimewatch* television programme aims to exploit this fact by broadcasting appeals directly to people who know the suspect.)

3 Facial features are processed holistically (all together as a single unit). This has implications for facial reconstruction.

4 Of the facial features, the eyebrows and hairline are most important. (Again, vital for effective reconstruction.)

5 Illumination changes influence recognition (If the suspect is seen in poor or side light they may look very different.)

6 Motion of the face helps recognition. (Obviously, facial reconstruction is a static feature at present.)

7 There appear to be specialised neurones for face recognition which appear to be developed in infancy. (Everyone seems to have the ability to recognise faces.)

8 Face identity and expression may be processed by two different systems. (Again this has implications for reconstructions, which tend to be expressionless.)

One of the more recent areas of research in a lifetime spent on the subject are Bruce's investigations into what she calls the internal and external features of a face. It is thought that when we look at someone familiar, faces are recognised more accurately from their internal features (the region including the eyes, brows, nose and mouth), than from their external facial features (head shape, hair and ears), but for unfamiliar faces, the external features dominate. An interesting test of this is the construction of a facial composite as required by a witness to a crime. The following study by Bruce and her colleagues is her most recent work on this subject.

Key study

Frowd et al., The importance of external and internal features in facial recognition

Aim To investigate the relative recognisability of internal and external features of a facial composite.

Methodology Three laboratory experiments.

Participants Experiment 1: 30 staff and students from Stirling University were paid £2 to sort the composites, 15 males and 15 females with a mean age of 29.2.

Experiment 2: 48 undergraduates at Stirling University, 21 males, 27 females all volunteers.

Experiment 3: 8 staff paid £10 to be participant witnesses, 54 volunteers did a sorting task and 16 a naming task.

Procedure

Experiment 1

The stimuli were target photographs of 10 celebrities and 40 composite images produced by E-FIT, PRO-fit, Sketch and EvoFIT (these are facial composite programs in common use by the police). Each face was clean shaven and spectacles were avoided. Three sets of composites were used: a 'complete' set, a set containing the internal features and another set containing the external features.

Try this ...

At first glance these two photos look like different people. In fact both show the same person, Radovan Karadzic. He was trying to evade capture for war crimes in Bosnia and let his hair and beard grow and wore spectacles. In this way he lived and worked for 12 years unrecognised in his country even though he had been their leader. If you were trying to recreate these faces as a witness you would almost certainly want to describe the hairline and face shape first. These are the external features of a face and are the most important when we are describing a stranger.

Try getting a wig from a fancy dress shop and photographing someone with and without it. Show the two photos to a sample of people mixed with other photos of your friends with their permission. Can your sample identify the correct pair of faces? Is there a difference between male and female face recognition ability? Does age make a difference?

Figure 1.8 The external features of a face are most important for recognition

Participants were tested individually on one of the three conditions (independent measures design). They were asked to place each composite in front of the celebrity face in their own time until the task was completed.

Experiment 2

This experiment used a photo array or photo line-up with distracter faces or foils making the task more difficult. The faces and foils were made easy (all very different) or hard (all very similar) to identify. The composites were then presented one at a time along with the photo array and the participant had to pick out the celebrity face from the array which matched the composite. As before, the composites were either of internal features or external features of the face.

Experiment 3

Familiar or unfamiliar target faces were presented to 'witnesses' who then created PROfit composites after seeing them for 30 seconds. Then images were 'photoshopped' to create internal and external only composites. These were then randomly presented to the sorters and the namers as before with whole faces.

Results

Experiment 1

Whole composites and those of external features were sorted similarly at approximately 35 per cent correct. The composites of internal features were only 19.5 per cent correct.

Experiment 2

Composites of external features (42 per cent) were identified more easily than internal features (24 per cent) and this was consistent across array type (whether easy or difficult).

Experiment 3

Sorting was accurate at 57 per cent and it did not matter whether the face was familiar or unfamiliar. External features more accurate than internal: 53.3 per cent against 32.6 per cent. The naming task was 22 per cent accurate whether familiar or non-familiar.

Conclusions In Experiments 1 and 2, participants performed just above chance with internal features on the tasks used. In Experiment 3, familiarity with the target improved the sorters' success to 57 per cent. In all cases, participants performed equally well with external features or whole faces. This could indicate that there is something about the internal features of a face that does not work well when trying

to create a reconstruction. This effect holds true even when the face is familiar, which sheds some doubt on previous research.

Facial recognition research faces the same problems as any other type of memory recall, for example:

◆ Delay – how long ago did you see the face?

◆ Exposure mode – in what context or emotion did you see the face?

◆ Stimulus variable – how much did the face mean to you?

◆ Subject variables – how good are you at remembering faces?

The difference here is that the accuracy of recall really matters and the witness will be cross-examined about how certain they are about what they saw.

Psychological research (Davies et al., 1978) has shown that artist's impressions are sometimes superior to photofit pictures for identifying people, but new developments in facial morphing should significantly improve effectiveness.

Key term

facial morphing taking several 'original' versions of a face and merging them together by using points mapped onto the face electronically. Each successive merging of the face makes it blander and eventually after 16 faces have been morphed there is a very stereotypical image, which oddly most people then find more attractive than any of the original images

EvoFIT Evolving the face of a criminal

Figure 1.9 Facial morphing

Weblinks

Have a look at a useful short guide to memory and forgetting (see Contents page).

You may like to take part in an experiment using a facial morphing example and many other fun experiments (see Contents page).

The *New Scientist* has also published recent research on facial recognition, so it is worth a look at the website if you have a subscription (see Contents page).

see Contents page

Check your understanding

1   Are you confident in the difference between the internal features and the external features of a facial composite?

2   What are distracter faces or foils?

3   Why do you think that the internal features of a face are much less important than the external features? To help answer this, imagine you are meeting someone in a crowded place and scanning the crowd for the person you want. How do you do it?

1.2 Factors influencing identification

One of the problems a witness faces in recalling a suspect is elaborated below: what happens when a weapon is involved in the crime?

Weapon focus

Weapon focus refers to the concentration of a crime witness's attention on a weapon and the resultant difficulty in remembering other details of the scene. Perception experiments have shown that people fixate their gaze for longer, faster and more often on unusual or highly informative objects. It is assumed that eye fixation data are a valid measure of someone's attention in these pieces of research. The participant is filmed while looking at slides or a video clip and minute accurate measurements are made of exactly where the eyes were scanning. These measurements can then be plotted to reveal the greatest gaze concentration. Using this technique, Loftus et al. (1987) have investigated weapon focus experimentally.

Aim To provide support for the 'weapon focus' effect when witnessing a crime.

Methodology A laboratory experiment.

Participants 36 students at the University of Washington, aged 18–31. Half were recruited through an advertisement and were paid $3.50 for their participation. The remainder participated in exchange for extra credit in their psychology classes.

Procedure Two sets of 35mm slides were shown. The 18 slides in each series showed people queuing in a Taco Time restaurant. In the control group, person B (second in the line) hands the cashier a cheque. In the experimental condition, person B pulls a gun (the independent variable or IV). All the other slides in both series were identical and shown for 1.5 seconds. The participants were told it was a study of proactive interference. The dependent variable (DV) was measured by a 20-item multiple-choice questionnaire. The participants were also given a line up of 12 head-and-shoulder photos in a random sequence and were asked to rate how confident they were of their identification on a scale of 1–6 (1 = guess, 6 = very sure).

Results Answers to the questionnaire about the slide show showed no significant difference between the two conditions. Chance performance on the photo line-up was calculated to be 8.5 per cent. In the control condition, 38.9 per cent chose the correct person B (7 people) against 11.1 per cent in the weapon condition (2 people). This result is significant ($\chi^2 = 3.71$, $0.06 > p > 0.05$). There was no difference in the confidence level of either group. Eye fixation data showed an average of 3.72 on the gun and 2.44 on the cheque, which is also significant at $p < 0.025$.

Discussion As expected, the participants spent longer looking at the weapon and therefore had more difficulty in picking the suspect from the line-up. A second experiment, using the same procedure with another 80 psychology students, supported the findings. This influence may be further enhanced in a real-world situation when a witness will be more aroused and is likely to have increased attentional narrowing.

From this study and those done by other researchers it becomes obvious that an unusual attack or one involving a weapon is going to affect the witness's ability to create a photofit or E-fit of the attacker. Witnesses are also highly suggestible during questioning and so the police have to be very careful not to lead them in any way which might later destroy a case going to court.

Key term

proactive interference when something that you learned earlier interferes with your memory of the present, e.g. your old phone number interferes with your new one and confuses you. This effect is strongest if the two memories are similar

Check your understanding

1   As this was a laboratory experiment with a strictly limited range of behaviour measured, low ecological validity and high demand characteristics could be anticipated. Does this invalidate the study?

2   In this study, Loftus reduced her IV to one slide in a series of 18 while keeping all other factors as constant as she could. Why did she do this?

3   Why did Loftus give both groups a questionnaire about the slide show?

1.3 The cognitive interview

Over the last 20 years the police have worked with psychologists to develop the cognitive interview, which is designed to take account of well-known cognitive functions and avoid any chance of leading the witness.

The cognitive interview (CI) is a set of instructions given by the interviewer to the witness to reinstate the context of the original event and to search through memory by using a variety of retrieval methods (Fisher et al., 1989). So why does it work?

Theoretically, the CI is rooted in cognitive psychology and rests upon two principal assumptions, first that memory of an event is made up of an interconnected network and that there should therefore be several ways of getting to the same point, and second that retrieval from memory will be more effective if at the

time of retrieval the context surrounding the original events can be reinstated. Remembering some aspects of experience leads, by association, to others, but the sequence cannot be predicted and may seem confused to a listener. Cognitive interviewing is designed to facilitate accurate recall through a set of instructions.

There are four basic principles, according to Fisher et al. (1989).

1   **Interview similarity**
    Memory of an event such as a crime is enhanced when the psychological environment at the interview is similar to the environment at the original event. The interviewer should therefore try to reinstate in the witness's mind the external (e.g. weather), emotional, (e.g. feelings of fear) and cognitive (e.g. relevant thoughts) features that were experienced at the time.

2   **Focused retrieval**
    One of the roles of the interviewer is to generate focused concentration. There should be no interruption to the chain of thought and plenty of encouragement to try hard.

3   **Extensive retrieval**
    Witnesses should be encouraged to make as many retrieval attempts as possible. Even if they say they cannot remember, they should be encouraged to try another angle, e.g. imagining the scene from another viewpoint. Even seemingly irrelevant details are requested.

4   **Witness-compatible questioning**
    Events are stored and organised uniquely for each witness. Successful retrieval therefore reflects how compatible the questioning is with the witness's unique mental representation. Interviewers should be flexible and alter their approach to meet the needs of each witness.

The following study replaces the one by Geiselmann 1985/6 that is listed on the specification. This is a more recent study that applies the original research to an actual field test.

Key study
Fisher et al., Field test of the cognitive interview

Aim To test the cognitive interview (CI) in the field.

Methodology Field experiment with actual interviews of real witnesses by serving police detectives.

Participants 16 detectives from the Robbery Division of Dade County, Florida. All were experienced, with a minimum of 5 years with the division.

Procedure In the first phase of the experiment, detectives were asked to record a selection of their next interviews using the standard techniques they normally used. This took 4 months and 88 interviews were recorded, mostly relating to bag snatches or robberies. The detectives were then divided into two groups and one group was trained in CI techniques.

Training was over four 60-minute sessions. Seven detectives completed the programme and were used in the results shown below. Over the next 7 months more interviews were recorded by the two groups. The post-training interviews were analysed by a team at the University of California, who were blind to the conditions (trained or untrained in CI).

Results

After training, the seven trained detectives elicited 47 per cent more information than before, and 63 per cent more information than the untrained detectives. In terms of accuracy, laboratory-based research had shown no difference between the CI and the standard interview, with approximately 85 per cent of all statements being correct in all conditions. In this field study, accuracy had to be established by corroboration with another source. In 24 cases with corroborating evidence (16 by pre-trained detectives and 8 by post-trained detectives) 94 per cent of statements were corroborated.

The time taken to interview witnesses was not significantly different, but CIs do take longer.

Discussion Strong support was obtained for the effectiveness of CIs in the field. More information was obtained from witnesses to real events with no loss of accuracy and a minimal increase in time taken to interview them. The results in the field replicated those of the laboratory and perhaps gave them more weight, although the sample is small and may have been particularly well motivated to run the trial.

The CI has since been applied to other clinical settings, with therapists using it to develop medical histories.

It is used by police forces in the UK and is still the subject of research and refinement by Fisher and others.

Check your understanding

1   Which types of crimes will work best with the cognitive interview?

2   The CI depends on the witness being cooperative. Why?

3   It does take a little more time to conduct, it requires more effort on the part of the witness and the interviewer and time delays or the age of the witness may affect its usefulness. Why?

4   It is possible that the post-trained interviews were affected by another variable such as better observing conditions. Why is this a problem?

5   The improved accuracy of recall by witnesses in real life over the laboratory has been found in other eyewitness research. Can you suggest why this might be?

Section summary

◆   The work of Bruce and others shows that the old ways of constructing photofits relied on a false idea of how we recognise faces. Her research is leading to seeing face reconstruction as a holistic process with much more satisfactory results.

◆   It has been known for some time that if a weapon is involved in a crime then a witness is likely to be less accurate at identifying a suspect, as the shock of seeing a weapon will dominate over recall of the suspect's facial features.

◆   When interviewing a witness it is important not to lead them in any way, yet prompts can help recall immensely. A cognitive interview approach allows the witness to improve recall by reconstructing the event in their mind, including sights, sound, smells, feelings and taking different perspectives on the event.

2 Interviewing suspects

The caution, which must be given on arrest, should be in the following terms:

'You do not have to say anything, but it may harm your defence if you do not mention when questioned something which you later rely on in Court. Anything you do say may be given in evidence.'

2.1 Detecting lies

After an arrest, the purpose of an interview with a suspect is to establish guilt or innocence by getting them to say something about the events in question which may then lead to a conviction. A big problem in conducting research in the field is that of ethics. In the study by Mann et al. (2004), it would have been ideal to have a control group of lay people to give a comparison for the police officers' ability to detect lies. This is not possible because it would not be right for people outside the force to see video clips of a suspect's interviews. Under the law, a suspect is innocent until proven guilty, and people interviewed under caution have the right to privacy until their case comes to court.

A review by Vrij of all earlier research has suggested that on average an accuracy rate of 57 per cent is obtained in detecting lies. This is not far above chance. Ekman (1991) found some specialist groups such as the Secret service (64 per cent), CIA (73 per cent) and Sheriffs (67 per cent) were better. However, typically these studies use students asked to lie and tell the truth in laboratory experiments. This might lead to poor mundane realism as these students have nothing to gain or lose and so might not be exhibiting the cues of a genuine liar. To raise the stakes, they are sometimes offered money to try to 'get away with it'. Interestingly, these liars are easier to detect. Therefore Mann et al. set out to use real police officers with real witnesses in an attempt to make their study more ecologically valid and overcome these problems. Police officers tend to think that they are good at detecting lies and believe that suspects give away small details through body language such as looking down, putting their hands over their mouths and being inconsistent under repetitive questioning when lying.

The following study replaces the study by Vrij 2000 which is listed in the specification. This is a more up-to-date study and uses British police officers.

Key study

Mann et al., Police officers' ability to detect suspects' lies

Aim To test police officers' ability to distinguish truths and lies during police interviews with suspects.

Methodology Field experiment.

Participants 99 Kent Police Officers, 24 females and 75 males with a mean age of 34.3; 78 were detectives, 8 were trainers, 4 were traffic officers and the remaining 9 were uniformed response officers.

Procedure Participants were asked to judge the truthfulness of people in real-life police interviews.

They saw video clips of 14 suspects showing their head and torso so that expression and movement were visible. These clips were backed up by other evidence which established whether the suspect was lying or telling the truth at any point. The 54 clips varied in length from 6 to 145 seconds. The police officers began by filling out a questionnaire about their experience in detecting liars. They watched the clips and after each one indicated whether they thought it was a lie or the truth and in addition how confident they were about their decision. Finally, they were asked to list the cues they had used to detect the liars.

Results The difference between the mean lie accuracy (66.2 per cent) and truth accuracy (63.6 per cent) is not significant, but both levels of accuracy are significantly greater than chance (50 per cent). Experience in interviewing was correlated with truth accuracy (r (99) = 0.20, p = 0.05) and lie accuracy (r (99) = 0.18, p = 0.07).

The most frequently mentioned cue to detect lying was gaze, second was movements; vagueness, contradictions in stories and fidgeting were also mentioned as cues.

Conclusion First, the levels of accuracy found in this study exceed those found in other studies and are the highest for a group of ordinary police officers. To establish whether they were any better than lay people would require a control group, but lay people could not be shown the sensitive material in the video clips. Secondly, the more experience an officer (by his or her own self-report) has, the better they get at detecting lies. Thirdly, good lie detectors rely more on story cues than the more popular stereotypical belief that liars give themselves away by covering the mouth or fidgeting.

Finally, police officers can detect liars above the level of chance, but often pay attention to cues that are not diagnostic cues to deceit. This may be because they appear in police manuals.

Check your understanding

1   This was a field experiment. What defines a field experiment?

2   Is the sample generalisable?

3   To ensure no breach of ethics occurred, there was no control group to view the police interviews. Can you suggest another way that this problem could be overcome?

In groups of three; prepare three endings to the following sentences about yourself, two of which are true and one which is a lie. Try to detect the lies in each others' answers.

◆ The most unusual thing I have ever done is…

◆ My most frightening experience was…

◆ I think it is wrong to…

As a class, can you summarise the results? Did you have a particularly good lie detector? Are girls or boys better at detecting liars in your class?

2.2 Interrogation techniques

As mentioned in the introduction to this section, the police have been accused of using too much force to obtain confessions and this is illustrated by the case of FC documented by Gudjohnsson et al. (1990) (see pages 33–34). In this case we can clearly see the effect of a pressurised interview scenario on a young man who was innocent of the crime he was accused of. As discussed previously, numerous cases of false confession have been identified, with a recent report by Davis and Leo (2006) citing more than 300 documented instances.

Since the 1984 Police and Criminal Evidence Act (PACE) all interviews have to be recorded on special machines that record in triplicate. One copy is sealed in front of the suspect and not touched until the trial, one is the working copy for the police and one is for the solicitor defending the suspect. By this means, the reading of rights and the right to a solicitor, the individual is protected as any undue pressure can be revealed to the court in the suspect's defence. Unfortunately, false confessions still happen.

In the USA, interrogation used to be known as being subjected to 'the third degree', a term derived from the Freemasons (an organisation for men concerned with moral and spiritual values and a belief in a supreme being) where there are three degrees of membership, the third requiring an interrogation to pass as a master mason. The equivalent of the UK's PACE code of practice in the USA are the Miranda rights, which came into force in 1966 after a case (Miranda v Arizona) that was thrown out by the Supreme Court because the defendant had not been warned of his rights. The right to remain silent in the USA is called 'taking the fifth amendment' and is part of the constitutional rights of citizens.

So where did all this concern about the dangers of interrogation arise from? We will look at just one type of interrogation technique here, but many others exist, including those used by the British police in Northern Ireland.

Weblink

You might like to read a true story of what happened when some non-violent activists threw custard pies at the mayor of San Francisco in protest at his spending money regilding the dome of the city hall while homeless people died on the streets. Be aware that this website may have a biased viewpoint (see Contents page).

The difference between an interview and an interrogation is that the interrogation is accusatory: the investigator tells the suspect that there is no doubt as to their guilt. The interrogation begins with a police officer making a series of statements that require little response from the suspect, as opposed to the question-and-answer format of a normal police interview. Contrary to TV depictions, the police interrogator is required to be understanding, patient and non-demeaning to the suspect.

Prior to the interrogation an interview will have taken place which raises the prospect of the suspect's guilt. The suspect will often then be left in isolation until the interrogation begins. This is designed to increase arousal and anxiety. The procedure is summarised below.

Key study
Inbau et al., The Reid 'nine steps' of interrogation in brief

Inbau developed an approach to interrogation which relied on presenting a mass of damaging facts to persuade criminals that they had no choice but to confess. He felt that it was justifiable for the police to lie, deceive or use tricks to force a confession. His techniques are described in a book written with John Reid, *Criminal Interrogation and Confessions* (1962), which is the most widely used interrogation manual in the USA. As you can imagine he was not in favour of the Miranda rights when they came out, and he formed an organisation to fight what he saw as a trend towards placing the individual's rights before those of society in criminal cases.

1. Direct confrontation – the suspect is told directly that they are thought to have committed the offence.

2. The suspect is offered the chance to shift the blame away from themself by being offered some suggestions or justifications for what happened. The interrogator should show sympathy and understanding for their plight. This is designed to make it easier to admit guilt.

3. The suspect should never be allowed to deny guilt. Interrupt any denial to prevent the suspect getting the psychological advantage.

4. At this point the suspect will often try to give reasons why they could not have committed the crime. Try to use this to move towards a confession by ignoring them. Eventually the suspect will give up trying.

5. Reinforce sincerity to ensure that the suspect is receptive by staying close, keeping good eye contact and using first names.

6. The suspect will eventually become quieter and listen; at this point move towards offering alternatives. If the suspect cries, infer guilt.

7. Pose the 'alternative question', giving two choices of what the suspect could do, one more socially acceptable than the other (it gives a reason why they could have done it) but whichever they choose they are admitting their guilt.

8. Get the suspect to admit guilt in front of witnesses.

9. Document their admission and get them to sign a confession to avoid them retracting it later.

Inbau justifies the use of psychological techniques in this way because he says that they are being used on people presupposed to be guilty through their preliminary interview. One of the main criticisms is that when used with young people or the mentally impaired, it is highly likely to obtain a false confession. In the UK the use of psychological techniques or deception and the use of false evidence is prohibited by police conducting interviews with criminals.

Check your understanding

1. Can you apply the situational versus dispositional explanations of behaviour debate to explaining how this technique works so effectively?

2. Can you see why you would be advised to remain silent right through this process?

2.3 False confessions

Kassin and Wrightsman (1985), cited in Gudjohnsson (1990), suggest three distinct types of false confession:

1. The 'voluntary confession' which is offered in the absence of any obvious external pressure.

2. The 'coerced compliant confession' which is elicited by forceful or persistent questioning and where the suspect confesses in order to escape from a stressful situation.

3. The 'coerced internalised confession' where the person becomes at least temporarily persuaded during interrogation that they did commit the crime they are accused of.

This persuasion is possible because of the nature of our memories, which are fragile and susceptible to suggestion, especially when we are in a vulnerable state and anxious. A whole field of research is now devoted to false memories and from the AS course you will be familiar with the work of Loftus, whose work is dominant in the field.

U3
1

Key study
Gudjohnsson et al., A case of false confession

Aim To document a case of the false confession of a youth who was at the time distressed and susceptible to interrogative pressure.

Methodology Case study.

Subject A 17-year-old youth accused of two murders (FC). He was of average intelligence, suffered from no mental illness and his personality was not obviously abnormal.

Background In 1987, two elderly women were found battered to death in their home. The women's savings were missing and there was evidence of sexual assault. A few days later FC was arrested because of some inconsistencies in his account of his movements during an earlier routine enquiry and that he was spending more money than usual. There was no forensic evidence to link him with the offence. After his arrest he was denied access to a solicitor and was interviewed at length by the police, leading to his confession. The next day he repeated this confession in front of a solicitor and later wrote a statement incriminating himself from jail. After a year in jail he was released by a court after another person pleaded guilty to the crimes.

The police interviews FC's first interview lasted for nearly 14 hours with breaks. He was questioned by officers. To start with, FC denied being near the scene, but after being repeatedly accused of lying he agreed. Many questions were leading and accusatory and many suggested he was sexually impotent, which he found distressing.

In a second interview the next day in front of a duty solicitor, he retracted his statement, only to confess again under pressure about his failure to have successful relationships with women. There were three further interviews.

Psychiatric examination In prison he was examined by psychiatrists and no evidence of mental illness was found but he did score 10 for suggestibility on the Gudjohnsson Suggestibility Scale, making him abnormal in this respect. His IQ was 94. Using Eysenck's Personality Inventory (EPI) he came out as a stable extrovert.

Conclusion This is a case of a 'coerced compliant' false confession, meaning that he gave in to pressure during the interviews in order to escape from an intolerable situation. It shows that this can happen to anyone, not just the mentally ill, mentally handicapped or illiterates. Following his release, FC appeared to undergo a change of personality, his experiences hardened him and his self-confidence improved.

Check your understanding

1 Look at the police questions in the case study and think about the psychological effect they would have. Which step on the interrogation scale are they?

2 What are the situational factors here which would induce a false confession?

3 Evidence shows that juries heavily value confessions. Can you apply 'belief in a just world' or the 'fundamental attribution error' to understanding why this should be?

3 Creating a profile

3.1 Top-down typology

The phrase 'top-down' refers to taking an approach to human behaviour that assumes that higher cognitive functions such as thinking and problem-solving are applied to new situations by first applying a kind of visionary or 'big-picture' method and then looking for smaller details that will support the big picture. On the other hand, bottom-up approaches focus on the small details at the bottom of your field of view and build up a picture from there. The organisation is imposed on it at a later stage but initially everything is seen and processed.

Here we are applying the concepts to profiling. The Americans have historically been associated with the top-down approach, which imposes a big picture onto a crime scene, which they call a typology. They then look for the details in the scene which will support their hypothesis.

The next study is outlined only and then followed by a more useful evaluation of Hazelwood's work on typologies by David Canter. This is because of the study's unsuitable content for an A-Level text.

In 1980, Hazelwood and Douglas published their account of the 'lust murderer', in which they advanced their theory of the organised and disorganised offender for the first time. It makes grisly reading and it is inappropriate to go into detail here, but it describes the beginnings of the typology approach to profiling which has continued to be developed since.

Douglas et al. (1992) are proponents of the approach that was elaborated by the FBI in 1986. At that time Ressler et al. claimed that a crime scene can be used in the same way as a fingerprint to help in identifying a murderer, saying that it is possible to categorise

Section summary

The police think they are good lie detectors and often rely on non-verbal cues to try and tell if a suspect is lying. Research suggests that this is not the case and that inconsistencies in stories are a better indicator. The police are better at this, but not as good as they think they are.

Interrogation is sometimes used to force a confession, but in the UK this is only done under special circumstances. Inbau advocates

using psychological techniques to break down suspects' resistance and his handbook is used by police in the United States.

The problem with strong interrogation techniques is that they can lead to false confessions. This can happen with anyone, not just those with lower self-confidence. To protect witnesses, the PACE guidelines must be followed throughout the legal process.

this fingerprint as 'disorganised' or 'organised' (the typology) from an examination of the crime scene. An organised offender leads an orderly life and kills after undergoing some sort of critical event, and their actions reflect planning and control, perhaps with the use of restraints and bringing a weapon to the scene. The crime scene will therefore reflect this order and the offender is more likely to use a verbal approach with victims. The offender is claimed to be of average to high intelligence, socially competent, and more likely to be in employment than a disorganised offender.

The disorganised offender is likely to have committed the crime in a moment of passion, with no pre-planning and using whatever is to hand. They may leave blood, semen, fingerprints and the murder weapon behind. This type of offender is thought to be less intelligent and socially incompetent.

In 1992, Douglas et al. introduced a third category called the 'mixed' offender who does not easily fit either of the earlier two typologies. This might be because there is more than one offender, unanticipated events may occur during the crime, the victim might resist more than expected and the offence might escalate into a different pattern.

The original dichotomy was an attractive prospect for investigators because they felt it would guide their search for the suspects' behavioural characteristics.

The problems with the typologies are first that they were based on interviews with an opportunity sample of 36 murderers in prison who agreed to talk to them. The interviews were unstructured and developed in an ad hoc fashion. The murderers were initially divided into 24 organised and 12 disorganised offenders from their answers to the interview questions.

No tests of the two typologies were ever done on a random sample of offenders, and no further tests of the study's reliability were carried out. To be fair to Ressler et al., they called it an exploratory study and others have cited it as established research, giving it a momentum they probably never expected.

A further problem is the practical difficulty of deciding where disorganisation begins and organisation ends. It must be difficult to classify crime actions as one or the other in all cases.

In an effort to test the reliability of the typologies, Canter et al. (2004) conducted a study where they applied the criteria of each typology to 100 cases to see if they reliably co-occurred.

Key study

Canter et al., Investigation of the organised/ disorganised theory of serial murder

Aim To test the reliability of organised/disorganised typologies.

Methodology A content analysis using the psychometric method of multi-dimensional scaling was applied to 100 cases to find out if the features hypothesised to belong to each typology would be consistently and distinctively different. The cases came from published accounts of serial killers in the USA and were cross-checked with court reports and officers where possible. They had been collected over several years by an independent researcher and were called the *Missen Corpus*. The third crime committed by each serial killer in each series was analysed for the research. *The Crime Classification Manual* (Douglas et al., 1992) was used to classify the crimes as organised or disorganised as far as was possible based on their replies to interviews.

Results Twice as many disorganised as organised crime-scene actions were identified, suggesting that disorganised offenders are more common or alternatively, easier to identify.

Only two crime-scene behaviours co-occurred in the organised typologies in a level significantly above chance, which were that the body was concealed in 70 per cent of cases and sexual activity occurred in 75 per cent of cases.

Similarly, only sex acts and vaginal rape occur in more than two-thirds of disorganised cases. Most of the other crime-scene behaviours co-occur regularly in less than half the crimes in which they happen. This suggests that acts that occur most often in serial murder are the consequence of most serial killings and not really distinctively different for each murderer.

Further statistical analysis (smallest-space analysis) failed to separate the two sets of variables. Instead the organised variables appeared central in the scattered plot, with disorganised variables spread widely around them (Figure 1.10).

Conclusion Canter concludes that instead of there being a distinction between two types of serial murder, all such crimes will have an organised element to them, as we might expect from the fact the killers were not caught after three killings. The distinctions between serial killers may be a function of the different ways in which they may exhibit disorganised aspects of their activities. He suggests a better way is to look at the individual personality differences between offenders.

Key terms

dichotomy a mutually exclusive division into two (here used to place crimes in two distinct categories)

ad hoc (literally 'to this') refers to something created to do a particular job in a particular context, in this case the interviews concerned

unstructured interviews interviews that do not follow a predetermined set of questions and instead are free-flowing, with one question leading from the previous answer

smallest-space analysis a way of interpreting data based on the assumption that the behaviour we are interested in (in this case murder) is being tested if the relationship between every variable and every other variable is examined. A computer program does these correlations and then presents the results as an image. The correlations are also ranked in terms of their importance and the closer the two variables appear, the better the 'fit' between them

multi-dimensional scaling a statistical technique that attempts to analyse relationships between several variables, each of which is allocated a value

Check your understanding

1. How is Canter's test of the organised/ disorganised typology different from the original methods used by Hazelwood and Douglas?

2. Why do you think the third crime in each series was used for the analysis?

3. Is this research reliable?

4. Is this research valid?

Take it further

- Why should we be cautious about the correlational data in this study?

- What everyday features of police work will affect the accuracy of a profile?

- Read about the work of Britton and Canter in their own books, which you may have in your library.

- Try a crime scene activity and be a profiler.

- Canter admits that statistical analysis of this type is difficult, as there is no clear definition of what would be expected by chance. Therefore how do you know when you have a significant finding? He has to use assumptions for this and bearing in mind his views, could he have set overly stringent criteria?

3.2 Bottom-up approaches

Canter is one of the UK's foremost profiling experts and runs the Centre for Investigative Psychology at Liverpool University. He began his career looking at environmental psychology, such as the behaviour of people in buildings, which did not deviate even in emergencies such as fires, where he noted that there was consistency in their behaviour. From this observation of human behaviour came his approach to profiling, which looks for consistencies in offenders' behaviour during the crime. These can be inferred from the crime scene or from surviving victims' accounts, and he has worked on murders and rapes in detail. His most famous case

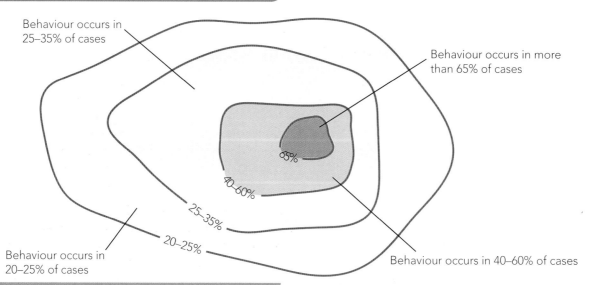

Figure 1.10 Graphical representation of smallest-space analysis

Behaviour occurs in 25–35% of cases

Behaviour occurs in more than 65% of cases

65%

40–60%

25–35%

20–25%

Behaviour occurs in 20–25% of cases

Behaviour occurs in 40–60% of cases

of profiling, that of the 'Railway Rapist', John Duffy, appears below.

In 1990, Canter and Heritage published a paper on a model of offender profiling. It was part of a series of studies carried out at the University of Surrey, and the central quest was to identify associations between aspects of the offender's characteristics and offence behaviour. This is a cognitive social approach in which the criminal's interactions with others are seen as the key to their behaviour. It is bottom-up because no initial assumption is made about the offender until a statistical analysis using correlational techniques has been carried out on the detail of the cases. It relies heavily on computer databases being accurate and powerful. Canter's methods can be considered more objective and reliable than top-down procedures because they are always based on data analysis and a theoretical basis of human behaviour. However, in practice the police will adopt a 'whatever works' philosophy and use elements of either approach.

Key study
Canter and Heritage, Developments in offender profiling

Aim To identify a behaviour pattern from similarities between offences.

Methodology A content analysis of 66 sexual offences from various police forces committed by 27 offenders was conducted to find 33 offence variables that were clearly linked to a potential behaviour characteristic, e.g. variable 2 was 'surprise attack'. It was possible to say 'yes' or 'no' to each variable. (Sexual offences are chosen because there is a great deal of information available about the perpetrator's actions.)

Analysis The data were subjected to a smallest-space analysis.

Results The following variables were found to be central to the 66 cases of sexual assault:

- vaginal intercourse
- no reaction to the victim
- impersonal language
- surprise attack
- victim's clothing disturbed.

This suggests a pattern of behaviour where the attack is impersonal and sudden and the victim's response is irrelevant to the offender. Less central were a further

four elements of the attacks which have been found to be important in other research. These were: attempted intimacy with the victim, sexual behaviour, overt violence and aggression, impersonal interaction and criminal behaviour and intent.

Conclusions Canter believes that the usefulness of this method is that all five aspects have now been shown to contribute to all sexual offences, but in different patterns for different individuals. This can lead to an understanding of how an offender's behaviour changes over a series of offences, or more usefully still to establishing whether two or more offences were committed by the same person. This has become known as his '5-factor' theory.

Check your understanding

1. All the data are correlational and cannot therefore be used in any way to explain the causes of the offender's behaviour. Why not?

2. This analysis has been done on sexual offenders but has since been extended to other crimes where it also shows up useful patterns of behaviour. Which crimes would you expect it to work well with?

3. It is dependent for its effectiveness on good record-keeping by the police. What factors can affect the accuracy of police records?

3.3 Case study

Key study
Canter, The case of John Duffy

In November 2000, John Duffy, who was serving life for the rape and murder of several women, confessed to his prison psychologist that in fact he was responsible for many more and that he had committed many of these acts with an accomplice, David Mulcahy. He therefore testified in front of the jury at Mulcahy's trial, giving the evidence to 'clear his conscience'.

He admitted committing 25 offences between 1975 and 1986, including 2 murders and 21 rapes. Most of the women, aged between 15 and 32 years, were targeted at railway stations in and around London; others were attacked on Hampstead Heath in north London. This was many more than the police had evidence for, although they had always known there was an accomplice.

Canter became involved in the early 1980s when he read about the cases in the *Evening Standard* and started to draw up a table of the cases chronologically and showing whether they had been committed by one or two people. The police were interested in his ideas and appointed two police officers to assist him in accessing the database of the crimes. This was to be the beginning of Canter's method of profiling which he later extended and developed.

Canter's starting point for his profile was that a violent crime can be seen as a transaction between at least two people and therefore must reveal something about the way the offender deals with people. One of the most significant themes is how prepared the offender is to try to relate to the victim, which can indicate previous similar attempts at relationships. The second main theme is how much dominance is used. In Duffy's case, this was the minimal amount needed to accomplish the rape, indicating a weaker individual who was actually insecure. A further breakthrough came when Canter suggested looking at the cases over the 4 years they had evidence for, placing the cases on a map and overlaying each year on an acetate film. This revealed distinctive patterns in the locations and types of his crimes and allowed Canter to speculate on where Duffy was likely to live. This was later developed into his circle theory of crime and then into a further hypothesis where he called perpetrators 'marauders' and 'commuters' depending on whether they strike out from their home base (marauder) or travel away from their home base to commit crimes (commuter). Duffy would be a marauder by these criteria. From his analysis of the database Canter drew up the following rough profile.

Preliminary profile

Possibly arrested some time after 1983.

Residence

◆ Has lived in the areas circumscribed by the first three cases since 1983.

◆ Probably lived in that area at the time of the arrest.

◆ Probably lives with a wife or girlfriend, possibly with no children.

Age etc.

◆ Mid- to late twenties.

◆ Light hair.

◆ About 5 feet 9 inches.

◆ Right-handed.

Occupation

◆ Probably semi-skilled or skilled involving weekend work or casual labour from July 1984 onwards.

◆ His job most likely does not bring him into contact with the public.

Character

◆ Keeps himself to himself but has one or two very close men friends and probably very little contact with women, especially in a work situation.

◆ Has knowledge of the railway system along which the attacks happen.

Sexual activity

◆ The variety of his sexual actions suggests considerable sexual experience.

Criminal record

◆ Was probably arrested some time between 24 October 1982 and January 1984 and this may have had nothing to do with rape but with having been aggressive and under the influence of drink or drugs.

This profile represents the first attempt to use behavioural characteristics to search for a criminal, instead of purely forensic evidence from the crime scene.

Duffy was already on the database and had already been interviewed in connection with an attack at knifepoint on his ex-wife. This was labelled a 'domestic' by the police and therefore not associated, even though it bore similarities to the attacks on the women in the case. Duffy was one of nearly 2000 suspects linked to the crime by their blood group, but when other factors from the profile were fed into the computer database, Duffy was the only one who lived in the Kilburn area of London predicted by the profile: he worked as a carpenter on the railway and was the right age. A surveillance team therefore watched him and in due course he was arrested for his suspicious activities. A search of his house revealed the unusual paper-based string that he used to tie up his victims.

It turned out that Duffy was a lot shorter than his victims had described and their varying versions of his appearance (ginger- to black-haired) was one of the difficulties the police faced in the original enquiry. There is a strong possibility that the victims were experiencing the 'weapons effect' described on page 28, because a knife was used to control them. However their memory of the actions and events of the attacks was very accurate and revealed the similarities in Duffy's modus operandi.

Key term

modus operandi ('way of working') the method used by a criminal while committing a crime, which is often distinctive to that criminal. It is sometimes associated with a 'signature' such as collecting a souvenir from the attack

Check your understanding

1   What is an offender profile?

2   When is an offender profile used?

3   What is the difference between Canter's approach to profiling and that of the FBI?

Take it further

◆   Find out more details of this case and read about Canter's work on other cases.

◆   Extend your knowledge of profiling by researching geographical profiling methods which have grown from the early beginnings in the Duffy case.

Weblinks

Many accounts of Duffy's case history can be read through a BBC website link (see Contents page).

You can read about the anthrax killer who is still at large. You will see all the evidence the FBI has and their profile based on this evidence (see Contents page).

Section summary

◆   Profiling has become more accepted in recent years as it has become more methodical and statistically based. It is still just one of many techniques used to solve crimes and is really only useful for particularly unusual or serial crimes.

◆   Top-down typologies look for common patterns in murder scenes and categorise them as organised or disorganised. From this decision, a series of behaviour patterns is assumed which can be helpful in reducing lists of potential suspects.

◆   Bottom-up approaches examine statistical correlations from clues found at the scene with other, similar crimes. Other correlations are looked for in geographical location and consistencies in behaviour patterns.

◆   The case study of John Duffy illustrates the style of profiling adopted by David Canter. This was his most successful attempt and gave hope that these techniques would transform the search for suspects in murder cases.

U3

1

Making a case

Reaching a verdict

Pause for thought

◆ Have you ever wondered how people are chosen for jury service?

◆ Have you ever wondered if a jury has got their verdict wrong?

◆ Can we believe the evidence of young children?

This area will consider how psychology can inform behaviour in the courtroom.

Introduction

The courtroom is the centrepiece of the criminal justice system. It is formal, with an elaborate language, and the action moves at a slow and meticulous pace. The main actors (judge, barristers, clerks and ushers) are in costume and the room is divided into sections for each player in the story (jury box, bench, witness box, gallery and dock). Into this situation come the ordinary men and women of the jury, who are usually experiencing it for the first time. (Do you remember the AS core study work on how situations affect behaviour, for example the BBC Experiment reported by Reicher and Haslam (2006) and the study by Piliavin et al. (1969)?)

It often surprises students that anyone has the right to watch a criminal trial, but this right comes from the ancient part of our law, which has always held an individual to account publicly for their actions. Hangings used to be a public entertainment, and many accounts in literature refer to the Assizes as major events in towns throughout the UK. If you wish to visit the Central Criminal Court (The Old Bailey) in London, where many big cases are heard, you will need to give notice so that you can be security checked, but this is usually only a formality.

What takes place inside the courtroom is part of an ancient process that was enshrined in Magna Carta and still holds that justice must be *seen* to be done. In the UK we have an adversarial system. The jurors have the final decision, but the judge has to make sure that there is a 'fair fight' and that one side does not get an advantage over the other. In France they have an inquisitorial system; clients are still represented by solicitors, but it is not an adversarial system.

Before trial by jury in 1215 we had trial by ordeal (sometimes called summary justice or trial by fire and

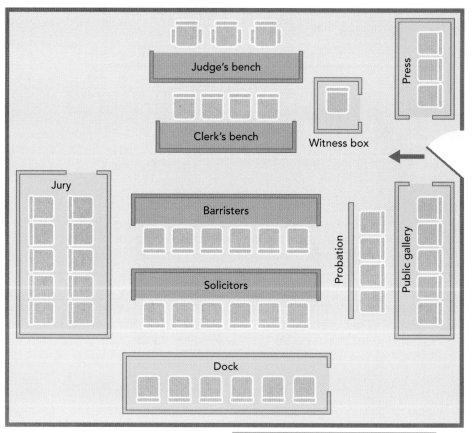

Figure 1.11 The layout of a courtroom

water). It often involved submerging someone in water to see if they would sink or float. If they sank they were innocent; if they floated God had rejected them and they were guilty (divine intervention).

How a jury is selected

Once you are 18 and you are on the electoral roll, you become eligible for jury service, which normally lasts about 2 weeks. Your name may come up on a computer selection program and you will get a letter inviting you to serve. You will have good notice so that you can rearrange other commitments, but you will be expected to turn up. Prisoners, ex-prisoners and those with mental illnesses are not eligible for service, and in some circumstances you can ask for your service to be deferred. Jurors are not paid, but they do get expenses. They are not trained in any way. On arrival at the court, jurors are allocated at random to a courtroom and take an oath to try the defendant fairly. In trials that are expected to be exceptionally long, the jury usher may ask for volunteers who can spare a long time.

Since 1989, jurors can only be challenged 'for cause' by the prosecution or defence, usually because of possible bias through a personal connection with the case. If the challenge is upheld by the judge, an alternative juror will be found. In the USA, jury selection involves *voire dire*, where a juror is interviewed about any preconceived ideas or attitudes that could bias the trial.

Key terms

adversarial where two sides argue the case in front of the judge and jury

inquisitorial where a judge calls their own witnesses and counsel and reaches a judgement independently

voire dire translates as 'to give a true verdict'. In the USA, when a potential juror is being questioned about their fitness to serve as a juror, they must respond truthfully to the questions from the defence barrister

There is a lot of information to absorb over a short period of time, even in a simple case, and the juror's task is not easy. The decision-making process might look something like that shown in Figure 1.12.

Here we will be looking at:

◆ persuading a jury

◆ witness appeal

◆ reaching a verdict.

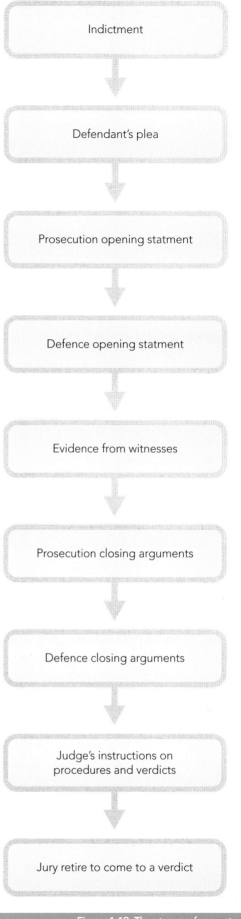

Indictment

Defendant's plea

Prosecution opening statment

Defence opening statment

Evidence from witnesses

Prosecution closing arguments

Defence closing arguments

Judge's instructions on procedures and verdicts

Jury retire to come to a verdict

Figure 1.12 The stages of a court case

This section examines the effect of order of testimony on the jury, whether it is more effective to present evidence in story order or witness order, the use of expert witnesses to persuade a jury and the effect on the jury's thinking of evidence being ruled inadmissible by the judge.

The next section will look in more detail at the witnesses themselves, what effect it has if they are attractive or confident when they give evidence and what happens if they are not in the courtroom at all, such as when a child gives evidence via video.

The third section will look in more detail at the stages of the jury's decision-making process and the influences of the majority and minority on an individual juror sitting with their peers trying to reach a verdict.

1 Persuading a jury

1.1 Effect of order of testimony

The adversarial system is all about persuading a jury, whichever side the counsel is representing. Psychologists have known for a long time that how we receive information affects how well we process and remember it. The primacy effect is one such factor. This was investigated by a researcher called Murdoch in 1962 in laboratory studies using word lists, where he demonstrated that the first words in the list were always more likely to be recalled than those from the middle or the end, hence the primacy effect.

This might be something to do with our arousal level at the start of a task, its novelty or how much effort we are using, but it is a robust finding that translates into the courtroom where the jury are fresh and interested at the start of a case when the opening statement is presented by the prosecution. This would suggest that the prosecution has an advantage over the defence at this point. Glanzer and Cunitz (1966) presented two groups of participants with the same list of words and got one group to recall immediately and the other to have their recall disrupted by counting backwards. The first group showed better recall of the words at the end of the list, whereas the disrupted group lost the benefit of the recency effect but retained the primacy effect. If we again apply this to the courtroom, in real life although the defence closes last, this is followed by the judge's summing up, which might wipe out any recency effect for the defence.

Also of interest to us is how counsel decide to structure their cases. Should they present their case as a story

unfolding in chronological order, or should they use the benefit of the primacy and recency effects to present their best witness first or last, even if this disrupts the order of events in the juror's mind?

The research on the order of testimony by Pennington and Hastie (1988) suggests that story order is best. However, in earlier work (in 1986), Pennington and Hastie showed that it is likely that even if the evidence is presented in witness order, the jury will make a chronological story out of it before they can reach a decision. In their research Pennington and Hastie use a case that they adapted from real life; you should read it to make the best sense of the experiment described below.

Try this ...

Ideally, enact the trial in your own class before going any further. Depending on your numbers, create one or two juries and discuss the case to reach a verdict. Allow plenty of time for this activity. You have to reach at least a majority verdict. It works well to have some observers who note down who becomes the leader and any minority/majority influence and primacy and recency effects.

Key study

Pennington and Hastie, Effects of memory structure on judgement

Aims To investigate whether or not story evidence summaries are true causes of the final verdict decisions and the extent to which story order affects confidence in those decisions.

Methodology A laboratory experiment, the second of two reported in this paper.

Participants 130 students from Northwestern University and Chicago University who were paid for participation in an hour-long experiment. They were allocated to one of four conditions in roughly equal numbers.

Procedure Participants listened to a tape recording of the stimulus trial (Commonwealth of Massachusetts v Caldwell) and then responded to written questions. They were told to reach either a guilty or not guilty verdict on a murder charge, and then asked to rate their confidence in their own decision on a 5-point scale. They were separated by partitions and did not interact with each other. In the story-order condition, evidence was arranged in its natural order. In the witness-order condition, evidence items were arranged in the order closest to the original trial. The defence items comprised 39 not-guilty pieces of evidence and the prosecution items, 39 guilty pieces of evidence from the original case.

So to summarise, we have four conditions:

| 39 prosecution items in story order | 39 defence items in story order |
| 39 prosecution items in witness order | 39 defence items in witness order |

In all cases the stimulus trial began with the indictment and followed the normal procedure, ending with the judge's instructions.

Results

Table 1.4 shows that story order persuaded more jurors of Caldwell's guilt in the prosecution case. If the defence presented its evidence in witness order, even more jurors would find a guilty verdict; if the positions were reversed and the defence had the benefit of the story order, the guilty rate drops to 31 per cent.

As predicted, the greatest confidence in their verdict was expressed by those who heard the defence or prosecution in story order. Least confidence was expressed by those who heard the two witness-order conditions.

Discussion Because the primacy and recency effect were controlled for, Pennington and Hastie are confident that they have shown the persuasive effect of presenting information in story order. In this case there is a difference in the defence case, which seems not to be as persuasive as the prosecution case, even when presented as a story. Pennington and Hastie account for this by referring to the case itself, in which they feel the defence case is less plausible (the victim was drunk and lunged forwards onto his assailant's knife). The case was adapted from a real-life case.

Check your understanding

1   Imagine carrying out this experiment yourself, listening to the tape and then going into a booth to give your answers with no contact with others to discuss the case. This is done to isolate the independent variable (in this case the story or witness order) under controlled conditions. In your opinion, does the experiment retain sufficient ecological validity to be generalised to a courtroom?

2   All the research that follows depends on some form of mock trial. Prepare some evaluation points which relate to the samples, how the trial is viewed/read or listened to and how the data are recorded.

3   Consider and inform yourself about the ethical issue of courtroom research.

1.2 Persuasion

So, having established that presenting evidence as a story works more convincingly, what happens to jury verdicts if an expert psychologist is called to give evidence about the research into all the psychological variables that affect an eyewitness giving evidence? We have covered some of this in the previous section (pages 25–30) and in the AS course, with Loftus and Palmer's study on leading questions (1974).

A psychologist called in to do this is likely to talk about the weapons effect, delays in giving testimony and the effect this has on memory, how when witnesses are given feedback it will affect their confidence in what they saw, how any ID parades were conducted and the effect this would have on accuracy, and so on. Overall, the research will suggest that any witnesses are likely to have an inaccurate or reconstructed version of the true events and that

	Defence evidence story order	Defence evidence witness order	Mean
Prosecution evidence story order	59	78	69
Prosecution evidence witness order	31	63	47
Mean	45	70	58

Table 1.4 Percentage of participants choosing a verdict of guilty of murder by prosecution and defence order conditions

therefore the jury should treat their testimony with some care. It was with some surprise therefore that Cutler et al. (1989) found that the jury were relatively unmoved by hearing all this, and retained confidence in the testimony of the witness.

The following study replaces the one by Krauss and Sales that is listed in the specification. This is a less complex study and has the benefit that the expert witness is a psychologist.

Key study
Cutler et al., The effect of the expert witness on jury perception of eyewitness testimony

Aim To investigate whether hearing about psychological research from an expert witness which casts doubt on the accuracy of eyewitness testimony would affect a juror's decision-making by making them more sceptical about such testimony.

Methodology A laboratory experiment using a videotaped mock trial.

Participants 538 undergraduates who were given extra credits for their introductory psychology course.

Procedure Participants viewed a videotaped robbery trial in groups of 2 to 8. Afterwards, they independently completed a questionnaire containing the dependent measures, which were the verdict, a memory test and rating scales for how confident they were in their verdict. There were four independent variables.

1 Witnessing Identifying Conditions (WIC) – whether the conditions were poor, i.e. the robber was disguised, brandishing a handgun (see page 28 for more about the weapons effect), there was a 14-day delay in the identification of the robber by the witness and the line-up instructions were suggestive; or the conditions were good – no disguise, a hidden gun, a 2-day delay and no suggestive instructions.

2 Witness confidence – the witness testified that she was (a) 80 per cent or (b) 100 per cent confident that she had correctly identified the robber.

3 Form of testimony – whether the expert psychologist described the results of eyewitness research in a descriptive way (small, medium or large effect) or whether it was quantified using percentages of correct or incorrect identifications.

4 Expert opinion – in half the trials the expert expressed his opinion on a scale from 0 (least likely to be correct) to 25 (most likely to be correct). These decisions coincided with the poor or good conditions in variable 1.

Results

Juror verdicts

When the WIC were good, more guilty verdicts were given and this effect increased if the expert witness had given descriptive testimony. All other variables were less significant or insignificant.

Juror memory

Of the participants, 85 per cent or more correctly recalled the testimony, so memory cannot be blamed for any lack of effect on jurors' judgments. In addition, memory for what the expert had said was also good, 50 per cent+ recalled the four stages of memory (perception, encoding, storage, and retrieval), 81 per cent recalled at least one stage. They also recalled correctly what the expert had said about weapons effects, disguises and delays in identification.

Juror confidence

Again it was under the good WIC that the jurors had more confidence in the accuracy of the identification. This effect was stronger if they had heard the expert witness and if the witness was 100 per cent confident rather than 80 per cent confident.

Discussion

The experiment showed that the expert testimony improved jurors' knowledge and made them pay more attention to WIC. It decreased the reliance on witness confidence alone and there was no evidence to suggest that expert testimony made the jurors sceptical about the witness's credibility, the accuracy of the identification or the defendant's culpability. With expert testimony, juror sensitivity to problems with evidence is improved and may help to prevent miscarriages of justice.

Check your understanding

1 Why were there three dependent variables in this experiment?

2 What is meant by good and bad WIC?

3 Why do you think the expert evidence was also varied?

4 Think about the sample used in this study. Can it be generalised?

- What happens if an opposing expert witness appears for either side, one saying that the evidence can be trusted and one saying it should be treated with caution, as is increasingly the case?

- Can you explain why the expert testimony appears to have so little measurable effect?

- Is this research ecologically valid enough to have meaningful application in the courtroom?

1.3 Effect of evidence being ruled inadmissible

Finally, this section will look at what happens when the judge tells the jury to disregard inadmissible evidence. The research that follows is American and based on the US legal system.

The laws of evidence say that, in order for evidence to be admissible in court, its relevance must outweigh its potential for prejudice. Inadmissible evidence includes such things as hearsay and prior conviction evidence (this is not supposed to be heard by a jury in case it biases them against the defendant on the grounds that if they have committed a criminal act before, they must automatically be guilty the second time) or evidence obtained by illegal means such as wire taps. Each trial is supposed to proceed on its own merits. However, since 2004 hearsay evidence and evidence of previous convictions is admissible in England and Wales subject to leave being given by the judge on specified grounds. Leave is commonly given.

If something is introduced which could be prejudicial, it is likely that the jury would be discharged for a re-trial by another jury. If counsel had introduced it deliberately they would be subject to severe discipline. Only a matter agreed to be of relatively minor significance would involve the jury being told to ignore it. Usually, when something slips out inadvertently no one makes an issue of it until a break occurs, the jury departs and its significance is then examined. The jury may not even notice it.

In the USA it may be that counsel 'drops in' something which the judge then directs should be ignored. The judge will then tell the jury to disregard what has just been said, but having had their attention drawn to it, the jury may pay even more attention to it. This is called reactance theory and it

is suggested that jurors perceive their instructions as undermining their freedom to take all the evidence into account.

In a study in 1977, Wolf and Montgomery used inadmissible evidence obtained through a stakeout to investigate this effect in a mock trial. They had three conditions, with inadmissible evidence favouring the prosecution, the defence or not present at all. The judge's ruling of admissible or inadmissible had very little effect on the guilty judgements reached by the jurors, except in the condition where he added an admonishment saying 'This evidence must play no role in your consideration of the case. You have no choice but to disregard it.' In this condition the jury members reacted against the instruction and used it to find the defendant guilty or not guilty, depending on which condition they were in.

The study by Pickel (1995) is one of three, and tests the effect of knowledge of previous convictions on the jury as well as the judge's instructions and finally looks at whether the credibility of a witness affects the jury's ability to disregard that witness's testimony.

The following study replaces the 1959 study by Broeder, which is listed in the specification. This is a more recent study which looks at what happened when an explanation for disregarding the evidence was given.

Key study

Pickel, Investigating the effect of instructions to disregard inadmissible evidence

Aims

1   To look at the effect of prior convictions

2   To look at the role of the judge's instructions when they were followed by a legal explanation.

3   To examine how much the credibility of the witness affects the juror's ability to ignore inadmissible statements.

Methodology An experiment using a mock trial of a fictional theft with a mock jury. The critical evidence was introduced 'by accident' by the witnesses. The item was objected to by the attorney and then either allowed or overruled by the judge. In the former case, when jurors were instructed to ignore the inadmissible evidence, this ruling by the judge was sometimes supported by a legal explanation: that the inadmissible evidence might be suggestive of bad character in the defendant and so bias the jury. Sometimes no legal explanation was provided.

Participants 236 Bali State University psychology students participated as part of a course requirement. They were assigned randomly to one of the conditions in an independent measures design.

Procedure On arrival, participants listened to an audiotape of the trial and then completed a questionnaire asking them to make several decisions about the case. One was the verdict, the second was their estimate of the probable guilt of the defendant, and the third was a rating on a 10-point scale of the extent to which knowledge of the prior conviction caused them to believe the defendant was guilty. Finally, they gave a rating on the credibility of each witness. There was a control group who did not get the critical evidence.

Results Mock jurors who heard the critical evidence ruled inadmissible and who received no explanation were able to follow instructions and ignore the evidence. Those who heard the evidence ruled inadmissible and who were given the explanation were more likely to find the defendant guilty and were clearly not able to disregard it. No evidence was found to support the hypothesis that the credibility of the witness would affect the juror's ability to disregard inadmissible evidence. In addition there was no significant effect on the use of prior conviction evidence as measured by the 10-point scale.

Conclusions It would seem that calling attention to inadmissible evidence makes it more important to the jury and they then pay it more attention. They apply their sense of fair play to decide whether or not to make use of it, which can create the 'backfire effect'. As long as the tactic is available to both sides and administered impartially by the judge, it could be a persuasive tool and is a minor matter.

Check your understanding

1   What is inadmissible evidence?

2   Make sure you understand how the application of the rules is different in the USA from England and Wales.

3   Why do you think there was a difference in hearing the evidence ruled inadmissible and hearing the ruling with an explanation?

Section summary

◆   The evidence about story order being more convincing is now well established and can be applied to understanding any body of knowledge. (It is usually easier to learn your A2 studies if you think of them as stories unfolding in some kind of context.)

◆   The use of expert witnesses in the courtroom is increasing and psychologists are being used to tell juries about the credibility of witness evidence. The research we looked at suggests that juries listen to the expert and remember what they have been told, but may still choose to ignore it when coming to a verdict.

◆   The research on evidence being ruled inadmissible suggests that juries feel confident in coming to verdicts irrespective of judges' instructions. It would be fascinating to be able to watch a real jury come to its verdict on a true case, but this is never likely to happen and so we have to use mock trials and mock juries. This creates many problems of generalisability and validity, which means we have to be cautious in applying the results in real life.

2 Witness appeal

2.1 Attractiveness of the defendant

Much has been made of the attractiveness of witnesses and defendants in court. This can be explained by psychological concepts such as impression formation, attribution and the 'halo effect' described by Asch (1946), where a positive halo of pleasant characteristics is imagined when one favourable characteristic is known about an individual (the reverse is also true). Another relevant theory is implicit personality theory as described by Dion in 1972 in the paper 'What is beautiful is good.' Dion hypothesised that the attractiveness stereotype attributed to beautiful people included the supposition that they must have attractive personalities.

What this means is that a jury may make decisions about witnesses and defendants based on their physical appearance, assuming that this relates to their personality, colouring their view of the evidence. This is why defendants' legal teams advise smart dress and a neat and clean appearance for a day in court. One piece of research into this effect was by Castellow in 1990, described below.

Key study

Castellow et al., The effects of physical attractiveness on jury verdicts

Aims To test the hypothesis that an attractive defendant is less likely to be seen as guilty. Secondly, when the victim is attractive, the defendant is more likely to be found guilty. Finally, to look for any gender differences in jury verdicts depending on attractiveness.

Methodology A laboratory experiment using the mock-trial format. It used an independent measures design.

Participants 71 male and 74 female students who participated for extra credit in their introductory psychology classes at East Carolina University.

Procedure Participants were told that they would be reading a sexual harassment case and would have to answer questions on it. With the case were attached photographs of the victim and defendant previously categorised as attractive or unattractive by a panel on a scale of 1 to 9, where 9 was very attractive and 1 was very unattractive. The dependent variable was measured by the answer to the question 'Do you think Mr Radford is guilty of sexual harassment?' Towards the end of the case booklet they were given, participants were asked to rate the defendant and the victim on 11 bipolar scales such as dull–exciting, nervous–calm, warm–cold.

Results Analysis of the ratings revealed that physically attractive defendants and victims were rated positively on other personality variables as well. When the defendant was attractive, guilty verdicts were found 56 per cent of the time against 76 per cent for an unattractive defendant. When the victim was attractive, the guilty verdict followed 77 per cent of the time with 55 per cent for the unattractive victim. No significant gender differences were found and both sexes were equally influenced by appearance.

Conclusion Although the findings come from a mock trial, when applied in the courtroom it seems that appearance does indeed have a powerful effect, and this finding has been supported by much other research. A defendant would be well advised to make the best of their appearance when appearing in court.

Check your understanding

1   Why was this experiment an independent measures design?

2   Is it ethical to ask people to rate others on a scale of attractiveness?

3   Why should attractive people be assumed to have positive characteristics?

2.2 Witness confidence

One of the most convincing features of a witness is their confidence when giving testimony. In a typical case, giving evidence is nerve wracking and it would be common for a witness to be hesitant or uncertain when answering questions under examination with all eyes upon them. When a witness is confident, the jury gain confidence in what they are saying and believe it to be more accurate. However this confidence can come from a system variable (how the police have conducted the earlier interviews and recording of evidence). Penrod and Cutler (1995) in a review of available evidence concluded that a major source of juror unreliability is reliance on witness confidence, even when measured at the time identification is made, when it should be at its most accurate. Confidence appears to be influenced by repeated questioning, briefings in anticipation of cross-examination and feedback about the behaviour of other witnesses (being told other witnesses had identified the suspect). This reliance on confidence appears to be unaffected by judges' instructions and cross-examination.

Key study

Penrod and Cutler, The effect of witness confidence on jurors' assessment of eyewitness evidence

Aim To examine several factors, including confidence, that jurors might consider when evaluating eyewitness identification evidence.

Methodology An experiment using a mock-trial scenario. Independent measures design.

Participants Undergraduates, eligible and experienced jurors.

Procedure A videotaped trial of a robbery was presented in which eyewitness identification played a key role. The witness testified that she was either 80 or 100 per cent confident that she had identified the robber.

Nine other variables, all at both high and low level, were introduced into the film, four of which are reported in Table 1.5. Participants experienced either the high or low condition variables on a random basis and after watching the film they were asked to decide whether the robber was guilty or not.

Results As can be seen in Table 1.5, witness confidence is the only statistically significant effect of these listed variables under the conditions of the mock trial (all the other six variables not shown were virtually identical).

In a further nine studies, Cutler et al. looked at the relation between confidence and accuracy. The correlations across the nine studies between the two variables were 0.00 to 0.20, which is very weak indeed.

Conclusion The evidence in the field is consistent in showing that confidence is a poor predictor of witness accuracy. It also shows that jurors' trust in it is undiminished, even if the judge advises the jury to be wary of it in their summing up.

Four of ten factors and levels	Percentage convictions
Suspect in disguise	
High – heavily disguised	63
Low – minimal disguise	63
Weapon focus – a weapon is used	
High – weapon clearly brandished	64
Low – weapon visible	63
Retention interval	
14 days	63
2 days	63
Witness confidence about identification	
100% confident	67
80% confident	60

Table 1.5 The influence of manipulated identification evidence on juror judgements

Check your understanding

1   Ten variables have been manipulated in this experiment. Most of them have shown little difference between the high and low conditions. How could you explain this?

2   Why do you think confident people are more believable?

2.3 Effect of shields and videotape on children giving evidence

In many cases involving sexual abuse, kidnapping and domestic violence, a child is the only witness. The experience of giving evidence in a courtroom is often traumatic for children, so they have been able to give evidence from behind a screen, or from outside the courtroom via a video link. It is hoped that by doing this, the psychological stress will be diminished. However, from the defendant's point of view, having the child give evidence via video link may suggest increased likelihood of guilt to a jury by the implication that the child needs protection from the defendant. The study by Ross et al. (1994) attempts to find some empirical evidence to help decide whether using a protective screen is prejudicial to the defendant and whether the use of such measures enhances a witness's credibility or makes them seem fragile and unreliable. This is an important study in an area of vital research, as the number of cases involving children continues to rise.

Key study

Ross et al., The impact of protective shields and videotape testimony on conviction rates

Experiment 1

Aims

1   To find out if the use of protective shields and videotaped testimony increases the likelihood of a guilty verdict.

2   To investigate the effect of protective devices on jury reaction to testimony – do they experience credibility inflation or deflation?

Methodology A mock trial based on an actual court transcript. A professional film crew recorded actors playing the roles in the case. Three versions of the case were created. The first was open court with the child in full view, the second had the child behind a 4 × 6 ft screen and in the third condition the child's testimony came via a video link.

Participants 300 college students (150 male, 150 female) from an introductory psychology class, the majority were white and middle class. They were told it was a study of psychology and the law. 100 students were assigned to each condition.

Procedure Participants watched one of the three versions of the 2-hour film of a court case of alleged abuse which had the child's father as the accused defendant, and the mother, two expert witnesses, one for either side and the child herself taking part as witnesses. The alleged abuse was a single touch while the father was giving the child a bath and the case focused on whether or not it was innocent or sexual in nature. The judge in the case read a warning before either the screen or the video monitor was used, clearly directing the jury not to imply guilt by their use. After the case, the participants gave their verdicts and rated the credibility of the child witness on various aspects of her story. They also rated the defendant on a variety of dimensions of his credibility.

Key terms

system variable variable that affects the accuracy of a witness's testimony by the delays it creates and the way statements are taken and given to the police and courts

credibility inflation where a child's testimony is enhanced because they are protected from negative effects of trauma

credibility deflation where a child witness is seen as fragile and unreliable because of the use of a shield

Results

The guilty verdicts show no significant differences between conditions. However there was a significant difference between male and female participants – 58.6 per cent of females against 38.6 per cent of males found the defendant guilty.

The jury's perception of the credibility of the defendant did not differ across the three conditions, although once again there was a gender difference with more female

	Open court	Shield	Video
Guilty (%)	51	46	49
Not guilty (%)	49	54	51

Table 1.6 Percentage of guilty/not guilty verdicts

students rating the defendant as less credible than the males. The same pattern emerged for the credibility of the witness, with no difference across the three conditions and a very significant difference between genders where again the female students rated the child as more credible.

Conclusions Before drawing the obvious conclusions from this study, it is worth looking at the follow-up research Ross et al. investigated in Experiment 2. All remained the same as before, but this time the tape was stopped immediately after the child testified. This time the results showed a clear difference, with participants in the open court condition far more likely to convict and this time the effect of gender was not significant. The effect on the credibility of the witness was the same as before, i.e. no significant difference between conditions.

The results of the two pieces of research suggest that the defendant is *not* more at risk if protective devices are used, with the video condition slightly less likely to produce a conviction. The biggest differences were found in the second experiment where the trial was artificially interrupted to test the jury's response. When a case is allowed to run its full course and the judge's warnings are in place there is no disadvantage to the defendant, which raises a dilemma – what of the position of the child witness?

U3
1

Check your understanding

1   In what way was deception used in this study? Why was it necessary?

2   Can we accept the conclusions from this research when we consider the sample?

3   Why do you think the second study produced the different response?

Section summary

◈ The effects of attractiveness and confidence are well researched and consistent, and create a worrying problem for a defendant who is unattractive and hesitant. Their legal counsel will do their best to prepare them for the courtroom experience, but these people may be treated more harshly by the jury.

◈ The issue of the use of shields is again a difficult issue in real life. The sight of a young child giving evidence in a courtroom would be emotional for the jury as well as the child, and it is thought better to protect the child from the experience. What if this means that the child's story is not properly heard? This is an ongoing dilemma for the court and it will come down to individual judges' discretion to ensure that each case is heard in the best possible way.

Take it further

Consider these points:

◈ This was a video, albeit very well made, not a real live case, and a real courtroom may produce different results. The case was also extremely over simplified.

◈ The sample of undergraduates may have similar views, which may not represent what would happen in a real case.

◈ The gender differences in the first experiment suggest that the balance of males and females on the jury may be more of an issue in a child-abuse case than how the child testifies.

◈ Watching a child testify on a video screen loses a lot of emotional impact and depends on the skill of the interviewing officer. Some interviewers are better than others at creating a rapport with the child and getting them to talk.

◈ Bearing in mind all of the above, how should psychological research be used in future to inform the courts about the testimony of children?

3 Reaching a verdict

The courtroom drama reaches its climax when the jury return to give their verdict after considering the evidence. All sorts of influences have been investigated by psychologists to explain the process of coming to a verdict. The problem for researchers is that actual jurors are sworn to secrecy about their deliberations, which are held behind locked doors, and they must not discuss the case even when it is over. Therefore once again investigations have to be done in mock fashion. Some of the influences are the size of the jury, cognitive processes, pre-trial publicity, the ethnic make-up, individual differences, the social processes which influence decision-making, leadership and gender.

The final section on how juries reach a verdict will consider the psychological processes that affect the jurors in the jury room. There is a lot of research into group processes and social psychology which can be applied here. Reaching a verdict involves complex processing of data, as shown in Figure 1.7.

3.1 Stages in decision-making

Key study

Hastie et al., Stages and influences on decision-making

According to Hastie et al. (1983), jury discussion goes through the stages described in Table 1.7.

Orientation period	◈ Relaxed and open discussion ◈ Set the agenda ◈ Raise questions and explore facts ◈ Different opinions arise
Open confrontation	◈ Fierce debate ◈ Focus on detail ◈ Explore different interpretations ◈ Pressure on the minority to conform ◈ Support for the group decision is established
Reconciliation	◈ Attempts to smooth over conflicts ◈ Tension released through humour

Table 1.7 Stages in jury decision-making

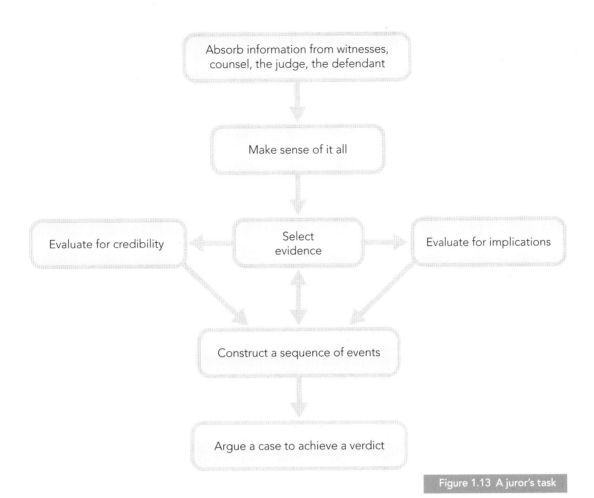

Absorb information from witnesses, counsel, the judge, the defendant

↓

Make sense of it all

↓

Evaluate for credibility ← Select evidence → Evaluate for implications

↓

Construct a sequence of events

↓

Argue a case to achieve a verdict

Figure 1.13 A juror's task

Hastie et al. are applying findings from social–psychological research of group dynamics to the jury here. The problem is that actual juries cannot be studied for the reasons mentioned earlier, and so it is an assumption that these processes apply. We need to question whether the special nature of being locked in a room until you come to a unanimous decision means that this research needs to be applied with caution.

Check your understanding

1   The orientation period begins when the jury are first locked into the jury room to begin their deliberations. They will have chatted to each other during coffee and lunch breaks before this, but never tried to have a formal discussion. Think about how this might feel.

2   Do you think it is always necessary to have confrontation in order to come to a verdict?

3   What outside pressures may be affecting the jury's decision-making?

3.2 Majority influence

In a now classic study (1955), Asch gave us an insight into the power of majority influence and conformity.

Key study

Asch, The power of majority influence and conformity

Aim To investigate the effects of conformity to a majority when the task is unambiguous.

Methodology A laboratory experiment.

Procedure Asch arranged for a naïve participant to be asked a question to which several stooges of the experimenter had already given clearly the wrong answer. ('Which of three lines, A, B or C matches the stimulus line X?') He was interested to see if even in a crystal-clear decision, an individual would defer to the majority.

Results Asch found that individuals conformed in one out of three occasions. This finding of approximately 32 per cent conformity is a robust one until just one

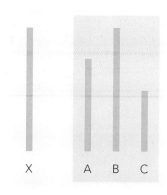

Which line, A, B or C, is the same length as X?

Figure 1.14 Asch's task

stooge in the group is instructed to disrupt this conformity, when it falls to about 5 per cent. Another finding is that majorities bigger than three make very little difference to the conformity effect. This may be because three is enough to create a group norm while two would be insufficient.

Discussion Why do we conform to majorities? The conventional view is that there are two reasons:

◆   the need to belong to a group

◆   the need to be right.

The need to belong is thought to be part of the socialisation process, which particularly influences those with poorer self-esteem who are insecure about their own worth and opinions. It has been linked to a conformist style of personality and it would be this type of person who would be one of the 32 per cent who conform. The need to be right arises when any ambiguous situation occurs and we look to other people's solutions to guide our own. Clearly in the Asch experiment we have an unambiguous stimulus and so it is more likely that the need to belong is prevalent. In a jury, the task is far more complex and an individual juror may be far more influenced by the need to make the right decision and give the correct verdict for the evidence. Research with over 225 juries has shown that the majority guilty view (8 to 11 jurors) expressed as a vote early in the deliberations led to a guilty verdict 86 per cent of the time, showing that the majority has the most powerful influence (Abbott and Batt, 1999). There is some informal evidence to suggest that the first thing many juries do is take a vote when they withdraw, as a starting point for their discussions. Obviously the suggestion of this research is that conformity effects might be better resisted if the vote was delayed until discussion about the evidence has taken place.

In 1966, Rotter distinguished between two types of person, the internally directed (internal locus) who see their effectiveness and behaviour in terms of their own actions, and the externally directed (external locus), who see no connection between their own behaviour and events which they see as beyond their control. Some students, for example, like to blame computer failure, absence from a particular lesson or a friend failing to pick them up as reasons for not managing to meet an essay or coursework deadline. In theory, the more autonomous, internally driven individual is more likely to resist conforming and this is borne out in research cited by Moscovici (1985).

Check your understanding

1   Asch's research suggests that the majority can have a huge effect on a minority when taking a show of hands. What does this suggest about how important votes are taken, not just in the courtroom but for any big decision?

2   Who is more likely to conform: someone with an internal locus or someone with an external locus?

3   Why is conformity sometimes very useful?

3.3 Minority influence

Moscovici carried out a set of experiments to test the minority influence. He got groups of six participants (four naïve, two stooges) to make colour perception judgements about a series of slides which were all blue. In the first condition his stooges declared the slides were all green. In the second condition two-thirds of the slides were declared green and in the final condition slides the stooges were completely inconsistent in their choices. The result of this was to find the expected 32 per cent conformity only in the first condition. So what does this tell us?

Moscovici believes that it is the *consistency* of the minority which is persuasive. Consistency creates an impression of certainty and confidence, and its uncompromising attitude induces everyone else to take it seriously and to make concessions – in this case people were persuaded to see blue as green.

In the following study, the concept of autonomy or internal locus is combined with consistency to find its effect on minority influence.

Aim To investigate the influence of perceived autonomy (choosing where to sit at a table) and consistency on minority influence.

Methodology A laboratory experiment as a mock trial.

Participants Groups of five participants (one is a stooge) drawn from an adult sample of students.

Procedure The group of five have to deliberate on the amount of compensation due for a victim of an injury. After hearing the facts, everyone makes an individual verdict and is then taken to another room where there is a rectangular table with two seats at either of the long sides of the table and one at the head of the table. In half the groups the participants are asked to sit at the table with the confederate or stooge choosing the seat at the head or the top of the table. In the other groups the experimenter tells everyone where to sit. They then deliberate on the case. During the discussion, the confederate consistently adopts a deviant position, suggesting a figure of $3000 in compensation instead of $10,000–$25,000 which was the view of the rest.

Results The confederate exerts influence when he is consistent and when he is perceived as autonomous, because he has chosen his seat, whereas when seated by the experimenter he has little influence (measured by the difference between the original individual verdicts and the later group ones). Moreover, when he has been influential, this effect continues into a second case. When he sits at the head of the table he is seen as more consistent and confident.

Discussion This has interesting repercussions for the jury room where people sit around a long table. Could the effect be replicated in the classroom? Many examples exist where minorities have influenced the majority into adopting their views by being consistent over time, for example gay civil partnerships (homosexuality used to be considered a mental illness), belief in global warming (this was originally an extreme view held by a few scientists), and cult music groups or programmes which become mainstream. However, it is possible that in the jury room in real life this effect is weakened by the need for unanimity in a limited time.

Check your understanding

1   What is the most important influence a minority can use to sway the majority?

2   Why would someone who was perceived to be autonomous be more convincing?

3   Why do people conform?

Take it further

Suggest some rules that a jury should follow when coming to their verdict, based on the research described above.

U3

1

Section summary

Once out in the jury room, many influences come into play in reaching a verdict and only a few have been covered in this book. Majority and minority influence are probably the best known, but there is much more research on decision-making which can be applied here.

After a guilty verdict

Pause for thought

◆ Does prison work?

◆ Why do prisoners usually serve only part of their full sentence?

◆ Should the death penalty be reintroduced?

This area will look at how psychology can inform the penal system.

Introduction

Once a guilty verdict has been announced, the defendant becomes part of the penal system and is then called an offender. Depending on the severity of the crime and whether or not this is a first offence, the offender will be sentenced to a punishment. This could be community service, being tagged, an ASBO (anti-social behaviour order), a fine, a probation order or a prison sentence. Psychologists have been interested in whether any of these punishments work and if so which are the most effective. To measure effectiveness it is usual to look at **recidivism rates** or **re-offending** rates as a whole for each type of punishment. This is rather a blunt instrument, as an individual offender may end up being sentenced to several different punishments before finally turning away from crime, so it depends when the statistics are recorded and whether the offender is caught for their re-offence.

Key term

probation order a general term given to a whole range of different punishment and treatment options which could include unpaid work, attendance on a treatment programme, a curfew, an exclusion, a residence requirement, electronic monitoring (tags) and any combination of the above. The offender has to meet the terms of the order administered by the probation officer or face a stiffer penalty

The penal system has two aims, first to punish and second to rehabilitate the offender. These two often seem to come into conflict in the public mind, especially when a particularly offensive crime has been committed. It is hard for the victim's relatives and the public generally to see criminals getting help and support which is costly when the victim generally gets nothing or may have lost their life. The idea of rehabilitation is that offenders who are safe to let out into the community can become useful citizens who contribute to society through working and paying taxes, instead of being a drain on resources.

1 Imprisonment

This section looks at imprisonment and its effects and effectiveness. The prison population hit an all-time high of close to 81,000 in the summer of 2007, while there was an official capacity of just 78,000. Such a discrepancy means that overcrowding is rife and prisoners are often held in police cells as a temporary measure. In prisons offenders are not getting as much time out of their cells as they should, nor are they receiving the education programmes and treatments they normally would, because they are frequently moved from prison to prison where there are different levels of provision. Some people may say 'so what?', taking the line that prisoners deserve all they get and there should be no sympathy for them. An opposing view however, is that whilst in prison these individuals are costing society money in many ways, such as supporting their families on the outside and paying a substantial amount to keep them inside (£40,000 p.a.).

If they can be turned around, educated and made employable, they are more likely to stay out of trouble and contribute to society instead. The first key study looks at this point and shows that if an offender has a planned route to freedom, their chances of success increase greatly. The second key study looks at what happens to some individuals psychologically when they experience their loss of freedom for the first time and the third examines what has happened since Zimbardo did his famous prison simulation study in 1973 and considers the US prison system as it is now.

Weblinks

You might like to view a walkthrough for prisoners, which will give you all the basic information about a prison sentence ... or watch a slide show about prison life (see Contents page).

1.1 Planned behaviours once freed from jail

Applying Azjen's theory (1988) to the likelihood of successful integration for offenders leaving jail, the outcome will depend upon the positive intention to stay out of prison. This will be influenced by the prisoner's beliefs about the value of their life on the outside and how much confidence they have that they can control what will happen to them. Their attitude to 'going straight' will in turn be influenced by their personality traits.

The amount of control they may feel they have will depend on many variables. It may be that they are poorly educated, cannot speak much English, have an addiction problem, etc.

Research has shown that leaving prison with no employment prospects and a lack of normal ambition are important risk factors for a return to prison. If we look at the typical profile of a prisoner in the UK, we find that 50 per cent of all prisoners are at or below the level expected of an 11-year-old in reading, 66 per cent in numeracy and 80 per cent in writing. More than 50 per cent of male and more than 66 per cent of female adult prisoners have no qualifications at all. Half of all prisoners do not have the skills required by 96 per cent of jobs. Nearly 50 per cent of male sentenced prisoners have been excluded from school and approximately 30 per cent of all prisoners have been regular truants whilst at school (Prison Reform Trust, 2007).

At this point it is worth pointing out why prisoners do not always serve all of their sentences. Once admitted to prison, the sentence is planned and there will come a point where the prisoner can apply for parole. Whether their application is successful will depend on the nature of the offence, the judge's directions at the time of the trial and the inmate's behaviour in the prison. This gives the prisoner an incentive to behave and comply with prison staff's directions. Without this incentive the prisoner has nothing to lose and may become more difficult to manage. In the context of our overcrowded prisons this would mean an impossible task for the staff and would probably lead to more 'lock downs' and unrest. In the USA, as we will see in Haney and Zimbardo's paper, public opinion has moved away from the idea of sentence remission and as a consequence, prisons have become harsher places.

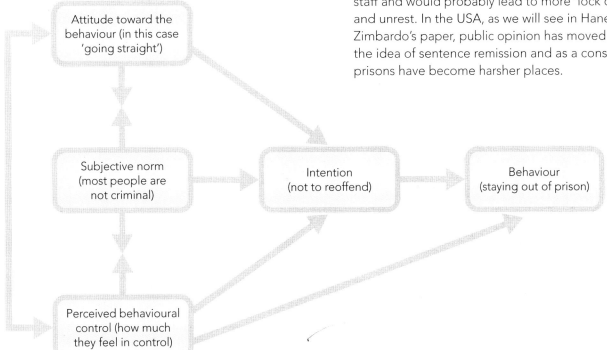

Figure 1.15 The theory of planned behaviour applied to an offender's likelihood of 'going straight'

The study described below was conducted in Canada on inmates who were about to be released, having completed their sentence. In their prison it was possible to start an employment programme in the final months of their sentence. The success rates of those with a planned exit from prison are compared using a matched pairs design with prisoners with no planned employment. As might be expected, having a job is more than just a means of survival, and it helps the ex-prisoners to become integrated into society by providing them with non-criminal contacts and friendships.

Key study

Gillis and Nafekh, The impact of community-based employment on offender reintegration

Aim To investigate the effect on recidivism rates of a community-based employment scheme.

Sample Federal offenders conditionally released between January 1998 and January 2005, 23,525 individuals, 95 per cent men and the rest women.

Methodology Content analysis of data from Canada's Offender Management System on the 23,525 offenders in the sample. A matched pairs design was used, where offenders were divided into those employed prior to release on a special programme and those who were unemployed. They were then matched for gender, risk level, release year, sentence length, family/marital relations, substance abuse, emotional orientation, community functioning and attitudes.

Results The average time for the whole sample to get employment on the outside was 6 months for men and 10 months for women.

Those on employment programmes prior to finishing their sentence were more likely to remain on conditional release and less likely to return to custody with a new offence. The median time to return was also longer for the employed group (37 months versus 11 months). At the end of the study period 70 per cent of the employed group remained on conditional release compared to 55 per cent of the unemployed group.

Conclusions This study responds to previous criticisms of similar research by having a strong sample and methodology so that its findings can be generalised. The implications are that employment-based programmes play an important role in the last few months of an offender's sentence, giving them some of the skills they need and helping them to integrate into the community. The programmes focus on job-search

techniques, individual psychometric assessments and on-the-job placements. Offenders with more severe deficits in learning should be offered more tailored programmes, which are just as important as drug-rehabilitation and anger-management programmes. This study shows that planning the return to the community addresses some of the points raised in Azjen's model and increases the likelihood of success.

In general, prison has a poor record for reducing re-offending: 64.7 per cent are re-convicted within 2 years of being released. For males aged 18–20 it is 75.3 per cent (Prison Reform Trust, 2007). Without a planned return to society it is all too easy to see life on the inside as an easier option where all decisions are made for you and you are automatically fed and sheltered, albeit in overcrowded conditions. If the alternative, the outside, is worse, it is not surprising that prison appears not to work.

Check your understanding

1. What is a content analysis?

2. What does the research suggest would reduce the chances of re-conviction for offenders?

3. What makes a matched pairs design a strong design to use in methodological terms?

1.2 Depression/suicide risk in prisons

Unnatural deaths, especially suicide, occurring in prison have been a cause of concern in recent years (92 deaths in 2007 with a further 100 resuscitated, a rise of 40 per cent (Howard League for Penal Reform, 2007). This is particularly likely to happen in the case of young offenders on remand (41 of the 92). At any one time, 1500 prisoners are on suicide watch, considered to be of high risk of killing themselves. To understand this, imagine yourself restricted to an area of your classroom for 23 hours a day for an unknown period of time. Then imagine you were confined there with two other people you did not like or were afraid of. You are probably only 15 or 16 and the bravado you showed to your mates has long since disappeared. You are lonely and afraid and you do not know how long you will wait for your case to come to trial because it is out of your hands and into a slow-moving and complex system. Occasionally you are allowed a visit, but this may be difficult for your family as due to overcrowding you may be hundreds of miles from your home

When that big steel door clangs shut on you it may feel like the end of your life.

As well as suicide, self-harm is common amongst prisoners and the study by Dooley attempts to investigate this by looking at all unnatural deaths between 1972 and 1987. If this figure is included, an even greater number of deaths would have to be taken into consideration. One example of a death by a consciously self-inflicted injury (CSI) is prisoner A cited in Dooley's (1990) paper.

Prisoner A had been convicted of manslaughter in 1977 and had received a 6-year sentence. He had apparently been depressed for a number of weeks prior to the offence. He had never overcome the strong guilt he felt for what he had done, and when considered for parole his guilt increased. A month before his death he had tried to hang himself and had stated at the time that he 'would rather be dead than endure the sufferings of a tortured conscience'. Though he was seen weekly by a visiting psychiatrist, he hanged himself from a coat hook in his cell. A verdict of misadventure, not suicide, resulted.

Dooley found that the most common method of suicide was hanging, despite care being taken to try to minimise this risk, and CSI deaths mostly occurred at night.

Key study
Dooley, Unnatural deaths in prison

Aim To investigate all unnatural deaths that occurred in prisons in England and Wales between 1972 and 1987.

Methodology A content analysis of Prison Department personal papers. A checklist that included social, psychiatric and forensic history was used to analyse the papers. The groups getting a verdict of suicide were compared to those who did not.

Results 442 unnatural deaths were recorded in prisons in England and Wales between 1972 and 1987. Of these, 300 got a verdict of suicide and the remainder a variety of verdicts including 52 from consciously self-inflicted injury.

The differences between the deaths classed as suicide and those classed as CSI were that significantly more of the suicide group were on remand. More of the CSI group were female and the deaths occurred mainly at night.

Discussion This study helps put into perspective the present level of suicide in British jails quoted

earlier, which is much higher than in previous years and is being attributed to overcrowding increasing prisoners' stress. We must also bear in mind that many prisoners suffer from mental-health problems and addiction when they are admitted. In his paper presented to the Commission on Safety and Abuse in Prisons in the USA, Haney (2006) highlights the psychological effects of overcrowding, particularly on younger inmates, stating that overcrowding increases stress on prisoners because it increases the number of interactions in a confined space that the prisoner must deal with. In the prisoner's mind this will increase uncertainty about what the other prisoners intend and may interfere with what the prisoner intends to do.

> ## Check your understanding
> 1 Why does overcrowding cause stress?
> 2 Why do you think there are there more suicides among prisoners on remand?

Weblink

The website of the Howard League for Penal Reform has news and information about life in English prisons (see Contents page). You may like to watch a film made by the Commission on Safety and Abuse in Prisons in the USA (the equivalent of the UK's Howard League for Penal Reform). The film is approximately 14 minutes long. You can see Haney giving evidence (see Contents page).

1.3 The prison situation and roles

The prison situation

Before beginning this section it is worth recapping Reicher and Haslam (2006), which was based on the Stanford Prison Experiment (SPE) carried out by Haney et al. in 1973. This part of the Forensic Psychology option looks at what has happened in US prisons 25 years on from the original Stanford prison study.

The researchers' original goal was to demonstrate the power of institutional environments on groups of people who pass through them, in contrast to the work of Milgram (1974) who looked at the effects on individuals complying with an authority figure's increasingly severe demands. Milgram was looking for an individual explanation of behaviour whilst Haney et al. believed that the situation was more important.

The behaviour of the prisoners and guards in the simulated prison bore a strong resemblance to the behaviour of similar people in real prisons, even though the people in the experiment could have chosen to behave in any way they liked. They researchers concluded that the pathological behaviour was created by the prison situation and not by the nature of the individuals who took part.

Since the end of the Stanford Experiment, Haney has continued to work in the prison setting and frequently testifies in hearings in his capacity as a prison expert. Zimbardo has moved into the area of what he calls 'psychological prisons' which constrict human experience and stop people reaching their full potential. The other original collaborator, Banks, is deceased.

In 1998, Haney and Zimbardo presented a paper in the *American Psychologist* on the changes that had taken place in the US prison system over 25 years. Below is a summary of this, ending with the six points that Haney and Zimbardo present as lessons to be learned.

Before beginning, it is worth pointing out that when the original study was published in 1973, it was expected to lead to improvements in the prison system. At the time there was much concern in US society about whether prisons were too harsh and whether they worked to rehabilitate the inmates. People were also looking for alternatives to prison and there was a moratorium on the building of any more jails. The Supreme Court had overall control of the prison system and monitored it closely, believing that a humane prison system was a sign of a cultured society.

Key study

Haney and Zimbardo, The past and future of prison policy in the USA

This study is in two parts, the first summarising changes and the second suggesting improvements to the prison system.

Part 1 Summary of changes to the prison system over 25 years

In the 1980s, political pressure mounted to put more and more criminals behind bars. A Republican government under Ronald Reagan declared a 'War on Drugs'.

The concept of rehabilitation was publicly discredited and replaced with 'incapacitation' and 'containment' and the prevailing idea was one of 'just deserts' – locking people up for no other reason than that they deserved it.

The other major change was towards determinate sentencing, which means that whatever tariff is imposed, it has to be served in full with no parole, thus removing the discretion of courts and the probation service to let anyone out early for good behaviour. Rigid sentencing guidelines or 'grids' are now in place.

The building of new prisons in the USA has escalated with the increase in the prison population. In 1998, it was 1,630,940 and in 2008 is over 2 million. The USA now puts more people in prison than any other modern nation. At the same time, recorded crime has fallen according to crime victimisation surveys.

The prison population also appeared to show racial bias because African-American men made up 48 per cent of the prison population although they represented 6 per cent of the general population. Hispanics and women were also over-represented compared with white men.

Most serious offences	Total % change 1985–95	White % change 1985–95	Black % change 1985–95
Total	119	109	132
Violent offences	86	92	83
Property offences	69	74	65
Drug offences	478	306	707
Public-order offences	187	162	229
Other	–6	–72	64

Table 1.8 A summary of Haney and Zimbardo's findings, clearly showing the over-representation of black inmates for drug offences compared to other offences

Another group who were over-represented were drug offenders, a result of Ronald Reagan's 'War on Drugs' policy, and black inmates were in the majority, with 64 per cent of black male defendants and 71 per cent of black female defendants convicted in drugs trials compared with 12 per cent of white defendants.

Haney and Zimbardo suggest that by emphasising severe sentencing instead of treatment and rehabilitation, the USA is perpetuating discrimination against black people and encouraging dispositional explanations of their behaviour. They also point out that in 1990 there were more black men in the prison system than in college.

A further development was the rise of the 'Supermax' prison, where special ultra-secure, long-term segregated confinement is imposed on the offender so that they live in extreme isolation with little stimulation and reduced privileges, and are locked up for 23 hours out of 24. The authors point out that here again a dispositional explanation has been used to categorise people as 'problem prisoners' instead of looking at the context and situation.

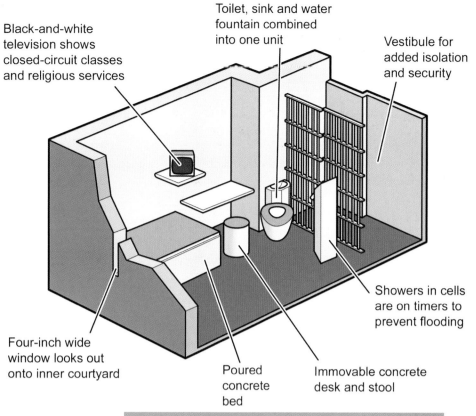

Black-and-white television shows closed-circuit classes and religious services

Toilet, sink and water fountain combined into one unit

Vestibule for added isolation and security

Four-inch wide window looks out onto inner courtyard

Poured concrete bed

Immovable concrete desk and stool

Showers in cells are on timers to prevent flooding

Figure 1.16 A 'Supermax' prison cell

U3

1

Key term

dispositional explanation an explanation of behaviour where blame is placed on the personality or traits of the individual rather than looking for an explanation in their environment, which would be a situational explanation

Finally, the Supreme Court had shown an unsympathetic stance on appeals from prisoners who used the Eighth Amendment, which states that 'no cruel and unusual punishments' should be imposed on a US citizen, thus setting a punitive tone which reflected current public attitudes towards crime.

Part 2 Suggestions for improvements to the prison system

1   Prisons should be used sparingly in the war on crime because they are psychologically damaging and more resources should be put towards alternatives to prison.

2   The SPE was populated with psychologically healthy young men, was minimalist in design and short lived, yet produced powerful effects on all the participants. Real prisons are crowded, violent and contain mentally unstable people and therefore should take account of individual differences in how a person adapts to confinement.

3   The conditions that exist when someone comes out of prison are as important as those on the inside. Therefore decompression programmes should be in place, gradually reversing the effects of the extreme environments inside. At present about 25 per cent of those sentenced for a non-violent crime are sentenced a second time for a violent offence.

4   More situationally specific assessments should be made of prisoners. At present they are given psychometric tests that ask about characteristic ways of responding in familiar situations and therefore have little predictive value for a prison environment. When prisoners have behaved violently, this should be seen more in the context of the event or the situation which caused it.

5. Haney and Zimbardo acknowledge that they got caught up in the SPE and lost their balanced perspective as objective experimenters They therefore suggest that reform has to come from people outside of the system who are empowered to act on it.

6. Finally, they suggest that psychological knowledge should be used to improve the nature and effects of imprisonment, and they encourage more use of the body of knowledge that exists already. They are obviously disappointed that lessons from the SPE have not yet been learned and in fact psychologists have been distanced from the system.

Check your understanding

1. In what ways have attitudes towards imprisonment undergone a major shift since the 1970s?

2. What is a dispositional explanation of behaviour?

3. Think of an example in which a situation has created aggressive behaviour.

Section summary

◆ This section has perhaps presented a depressing picture of the penal system. We have seen that despite much effort and real commitment by researchers and prison staff, re-conviction rates after imprisonment stubbornly remain at around 60 per cent.

◆ The picture in the USA is one of a movement to a more extreme regime which at present prioritises containment and control above rehabilitation.

◆ Overcrowding has led to more suicides and deaths in prisons both in the USA and in the UK, increasing the stress on prisoners and staff.

◆ Prisons and treatment programmes have to be seen within the legal and political frameworks of the country in which they exist.

2 Alternatives to imprisonment

Having looked at the negative effects of imprisonment, we now consider alternatives that are offered alongside a custodial sentence. Probation has been used for many years and works within and outside prisons as a well-established programme intended to help the offender to adjust to life on the outside and not re-offend. Restorative Justice is a more recent concept and still somewhat controversial, as it moves away from pure punishment of the offender independently of the victim towards involving all the people affected by the crime in a discussion about its effects on them. In some cases the punishment is agreed by the police, victim and offender together. In the case of more minor crimes, it puts the police in command of the whole process of crime control and punishment, and some people are not comfortable with this idea. The death penalty is even more controversial; the UK abandoned it in 1969, but 36 US states still use it and 1099 people have been executed in the USA since 1979. Most are killed by lethal injection, and this is presently in dispute under a case brought using the Eighth Amendment of the US constitution, which says that cruel and unusual punishments should not be used against its citizens. The case does not dispute the death penalty as such, but is arguing that the injection itself is unnecessarily cruel because of the intense pain inflicted by the curare-type drug used to paralyse muscles, one of three drugs in the injection. Apparently, it sometimes happens that the vein is missed and the drugs go into tissue instead. Patients in hospitals who receive the same drug during operations have sometimes reported a failure to lose consciousness and experience of terrible pain while being unable to tell anyone because they are paralysed. Until the case is resolved, no executions by lethal injection are taking place in the states affected.

2.1 Probation

In 1896, a gift of 5 shillings to the temperance society of the Church of England to reform alcoholics was the beginning of today's probation service. In those days alcohol was seen as 'the root of all evil' and offenders were made to sign the pledge (swear to give it up) and follow the teachings of the Bible to keep them away from crime.

Today the probation service supervises over 200,000 offenders on four main types of community sentence:

◆ Community rehabilitation orders

- Community punishment orders
- Community punishment and rehabilitation orders (combined orders)
- Drug treatment and testing orders.

Approximately 90 per cent of cases are male and 10 per cent female. Just over 25 per cent are aged 16–20.

Approximately 70 per cent of offenders supervised will be on community sentences, and 30 per cent imprisoned with a period of statutory licensed supervision in the community as an integral part of the sentence. The purpose of the order is to continuously manage the risk of the offender to the community and at the same time to provide programmes designed to reduce re-offending.

Each year the National Probation Service (NPS) assists magistrates and judges in their sentencing decisions through the provision of about 246,000 pre-sentence reports, and 20,000 bail information reports.

Each year probation service staff find and supervise some 8 million hours of unpaid work by offenders in local communities, to ensure that they meet the requirements of their community punishment orders.

One hundred approved probation hostels play a major role in the NPS public protection strategy, providing controlled environments for offenders on bail, community sentences and post-custody licences.

Many probation staff are seconded to work in youth offending teams, prisons and a wide range of other public protection and crime prevention or reduction partnership agencies. Their skills, particularly in assessing risk and dangerousness, are highly valued.

What you must do when placed on a probation order

- Stay out of trouble.
- Tell your supervisor immediately, if you change your address or phone number.
- Be on time for appointments you are given.
- Let staff visit you at home.
- Keep to any extra requirements ordered by the court.
- Keep to any extra requirements on your licence if you have been released from prison.
- Take part fully in anything else your supervising officer asks you to do. This may be taking part in a one-to-one or group work programme.

What you must not do

- You must not miss an appointment or be late.
- You must not turn up under the influence of drugs or alcohol.
- You must not upset or threaten other people.
- You must not make racist, sexist or other offensive remarks.

Does probation work?

To answer this we can look at the work of Mair and May which follows. They surveyed a cross-section of probation officers to find out how well they were working with offenders. As we will see, they found a mixed picture of success.

Key study

Mair and May, Investigation of the experiences of offenders on probation orders

Aim To investigate the experiences of offenders on probation orders in a cross-section of offices in England and Wales.

Methodology A survey using a questionnaire that was piloted initially with seven offices and 24 offenders, then improved before being given to the final sample.

Sample A total of 3299 offenders were selected at random from 22 probation offices across England and Wales to be representative of all crimes and age groups. Of the original selected sample, 40 per cent failed to take part for various reasons, with more failing to turn up for appointments in the London area. This means that the smaller offices are over represented and a corrective weighting has had to be employed.

Procedure Interviews were conducted by independently employed researchers visiting the selected offices and covered a vast range of questions about the offender's life as well as their likelihood of re-offending. Many questions had Likert scale responses, otherwise they were all closed, multiple-choice type.

Selected results An average of 88 per cent of the sample felt probation was extremely or very useful. Over 60 per cent of the sample felt that the probation officer would help them to sort out problems and was there to talk to, but only 37 per cent felt that this would stop them re-offending altogether. Having someone independent to talk to seems to be the most useful function of the probation officer, and the topics discussed included: things to do, problems with accommodation, problems with money, employment, family problems, why they committed the offence, drugs and alcohol problems and their health generally.

Conclusions Probation is seen in a positive light by offenders. However, the percentage who failed to keep all of their appointments and are therefore excluded from the analysis may have more negative views. This survey confirms the previous research, which shows that those on probation tend to be unemployed, on benefits, poorly qualified and in poor health, so that much of a probation officer's time is spent discussing these factors. It was disappointing that not one offender in the survey thought that their order was intended to stop them re-offending and nearly one-third went on to commit another offence.

Probation is seen as a 'soft sentence' by some offenders. The sheer volume of an individual officer's case load means that the individual help that the offenders value most may not be happening as it should. In many cases the service has been criticised for failing to assess the risk to the public of offenders who have committed serious offences while on a probation order. This risk is partly assessed using the eOASys (a psychometric inventory), which examines factors such as offending history and current offence, financial management and income, relationships, lifestyle and drug and alcohol misuse. If any of these factors come up as high risk, further specialist assessments can be made.

As in all assessments, an honest answer by the offender is essential to its effectiveness and there must always be a question mark over whether this happens in practice.

2.2 Restorative justice

Historically in the justice system, the offender is seen as committing an offence against the state. Victims have little chance to say how they have been affected by the crime and the offender is not encouraged to accept responsibility. Under the principles of restorative justice (RJ) the crime is seen as being against the person or organisation, and victims are allowed to be a part of what happens as a result. Under the control of an impartial facilitator, the offender is encouraged to accept responsibility and be re-integrated into the community. There are four types of restorative justice systems in use:

◆ victim–offender mediation

◆ group conferencing

◆ restorative conferencing

◆ indirect mediation/reparation.

In addition, RJ has to be voluntary for all parties, seeks a positive outcome for all parties, and is respectful and not degrading.

It can provide victims with:

◆ an opportunity to explain the impact of the crime

◆ an acknowledgement of the harm caused

◆ a chance to ask questions

◆ some control and choice

◆ peace of mind about the future.

Sometimes an apology/reparation/recompense is agreed.

A major analysis by the Smith Institute was published in 2007, which looked at RJ across the world. To analyse these data is extremely difficult because in every country RJ applied under different circumstances. The researchers therefore present their findings in a relatively raw state, having selected their sample in the most representative way they could.

Aim The purpose of this review is to look at good practice in RJ and to reach a conclusion on its effectiveness with reference to re-offending.

Sample An internet search including the words 'restorative justice' with 're-offending' or 'recidivism' or 'mediation' was applied to many databases of abstracts and academic periodicals worldwide. This yielded 424 hits.

Procedure Two researchers analysed the content of all the research found by the above search where a sample of offenders on an RJ programme was compared with a similar sample who did not experience RJ, which is the minimum standard used by the Home Office in assessing re-conviction rates to arrive at what they call 'reasonably unbiased' results. This yielded 36 studies, which form the basis for the analysis.

Summary of results Reductions in re-offending were found for violence and property crime but RJ does not work in all cases. It is more effective for cases with a personal victim. It also seems to be more effective when violence has been part of the crime. From the victim's viewpoint, provided they have been willing participants it can improve their mental health by reducing post-traumatic shock symptoms and helping them to come to terms with what has happened to them.

Conclusions There is strong evidence that RJ is effective in some cases and support for its increased use, perhaps beginning with young offenders. One of the advisors to the report is a senior police officer with the Thames Valley Police, leaders in the field in the UK for RJ who have developed expertise in RJ conferencing which they are now cascading out to other police forces. The report also points out that it is also becoming widespread in schools with the publication of Daniel Goleman's book *Emotional Intelligence* (1996) as a theoretical basis.

Take it further

Research an RJ project in the UK.

Check your understanding

1   What difficulties could be encountered by relying on the internet to find a sample of research?

2   The complicated nature of this report meant that the data had to be presented both qualitatively and quantitatively. Is this an advantage or a disadvantage?

Weblinks

You can read more about RJ at the restorative justice website (see Contents page).

Several case studies of RJ can be found on the internet. It is a good idea to read some of these to get a clear idea of how RJ works (see Contents page).

2.3 'Looking deathworthy'

'Looking death worthy' is the title given to a piece of research by Eberhardt et al. (2006), which investigates whether it is true that the more stereotypically black your features, the more likely it is that you will be given a death sentence for your crime.

This seems a startling proposition when you first read it, but when seen in the context of the US justice system we can see why it happens. Stereotypes are associated with positive or negative characteristics, and the stereotypical black face is seen as less attractive by white people and therefore attributed with more unattractive characteristics. White people dominate the criminal justice system in the USA (98 per cent of the chief district attorneys in death penalty states are white; only 1 per cent are black: Pokorak, 1998).

In the UK too there have been theories of facial and physical stereotypes being associated with criminality and the idea of a subset of the human population who were born criminal was around until discredited in the 1950s. We are all too ready to categorise someone as criminal on appearance alone.

If we look at where the death penalty is still practised, we see it is very much in the southern states of the USA, which have a history of prejudice and discrimination

Figure 1.17 The face on the right would be considered more stereotypically black than the face on the left

dating back to the days of slavery in the southern plantations. The overall statistics on the death penalty are shown in Figure 1.18.

About 80 per cent of the murder victims in cases resulting in an execution were white, even though nationally only 50 per cent of murder victims generally are white.

Researchers have found that controlling for all other factors, murderers of white victims are more likely to get the death sentence than murderers of black victims, and being black and killing a white victim is even more likely to lead to a death sentence. Criminality is associated with the black facial stereotype and such criminals get 8-month longer sentences on average when all other variables are controlled.

Race of defendants executed 1967–2008

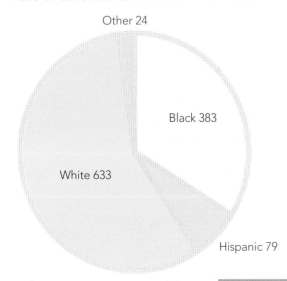

Other 24

Black 383

White 633

Hispanic 79

Race of victim 1976–2008 in death-penalty cases

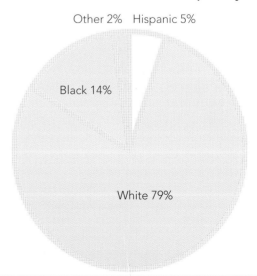

Other 2%   Hispanic 5%

Black 14%

White 79%

Figure 1.18 Ethnicity of defendants and victims executed in the USA between 1967 and 2008 (Source: Death penalty fact sheet from http://www.deathpenaltyinfo.org/)

Key study

Eberhardt et al., Investigation of the relation between stereotypically black features in offenders and the likelihood of receiving the death sentence

Aim To investigate whether there was support for the hypothesis that black offenders with stereotypically black features were more likely to get the death sentence than white offenders.

Methodology Laboratory experiment.

Procedure Analysis of the database of death-eligible cases in Philadelphia, Pennsylvania that advanced to penalty phase between 1979 and 1999. In 44 cases a black man had murdered a white victim. Their photographs were shown to naïve raters who were asked to use their facial features to give them a rating of stereotypicality from 1 to 11, where 11 was very stereotypical. There were 51 raters from Stanford University (32 white, 15 Asian and four of other ethnicities), who watched the black and white photographs one at a time for 4 seconds each.

Results An analysis of covariance (where multiple variables are analysed at once to look for relationships between them) was carried out which allowed the researchers to input many different variables to test for their effects on sentencing decisions such as: aggravating circumstances, mitigating circumstances, severity of the murder, socioeconomic status of victim and defendant and the defendant's attractiveness. Final analysis showed that of all the variables the most significant was that the most stereotypically black defendants were 57.5 per cent more likely to receive the death sentence than the less stereotypically black at 24.4 per cent.

In a second study where there was a black defendant and a black victim, the same analysis produced no significant effect, suggesting that a black victim is in some way seen as less important.

Discussion Why the difference between the results if the victim is black or white? The authors suggest that it is possible that the jurors see the race of the defendant as a blameworthy factor in the trial. This could be explained by intergroup conflict in the case of a black defendant/white victim and interpersonal conflict when both defendant and victim are black (Prentice and Miller, 1990). Black physical traits are associated with criminality, and in this case it appears that they influence sentencing decisions.

Check your understanding

1 Why were the photographs rated by non-black raters?

2 The data were drawn from just one state in the USA. Can you suggest a problem with this?

3 It would appear that some states in the USA are moving away from the death penalty as public opinion swings away from the right-wing conservative Republican stance of the last 8–10 years. What does right-wing mean?

Take it further

Research such as the above has socio-political impact. What does this mean and how does it affect the psychologist's role as investigator in whatever political system they find themselves?

Weblinks

The website of the Death Penalty Information Center has information and discussion about the death penalty in the USA (see Contents page).

The website of the US Department of Justice has a wide range of statistics about the US criminal justice system (see Contents page).

Section summary

- Probation offers a chance to integrate back into society if it happens as intended. Unfortunately, pressures on the system mean that insufficient time is spent with offenders pre- and post-release and so the offenders often slip back into old patterns of behaviour.

- Courses of significant treatment are not usually available to short-term prisoners because there is not much time for impact. There are sometimes indications in pre-sentence reports that a longer sentence will mean that a prisoner will get some appropriate and effective treatment.

- Prisoners must consent to drug and alcohol rehabilitation orders because these come under the category of medical treatment. They are not good at coming to weekly blood tests and there is a high attrition rate on these programmes.

- A positive note comes from the research on restorative justice, which seems in the right cases to offer victims of crime a way to come to terms with what has happened to them and to increase an offender's awareness of their personal responsibilities.

- Being black is still likely to create negative stereotypical responses from the largely white members of the jurisdiction in the USA, leading to stiffer sentences and a greater likelihood of the death sentence.

3 Treatment programmes

There have been many attempts to treat offenders while in prison and on probation orders. It is acknowledged that the only way to break the 'revolving door' phenomenon of repeated offending is to interrupt this cycle and criminal lifestyle. In the 1980s and 1990s the realisation of prisons' poor success rates in rehabilitating offenders led to a change in the ethos of dealing with prisoners. Even so, after much effort and trying many different programmes, the re-offending rate in the UK today is approximately 64 per cent. The re-offending rate is used as a measure of success for all treatment programmes, and the Home Office compares the expected risk of being re-convicted against what actually happens in treated and non-treated groups, to see if the difference is significant 2 years later. This of course is dependent on having accurate statistics: some offenders may re-offend but not get caught, while others may be picked up repeatedly, thus distorting the picture; the re-conviction rate for sexual offenders is so low that it is difficult to find a statistically significant difference between the treated and non-treated groups.

3.1 Cognitive skills programmes

Psychologists believe that one way to stop the cycle is to break down the faulty thinking patterns which they believe underlie criminal behaviour. Before a criminal act can occur, it must be preceded by criminal thoughts. Therefore if this pattern is broken, progress can be made towards a non-criminal lifestyle. This ideology is the rationale behind cognitive behavioural therapy (CBT), and it is this approach that has shown the most success in treating prisoners. In the earliest assessments of it in practice in the USA, it was estimated that re-conviction rates of people on the programmes went down by 10 percentage points. This led to optimism and in 2002, Friendship reported on a group of offenders who appeared to have benefited greatly from being on the programmes in British jails between 1992 and 1996 with a re-conviction rate 2 years after leaving prison of up to 14 percentage points lower than the control group.

Following this publication, the programme was extended and rolled out across the prison service in the belief that here was a cost-effective way of reducing the prison population. Then in 2003, Falshaw working with Friendship and others failed to find a significant difference between a treatment and a matched control group who had experienced the programmes between 1996 and 1998. Falshaw et al. suggest the following reasons for this turnaround:

- It could be just normal variation in populations, rather like good and bad cohorts in schools.

- The programme leaders in the original studies were more highly motivated and did a better job.

- The rapid expansion of the programmes affected their delivery quality.

- The treatment and control groups could have differed on risk factors that were not assessed in the study (confounding variables).

- The programmes had been targeted at lower-risk offenders than the earlier study. These were people who were less likely to be positively affected by them because the fact that they were already at lower risk of re-offending meant that they would not show much difference from the control group.

- The 2003 programmes may have been affected by the movement of prisoners to local prisons, which do not have the same facilities for treatment and training and are thus unable to complete a treatment.

Both the 2002 and the 2003 studies had samples of over 600, with comparison groups of over 1800 offenders; they are two of the biggest studies assessing effectiveness of the programmes, which means that the findings can be assumed to be representative.

Naturally enough, bearing in mind the gender balance in the criminal population, most of the research has been based on males. However, in the report which follows, cognitive skills training, which is an established part of CBT, is applied to a sample of female offenders. The two programmes mentioned in the research are described below.

After a guilty verdict

Reasoning and rehabilitation (R&R)

Reasoning and rehabilitation is available in 23 adult prisons and is intended to develop prisoners' cognitive skills. Prisoners are chosen for the programme if they have sufficiently high IQ (it must be above 80) and basic literacy skills. It targets thinking style, self-control or impulsivity, interpersonal problem-solving, critical reasoning, moral reasoning and social perspective-taking. The programme should last for 36 sessions of 2.5 hours each, with assignments set for prisoners to work on between sessions and when the programme is over. Prisoners are assigned to it as low risk, medium-low risk, medium-high risk and high risk of re-conviction. Their sentence type will be violent, sexual, acquisitive and other and they will have served sentences varying from a few months to 4 years or more.

Key study
Cann, Impact of cognitive skills programmes in reducing re-conviction

Aim To find out if cognitive skills programmes were effective in terms of lower re-offending rates for a sample of women prisoners.

Sample 180 offenders who started enhanced thinking skills (ETS) or R&R between 1996 and 2000, including 14 non-completers. The comparison group comprised 540 female offenders who did not participate in these programmes. All offenders were discharged in 1996–2000 and spent at least a year in the community following a custodial sentence of 6 months or more.

Procedure Expected 2-year re-conviction rates were calculated for all the women who were matched by whether they were at high, medium or low risk of re-conviction. Also, actual re-conviction rates were calculated for 1 and 2 years after release. Each individual programme (ETS or R&R) was also examined for effectiveness.

Results No significant difference was found between the treated group and the comparison group on expected re-conviction.

No significant difference was found between the groups for actual re-conviction after 1 or 2 years.

No significant differences were found for ETS, but for R&R the treated group actually fared worse and were significantly more likely to re-offend.

Discussion These results add to a mixed picture for the effectiveness of treatment programmes. In an earlier

study with male offenders, Friendship et al. (2002) found a significant result for their effectiveness but other researchers (including Friendship a year later) have failed to find a positive effect. Cann (2006) suggests the following reasons in the case of females:

- Women offend for different reasons from men and while they may have cognitive skills deficits, these are not necessarily criminal in nature. Women offend because of drug abuse, relationship problems, emotional factors and severe financial hardship.

- The programmes were inappropriate for the women's needs, having been developed for men and with men's risk factors in mind.

- The programmes were not delivered consistently in the women's prisons and were limited in length, not meeting the standards in the description above.

Check your understanding

1   What other factors could have influenced the success of these women in staying out of prison (e.g. many women in prison have severe drug dependency problems)?

2   What is the problem with using re-offending rates as a measure of success of a programme such as this?

3   Why do you think the R&R group of women might have got worse and were more likely to offend? Hint: look back at what the programme entails and think about the typical female offender.

3.2 Anger management

Anger is a strong emotion which produces an equally obvious physical response in the body. Psychologists distinguish between instrumental aggression, and hostile aggression. In the prison setting it is hostile aggression that is worked on because it is usually the hot-headed individual who gets into fights and causes injuries and ends up behind bars. There would be no point in working on instrumental aggression, which is by definition controlled.

To manage aggression, the prison service uses another cognitive behavioural accredited programme called CALM.

Key terms

enhanced thinking skills (ETS) this is similar to reasoning and rehabilitation and is available in 78 establishments; there are 20 sessions in a programme

instrumental aggression aggression that is a means to an end, for example an aggressive tackle to gain the ball in a rugby game

hostile aggression aggression that is an uncontrolled reaction to a person or stimulus, such as road rage

Weblink

You might like to find out more about CALM (see Contents page).

CALM is a cognitive behavioural programme aimed at prisoners who have problems in managing their emotions and for whom this had been an important part of their offending behaviour. The prisoner may also show a lack of emotional control in the prison and therefore be difficult to manage. Prisoners who have a psychotic illness, those with no literacy skills and those who use aggression solely to achieve a purpose (e.g. control during a robbery) are excluded. There are six modules with a total of 26 sessions.

The anger-management programme module by module (The Prison Service)

Module 1 The programme begins by focusing on motivating the prisoner to take part in the programme and to want to change.

Module 2 Group members are introduced to the concept of physiological arousal and the relationship between arousal and performance. They are taught how to identify physiological changes that they experience when becoming angry and are provided with a range of arousal management techniques which they practise and receive feedback on from peers and course leaders.

Module 3 The course leaders work with participants to understand how their irrational, hurtful and unhelpful thoughts contribute to their feelings and actions (anger and aggression). Participants learn to recognise irrational thinking, to argue against it and replace it with more rational thinking. This in turn leads to more helpful and less disturbing feelings and behaviour.

Module 4 Participants learn a number of skills to enable them to communicate with others more effectively, for example in response to provocation from others. They also learn how to communicate and take responsibility for how they feel about a situation without blaming others and remaining in control of their emotions.

Module 5 The prisoners practise applying the skills learned so far to other emotions that can lead to problematic or offending behaviour. These include jealousy, depression, anxiety (social threats and fear of losing control), and 'superman feelings' (feelings of unlimited power).

Module 6 Requires participants to identify the situations which are likely to be of highest risk for them in the future in terms of a return to anger and aggression. Programme leaders then support participants in developing relapse-prevention plans which incorporate skills learned on the programme and other skills as appropriate to the situation. Included in this module is preparation for what happens if they do relapse and exploration of 'healthy' and 'unhealthy' ways of coping following a relapse.

CALM is currently offered in 24 establishments. Approximately 550 prisoners completed the programme in 2006/07. CALM is also available in 14 probation areas.

Case studies of CALM

John was in his late forties and was serving a 4-year term for attempted arson. He had served most of his sentence by the time he entered the programme. His story varied on each telling, but it seems he was in a pub and had an argument with the landlord, who threw him out. As he was being thrown out, he threatened to burn the place down. Sometimes in his story he changed his mind on the way to the petrol station; in other versions, he bought the petrol, abandoned it and was arrested on his way home; in fact he was arrested with a can of petrol on his way back to the pub. John remained in prison and served his sentence but got into far less trouble on the wing.

John had the typical profile of a subject for anger management – prone to spontaneous, manifestly self-destructive bursts of rage, and full of delusional notions about where they came from. He had some strange theories, among them that he had a psychic ability not to feel pain down one side of his body, as long as he decided not to.

Following his treatment, John left prison to live in a hostel on probation and under supervision. The

U3
1

After a guilty verdict

techniques that he was taught in order to manage his aggression were simple and can help anyone in a confrontational situation.

1   Thought-stopping – where the prisoner learns to stop thinking negative aggressive thoughts and direct them somewhere else.

2   Fogging – where the prisoner learns to hear criticism without over reacting and learns to ignore it.

3   The broken-record technique (much used by teachers!) – where repetition is used to gain what you want without escalation into anger and retaining control of the voice and body language.

So does it work in general?

U3
1

Key study

Ireland, Investigation of whether anger-management courses work

Aim To assess whether anger-management programmes work with a group of young male offenders.

Sample 50 prisoners who had completed an anger-management course and a control group of 37 prisoners who had been assessed as suitable for such a course but had not actually completed one. They were matched therefore on the following three criteria:

◆   their responses to a cognitive behavioural interview

◆   the Wing Behavioural Checklist (WBC) which was completed by prison officers rating 29 angry behaviours with scores of 0, 1 or 2 for the week before the interview

◆   a self-report questionnaire on anger management (AMA) with 53 items completed by the prisoners themselves.

Methodology A quasi-experiment taking advantage of the two naturally occurring groups. The measures above were given to the prisoners in the treatment group before and after they completed the programme; the control group also got them twice but without any intervention in between.

Results There was a significant reduction in prison wing-based aggression in the experimental group but not in the control group. The experimental group scored lower on the self-report measures after completing the course but there was no difference in the control group.

Overall, 92 per cent of the prisoners in the experimental group showed improvement on at least one measure, 48 per cent on two measures and 8 per cent showed deterioration on both measures upon completing the course.

Conclusions In the short term these prisoners appeared to be helped by the programme, but in this case we have no re-conviction data further down the line. It is interesting that 8 per cent actually got worse, which would require further investigation.

Check your understanding

1   What weight can we give to the self-report data from the prisoners before and after they completed the programmes? Is it valid and reliable?

2   It appears that attending these programmes improves behaviour on the wings. Can you suggest any other variables which might be causing this effect and confounding the research variable?

Try this ...

You have been asked by the prison service to come up with a reliable and valid way of measuring a change in aggression before and after a treatment programme. Think about how you could measure someone's anger. Design a piece of research to do this using your knowledge of psychological methodology.

Take it further

The research on all CBT programmes presents a mixed picture of success. It could be argued that making someone aware that they have an anger problem excuses them from full responsibility for their actions and that their behaviour is being determined. How far would you agree?

3.3 Ear acupuncture for drug rehabilitation

Ear acupuncture is an alternative treatment that has been used in prisons for 5 years and is popular with staff, management and prisoners because it is cheap, easily taught and does not depend on the prisoner to be highly motivated to work. Drug-addicted prisoners are often highly confrontational, so to try to begin a programme of talk-based therapy is difficult initially but can successfully follow the acupuncture treatment.

Key study
Wheatley, Use of acupuncture to treat drug addiction in prisoners

Sample 350 prisoners in six high-security prisons who received acupuncture and the standard care programme which is called FOCUS, with a control group who did not receive acupuncture but did get the standard care.

Procedure Two trained practitioners worked with groups of 10–15 prisoners in a relaxed setting. Fine needles were inserted into five acupuncture points in the ear and prisoners relaxed for a 40-minute period. They then returned to normal duties. Qualitative and quantitative data were collected.

Results Qualitative data: prisoners reported better sleep, improved relaxation, better coping skills, reduced cravings for nicotine, amended cognitions and health improvements. They made more effort to communicate with their families and attend classes. Staff commented that they could tell when prisoners had been to acupuncture because the wing was calmer and there was less demand for healthcare services.

Quantitative data:

- a 70 per cent reduction in drug-related incidents from 6 months pre- to 6 months post-treatment
- 41 per cent reduction in serious incident reports
- 42 per cent reduction in positive drug testing results (mandatory)
- 33 per cent reduction in positive drug test results (voluntary).

Figure 1.19 Wheatley found that acupuncture improved prisoners' sense of well-being

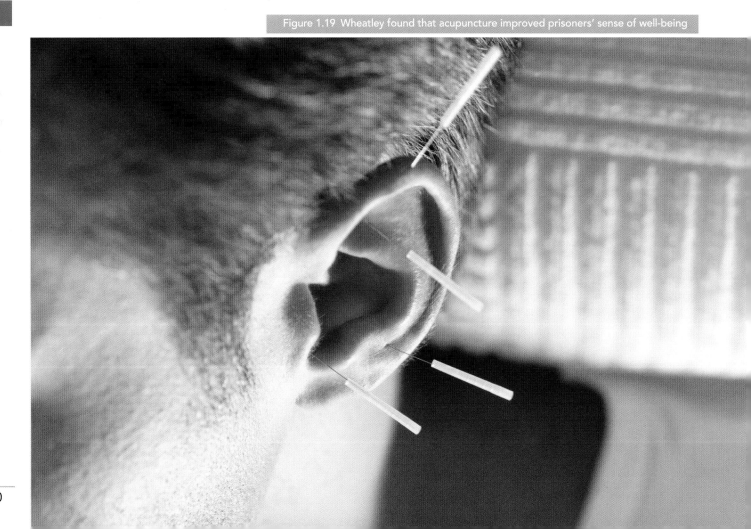

Conclusion Wheatley feels there is enough evidence to expand the delivery of the programme throughout the prison system and believes that acupuncture works as a complementary therapy with other programmes.

Check your understanding

1   What other variables could account for the improved relaxation and attitude of these prisoners after treatment?

2   This study gives us qualitative and quantitative data. Which would you find more convincing if you were the governor of a prison who had been asked to try acupuncture?

3   What is the expectancy effect and how could it be related to the results of this study?

Take it further

Research by Gates et al. in 2006 found no significant effect for genuine acupuncture versus sham acupuncture (where the needles were placed randomly in the ear) for a sample of cocaine addicts in randomised controlled trials. The authors found seven studies with 1433 participants by searching a register of controlled trials and online computer databases. However, the needles were sometimes placed in only two or three of the five official acupuncture points in the various studies, so there were problems of comparison. They conclude that more trials are needed to be sure of the lack of effect.

This is typical of peer-reviewed research where one researcher's findings are tested against another's until a body of knowledge is accepted and agreed upon. Alternative and complementary therapies have been difficult to test formally in this way. Why is this?

Should we test a therapy which by definition is part of a holistic way of treating a person, by isolating part of it as an independent variable in the usual way of a laboratory experiment within a scientific paradigm?

Do we have to develop different ways of assessing alternative treatments which may be less scientific and therefore less credible?

A further interesting phenomenon is the placebo effect. How could this be used to interpret the data in this experiment?

Section summary

◆   Treatment programmes are a real problem to assess. It seems that when a programme is well conducted, completed in full and properly targeted on the right offender, it works, but when extended to larger groups and often incomplete because of the overcrowding in the system, the positive effects disappears.

◆   However, both cognitive skills programmes and anger-management programmes rely on self-reports and observation to evaluate their effectiveness. This means that a prisoner could show high demand characteristics and present a favourable impression of their effectiveness to secure an early release.

◆   Psychologists and prison staff are willing to try alternative therapies such as ear acupuncture with drug offenders. This in itself is not psychological unless one views it as a placebo, but in practice it is used with so-called 'talking cures' or more standard therapeutic approaches.

◆   In the end, all concerned look for 'whatever works' and put it into practice wherever they can. Unfortunately the present overcrowded system works against the prison staff and psychologists, meaning that prisoners rarely get to finish programmes or that insufficient time and expertise are put into them.

ExamCafé
Relax, refresh, result!

Relax and prepare

Student tips

Linda

Get a set of index cards from a stationer. Summarise the research on one side and put evaluation issues on the back. When you have a set, pair up with a friend and test each other, or get your parents involved – then they can really see that you are working!

Anya

I need to practise changing my answers for different questions. This will help me focus on exactly what the question is asking in the exam. First, I need three questions on the same topic from my teacher.

If I have put my research onto cards I can move them around on the table in front of me to suit the different questions and I can see at a glance what would work. Because I have the evaluation issues on the back, I can also create a discussion section with ease.

Refresh your memory

Revision checklist: approaches to teaching

A simple revision aid is to make a checklist summarising the key points of a study and taking four issues which you will prepare to evaluate it. Below is a partially completed example for you to copy and complete.

Explanation/study	Issue – reductionist?	Issue – methodology?	Issue – nature/nurture?	Issue – perspective?
Farrington	Takes a holistic view, looking at many factors that influence crime. Main one is transmission through families	Longitudinal Interviews – advantages and disadvantages Crime data – advantages and disadvantages Subject attrition		
Sutherland				
Peterborough study				

Get the result!

Example answers

Below is a student response written under exam conditions in answer to the following question:

Describe, using evidence, any two influences that explain why a person turns to crime. (10 marks)

Student answer

Two influences which explain why a person turns to crime are upbringing and biology. Within the influence of upbringing, there are several strands. First, there is family transmission, as described by David Farrington, who conducted a longitudinal study of 411 East End boys all born in 1953. He followed them through their lives into the second and third generation because he wanted to see if criminal behaviour was passed on from parent to child or whether other influences were as important. He found that the boys who became involved with crime early committed the most offences and had the longest convictions.

As he expected, he found that the most important childhood risk factors at age 8–10 for later offending were that the family was involved in crime and they were daring or risk-taking, with low school attainment, poverty and poor parenting.

A second strand of upbringing would be the relationships young people have with each other. This was investigated by Edwin Sutherland, who believed that criminality was learned from peers. He thought that if a child had more reasons to be criminal than non-criminal then it would follow that they would become criminal. How the reasons were defined was affected by the child's culture and what rules they thought were worth sticking to.

Another influence which explains criminal behaviour is biology. Adrian Raine has done much work in this area by using PET scan technology to look for differences in the brains of violent murderers and also for other biological measures such as a low resting heart rate and birth problems. He believes that this combination of factors increases the risk of becoming criminal by explaining the likelihood of risk taking and lack of control over impulsive behaviour.

However all the influences must interact in some way to explain criminal behaviour.

Examiner says:

The first paragraph is really strong and just what we are looking for. We can clearly see how this study was carried out and the scene is set for the results.

The second paragraph concisely draws attention to the most important findings, although more detail would improve the answer.

The third paragraph concisely describes the main point of Sutherland's work; it adds to the argument begun in the first paragraph and supports it. Good structure developing.

The fourth paragraph sums up Raine's work but this time it does not quite do the job. We are left wondering how the low heart rate and birth problems explain criminal behaviour.

The final paragraph needs one more sentence explaining the evolutionary link to risk-taking.

Overall a strong answer.

Below is a student response written under exam conditions in answer to the following question:

Using the issue of reductionism, evaluate any two explanations of crime. (15 marks)

Student answer

Reductionism is the idea that complex phenomena, in this case criminality, can be explained by taking them apart and examining each contributory factor individually. This idea is attractive to psychologists because by doing this they hope to find the cause or causes of criminality. It is also attractive because it encourages a scientific approach which is more objective and convincing to the outside world.

A very reductionist idea is that we will one day find a gene or genes for criminal behaviour. An example is the work of Brunner. He found mutations on the genes of a family who were prone to extremes of aggression and criminal behaviour. The problem with this is that mutations are unpredictable and may be unique to families or small populations, as in this case. It is also the case that in this study and in earlier ones there is alteration of appearance which might also influence how these people turn out and how they are treated by society.

Not so reductionist is Adrian Raine's approach to explaining criminality because he breaks down criminal behaviour into lots of factors and then systematically seeks to investigate them. He never says that one factor on its own is enough to produce criminal behaviour. He believes that they co-occur and he also believes that the environment is important in switching these factors on or off. One such factor is a low resting heart rate and in his recent work he finds this to be consistent in young offenders. His suggestion is that there is a link to risk-seeking behaviour as these individuals want to raise the level of functioning of the nervous system. The advantage of finding this to be true would be to help us understand and perhaps provide more legal thrill-seeking opportunites for young males.

Examiner says:

The first paragraph shows a reasonable level of understanding, although there is a lack of detail. It would have been interesting to know more about how this gene changed these individuals, but it is answering the question.

The second paragraph is more detailed and again well focused. No disadvantages are mentioned, though this would have added to the strength of the paragraph. It would be good to know more about the functioning of the nervous system and why low resting heart rate matters.

Overall a reasonable attempt at the question which stays focused.

Health and Clinical Psychology

Contents

Studies used in the Health and Clinical Psychology option

Healthy living

Stress

Dysfunctional behaviour

Disorders

Full references for the studies can be found in the References section on page 330

Introduction

Figure 2.1 How do we define health?

Health psychology is a relatively new area of psychology, encompassing not only dysfunctional behaviour (or mental-health issues), but also the whole area of human health.

Health can be considered to be a lack of illness, both physical and mental. It can relate to many aspects of the mind and body, including physical trauma, reduction in ability or disease. But health psychology is not only to do with these aspects of health; it also looks at health behaviours such as eating well and not drinking to excess, and unhealthy behaviours such as smoking or taking on too much and becoming stressed. If psychologists are fundamentally asking 'Why do people do that?' then health psychologists are asking why people do or do not adopt particular health behaviours.

But health psychology goes beyond this. Being psychology, it relies on empirical research to support theories of health, models of health behaviours, and health interventions and promotions. Much health research in psychology is fairly recent, although some long-standing theories still have credence today, such as Watson and Raynor's (1920) research into phobias (see pages 115–116). Once research has established the antecedents that cause us to adopt health behaviours, the applications can be fully explored. Health-promotion campaigns are based on theories of communication and behavioural change. Legislation has been seen to be effective in changing behaviour, hence the law prohibiting smoking in public areas. All this should make for a healthier society and less public spending on health, although of course living longer brings with it the problem of an increasing elderly population – lifespan psychology has taken on this area of research.

> **Key terms**
>
> dysfunctional unable to function emotionally or as a social unit
>
> credence credibility or authority
>
> antecedent something that happens or exists before something else
>
> aetiology the cause or origin of a disease or disorder as determined by medical diagnosis

Health psychology also includes the study of mental health (more properly called clinical psychology). This looks at the diagnosis, causes and treatments of a wide range of dysfunctional behaviours: anything that interferes with a person's day-to-day functioning. These are not simple to define or diagnose, and when it comes to treatments, every approach has something to offer, creating a bewildering array of therapies. However, the individual differences that make each human unique require a unique approach to ensure that we remain healthy, and a variety of therapies can help to meet our needs.

What do health psychologists do?

Health psychologists apply psychological research and methods to:

◆ the promotion and maintenance of health

◆ the prevention and management of illness

◆ the identification of psychological factors contributing to physical illness

◆ the improvement of the health-care system

◆ the formulation of health policy.

In practice this might mean devising programmes for preventing smoking or drug abuse, making work settings healthier, promoting healthy behaviours such as eating fruit and vegetables. Health psychologists may also be able to predict high stress levels, and reduce stressors or introduce stress-management techniques. There are many areas of health psychology that this text cannot cover; further areas include disability and its psychological effects on patients and their families, management of illness and pain, and how to improve communication between patients and health practitioners to ensure that health intervention produces the best outcomes.

Where do health psychologists work?

In hospitals and health authorities, and also in academic and research situations in hospitals and universities. They may deal with specific problems identified by health-care agencies or professionals. In addition they may work in government health departments or any of the health-care charities and organisations.

How do you become a health psychologist?

The British Psychological Society governs the training and study of chartered psychologists. Currently (2008) to become a chartered health psychologist you need two qualifications after gaining a Psychology degree:

◆ the Stage 1 Qualification in Health Psychology provides the necessary underpinning knowledge (equivalent to an MSc)

◆ the Stage 2 Qualification in Health Psychology consists of structured and assessed supervised practice and written assignments.

What do clinical psychologists do?

Clinical psychologists may see patients with depression, relationship problems, learning disabilities and serious mental illness. (They are not psychiatrists, who are doctors who then specialise in the area of psychiatric disorders.)

A clinical psychologist would assess a patient using methods that might include interviews, observations and psychometric tests. This may lead to a therapy regime that could include counselling or interventions such as cognitive behavioural therapy.

Where do clinical psychologists work?

In hospitals, or with community mental-health teams, child and adolescent mental-health services, or privately with self-referred patients.

Introduction to Health and Clinical Psychology

U3
2

How do you become a clinical psychologist?

After gaining a Psychology degree you would go on to a three-year, full-time course leading to a doctorate in Clinical Psychology.

The areas of health psychology covered in this book are:

- Healthy living
- Stress
- Dysfunctional behaviour
- Disorders.

Healthy living

Healthy living considers theories that might explain our health behaviours, such as the health belief model, and then looks at health-promotion campaigns. This section also looks at adherence: understanding why people adhere to medical advice and how adherence can be improved are important in ensuring the long-term health of society.

Stress

One of the most common health problems is stress. Health psychologists try to identify what will help to reduce stress, and also to teach people stress-management techniques. There are problems with measuring health behaviours such as stress, and these are also considered, as without effective measurement there is little validity in what we know about health behaviours.

Dysfunctional behaviour

How society defines dysfunctional behaviour will to some extent predict its treatment of disorders, based on whichever approach is prevalent. This section looks at biological, cognitive and behaviourist explanations, although other explanations such as the psychodynamic also contribute to our understanding and treatment of dysfunctional behaviour. The definitions and categorisation of disorders are covered in this section, with an overview of the two main diagnostic manuals.

Disorders

This section looks at three types of disorder in more detail. The characteristics of psychotic, affective and anxiety disorders are identified, then one disorder from each category is studied in greater depth. The aetiology of one disorder from each category is covered and the explanations and treatments for this disorder are detailed, along with research in support of these explanations.

U3
2

Healthy living

Introduction

In studying healthy living, we need to consider what makes people behave in a healthy or non-healthy way. The three areas of healthy living covered here are:

◆ theories of health belief

◆ methods of health promotion

◆ features of adherence to medical regimes.

Theories of health belief

Some health psychologists are concerned with trying to find out why individuals adopt certain health behaviours. As with all aspects of psychology there are many explanations, for example social psychologists would look at how others might influence our behaviour. Cognitive psychology is one of the main approaches in this area. However, it assumes that we think through our actions logically before rationally coming to a decision as to which behaviour to adopt. Anyone who has broken their New Year's resolution will know that, however convincing the argument for adopting healthy behaviours, there are still times when we choose, illogically, to adopt unhealthy ones. If we could all be depended upon to do the logical thing, there would no longer be anyone who smoked; drinking to excess would be a thing of the past; and obesity would not be a threat.

Methods of health promotion

Consider media campaigns you have seen. What messages are they trying to convey? Don't drink and drive? Don't drive too fast? Eat five portions of fruit and vegetables a day. But do we all follow the advice we are given? Not really! So why bother with health-promotion campaigns? Research shows that they can work, and that while they may not cut out unhealthy behaviour completely, they can have some positive effects.

Features of adherence to medical regimes

Adherence to medical regimes can be linked to healthy living, as medical regimes might include health behaviours such as giving up smoking or eating healthily. Adherence can be thought of as being conscientious in following something like a medical regime prescribed by the doctor, and this subsection looks specifically at adherence to taking medication.

Adherence is an important issue for health psychologists, as there is much evidence to show that adherence rates are low. Even for statins (drugs which reduce cholesterol and have few side effects), the adherence rate is only 70 per cent, as shown by Simons et al. (1996) who researched this in Australian adults. They found that there was a lot of wastage of resources, and opportunities to prevent heart disease were lost.

Try this ...

1. Find examples of health-promotion materials. You could look in doctors' waiting rooms, libraries, or on the internet.

2. What do you think makes these materials effective?

3. Is there anything in them that you feel would or would not have a strong effect on your behaviour?

Themes and perspectives

The individual's rights versus the rights of society is an ethical dilemma for people promoting healthy lifestyles. Why shouldn't people smoke or drink without being shown gruesome images or frightening media campaigns? In addition, the methodological problems of researching health behaviours can cause problems with validity of research. Self-report is a key method of data-gathering, but can be susceptible to social desirability bias and demand characteristics. However, the qualitative nature of the data gathered by self-report may outweigh these problems. In health psychology, understanding the reasons behind people's choices can lead to the development of cognitive models which are useful in predicting behaviours and promoting healthy lifestyles.

Reductionism is an issue as there are many factors influencing areas as complicated as health behaviours. To suggest that just one personality trait, such as locus of control, could substantially influence something like giving up smoking is too simplistic. Biological factors such as addiction and social phenomena such as peer pressure, together with habit formation, denial and illogical cognitions, must all play a part in a person's decision to smoke, not to mention the economic factor of cost! So it would be limited to adopt only one stance in health psychology, and a holistic approach to health must be beneficial.

Weblinks

Have a look at examples of health promotion campaigns (see Contents page).

1 Theories of health belief

There are many theories that might explain our adoption of health behaviours. This section will look at three lifestyle models that contribute to our understanding of health behaviours:

- the health belief model, which can predict the uptake of health behaviours based on several factors

- locus of control, which considers where people believe the control of their health is located: within themselves or with others

- self-efficacy: how effective a person thinks they can be in changing their behaviour will directly influence their tendency to try to change their behaviour.

1.1 Health belief model

One major theory which mainly adopts the cognitive approach is the health belief model (HBM). A study in 1954 on why people did or did not go for tuberculosis (TB) screening seemed to indicate that a main consideration was how serious they perceived TB to be. If it was seen to be a serious threat to health, the logical thing was to be screened and then treated if necessary. From this Becker and Rosenstock developed the HBM in 1970 (Becker et al., 1978).

The HBM is a cognitive model which identifies factors that indicate the possibility of an individual adopting a health behaviour.

There are two aspects of this threat to health: the *perceived seriousness* (Will it actually kill me?) and the *perceived susceptibility* (Am I likely to get it?). In addition to the perceived threat is the cost–benefits analysis which is thought by psychologists to influence our behaviour in many situations. The costs and benefits of adopting the behaviour are weighed up and the individual decides whether the costs outweigh the benefits. But the logical process of deciding on the health behaviours we adopt (or do not adopt) is complicated. Demographic variables might all influence the final decision, and external cues such as TV adverts and posters or internal cues such as a period of ill health might remind us about the behaviour. The HBM takes into account some social aspects such as culture, and is not only a cognitive model, which must make it more useful when assessing complex human behaviour. Figure 2.2 illustrates the factors that affect our likelihood of adopting a health behaviour.

Key terms

cost–benefits analysis a process by which decisions are made. The benefits of a given situation are taken into account and then the costs associated with taking that action are subtracted

demographic variables population characteristics such as age, income, sex, occupation, education, family size

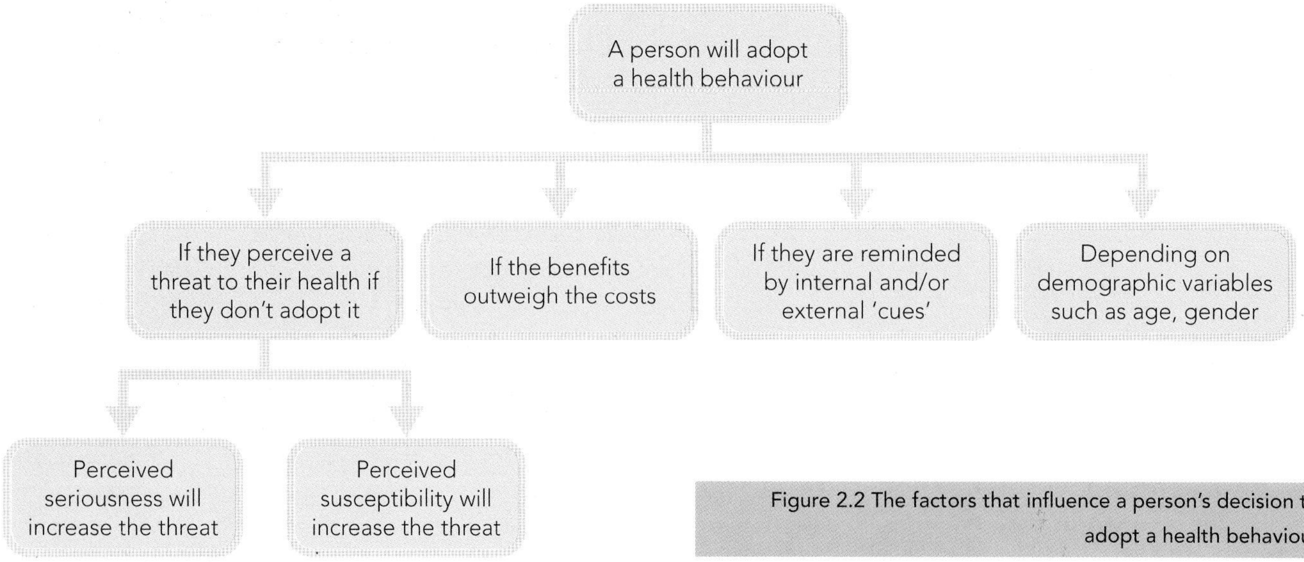

Figure 2.2 The factors that influence a person's decision to adopt a health behaviour

As Figure 2.2 shows, if a person perceives a threat to their health they will adopt a health behaviour. So, for example, if you think smoking will damage your health, you are more likely to give it up. This might also apply to adopting health behaviours such as breast self-examination.

Becker's study on the use of asthma medication (Becker, 1978) tested the HBM, and found that the belief that their child was susceptible to asthma attacks was one reason why a parent would administer medication. Compliant parents tended to see their child's asthma as interfering with their own activities, so the benefits of giving the medication were high. Factors such as the perceived seriousness of the child's asthma and demographic variables such as education and marital status also confirmed the HBM to be an accurate predictor of the likelihood of a parent administering the medication.

Key study

Becker, Compliance with a medical regimen for asthma

Aim To use the HBM to explain mothers' adherence to a drug regimen for their asthmatic children.

Methodology A correlation between beliefs reported during interviews and compliance with self-reported administration of asthma medication. For some participants, a blood test was also used to test the level of medication; this confirmed the validity of the mothers' answers in the interview.

Participants 111 mothers responsible for administering asthma medication to their children. They were aged 17–54 years and the children were aged from 9 months to 17 years.

Design Correlational design.

Procedure Each mother was interviewed for about 45 minutes; mothers were asked questions regarding their perception of their child's susceptibility to illness and asthma, their beliefs about how serious asthma is, how much their child's asthma interfered with the child's education, caused embarrassment and interfered with the mother's activities. They were also questioned about their faith in doctors and the effectiveness of the medication.

Findings A positive correlation was found between a mother's belief about her child's susceptibility to asthma attacks and compliance with a medical regimen. This positive correlation also existed between the mother's perception of the child's having a serious asthma condition and her administering the medication as prescribed. Mothers who reported that their child's asthma interfered with their own activities also complied with the medication.

The costs which negatively correlated with compliance were disruption of daily activities, inaccessibility of chemists, the child complaining about the medication and the prescribed schedule for administering the medication.

The two demographic variables correlated with compliance were marital status and education. Married mothers were more likely to comply, and the greater the mother's education, the more likely she would be to keep to the prescribed routine for administering the medication.

Conclusion The HBM is a useful model to predict and explain different levels of compliance with medical regimens.

1.2 Locus of control

A second, much simpler, theory about why we might or might not adopt a health behaviour is Rotter's locus of control theory (1966). This simple explanation is reductionist in that it reduces the explanation down to a person's locus of control. *Locus* (from the Latin meaning 'place') suggests that where a person thinks the control of their health lies will influence whether they adopt a health behaviour. If a person has an *internal* locus of control, this would suggest that they control their health themselves. It follows that if you believe you have control over your health, then you will do what you think will make you healthier. You might eat five portions of fruit and vegetables a day, cut down on saturated fats, or follow any other advice to keep yourself healthy. On the other hand, some people have an *external* locus of control, seeing their health as being in someone else's hands (this might be doctors, parents, fate or religious leaders). If you believe you have no control over your health, then it really does not matter what you eat or how you live: 'fate' will decide whether you live or die. This rather deterministic theory is quite pessimistic, as it would seem that your locus of control will predict your health behaviours, or lack of them. A study by Rotter (1966) investigated internal versus external locus of control.

Key study

Rotter, Internal versus external locus of control

Methodology Review article.

Sample Initially six pieces of research into individual perceptions of ability to control outcomes based on reinforcement.

Findings Rotter found that results from the studies reviewed consistently showed that participants who felt they had control over the situation were more likely to show behaviours that would enable them to cope with potential threats, than participants who thought that chance or other non-controllable forces determined the effects of their behaviours.

Conclusions Rotter concluded that locus of control would affect many of our behaviours, not just health behaviours. He included in his article a summary of research by James et al. (1965), which found that male smokers who gave up and did not relapse had a higher level of internal locus of control than those who did not quit smoking. Interestingly there was not a significant difference for female smokers, indicating that factors such as weight gain were influential in giving up smoking.

1.3 Self-efficacy

Linked to the cognitive idea of locus of control is a final theory to consider: Bandura's concept of 'self-efficacy'. Bandura (one of the team who in 1961 studied aggression in children) considered self-efficacy as being a strong indicator of a person's potential to adopt health behaviours. Self-efficacy simply means how effective a person thinks they will be at successfully adopting a health behaviour. This is another cognitive model based on the thought processes of the individual. Bandura agreed that concepts such as locus of control affect behaviour, but felt that determining behaviour went beyond such a simple explanation. His view of self-efficacy is a theory which he sets out in the article described on page 84. He uses many other pieces of research as evidence for his theory, in particular how treatments of disorders such as anxiety can be helped by increasing self-efficacy.

Bandura (1977) felt that learning from consequences was a cognitive process and would result in an *outcome expectancy*. This means that based on previous experiences a person could estimate the likely outcome in any situation. The other key concept Bandura identified as affecting behaviour is the *efficacy expectation*. This is a person's belief that they can successfully do whatever is required to achieve the outcome.

The key factors that affect a person's efficacy expectation are:

- *vicarious experiences* – seeing other people do something successfully

- *verbal persuasion* – someone telling you that you can do something

- *emotional arousal* – too much anxiety can reduce a person's self-efficacy.

In addition, *cognitive appraisal* of a situation might also affect expectations of personal efficacy. Factors such as social, situational and temporal circumstances are contextual factors that could influence such an appraisal. This means that a person's self-efficacy can alter depending on the situation. Bandura cites the example of public speaking, and how the time, audience, subject matter and type of presentation might all influence the microanalysis of perceived coping capabilities which represents self-efficacy. This is not simply dependent on personality traits.

Bandura suggests that locus of control is often thought to be the same as self-efficacy, but that locus of control is concerned with the cause of an outcome, whereas self-efficacy is actually a person's conviction that their own behaviour will influence the outcome.

Evidence from a 1977 study by Bandura and Adams is used to support this theory. They found that self-efficacy was an accurate predictor of performance on tasks that the participants thought they were able to do, whereas low self-efficacy was linked to failure when participants thought the tasks were beyond their capability.

Key study

Bandura and Adams, Analysis of self-efficacy theory of behavioural change

Aim To assess the self-efficacy of patients undergoing systematic desensitisation in relation to their behaviour with previously phobic objects.

Methodology A controlled quasi-experiment with patients with snake phobias.

Participants Ten snake-phobic patients who replied to an advertisement in a newspaper. There were nine females and one male, aged 19–57 years.

Procedure Pre-test assessment: each patient was assessed for avoidance behaviour towards a boa constrictor, then fear arousal was assessed with an oral rating of 1–10 and finally efficacy expectations (how much they thought they would be able to perform different behaviours with snakes). Their fear of snakes was also measured on a scale, along with their own rating of how effectively they would be able to cope.

Systematic desensitisation: a standard desensitisation programme was followed, where patients were introduced to a series of events involving snakes and at each stage were taught relaxation. These ranged from imagining looking at a picture of a snake to handling live snakes.

Post-test assessment: each patient was again measured on behaviours and belief of self-efficacy in coping.

Findings Higher levels of post-test self-efficacy were found to correlate with higher levels of interaction with snakes.

Conclusion Desensitisation enhanced self-efficacy levels, which in turn led to a belief that the participant was able to cope with the phobic stimulus of a snake.

Check your understanding

1. What does self-efficacy mean?

2. What factors influence a person's self-efficacy?

3. What were the conclusions in Bandura and Adams's study?

Try this ...

Design a piece of health promotion material using the three theories. For example, what would you put on a poster to make sure someone perceives smoking to be a serious threat to their health?

Section summary

◆ A person's lifestyle choices may be healthy or not healthy. They may choose to give up smoking, eat healthily or exercise regularly.

◆ There are many theories that would explain such choices, and the ones we have looked at concentrate on the logical cognitive approach to such behaviour.

◆ All the theories are linked, in that there are individual perceptions based on previous information which might affect a person's locus of control, their self-efficacy, and how susceptible they think they are to ill-health.

◆ These cognitive models or theories successfully explain how individuals might adopt one or more behaviour, but not necessarily all of them.

Try this …

How would you explain one person's decision not to give up smoking, using the three theories outlined previously?

Take it further

Each of these theories can be applied to issues such as reductionism and nature–nurture. Draw a chart or write an essay, comparing and contrasting these theories in relation to at least three evaluation issues from the A2 specification, or use the issues that you studied at AS.

2 Methods of health promotion

This section considers the topic of health promotion. Government agencies, health agencies, charities and businesses all try to encourage people to adopt a healthy lifestyle. The many cognitive factors that influence health behaviour mean that any health-promotion campaign is going to be more successful for some people than for others.

This section looks at three methods of health promotion and the research that indicates that they are effective. The methods are:

◆ media campaigns: it would be a waste of money if there was no evidence to demonstrate the effectiveness of health promotion by the media

◆ legislation: how passing laws to prohibit unsafe behaviours or ensure safe behaviours can encourage people to change

◆ fear arousal: underlying psychology that can increase the impact of health-promotion campaigns. This can link to the 'perceived seriousness' concept in the HBM (see page 81).

It will be interesting to see how the lifestyle models that were considered in the previous section fit with the methods described in this section. Validity of research is a problem, as people generally overemphasise either their health or their illness, depending on who is asking. It is unlikely that we would admit to not following a healthy diet, as this could lead to lack of sympathy, and even lack of health care. On the other hand, if we want to appear better, then we might overstate our adherence and a reduction in our symptoms. After any health-promotion campaign, it is a brave person who stands up and admits to going against advice, or ignoring legislation.

The issue of ecological validity can also be considered. Most research in health psychology takes place in real-life situations, for example Watt's (2003) research on improving adherence, Lustman's (2000) research on measuring adherence in patients with depression and Cowpe's (1989) research on media campaigns to reduce chip-pan fires (see pages 86–87). High ecological validity can give us useful insights into human behaviour. However, alongside this we must consider the lack of control of extraneous variables. For example, *if* the local cycle store in Howard County had a sale of helmets just as Dannenberg's (1993) study on cycle-helmet wearing and legislation was starting (see page 87), would this affect the wearing of helmets?

2.1 Media campaigns

Try this …

Television adverts, posters and leaflets are all common means of getting health messages across to the general public. Try to think of campaigns that have used different media.

Figure 2.3 An image from a television 'Don't drink and drive' campaign

Television campaigns

A Scottish media campaign on drink-driving showed that the numbers of people drinking at home between August 2006 (before the campaign) and December 2006 (after the campaign) did not change significantly. There was, however, a gradual decline among those who claimed to drink at home at least once a week, from 75 per cent in December 2005, to 73 per cent in August 2006 and 71 per cent in December 2006 (Scottish Government, 2007). This might show less of a behaviour change than governments would hope for, but it is a move in the right direction. The objective to change behavioural patterns in relation to drinking is a long-term one and significant year-on-year changes in attitude are not expected.

A review of media campaigns shows what does and does not appear to work in media campaigns (Gallichan, 2002) and some studies do show positive results. Often major changes in attitude occur which do not always translate into behavioural change (Whelan and Culver, 1997). Occasionally, campaigns in areas such as health and safety can show some effectiveness, for example Cowpe's research into chip-pan fires (1989).

Key study

Cowpe, Chip-pan fire prevention

Aim To test the effectivness of an advertisng campagin which demonstrated a procedure, provided information, challenged perceptions about lack of ability to cope and encouraged preventative actions.

Methodology A quasi-experiment where a media campaign was shown in ten UK regional television areas from 1976 to 1984. An analysis of the number of chip-pan fires reported between 1976 and 1982, plus two quantitative consumer surveys in 1976 and 1983, was used to gather the data.

Participants People living in the television areas.

Procedure The campaigns were shown on television. There were two 60-second commercials, one called 'Inattendance' and one called 'Overfilling'. These showed the initial cause of the fire and the actions required to put it out. There were real-time and slow-motion sequences to heighten the effect. Each region was shown the chip-pan campaign, and three areas (Granada, Harlech and Tyne Tees) were shown reminders in another year. The number of reported chip-pan fires was analysed for each area.

Findings The net decline in each area over the 12-month period of the campaign was between 7 per cent (Central television area) and 25 per cent (Granada television area).

The largest reduction was during the campaign. In Tyne Tees television area there was a reduction of 33 per cent during the campaign, a reduction of 17 per cent over the next six months and then 15 per cent over the following 15 weeks.

Interestingly, if an area received more than one television channel, i.e. Granada and Central, the 'overlap' areas showed less impact, probably due to the reduced impact of seeing the campaign more than once.

The questionnaires showed an increase in the awareness of chip-pan fire advertising from 62 per cent in the Yorkshire TV area before the campaign to 90 per cent after the first adverts, and stayed at 96 per cent after the campaign.

People mentioning chip-pan fires as a danger in the kitchen also increased from 12 per cent before the campaign to 28 per cent after the campaign in the Yorkshire TV area.

Conclusion The advertising proved effective as shown by the reduction in chip-pan fires. The behaviour change is seen most during the campaign and reduces as time passes after the end of the campaign. Viewers are less likely to be influenced by the campaign if overexposed to it, as in the overlap areas.

Confidence in the data is shown by the change in awareness both of chip-pan fire adverts and the danger of chip-pan fires in the kitchen.

> ## Check your understanding
>
> 1 This research was a field experiment. What are the strengths and weaknesses of this research method?
>
> 2 What extraneous variables do you think could have influenced the results?

2.2 Legislation

Legislation varies from country to country, or state to state in the USA. In 2007, the maximum blood alcohol limit in the UK was 80mg of alcohol per 100ml of blood. but the Royal Society for the Prevention of Accidents suggested that this should be lowered, in particular for new drivers (ROSPA, 2007). An increase in alcohol-to-blood ratio of 20mg per 100ml has been shown to substantially increase accidents in young drivers, and legislation could be used to reduce this risk. The problem with any legislation is that it needs effective enforcement: would the laws be obeyed if there was no chance of being caught? In 2007, the police in the UK could stop any driver for any reason, but could not ask them to take a breath test without some evidence or suspicion that they had been drinking. They could breathalyse any driver who had committed a traffic offence or been involved in an accident.

A study by Dannenberg et al. (1993) looks at legislation in Maryland, USA, to see how legislation to compel young cyclists to wear helmets affected health behaviours.

Key study

Dannenberg et al., Bicycle helmet laws and educational campaigns

Aim To review the impact of the passing of a law requiring cycle helmet wearing in children.

Methodology Natural experiment when laws were passed in Howard County, Maryland, USA requiring children under 16 years of age riding bicycles on roads and paths to wear an approved safety helmet.

Participants Children from 47 schools in Howard County, and two control groups: one from Montgomery County and one from Baltimore County, all in Maryland, USA. They were aged 9–10 years, 12–13 years and 14–15 years. In the control group of Montgomery County there was already a campaign to promote bicycle safety. In all, 7322 children were sent questionnaires.

Design Independent design with each child naturally falling into one of the three counties.

Procedure Questionnaires containing a four-point Likert scale were sent. The topics covered included bicycle use, helmet ownership and use, awareness of law, sources of information about helmets, and peer pressure. Parents were asked to help children complete the questionnaire, so consent was obtained.

Findings Response rates were between 41 and 53 per cent across the three age groups and three counties.

The important data were on changes in wearing of cycle helmets. Participants were asked about use 1 year previously and on their most recent bike ride. In Howard County (the one with the law) reported usage had increased from 11.4 to 37.5 per cent, compared with 8.4 to 12.6 per cent in Montgomery County and 6.7 to 11.1 per cent in Baltimore County. Again, young children increased their usage most. Most children (87 per cent) in Howard County were aware of the law, and 38 per cent of those had worn their helmets on the last ride, as opposed to 14 per cent of the children who did not know there was a law (4 per cent of the respondents).

Conclusions Although many children did not routinely wear a helmet when cycling, the Howard County legislation did show a large increase in the reported rate of cycle helmet wearing. The slight rise in the area where there was an educational campaign was not significantly different from the area where there was no campaign. We might conclude from this that passing legislation has more effect than educational campaigns alone, and educational campaigns are not necessarily effective at all in increasing health behaviours.

It is interesting to note that the self-report method in this study was correlated with an observational study by Coté et al. (1992), which found similar rates of cycle helmet usage.

2.3 Fear arousal

What frightens you about poor health? Is it the possibility of pain of getting a disease, the possibility of dying young, or the treatments you might have to undergo? How could you show someone the consequences of their unhealthy behaviour in a way that would frighten them into changing? A longitudinal study over 2 ½ years by Hammond (2003) showed that pictorial warnings on cigarette packets in Canada had a greater impact on reducing smoking than written warnings on packets in the UK.

Janis and Feshbach's (1953) research into the effect of fear arousal on dental hygiene shows how important it is to get the 'fear factor' just right: too much fear just makes people switch off, while with too little fear the impact is lost. Bearing in mind each individual's fear threshold, we could assume that any fear arousal will work with only a proportion of the target population.

Key study

Janis and Feshbach, Effects of fear arousal

Aim To investigate the consequences on emotions and behaviour of fear appeals in communications.

Methodology Laboratory experiment, which showed fear-arousing material and then collected data by a series of questionnaires on emotional reactions and changes in dental practices.

Participants An entire 9th grade Freshman class at a US high school, aged 14.0 to 15.11 years, mean age 15 years. Divided into four groups, including a control group.

Design Independent design. Each participant was in one of three lectures. Group 1's lecture had strong fear appeal, emphasising the painful consequences of poor dental hygiene, such as tooth decay and gum disease; it included direct statements such as 'This could happen to you'. Group 2's lecture had moderate fear appeal with little information on the consequences of poor dental hygiene; statements were more factual than audience-focused. Group 3's lecture had minimal fear arousal. It consisted mostly of neutral information on tooth growth and function rather than the consequences of poor dental hygiene. Group 4 – the control group – had a similar lecture on the functioning of the human eye.

Procedure A questionnaire was given one week before the lecture, including some questions on dental-health practices.

A 15-minute illustrated lecture, as described above, delivered in a standard manner by the same lecturer. Immediately after the lecture, a questionnaire asking for emotional reactions to the lecture was handed out. One week later a follow-up questionnaire asked about longer-term effects of the lecture.

Findings The amount of knowledge on dental hygiene did not differ between the three experimental groups, so all lectures had conveyed the required information.

Interestingly, the strong fear-appeal lecture was generally seen in a more positive light, with students more likely to agree that the talk was interesting, easy to follow, and should definitely be given to all schools in Connecticut. However, they also reported higher levels of dislike, with more saying they disliked something in the talk, and that the slides were too unpleasant.

With regard to changes in dental hygiene, however, the strong fear-appeal group showed a net increase in conformity of 8 per cent. This was measured by comparing the number of recommended dental practices, such as brushing for 3 minutes, shown before the lecture, with the number reported one week after the lecture. The percentages of higher conformity, lower conformity and no change were added up and the result was a net increase in conformity. The net increase in the other groups was 22 per cent in the moderate fear group and 36 per cent in the minimal fear group, with the control group showing 0 per cent change. The difference between the strong fear group and the control group was not significant.

Conclusions Fear appeals can be helpful in changing behaviours, but it is important that the level of fear appeal is right for each audience. Minimal fear was the

◆ Draw a diagram of this study. Start with a box with the participant details, then add four boxes with the groups in, then go through the procedure, and add the findings. A sample diagram for Dannenberg et al.'s research is shown in Figure 2.4.

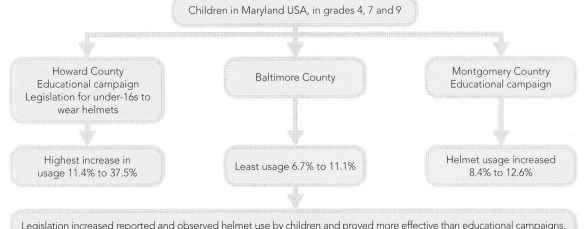

Figure 2.4 Dannenberg et al.'s study on the use of cycle helmets

◆ Take a current health-promotion campaign such as a recent drink-driving campaign and analyse it from a psychological perspective.

◆ You could look at any fear arousal in the campaign. How strong is it? How would you make it stronger or milder if you needed to? Is there anything from the HBM in the campaign, such as emphasising the benefits of adopting a healthy lifestyle?

most effective form of lecture, with more conformity to recommended practices. The moderate and strong appeals had no unique effect on the behaviour of the participants, which means they both had much the same effect. As Janis and Feshbach point out, the use of strong fear presentations did increase emotional arousal and positive feedback, and in some situations, such as getting people to donate money, this might be a good method to use, but they conclude that relatively low fear arousal is likely to be the optimal level for promoting health.

Health promotion is expensive. Elder et al. (2004) found that one campaign in Australia in 1992–95 cost $403,174 per month for advertisement development, supporting media, media placement, and concept research.

The benefits appear to justify the expense in economic terms at least. The estimated savings from health-care costs, loss of productivity, pain, suffering, and property damage were $8,324,532 per month. Not only did the population of Victoria, Australia have healthier lives, the community saved money as well.

Check your understanding

1 What evidence is there that legislation can help with promoting health?

2 How would you organise a media campaign to discourage drinking and driving?

3 What might be the problems of using fear arousal to reduce smoking?

Section summary

◆ There may be ethical considerations in dictating or compelling behaviours for an individual's own benefit, and perhaps individuals should make their own choices when it comes to adopting health behaviours.

◆ It seems that a variety of health promotion methods can be effective in ensuring healthy lifestyles, and one could argue that governments have a duty of care to ensure that their citizens are as healthy as possible.

3 Features of adherence to medical regimes

We need to consider why people do not adhere to medical advice, and this section will look at patients who make a rational decision not to adhere. There is also the question of how to improve adherence and how to measure adherence. This section will look at:

- rational non-adherence: how weighing up the pros and cons of adherence may logically lead to non-adherence

- physical methods of measuring adherence: a study that measures adherence to a medical regime for diabetes by measuring glycohaemoglobin (GHb) levels

- reinforcement to improve adherence: using an adapted inhaler to make asthma medication fun can help to increase adherence rates in children.

3.1 Reasons for non-adherence

Rational non-adherence is the logical decision not to adhere to medical advice. It may be linked to the HBM (see page 81) whereby if the costs and benefits are considered and the costs of adhering outweigh the benefits, then the rational decision might be not to continue with medication.

Bulpitt et al.'s (1988) study on males with hypertension (high blood pressure) found they felt the cost of the side effects of taking anti-hypertension drugs outweighed the benefits of having lower blood pressure. In the long term, high blood pressure is linked with heart disease and stroke, but there are often no real adverse short-term effects. Anti-hypertension drugs can reduce the circulation of blood. This can cause erectile dysfunction (impotence) in males, which could outweigh the long-term benefits of not having a heart attack or stroke. In this case the males rationally made the decision to stop the anti-hypertension drugs so that they would not have the problems caused by the medicine.

There are cases in the media where patients have refused potentially life-saving treatment, as the costs in terms of lower quality of life outweigh the less-than-certain, often short-term, effects of prolonging life. Who is to say that this is irrational? The key study by Bulpitt et al. (1988) confirms the cost–benefits analysis that patients undertake before deciding whether to adhere to medical advice. Their study uses a qualitative approach and so gives us much insight

into the patients' beliefs about medication, and how they weigh up the outcomes of taking their anti-hypertension medication.

Aim To review research on adherence in hypertensive patients.

Methodology Review article of research identifying problems with taking drugs for high blood pressure.

Procedure Research was analysed to identify the physical and psychological effects of drug treatment on a person's life. These included work, physical well-being, hobbies etc.

Findings Anti-hypertension medication can have many side effects, including physical reactions such as sleepiness, dizziness, lack of sexual functioning. They also affect cognitive functioning, so work and hobbies are curtailed.

In one study by Curb et al. (1985) 8 per cent of males discontinued treatment because of sexual problems.

Research by the Medical Research Council (1981) found that 15 per cent of patients had withdrawn from taking medication due to side effects.

Conclusion When the costs of taking medication, such as side effects, outweigh the benefits of treating a mainly asymptomatic problem such as hypertension, there is less likelihood of the patient adhering to their treatment.

Check your understanding

1   What method did Bulpitt et al. use for this research?

2   What did they find that supported the health belief model?

3.2 Measures of non-adherence

Even if it is assumed that adherence rates are low, psychologists still need to consider how adherence can be measured. There are numerous ways of measuring adherence and, as in all psychological research, no perfect research method. Self-reporting by patients lends itself to social desirability bias, where a person might not want to admit to not taking medication in case the doctor refuses to help any more. This can be overcome by using a physiological measure, which is how Lustman et al. (2000) measured adherence in their research into diabetes and depression. They found that people being treated with an anti-depressant called Fluoxetine were likely to have less depression, measured by psychometric tests, but also better glycemic control, indicating a better adherence to the regime required by their diabetes. However, a physiological measure might not be useful in all cases, although it is perfectly possible in diabetes patients, as Lustman et al. showed.

Most commonly, monitoring of adherence is done by doctors who look at the therapeutic outcomes, that is, the medicine's effect on the person's health. If a patient is given antibiotics to eliminate an infection and the infection does not return, then it is fairly safe to assume that they took the antibiotics as prescribed. Of course, there are cases when, despite strict adherence to medical regimes, the outcome is not so positive, so this method is a rather rough-and-ready measurement of adherence.

Try this …

Consider other ways of measuring adherence. What might be the strengths and weaknesses of the following methods?

1   Pill and bottle counts, i.e. comparing what is left in the bottle with what should be left in the bottle.

2   Mechanical methods, e.g. a device for measuring the amount of medicine dispensed from a container.

3   Biochemical tests, e.g. blood or urine tests.

The study by Chung and Naya (2000) looks at how effective a mechanical device for measuring adherence was. Although they found high compliance rates, we have to consider whether simply being told that their compliance was being assessed may have influenced the patients' behaviour. Lustman et al.'s (2000) study shows how physical measurements such as blood sugar levels can indicate adherence to the regimen necessary for the control of diabetes. Glycohaemoglobin (haemoglobin with glucose attached to it, GHb) levels will show the amount of glucose in the blood; in non-diabetics about 4–6 per cent of the haemoglobin in the blood has glucose attached to it, whereas diabetics have higher levels of GHb. The regime a diabetic

has to adopt, which could include changing diet and administering insulin by injection, should keep GHb levels near to normal. Therefore adherence to medical advice can be measured by measuring the GHb levels. This study encompasses the assumption that treating depression can aid adherence.

U3

2

Key terms

asymptomatic not showing any indications of a disease or other medical condition

placebo something that is inactive, but is given to people who believe it may contain an active substance

haemoglobin a substance in red blood cells that carries oxygen

double blind study a study in which neither the participants nor the researchers know who belongs to the experimental group and who to the control group until all the data have been recorded

3.3 Improving adherence using behavioural methods

This follows on from what we know about why people do not adhere. We may need to reduce the costs of taking medication (whatever they might be) and increase the benefits. However, if we look at the study by Simons et al. (1996) there seems to be no rational reason for people not taking statins. Simons et al. suggest that the reasons are irrational and therefore may be more open to interventions to improve adherence rates. Ley et al. (1973) and Banyard (2002) found that patients forget most of the information they are given. Ley et al. found that if doctors are trained to structure their information and write down instructions, adherence rates can be improved, particularly for the elderly. We could look at the lifestyle models for further enlightenment. The demographic variables of the HBM may be useful, for example females are less likely to be troubled by anti-hypertensive drugs and their effects on blood flow. But we could also consider how perceptions of seriousness or susceptibility might also influence adherence. Locus of control might also be an issue here – a person who believes that fate maps out their life will not be easily convinced of the efficacy of medicines.

Health psychologists have investigated how interventions might improve adherence rates, and one technique based on behaviourism uses the idea of reinforcement for correct adherence. A study by Watt et al. (2003) on using a Funhaler® with a whistle and spinner to reward children for using their asthma inhaler correctly, shows how such reinforcement can improve the children's adherence. This study does of course highlight the issue of using self-report to measure adherence. How do we know that the children's parents did not realise what was going on and simply gave the answers they thought the researchers wanted to hear (demand characteristics)?

Key study

Watt et al., Improving adherence to taking medication for asthma

Aim To see if using a Funhaler can improve children's adherence to taking medication for asthma.

Figure 2.5 The Funhaler used in the study by Watt et al.

Methodology A field experiment, although as it uses children with asthma it can also qualify as a quasi-experiment. The experiment sets up two conditions, then uses self-report to measure the adherence rates.

Participants 32 Australian children (10 boys and 22 girls) aged 1.5 to 6 years, mean age 3.2 years. They had all been diagnosed with asthma and prescribed drugs delivered by pressurised metered dose inhaler (pMDI). The parents gave informed consent.

Design A repeated design as each participant had one week using the normal pMDI inhaler Breath-a-Tech®, then one week using the Funhaler.

Procedure Each child was given a Breath-a-Tech to use for one week, and the parents were given a questionnaire to complete. The second week, the children used the Funhaler, and the parents were given a questionnaire with matched questions at the end of the second week.

The Funhaler has incentive toys (spinner and whistle), which function best when the child uses the deep breathing pattern that ensures the effective inhalation of the medication.

Findings 38 per cent more parents were found to have medicated their children the previous day when using the Funhaler, compared to the existing treatment.

Conclusions Previous research had given reasons for non-adherence in children with asthma such as boredom, forgetfulness and apathy. The Funhaler set out to remedy this by reinforcing correct usage of the inhaler with a spinner and a whistle. This did improve adherence to the medication. So by making the medical regime fun, adherence, certainly in children, can be improved.

Try this ...

1   Try making a leaflet to help parents encourage their children to take their medication. You could suggest the use of the behavioural technique of reinforcement.

2   Make notes of the key points of each study or theory covered in the healthy lifestyles section on revision cards or with mind-maps. See how much you can do without looking back.

Check your understanding

1   Which technique did Watt et al. use to improve adherence?

2   What approach is this based on?

3   What are the strengths and weaknesses of using self-report to measure health behaviours?

Take it further

Research into health psychology has many evaluative issues. Make a chart listing every piece of research you have covered so far in one column, then add a column for every methodological evaluation issue you can think of from the AS course, such as validity, control of variables, ethics. Now apply each issue to each piece of research to provide a comprehensive evaluation chart of the research covered so far.

Section summary

◆   It is interesting to break down something as commonplace as adhering to medical advice into its psychological components.

◆   Why do we adhere or not? There are many reasons.

◆   There are also many ways to improve adherence.

◆   It would be possible to use the HBM to explain why people do not adhere and also to improve adherence.

◆   This section has touched on just one or two ideas from a plethora of ideas, models and research. Given the high cost of medication that is prescribed but not taken, in addition to the health costs of people not adhering to regimes, the importance of this area of health psychology can be seen not only in healthier patients, but in less wastage of resources.

Stress

Pause for thought

◆ In 2005–2006, 420,000 people said they had been ill with stress (Health and Safety Executive, 2006).

◆ Do you think that stress-management techniques work?

◆ Are modern drugs as good as ancient techniques such as acupuncture?

Stress is one of the most commonly cited problems in western society. It has many aspects that interest psychologists. What causes stress? How does it affect us? How can we reduce or manage stress? Stress is often used to represent the reaction we have both psychologically and physiologically to stressors. These may be major, life-threatening events such as earthquakes, life events such as divorce or bereavement, or the minor hassles of day-to-day life, such as not being able to find a parking space, or dropping your Psychology folder in a puddle.

You can probably think of many things that cause you stress either daily or occasionally. We are programmed to respond physically to stress by producing adrenaline, which prepares our bodies for flight or fight by:

◆ increasing heart rate and respiration so that more blood can be carried to the brain to help us think more clearly

◆ closing down functions that are not immediately vital, such as digestion

◆ dilating our pupils so that our vision becomes clearer.

All these reactions might have been useful when our ancestors were hunting woolly mammoths, but our stressors are more likely to be less life threatening but longer lasting, such as financial worries, relationship problems and exams. Adrenaline is still produced, but our bodies become used to it and the physiological reactions calm down. The big problem, however, lies in the continuous production of adrenaline, which attacks our immune system and reduces our ability to fight disease. There is much evidence to suggest that stress is linked to illness, and Kanner et al.'s (1981) research illustrates this. In addition there are the psychological reactions to stress, such as anger, crying, insomnia and depression. Perhaps it is easy to see why stress is such

a problem, and why so many days are lost from work due to it. The UK Health and Safety Executive suggests that approximately 1.4 million working days per year are lost due to work-related stress. For more information on the effect of stress on our health, Selye's General Adaptation Syndrome (1936) is a useful place to start.

This area will look at:

◆ causes of stress

◆ measuring stress

◆ managing stress.

Causes of stress

If you tried listing your stressors, you would probably find there were many, but perhaps they were not all equally serious. Being nagged to tidy your bedroom may or may not be as stressful as meeting deadlines for homework, or driving lessons. Psychologists need to find out what causes stress so that stressors can be reduced as far as possible.

Measuring stress

There are various ways in which psychologists can find out about stress. The obvious ones are by asking people through self-report, observing people, or measuring a person's physiology. Some researchers like to adopt a less reductionist approach and use a combination of methods; this may increase the validity of their measurements.

Managing stress

The application of psychological knowledge to practical situations must be one of the main goals of psychological research. If we can understand health behaviours and their antecedents, we can help people to lead healthier lives. This can not only enhance people's quality of life, but can also save society the costs of health care and lost productivity. If you glance at the self-help section of any bookshop you cannot help but notice the range and number of stress-reduction books available.

Themes and perspectives

The methodology of studying stress has a direct influence on the stress levels of the participants and so cannot be discounted as a confounding variable. Also the limitations of studies into certain target populations restrict the generalisability of techniques and explanations to those groups in the research. People have their own agendas for hiding or exaggerating their stress levels: they may be seeking compensation from an employer for causing stress, or they may be unwilling to admit stress in case their employer thinks they are unable to do their job. These factors have to be taken into account when considering the validity of measuring stress, to find either the cause of the stress or the effectiveness of treatments.

A key theme that is inherent in health psychology is the problem of measuring health behaviour. The validity of any measurement must be questioned: the most valid research should use a combined method or two or more techniques to ensure that detailed and accurate data are obtained. The effectiveness of any technique in changing behaviour, such as improving adherence or managing stress, also has to be considered. Health psychologists need to know how effective any such strategies are, in both the short and long term, but participant attrition or drop-out could make this difficult to measure, and again the measurement of behavioural change may lack validity. In health psychology, ethical considerations are paramount. Patient–practitioner relationships are bound by legal confidentiality and any information gained may be sensitive and must remain confidential.

Weblinks

You can read more information on the causes and management of stress (see Contents page).

Try this …

Rate your stress level on a scale of 1–10, where 1 is totally laid back and 10 is breaking point.

Make a list of all of the things that cause you stress.

Ask a friend or two to do the same. Is there a correlation between the number of stressors and the stress rating scale?

Can you identify an area of your life that is causing you most stress?

Key terms

stressor anything that causes stress

immune system the body's recognition of cells that are not its own, such as illness-inducing bacteria, and its response to fight them

1 Causes of stress

Psychologists realise that almost any area of our lives could cause stress, but this section looks at three of them:

◆ work: where the pressures of a repetitive and responsible job are compared to a less pressured one

◆ hassles: the minor irritations that occur daily can predict stress-related illnesses

◆ lack of control and how this can cause a physical stress response.

1.1 Work

Johansson's (1978) research with Swedish sawmill workers found that people whose jobs involved responsibility for meeting targets and lack of social contact, were more stressed. However, even the people with less stressful jobs were found to be more stressed at work than at home, suggesting that any job is going to cause some level of stress.

Try this …

If you have a job, think about how stressful your job is. Are there other jobs that you would think are more or less stressful than yours?

Key study

Johansson, Measurement of stress response

Aim To measure the psychological and physiological stress response in two categories of employees.

Methodology A quasi-experiment where workers were defined as being at high risk of stress or in a control group. Data were collected through physiological measures of chemicals in urine and self-report of mood.

Participants 24 workers at a Swedish sawmill. The high-risk group were 14 workers who had to work at a set pace, governed by the production line; their job was complex and required a great deal of knowledge about raw materials. They were responsible for the rate at which the finished objects were completed and so responsible for their own and their team's wages. The control group were 10 workers who were cleaners or maintenance workers.

Design An independent design with participants already working in one of the two categories, so no manipulation of the independent variable. The high-risk group were classified as having jobs that were repetitive and constrained, had little control of pace or work routine, were more isolated and involved more responsibility.

Procedure Each participant was asked to give a daily urine sample when they arrived at work and at four other times during the day. They also gave self-report of mood and alertness, plus caffeine and nicotine consumption.

The baseline measurements were taken at the same time on a day when the workers were at home:

◆ catecholamine (adrenaline) levels were measured in the urine

◆ body temperature was measured at the time of urine collection

◆ self-rating scales of words such as *sleepiness, well-being, irritation, efficiency* were made on scales from zero to maximal (the highest level the person had ever experienced)

◆ caffeine and nicotine consumption were noted.

Findings In the first urine samples of the day, the high-risk group had adrenaline levels twice as high as their baseline and these continued to increase throughout the day. The control group had a peak level of 1.5 times baseline level in the morning and this declined during the rest of their shift. Figure 2.6 shows this graphically.

In the self-report, the high-risk group felt more rushed and irritated than the control group. They also rated their well-being as lower than that of the control group.

Conclusions The repetitive, machine-paced work, which was demanding in attention to detail and highly mechanised, contributed to the higher stress levels in the high-risk group.

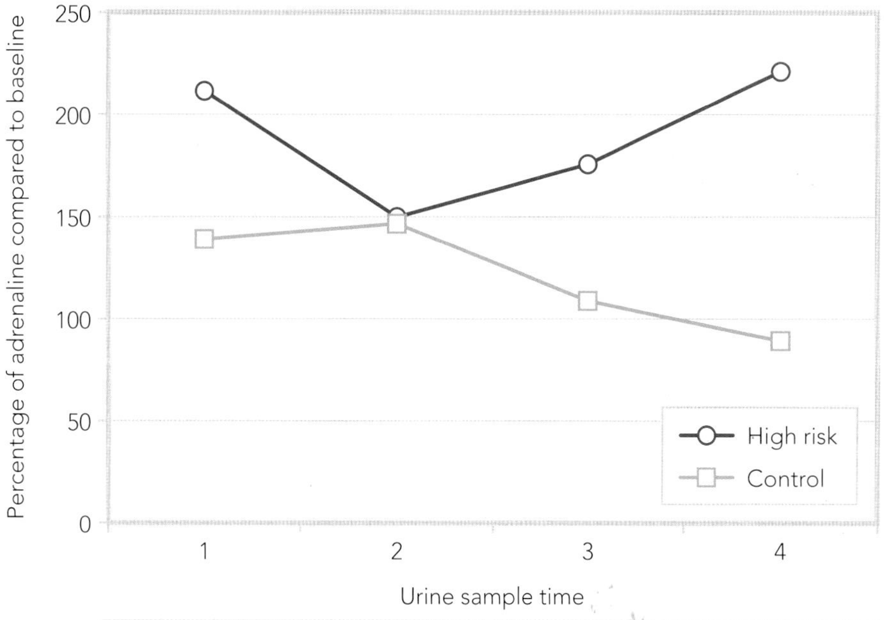

Key term

quasi-experiment an experiment where the independent variable is naturally occurring

Check your understanding

1 Which two methods did Johansson use to measure stress?

2 What were the key factors of the jobs in the high-risk group which Johansson believed contributed to stress?

3 What problems are there when self-report is used to measure behaviour?

Figure 2.6 Graph to show levels of adrenaline (catecholamine excretion) in urine throughout the four urine sample times

1.2 Hassles

Try this …

Think of ten things that have caused you minor irritation today. You may have had to wait to use the bathroom, not got your favourite seat on a bus, had a lesson you don't like, been nagged to hand in homework.

There is evidence to suggest that minor stressors can combine to become one large cause of stress. Kanner et al.'s (1981) study shows how stress can affect all of us, by seeing how hassles can predict psychological symptoms of stress. Kanner et al. also compared using hassles as predictors of stress (illness) with life events, using the Holmes and Rahe (1967) Social Readjustment Rating Scale (SRRS). For more detailed information on how the SRRS was devised, see the text on measuring stress on pages 100–101.

Key study

Kanner et al., Comparison of two methods of stress measurement

Aim To compare the Hassles and Uplifts Scale and the Berkman Life Events Scale as predictors of psychological symptoms of stress.

Methodology A repeated design in that each participant completed the Hassles rating scale and the Life Events scale. They then assessed their psychological symptoms of stress using the Hopkins Symptom Checklist (HSCL) and the Bradburn Morale Scale.

Participants 100 people who had previously completed a health survey in 1965. They were from California, were mostly white, protestant, with adequate or above income and at least 9th-grade education. 216 were initially contacted, 109 agreed to take part and nine dropped out.

Hassles	Somewhat severe	Moderately severe	Extremely severe
1 Misplacing or losing things	1	2	3
2 Troublesome neighbours	1	2	3
3 Social obligations	1	2	3
4 Inconsiderate smokers	1	2	3
5 Troubling thoughts about your future	1	2	3
6 Thoughts about death	1	2	3
7 Health of a family member	1	2	3
8 Not enough money for clothing	1	2	3
9 Not enough money for housing	1	2	3
10 Concerns about owing money	1	2	3

Uplifts	Somewhat frequent	Moderately frequent	Extremely frequent
1 Getting enough sleep	1		
2 Practising your hobby	1	2	3
3 Being lucky	1	2	3
4 Saving money	1	2	3
5 Nature	1	2	3
6 Liking fellow workers	1	2	3
7 Not working (on vacation, laid-off etc.)	1	2	3
8 Gossiping: 'shooting the bull'	1	2	3
9 Successful financial dealings	1	2	3
10 Being rested	1	2	3

Table 2.1 The Hassles and Uplifts Scale (Source: Kanner et al., 1981)

Design A repeated design as participants completed both the hassles and life events scales.

Procedure All tests were sent out by post one month before the study began. The participants were asked to complete:

- the hassles rating every month for 9 months

- the life events rating after 10 months

- the HSCH and the Bradburn Morale Scale every month for 9 months.

Findings Hassles were consistent from month to month.

Life events for men correlated positively with hassles and negatively with uplifts. This means the more life events the men reported on the SRRS, the more hassles they reported on the hassles rating scale and the fewer uplifts they reported.

For women, the more life events they reported, the more hassles and uplifts they reported.

Hassle frequency correlated positively with psychological symptoms on the HSCL. This means that the more hassles the participant reported, the more negative psychological symptoms they reported. Hassles correlated positively more with psychological symptoms than life events did.

Conclusions Hassles are a more powerful predictor of psychological symptoms than life events. Hassles contribute to psychological symptoms whatever life events have happened.

Table 2.1 shows an extract from the hassles and uplifts scale. Participants are asked to circle hassles and uplifts that they have experienced in the past month and then to indicate severity for hassles and frequency for uplifts by circling 1, 2 or 3 in the appropriate column.

Check your understanding

1   This study used a longitudinal method. What are the strengths and weaknesses of this method?

2   What were the three variables correlated?

3   Which measure of stress was a better predictor of morale?

1.3 Lack of control

Tangible stressors are one cause of stress, but we can also consider situations that might contribute to our stress. For example, if your neighbours are playing loud music while you are trying to go to sleep, what is it that makes the situation stressful? It could be the level of the noise (there is some evidence to suggest that noise is a stressor), but the most likely cause of stress is our lack of control over the noise.

Geer and Maisel (1972) set up an experiment to see if perceived control over something aversive (unpleasant) reduces stress, or put another way, if thinking that we lack control over a situation makes it more stressful. As you read their study, you might like to consider the ethics of showing students unpleasant photographs of car-crash victims!

Key study

Geer and Maisel, The effect of control in reducing stress reactions

Aim To see if perceived control or actual control can reduce stress reactions to aversive stimuli.

Methodology Laboratory experiment, in which participants were shown photographs of dead car-crash victims, and their stress levels were measured by galvanic skin response (GSR) and heart-rate electrodes.

Participants 60 undergraduates enrolled in a psychology course from New York University.

Design Independent design, as participants were randomly assigned to one of three conditions:

Group 1 were given actual control over how long they saw each photograph for; they could press a button to terminate the photograph (max. 35 seconds) and were told that a tone would precede each photograph.

Group 2 were yoked to Group 1 (they saw the photos for exactly the same time as Group 1), but were warned that the photos would be 60 seconds apart and for how long they would see each photo. They were also told that a 10-second warning tone would precede each photograph. This group had no control but knew what would happen.

Group 3 were also yoked to Group 1, but were told that that from time to time they would see photographs and hear tones. This group had no control and no predictability.

Procedure Each participant was seated in a sound-shielded room and wired up to GSR and heart-rate monitors. The machine calibrated for 5 minutes while the participant relaxed and then a baseline measurement was taken. The instructions were then read over the intercom and after 1 minute's rest the stimuli were presented. Each photograph was preceded by a 10-second tone then flashed up, and when the button was pressed (Group 1) or after the predetermined length of time (Groups 2 and 3) the photograph disappeared. The GSR analyses were taken at the onset of the tone, during the second half of the tone and in response to the photograph.

Findings The heart-rate monitors proved inaccurate and so data from these were discarded.

The predictability group (Group 2) showed most stress with the tone, as they knew what was coming, but did not have control over the photograph.

The control group (Group 1) experienced less stress in response to the photograph than the predictability and no-control groups (Groups 2 and 3).

Conclusions Participants showed less GSR reaction, indicating less stress, when they had control over the length of time they looked at the disturbing photographs. It is likely that being able to terminate aversive stimuli reduces their stressful impact.

These studies have shown that there are many causes of stress, and that not only the stressors in our lives, but the situation we are in can affect our stress levels.

Key terms

galvanic skin response (GSR) the electrical current conducted by the skin, which varies according to moisture on the skin. Anxiety causes sweating and so increases the moisture on the skin and its conductance

calibrated a machine is set so that the individual's baseline behaviour is the starting point. A person's heart rate at rest will become the baseline, which may differ from another person's heart rate and so their calibrated baseline

Check your understanding

1   What were the three conditions in Geer and Maisel's study?

2   Why were the participants in Groups 2 and 3 yoked to participants in Group 1?

3   Which group showed most stress?

Section summary

◆   Each of us would probably realise that a cause of stress for one person may not be a cause of stress for another.

◆   Some people in high-powered jobs seem to thrive on the pressure, while others would soon burn out and show signs of physical and/or mental illnesses.

◆   Individual differences are a major problem for any researcher looking at stress.

◆   Cultural norms and expectations can also influence how stressful events might be; this means that ethnocentrism is also an issue psychologists need to consider.

2 Measuring stress

The ways in which psychologists measure stress can be seen in the previous research, using physiological measures to assess the biological reaction; asking people to assess their own stress levels or stressors is also used. Of course there are methodological problems with both of these. A better way may be to combine them to create a more holistic measure.

2.1 Physiological measures

Physiological measures of stress can overcome the subjectivity of the self-report by relying on scientific measurements of hormones, chemicals, heart rate, blood pressure etc. The main problem with these measurements can be validity. How do you know you are measuring a person's stress levels? Think what other factors could cause physiological changes that may mimic stress reactions. Caffeine, for example, can make the heart race, recreational drugs or alcohol can cause pupils to dilate and make people sweat. And how stressful do you think it is to be wired up to a stress monitor? Having said that, it is probably as good a way as any to measure stress, as there are problems with any method. Simply asking someone about stressors can be stressful. The research by Geer and Maisel is an example of using the physiological approach to measurement.

Re-read Geer and Maisel's study on pages 98–99 and identify how they measured stress in their participants.

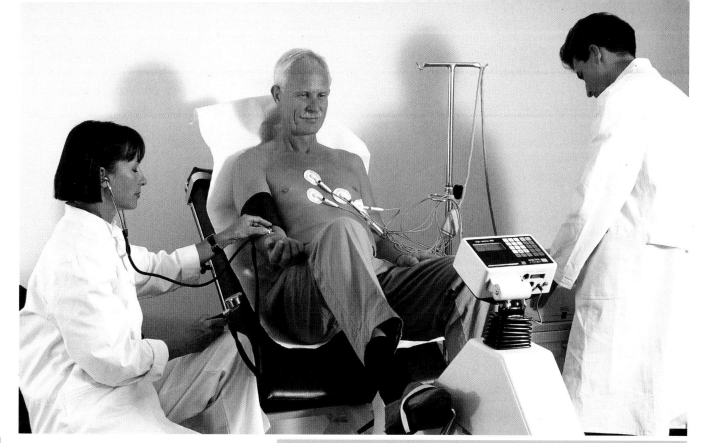

Figure 2.7 A person wired up to a polygraph to measure psychophysiological data

Key study

Geer and Maisel, Stress measurements for evaluating the effects of prediction and control

Participants' stress levels were measured by GSR and heart-rate electrodes.

A Beckman Model RB Polygraph was used to collect psychophysiological data. The data are converted from a voltmeter to a printout. Each recording was performed in a sound and electrically shielded room to ensure no audio or visual input from the projector would interfere with the data collection. The heart monitors were attached in standard positions, and the GSR electrodes were placed between the palm and forearm of the participants' non-preferred arm (i.e. the left arm for right-handed people).

Check your understanding

1   What is the link between stress and galvanic skin response?

2   What are the strengths of obtaining objective data?

Take it further

When you have read the study by Budzynski on biofeedback (pages 104–105), you will have details of another physiological method of measuring stress through muscle tension, which you could use to supplement your knowledge. Try to compare and contrast these two methods, and evaluate them in comparison with other non-physiological measures of stress.

2.2 Self-report

Self-report methods can include questionnaires, interviews and diary-keeping. All of these have the strengths and weaknesses of this method. You may recall these from AS psychology.

Holmes and Rahe (1967) used a self-report measure with their Social Readjustment Rating Scale (SRRS). This looks at the events that have occurred in a person's life, and rates their impact. The readjustment needed to cope with such an event causes stress, so it follows that the more life events you experience, the more readjustments you have to make and so the more stressed you are.

Life event	Life change units
Death of a spouse	100
Divorce	73
Marital separation	65
Imprisonment	63
Death of a close family member	63
Personal injury or illness	53
Marriage	50
Dismissal from work	47
Marital reconciliation	45
Retirement	45
Change in health of family member	44
Pregnancy	40
Sexual difficulties	39
Gain a new family member	39
Business readjustment	39
Change in financial state	38
Change in frequency of arguments	35
Major mortgage	32
Foreclosure of mortgage or loan	30
Change in responsibilities at work	29
Child leaving home	29
Trouble with in-laws	29
Outstanding personal achievement	28
Spouse starts or stops work	26
Begin or end school	26
Change in living conditions	25
Revision of personal habits	24
Trouble with boss	23
Change in working hours or conditions	20
Change in residence	20
Change in schools	20
Change in recreation	19
Change in church activities	19
Change in social activities	18
Minor mortgage or loan	17
Change in sleeping habits	16
Change in number of family reunions	15
Change in eating habits	15
Vacation	13
Christmas	12
Minor violation of law	11

Score of 300+: risk of illness
Score of 150–299+: moderate risk of illness (reduced by 30 per cent from the above risk)
Score 150–: only a slight risk of illness

Table 2.2 The Social Readjustment Rating Scale
(Source: Holmes and Rahe, 1967)

Remember that the SRRS is only one measure of stress, and may lack validity if it is not standardised for age or culture. Also, psychology looks at trends, not certainties, so there is no definite outcome, whatever the score on the SRRS.

Key study

Holmes and Rahe, Life events as stressors

Aim To create a method that estimates the extent to which life events are stressors.

Methodology A questionnaire designed to ascertain how much each life event was felt to be a stressor.

Participants 394 subjects (179 males and 215 females), from a range of educational abilities, ethnic groups and religions.

Procedure Each participant was asked to rate a series of 43 life events. Marriage was given an arbitrary rating of 50 and each event was to be judged as requiring more or less readjustment. Ratings could be based on personal experience and perceptions of other people's experiences. The amount of readjustment and the time it would take to readjust were both to be considered.

Findings The final SRRS was completed based on the mean scores allocated by the participants (see Table 2.2).

Correlations between groups were tested and found to be high in all but one group. Males and females agreed, as did participants of different ages, religions, educational level, but there was less correlation between white and black participants.

Conclusions These events are mostly ordinary (some are extraordinary, for example going to jail, but they do pertain to the western way of life). There are also some socially desirable events which reflect the western values of materialism, success and conformism. The degree of similarity between different groups is impressive and shows agreement in general of what constitutes a life event and how much they cause stress (or readjustment).

Check your understanding

1   List the strengths and weaknesses of self-report techniques.

2   Consider why these might be particularly relevant to asking people about their stress.

2.3 Combined approach

The combined approach of Johansson, which showed work as a cause of stress, used both self-report and physiological measures. You can use the Johansson et al. study outlined on page 96 to support the combined technique. The key points to make notes on are the techniques used to measure the workers' stress.

Key study

Johansson et al., Measurement of stress response

Re-read this study on page 96 and note how the researchers measured stress.

Each participant was asked to give a urine sample four times during the day, so that their adrenaline levels could be measured. This is a physiological measure. Their body temperature was recorded at the same time (this can give an indication of how alert a person is). These measures were combined with a self-report where each participant had to say how much caffeine and nicotine they had consumed since the last urine sample. They also had a list of emotions and feelings such as sleepiness, well-being, calm, irritation and efficiency. These were on a continuum from minimum to maximum and on a millimetre scale. The score was how many millimetres from the minimum base point the participants had marked themselves to be feeling. This combined method of physiological measures and self-reports gave some good qualitative and quantitative data that enabled Johansson et al. to compare the two groups, and have some understanding of the impact of higher stress levels on the participants.

Check your understanding

Compare the three methods of measuring stress in terms of their validity.

Section summary

- As with measuring any behaviour, each method has its strengths and weaknesses, yet if psychology aspires to be accepted as a science we must acknowledge the objectivity of scientific methods.

- Just measuring chemicals or physiological responses will yield less information than the more qualitative data that self-report techniques can give us.

- Richer qualitative data can help us understand behaviours such as stress.

- Perhaps the combined approach is the most useful, though it may also be the most costly in terms of resources and time.

3 Managing stress

The research cited below gives credence to three stress-management techniques, though many others are just as reputable. If a stress-management method can stand up to scrutiny in valid research, then it can be seen as having some authority. In order to understand the techniques used in stress management, it is good to have some idea of how psychological approaches might view stress, as this will give some indication of how each approach might suggest that stress can be reduced.

Try this ...

Consider how the social, cognitive and behavioural approaches might suggest stress is caused.

Now take those same assumptions and think how they could be used in stress-management techniques.

The research in this section shows three techniques based on three different approaches:

- stress inoculation therapy is a cognitive approach to restructuring thoughts that contribute to stress
- biofeedback uses the behavioural concept of reinforcement of stress reduction
- social support shows how a person's social networks can reduce stress.

Each of these approaches has been validated by empirical research, to support its theoretical assumptions about stress management.

3.1 Cognitive

Meichenbaum's stress inoculation therapy (SIT) (1972) adopts a cognitive approach. His assumption is that stress is caused by faulty processing of information. For example, we might be stressed by exams, because we think we will not do well. This might be based on

Figure 2.8 Can we learn not to be stressed by exams?

previous experience (memory) or what we are being told (perception). Whatever the cause, the exam situation proves to be unrealistically stressful.

Meichenbaum suggests that there are three components of SIT:

1 The patients with the stress have to become aware of the thoughts they have in a stressful situation. These might be self-instructions or self-verbalisations that contribute to the poor performance that is causing stress. So if a person is stressed by exams they may tell themselves that they cannot pass exams, that they might as well not even bother as they don't know anything. This will lead to poor performance and so confirm their negative thoughts about their performance in exams.

2 The second component is the coping strategies that patients are taught to enable them to restructure their thoughts. They are taught to relax when they become tense, they imagine themselves in situations that cause them stress and learn how to relax. They then learn self-instructions that will help them to relax rather than be stressed.

A person who is stressed by exams might tell themselves that they have revised, that they know the structure of the paper, and just have to take one question at a time. They will also have practised deep slow breathing and maybe muscle relaxation, which will help them in the stressful situation. This helps them to believe that they can succeed in the exam.

3 Finally, the person puts what they have learnt into practice in a real-life stressful situation. So, having practised how to cope with exams, in the exam situation the person uses positive self-instructions and relaxation techniques to succeed.

The evidence to support this comes from Meichenbaum's study on college students.

Key study

Meichenbaum, Stress Inoculation Therapy (SIT)

Aim To compare SIT with standard behavioural systematic desensitisation and a control group on a waiting list.

Methodology A field experiment where students were assessed before and after treatment using self-report and grade averages. It was a blind situation in that the people assessing them did not know which condition they had been in.

Participants 21 students aged 17–25 who responded to an advert for treatment of test anxiety.

Design Matched-pairs design with random allocation to the SIT therapy group, the waiting list control group or the standard systematic desensitisation (a behaviourist treatment) group. Although randomly allocated, gender was controlled to be equal in each group and also anxiety levels were matched in the three groups.

Procedure Each participant was tested using a test-anxiety questionnaire. They were then told they would be doing some IQ tests and would be assessed using an Anxiety Adjective Checklist. After the IQ tests participants were given a baseline score and allocated to their group.

In the SIT group, participants received eight therapy sessions. They were given the 'insight' approach to help them identify their thoughts prior to the tests. The were then given some positive statements to say and relaxation techniques to use in test situations.

In the systematic desensitisation group, participants were given eight therapy sessions with progressive relaxation training which they were encouraged to practise at home. They were told to practise relaxation while imagining progressively more anxiety-causing situations.

The control group were told they were on a waiting list and that they would receive therapy in the future.

Findings Performance on the tests improved in the SIT group compared with the other two groups, although the significant difference was between the two therapy groups and the control group.

Participants in the SIT group showed more reported improvement in their anxiety levels, although both therapy groups showed overall improvement compared with the control group.

Conclusions SIT is a more effective way of reducing anxiety in students who are anxiety prone in test situations. It is more effective than behavioural techniques such as systematic desensitisation, as it adds a cognitive component to the therapy.

> **Check your understanding**
>
> 1   What are the three stages of stress inoculation therapy?
>
> 2   Which psychological approach does stress inoculation therapy relate to?
>
> 3   In his research, how did Meichenbaum know that SIT was effective?

3.2 Behavioural

A different approach to stress reduction is seen in biofeedback, which has a behavioural perspective as its basis. One aspect of the behaviourist approach is the idea that consequences of behaviour can lead to it being repeated or not, i.e. reinforcement. If something is pleasurable or rewarding we are much more likely to repeat it. Biofeedback is simply feedback on one's biological functioning. We looked earlier at the physiological response to stress (increased heart rate, high blood pressure), and we can all think of times when stress has made us tense our muscles, ready for fight or flight. By giving visible or audible feedback on the state of the body, and rewarding us for reducing the stress reaction, biofeedback would assume that we would be more likely to repeat the method of reducing stress. This is the technique used in Budzynski et al.'s (1970) research on patients with tension headaches, who were taught to relax and given feedback on how successful they were at reducing muscle tension. The tension headache is felt across the top of the head and sometimes in the forehead; it gradually becomes worse and can last for weeks. These headaches are thought to be caused by sustained contraction of the scalp and neck muscles, which is associated with stress. Therefore by relaxing these muscles (reducing the stress response), the headaches should be reduced.

Key study

Budzynski et al., Biofeedback and reduction of tension headaches

Aim To see if previous research on biofeedback as a method of reducing tension headaches was due to the placebo effect or whether biofeedback was an effective method of reducing tension headaches.

The term 'placebo' refers to a treatment that contains nothing that should affect a patient, but may have a positive psychological effect because patients believe that they are receiving treatment.

Methodology Experimental method, with patients being trained in a laboratory, and data collected by measuring muscle tension using an EMG (electromyography) feedback machine with electrodes on the muscles producing a graph of muscle tension. Patients were also given a psychometric test of depression (MMPI) and asked to complete questionnaires on their headaches.

Participants 18 participants who replied to an advertisement in a local newspaper in Colorado. Respondents were initially screened by telephone, and then underwent psychiatric and medical examinations to ensure there was no other reason for their headaches. There were 2 males and 16 females, aged 22–44 with a mean age of 36.

Design Independent design. The participants were randomly placed in three groups of six.

Group A had biofeedback sessions with relaxation training and EMG feedback.

Group B had relaxation training but only had pseudo-feedback. This was a tape recording of real biofeedback, from another person's session, but it was obviously not linked to the participant's relaxation. It controlled the use of noise, which might have influenced the outcome.

Group C were the control group who were told they were on a waiting list, but asked to come to the laboratory for appointments to keep them in the study and to control for attention the others might be getting.

Procedure For 2 weeks, patients kept a record of their headaches, rating them from 0 (mild) to 5 (severe) every hour. This gave a baseline headache reading. They also completed the MMPI which tested depression, hysteria and hypochondria.

Groups A and B were given 16 sessions of training, with two sessions each week for 8 weeks. Group A were taught relaxation and told that the 'clicks' of the biofeedback machine would reflect their muscle tension, with slower clicks indicating less muscle tension. Group B were told to concentrate on the varying clicks. Both groups were told to practise relaxation at home for two 15–20 minute sessions each day.

Group C were given no training but were told they would begin training in 2 months.

Each participant recorded their headache activity.

After 3 months Groups A and B were given an EMG test and completed a questionnaire, plus the MMPI.

Findings Group A's muscle tension was significantly lower than Group B's by the end of the training, and after 3 months Group A's tension was still significantly lower than Group B's.

Group A's reported headaches dropped significantly from their baseline, whereas the others did not. Group A's reported headaches were also significantly less than those of Groups B and C.

The MMPI tests showed high levels of hysteria, depression and hypochondriasis for all groups at the beginning of the study. After the training period, all of these had reduced for all groups, however only Group A showed a significant reduction in hypochondriasis.

The follow-up questionnaire for Groups A and B showed that Group A had more reduction in symptoms than Group B. This included a drop in depression, insomnia, fast heart rate, apathy and fear of crowds.

Interestingly, both groups reported better social relationships.

Drug usage in Group A decreased, more than in Group B.

There was a follow-up for Group A after 18 months, when four out of the six participants were contacted. Three reported very low headache activity, and the fourth reported some reduction.

Conclusions Biofeedback is an effective way of training patients to relax and reduce their tension headaches, so can be seen as an effective method of stress management.

Relaxation training is also more effective than just being monitored, but is better when used together with biofeedback.

NB Group B was offered 'different' training, i.e. with real biofeedback, and Group C started their biofeedback training after their 2 months on the 'waiting list'.

> **Key term**
>
> hypochondriasis an excessive preoccupation with one's own health

3.3 Social support

The two previous techniques require some intervention
by a therapist, which might make them less readily
available. However, the final technique is less an
intervention than a social situation. Support networks
are used for a variety of problems: slimming clubs,
Alcoholics Anonymous, cancer clubs, are all ways in
which people with problems can increase their social
support, which in today's society is less likely to come
from family members. It is perhaps a little unclear how
social support networks can help reduce stress caused
by something like illness. Waxler-Morrison et al.'s (1993)
research into women with breast cancer and their
survival rates, does show how having extended social
support networks can increase the positive outcome
of survival after diagnosis of breast cancer. Sklar
and Anisman (1981) review a large body of literature
which has concluded that cancer growth is amplified
by stress, so we can assume that stress is directly
linked to cancer. However, there are too many factors
involved in any human behaviour to assume that the
reductionist approach of one technique or explanation
will be sufficient to encompass the complexities of our
activities.

Key study

Waxler-Morrison et al., Social relationships and
cancer survival

Aim To look at how a woman's social relationships
influence her response to breast cancer and survival.

Methodology A quasi-experiment with women who
were diagnosed with breast cancer. The information was
gathered using questionnaires and 18 interviews, plus
examination of medical records. The women naturally
fitted into categories based on their existing social
support networks.

Participants 133 women under 55 years (pre-
menopausal) who had been referred to a clinic in

Vancouver with a confirmed diagnosis of breast
cancer.

Design Independent design of women with
different levels of existing and ongoing social
networks.

Procedure Patients were sent a self-administered
questionnaire to gather information on their
demography and existing social networks. It also
included questions on their educational level,
who they were responsible for (i.e. children),
contact with friends and family, perception of
support from others, and a psychometric test
of social network that combined martial status,
contact with friends and families and church
membership.

The details of their diagnosis were abstracted from
their medical records between June 1980 and May
1981, and then their survival and recurrence rates
were checked in their medical records in January
1985.

Findings The six aspects of social network
significantly linked with survival were: marital status,
support from friends, contact with friends, total
support, social network and employment.

The qualitative data from the interviews showed
that practical help such as childcare, cooking and
transport to hospital was the concrete aspect of
support. Married women who survived tended to
report supportive spouses, although there were often
complex relationships with children, who themselves
needed support. Jobs were seen as important, even
if they were not financially important, as they were a
source of support and information.

Conclusions The prospective aspect of the study
– choosing a sample, assessing social networks
and then waiting to see outcomes for patients
– removed the biases of retrospective studies.
Several characteristics of the women's social
networks, including marriage and employment
status, are significantly related to survival, so the
conclusion is that the more social networks and
support, the higher the survival rate of women with
breast cancer. The assumption is that therefore the
participant's stress has been reduced. However, it
is acknowledged that the main factor influencing
survival is still the state of the cancer at the time
of diagnosis, with nodal status and clinical stage of
cancer being significantly linked with survival.

prospective a study that starts with participants and follows them to find out which behaviours they show in the future

retrospective a study that asks participants to recall their behaviours in the past

Check your understanding

1   How would you suggest someone should manage their stress on a daily basis?

2   What evidence is there for your answer?

Take it further

Evaluate the methods used in the research on stress by comparing and contrasting them using any of the evaluation issues you have studied in AS or A2, such as usefulness, approach, ecological validity.

Section summary

◆   It appears that there is no one cause of stress and no uniform reaction to stress; it is difficult to measure accurately, and there are many stress-reduction techniques, all of which can claim some success, at least on the participants in the supporting research.

◆   It is perhaps one of the joys of being human, that no one can really explain our behaviour; we are complex animals and we need to have a variety of tools at our disposal to explain, measure and treat any atypical behaviour. However, we would have to ask: is being stressed atypical?

U3

2

Dysfunctional behaviour

Pause for thought

◆ 'Dysfunctional behaviour' is a more up-to-date term than 'mental illness'. What do you think is the difference between the two labels?

◆ What do you know about dysfunctional behaviour or mental illness? How much of this has been gained from watching television or reading the newspapers? Do you think it is accurate?

Introduction

First, it is important to understand that psychology is a science that looks at trends, not certainties, so for every piece of evidence that appears to explain human behaviour, there is probably another that refutes it. This is particularly important in the case of dysfunctional behaviour and disorders. No psychologist can say for certain what causes dysfunctional behaviours; the evidence can point to factors that may cause a disposition or tendency towards a disorder, but as humans are all individuals, and more complex than animals, it is clear that not everyone will behave in the same way. Having said that, any concerns about dysfunctional behaviour are genuine, and the weblinks below may be helpful in reaching a better understanding of disorders and their implications.

Dysfunctional behaviour has been called many things – abnormal, atypical and currently dysfunctional – which seem to reflect society's view of the individual. If someone is not able to function as a human being, the label 'dysfunctional' carries less stigma than the label 'abnormal'. Clinical psychology looks at people with problems, such as stress and bizarre mood swings.

The first part of this area of the course will look at dysfunctional behaviour in general terms, from the basic question of what dysfunctional behaviour is and how to diagnose it, to some of the main approaches and how they explain and treat dysfunctional behaviour.

What is dysfunctional behaviour? This question has many answers, and clinical psychologists may disagree as to which dysfunctional behaviour one person is displaying. Records about the painter Vincent van Gogh (1853–90) have shown that he appears to have had an eccentric personality and unstable moods; he also had psychotic episodes during the 2 years that preceded his suicide at the age of 37. Doctors diagnosed him with a variety of illnesses such as epilepsy, depression, schizophrenia (Blumer, 2002). Research by Zigler and Phillips (1961) found that agreement on diagnosis of broad categories such as depression or anxiety was frequent (up to 84 per cent), but when it came to more precise classification within each category, the reliability between doctors' diagnoses dropped to less than 57 per cent (Kendell, 1975). This shows the problems with classifying or diagnosing dysfunctional behaviour.

Psychologists from various approaches will have their own explanations for dysfunctional disorders. It will not surprise you to know that behaviourists would consider the cause to be learned behaviour, and the second section of this topic will explore three explanations: the behaviourist, the biological and the cognitive. It follows that the treatments adopted by each approach will be based on the assumptions of that approach, so for example behaviourists believe that to treat dysfunctional behaviour, the patient needs to re-learn functional behaviours. Some psychologists believe that there is no such thing as mental illness. Szasz (1973) suggested that if people acted eccentrically they were labelled as 'ill' by a society that wants to control behaviour. For example, it is acceptable for a person to speak to God while praying, but if they hear God talking to them, they are considered schizophrenic. However, if we accept that mental illness does exist and needs treatment, then we first need to define what is abnormality. This area of the specification covers:

◆ diagnosis of dysfunctional behaviour

◆ explanations of dysfunctional behaviour

◆ treatments of dysfunctional behaviour.

Diagnosis of dysfunctional behaviour

Psychologists sometimes define something by saying what it is not, so abnormal behaviour is something that is not normal. This does not explain what 'normal' is. There are many concepts of normality and historically the main four that psychologists have used are: statistical infrequency, deviation from social norms, failure to function adequately and deviation from ideal mental health (Hill, 2001). But what about train-spotting? Is this infrequent, and deviation from the social norm? If so, it fulfils two of the criteria for mental illness. Depression is not statistically infrequent, so the boundaries between what we would call dysfunctional behaviour and 'normal' behaviour can be quite blurred. It is not surprising that it is difficult to diagnose dysfunctional behaviour (remember the problems the doctors had in Rosenhan's (1973) study in the AS course).

Explanations of dysfunctional behaviour

You will know from your study of AS Psychology that there are different explanations for human behaviour. These are based on approaches such as the cognitive or biological approach and perspectives such as the behaviourist perspective. Basic assumptions about behaviour should be transferable to any behaviour, including dysfunctional behaviour, if the approach is to stand up to scrutiny. You will have looked at Freud's psychodynamic approach to abnormality in the case study of Little Hans in the AS course. More modern approaches would identify other ways of explaining dysfunctional behaviour. Cognitive psychology, which has formed the basis of cognitive behavioural therapy (CBT), is one of the stronger contemporary explanations, but it is difficult to see how it can be applied to all disorders.

Treatments of dysfunctional behaviour

There are many treatments of dysfunctional behaviour in use today. Things may have moved on from the days when people who showed some dysfunctional behaviour were labelled 'mad' and were believed to be possessed by evil spirits. By cutting holes in their skulls (trepanning), these evil spirits could be allowed out. We may not use this technique now, but it does clearly show that the treatment of any disorder depends on what is perceived to be causing it.

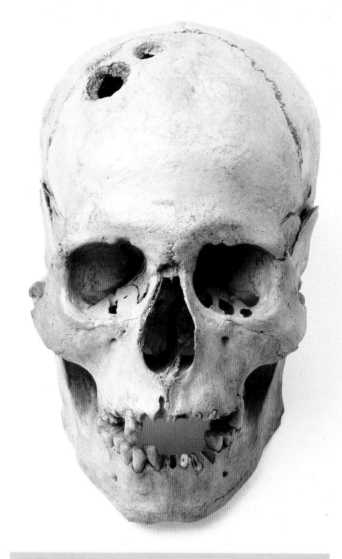

Figure 2.9 Trepanning dates from prehistoric times, and may have been carried out to allow evil spirits to leave a person's brain. The regrowth of bone around the incision shows that people survived the operation

We have seen that the biological, cognitive and behaviourist explanations derive from their respective assumptions about human behaviour. This naturally leads on to assumptions about treatments. If the cause is biological, there must be some biological intervention, such as drugs; if the cause is maladaptive learning, then the behaviourist would see the re-learning of appropriate behaviours as the way to treat behaviours such as phobias. The cognitive psychologist would believe that restructuring cognitions would reduce the faulty thinking that caused the disorder in the first place. Sometimes cognitive and behavioural therapies are combined, and one of the more common contemporary therapies is CBT. Perhaps it is better to have two approaches when looking at treatments, as a less reductionist approach might help with complex disorders.

Themes and perspectives

Ethics must be a strong consideration in health psychology research. What would you do as a psychologist if you found out that someone regularly drank and drove, or did not use condoms despite having a sexually transmitted disease? If a particular group were highlighted as engaging in risky health behaviours, would society discriminate against them? It is important that data are kept confidential and handled sensitively.

In this area one of the main issues is the ethics of labelling someone as having a disorder. You have read about the 'stickiness' of labels in Rosenhan's study in the AS course, and if society's views of dysfunctional behaviour lead to discrimination, such diagnoses need to be valid and safe. Also, the ethics of 'treating' a mental condition with drugs that might have side effects need to be considered in the light of an individual's rights.

However, there is an argument for a society's right to ensure the safety of its individuals. There are many media stories about people who have been diagnosed with a disorder but have not taken their medication and have gone on to harm themselves or others, though of course it is important to remember that media stories are not always to be trusted.

Weblinks

If you need help in understanding disorders and their implications, the MIND website may be a good place to start (see Contents page).

More information on clinical psychology can be found on the British Psychological Society (BPS) website (see Contents page). Membership is required for access.

1 Diagnosis of dysfunctional behaviour

Categories of dysfunctional behaviour

Two main diagnostic manuals have been used to help categorise dysfunctional behaviour with some consistency (or reliability) in diagnosis. These are the *Diagnostic Statistics Manual* (*DSM*) which tends to be used in the USA, and the *International Classification of Disorders* (*ICD*) which tends to be used outside the USA.

Definitions of dysfunctional behaviour

Rosenhan and Seligman's definitions extend these criteria to make defining abnormality a bit easier. Once society has agreed that certain behaviours are causing a person to lose their ability to function effectively in society (and what exactly is 'effectively'?) then comes the business of labelling the disorder. The problem of labelling people with disorders was also explored in Rosenhan's research.

Biases in diagnosis

This area is further confounded by the biases that have been shown to exist among practitioners when diagnosing disorders. This is not to say that these biases are conscious or discriminatory, but they may reflect society's view of what is dysfunctional. Cultural and gender biases in diagnosis have been shown to exist, and this section looks at one piece of research that appears to identify sex biases in diagnoses.

1.1 Categorising disorders

DSM (American Psychiatric Association, 2005) and *ICD* (World Health Organisation, 2000) are diagnostic tools designed to enable practitioners to identify and treat a particular disorder. These are updated (the 2008 versions being *ICD-10* and *DSM-IV*; *ICD-11* should be drafted by 2008 and published in 2011). Disorders will change with time, for example until 1973 homosexuality was perceived as a mental disorder. As society became more enlightened, the view that it was not something to be cured led to its being removed from *DSM-II* and replaced by 'sexual orientation disturbance'. This changed to 'ego-dystonic homosexuality' in *DSM-III* in 1980. In *DSM-III-Revised* in 1987 a category of 'sexual disorder not otherwise specified' was introduced, and this has continued in *DSM-IV*. The criteria here include 'persistent and marked distress about one's sexual orientation', so it would appear now that society is not labelling homosexuality as a disorder, but that distress about one's sexuality may lead to a disorder or to a diagnosis of a disorder. Binge-eating disorder (BED) was introduced in 1994 into the 4th edition of *DSM*. However, newer disorders such as eating disorders are included as they become more identifiable. Bulimia was introduced as a disorder in *DSM-III* in 1980, and the criteria for disorders such as anorexia can change over time. Denial of having the disorder is now a criterion included in *DSM-IV*, and the Body Mass Index for anorexia was changed to allow for cross-cultural consistency.

International Classification of Diseases and Related Health Problems (ICD-10)

This manual is published by the World Health Organisation (WHO) and is used in many countries throughout the world in diagnosing both physical and mental conditions. Chapter V of *ICD* is concerned with mental and behavioural disorders. Version 10 of *ICD* was first published in 1992, and was a revision of previous versions. In 1978 *ICD-8* was used as a basis for many cross-cultural collaborations in the 1980s with the aim of refining the definitions for disorders in the 10th version. This allowed for inconsistencies and ambiguities to be removed and resulted in the clear set of criteria now in *ICD-10*. The draft in 1987 was used in 40 countries to see if this improved psychiatric diagnoses across cultures. Of course *ICD-10* is only a snapshot of the field of dysfunctional behaviour, and as cultures change so definitions and criteria must continue to be revised.

In *ICD-10* each disorder has a description of the main features, and any important associated features. The diagnostic section indicates how many of each feature and the balance required between different types of features are needed to make an accurate diagnosis (see page 123). It is possible to be 'confident' in diagnoses; if a diagnosis is less certain due to some ambiguities, it is termed 'tentative'. Each disorder is then given a code and the numerical coding of 001–099 in *ICD-9* has been replaced by A00–Z99, which gives more possible categories. *ICD-9* had 30 such categories, *ICD-10* now has 100. Some of the categories relate to specific childhood or developmental disorders, while others, such as eating disorders, are applicable to both children and adults.

The categories include:

◆ dementia

◆ schizophrenia

◆ mood (affective) disorders

◆ personality disorders.

Diagnostic and Statistical Manual of Mental Disorders, 4th Edition (DSM-IV)

DSM-IV was compiled by over 1000 people who collaborated to produce a practical guide to clinical diagnoses. Field trials were used before publication to compare *DSM-III* with *DSM-IV* and also to compare it with *ICD-10*. This resulted in simpler classifications using criteria sets. Empirical research was used to support the criteria. Some new diagnoses were included, especially if they already appeared in *ICD-10*. *DSM-IV* now recognises the limitations in calling itself a manual of mental disorders, as this implies a mind/body split

that may not exist, although it is not clear what could replace it. There are some acknowledged problems with individual differences, as no individual's situation is the same as another's, and therefore the features of their illness may be different. As this manual is the main diagnostic tool used in the USA, there is also an attempt to highlight the ethnic diversity of the US population and suggest that diagnosing may be more difficult if the culture of the patient is different from that of the clinician.

The major difference between *ICD-10* and *DSM-IV* is that *DSM* is a multi-axial tool. Clinicians have to consider whether the disorder is from Axis 1, clinical disorders and/or Axis 2, personality disorders. Then the patient's general physical condition is considered, plus any social and environmental problems. This is used to assess the patient's functioning on a scale from 1 to100. This makes the *DSM* much more holistic in relation to diagnosis than the *ICD*'s rather reductionist approach to criteria-based diagnoses. Many clinicians would use the two diagnostic tools side by side before diagnosing a patient. It takes many years of study and training to be able to accurately and professionally diagnose patients with any illness, physical or mental.

The *DSM-IV* has classifications such as:

◆ learning disorders

◆ communication disorders

◆ dementia

◆ substance-related disorders

◆ sleep disorders

◆ sexual and gender identity disorders.

Other cultures have their own diagnostic manuals, for example the *Chinese Classification of Mental Disorders (CCMD)* is published by the Chinese Society of Psychiatry. The current version is *CCMD-3*, which follows the same format as *ICD* and *DSM*, but includes about 40 culturally-related diagnoses.

> **Check your understanding**
>
> What similarities and differences are there between the two diagnostic manuals, *ICD-10* and *DSM-IV*?

1.2 Definitions of dysfunctional behaviour

Rosenhan and Seligman's (1995) criteria cover a range of general behaviours that might help to diagnose dysfunctional behaviour. These include such things as showing self-knowledge and having a realistic view of life. They are summarised below.

1 Statistical infrequency

'Abnormality' would refer to any behaviour that is not seen very often in society. However, it is difficult to use on its own, as this might encompass behaviours such as exceptionally high IQ, or stamp-collecting. Other behaviours which are regarded as abnormal might be quite common, such as substance abuse, but it could be argued that this illness is 'abnormal'. There has to be more to it than just numbers.

2 Deviation from social norms

Here we have the definition that if society does not approve of a behaviour then it is dysfunctional. However, this will make some behaviours dysfunctional in some cultures and not in others. In western society we may consider women who wear trousers as perfectly normal, but this is not the case in every culture. It also has a sense of 'rightness', in that what society says is right and everyone else is wrong. If this was the case, societies would not be changed by forward-thinking people.

3 Failure to function adequately

Perhaps a more useful definition is that if a person is not functioning in a way that enables them to live independently in society then they are 'dysfunctional'. There are several ways a person might not be functioning well. These might be:

dysfunctional behaviours such as obsessive compulsive disorder, where a person cannot go out because of the rituals they need to undertake before they can leave

behaviour that distresses the person experiencing it – not being able to go out of the house is distressing for agoraphobics

behaviour that makes a person observing the patient feel uncomfortable – such as when a person is talking to themselves while sitting next to you on the bus

unpredictable behaviour – dramatic mood swings or sudden impulses can be seen as dysfunctional

irrational behaviour, where a person thinks they are being followed, or that people are talking about them, could lead to a failure to function adequately. Failure to function adequately might be the most useful definition. However, there are problems in that the context of the

behaviour might influence our view of it. We probably all talk to ourselves at times. Maybe a person who has been involved in a fire will obsessively check appliances before leaving the house. It can be quite a subjective view as to whether a person is not functioning adequately.

4 Deviation from ideal mental health

Psychologists often take the view that if you lack one thing, i.e. health, then you must have the opposite, i.e. illness. This might make logical sense, but we would have to consider what we mean by ideal mental health.

Jahoda (1958) suggests that to have ideal mental health you should:

- have a positive view of yourself
- be capable of some personal growth
- be independent and self-regulating
- have an accurate view of reality
- be resistant to stress
- be able to adapt to your environment.

These criteria are probably more relevant when we are considering what dysfunctional behaviour is. However, there is still a problem with culture bias, in that Jahoda's ideal mental health image is based on western individualist cultures. It also relies on the subjective view of the clinician as to whether the person has ideal mental health.

Check your understanding

1. What are the four main definitions of abnormality, according to Rosenhan and Seligman?

2. How might a person be considered to be functioning inadequately?

1.3 Biases in diagnosis

There is a lot of pressure from society on practitioners to ensure that people with disorders are helped. This may reflect a genuine belief that everyone has a right to mental health care, or it may be a media-induced idea that people who are not 'normal' should be removed from society. This belief can change with culture, and in each culture over time. It may be influenced by events, for example if someone who has been diagnosed with a disorder commits a crime, this may be taken as indicative of the behaviour of everyone with this disorder. Society's view of genders or cultures may also bias views of what is normal or not.

In some cultures, hearing voices is thought to be a good thing, as communicating with ancestors. Even Freud (1901) admitted this: 'During the days when I was living alone in a foreign city – I was a young man at the time – I quite often heard my name suddenly called by an unmistakable and beloved voice…'

The Mental Health Act Commission's 'Count Me In' Census (2005) identified that certain groups are significantly overrepresented in the mental-health system. For example, it found that rates of admission to hospital of both genders from the White British and Indian groups were lower than average, whereas the admission rates for people from the Black and White/Black Mixed groups could be three or more times higher than average. It is important to consider the extraneous variables that might affect this; socioeconomic status might be one.

Try this …

What extraneous variables do you think could make some groups more likely to be diagnosed as dysfunctional?

Culture-bound disorders are said to be disorders that are typical of one culture. An often-cited case is that of *dhat*, which is a neurotic illness found on the Indian subcontinent. Men believe that their fatigue and depression are caused by too much semen in their blood. However, by using diagnostic tools Chadda and Ahuja (1990) found that the men seem to be suffering from the much less culturally specific disorder of depression, and it is this that is causing

their lethargy. Of 52 patients, 21 were diagnosed with neurotic depression, 19 with anxiety neurosis, and three with hypochondriacal neurosis, so perhaps this was not a culture-bound syndrome but more a cultural explanation for global disorders, although the seven patients who were diagnosed with *dhat* may confound this theory.

Broverman et al. (1970) found that mental-health professionals used different adjectives to describe the normal male and normal female, with the normal female seen as submissive and concerned about her appearance. This would make any female who is not submissive appear to be abnormal and therefore more likely to be diagnosed with a disorder. However, the date of the research may indicate that a different view might be found today. This stereotypical view of genders is one way in which diagnoses can be biased. Ford and Widiger's research (1989) described below shows how even 19 years after Broverman such biases were appearing in diagnoses. Of course, the whole idea of the validity of diagnosis is also shown up, as only 20 per cent of some cases were diagnosed correctly!

Key study
Ford and Widiger, Sex bias in the diagnosis of disorders

Aim To find out if clinicians were stereotyping genders when diagnosing disorders.

Methodology A self-report, where health practitioners were given scenarios and asked to make diagnoses based on the information. The independent variable was the gender of the patient in the case study and the dependent variable was the diagnosis made by the clinician.

Participants A final sample of 354 clinical psychologists from 1127 randomly selected from the National Register in 1983, with a mean of 15.6 years' clinical experience; 266 psychologists responded to the case histories.

Design An independent design as each participant was given a male, female or sex-unspecified case study.

Procedure Participants were randomly provided with one of nine case histories. Case studies of patients with antisocial personality disorder (ASPD) or histrionic personality disorder (HPD) or an equal balance of symptoms from both disorders were given to each therapist.

Therapists were asked to diagnose the illness in each case study by rating on a seven-point scale the extent to which the patient appeared to have each of nine disorders:

- dysthymic
- adjustment
- alcohol abuse
- cyclothymic disorder
- narcissistic
- histrionic
- passive-aggressive
- antisocial
- borderline personality disorder.

Findings Sex-unspecified case histories were diagnosed most often with borderline personality disorder.

ASPD was correctly diagnosed 42 per cent of the time in males and 15 per cent in females. Females with ASPD were misdiagnosed with HPD 46 per cent of the time, whereas males were only misdiagnosed with HPD 15 per cent of the time.

HPD was correctly diagnosed in 76 per cent of females and 44 per cent of males.

Conclusions Practitioners are biased by stereotypical views of genders, as there was a clear tendency to diagnose females with HPD even when their case histories were of ASPD. There was also a tendency not to diagnose males with HPD, although this was not as great as the misdiagnosis of women.

The characteristics of HPD (a pattern of excessive emotional behaviour and attention-seeking, together with a need for approval and inappropriate seductiveness) might be considered by some clinicians to be gender specific, and so any behaviour that fits these criteria leads more readily to a diagnosis of a 'female typical' disorder.

Check your understanding

1. Ford and Widiger believed that histrionic personality disorder was seen as more likely in women. How could this be explained?

2. What were the three conditions in this research?

Section summary

- It is clear that diagnosing and categorising dysfunctional behaviours is not an exact science.

- Diagnosis often depends on how society views any particular disorder at any one time, and the biases inherent in that society.

- There are dysfunctional behaviours that cause distress to patients and their families, and which can be treated to facilitate a better quality of life.

2 Explanations of dysfunctional behaviour

This section will look at three approaches and their assumptions about dysfunctional behaviour, and what evidence there is to support these assumptions. Although these are general explanations, there is some overlap with the next section, which looks at each approach and its explanation and treatment of specific disorders. The approaches covered on the specification are:

- behavioural
- biological
- cognitive.

Behavioural

The behaviourist perspective is that we are born blank slates and all behaviour is learnt. Therefore any dysfunctional behaviour is learnt, by operant conditioning, classical conditioning, or social learning. This places the responsibility on us to ensure that we do not 'teach' dysfunctional behaviours to others.

Biological

The biological approach, which is part of biopsychology, would favour the nature side of the nature–nurture debate. Biological explanations of behaviour assert that something in our biology is the fundamental cause of dysfunctional behaviour. There could be a genetic cause, or a malformation of brain structures.

Cognitive

The third, but by no means least popular or effective, approach to explaining dysfunctional behaviour is that of cognitive psychology, which sees our behaviour as being a consequence of some internal processing of information. Much like a computer, we take in information, process it and respond in some way. If however there is a problem with the circuit boards in a computer, the response may not be what we would expect, and this is the same with humans. If something goes wrong with what information we attend to, and how we perceive and store it, then the response may not be what everyone expects, and this could lead to a label of dysfunctional behaviour.

Try this …

Having seen what constitutes dysfunctional behaviour in the previous section, how do you think the assumptions of cognitive, biological and behaviourist psychologists would explain dysfunctional behaviour? Try putting your thoughts in a chart like the one below.

	Assumptions	Related to dysfunctional behaviour
Behavioural		
Biological		
Cognitive		

2.1 Behavioural

The foundations of operant conditioning are Skinner's (1938) belief that animals (including humans) would determine their likelihood of repeating behaviour depending on its consequences. So if you are rewarded for dysfunctional behaviour, you are more likely to repeat it. This is quite a simplistic explanation for what can be very complex behaviours. Classical conditioning would suggest that associations are made between one act and another, see the example below of how Little Albert learned to associate a rat with fear caused by a loud noise and finally developed a fear of rats (Watson and Raynor, 1920). Your knowledge from the AS course of the research by Bandura et al. (1961) should enable you to understand the role of modelling. Obviously to go into all of these in detail would be beyond the remit of the specification, so this section will concentrate on the classical conditioning explanation of phobia acquisition.

Key study

Watson and Raynor, Study of classical conditioning

Aim To see if it is possible to induce a fear of a previously unfeared object, through classical conditioning.

To see if the fear will be transferred to other, similar objects.

To see what effect will time have on the fear response.

To see how it is possible to remove the fear response in the laboratory.

Methodology A case study undertaken on one child: 'Little Albert', in controlled laboratory conditions.

Participants Little Albert was a child of a wet nurse (someone who breastfeeds babies when the mother cannot) and so lived in a hospital environment. He was, according to Watson and Raynor, stolid and unemotional. Albert had no fearful reactions to a rat, a rabbit, a dog, a monkey, a mask with hair, or cotton wool.

A test when Albert was 8 months old showed that he reacted violently when a suspended steel bar was hit by a hammer. He was startled, held his breath, and then began to cry. The response was used to condition Albert to fear rats and other stimuli.

Design A single-subject design. The behaviours measured were Albert's reactions to various stimuli before and after the conditioning.

Procedure Albert's baseline reactions to the stimuli were noted as having no sign of a fear response in any situation. When Albert was 11 months old the experiments started.

Session 1 When Albert was presented with the rat in the laboratory, the steel bar was struck just as he reached for the rat. This was repeated.

Findings The first time the steel bar was struck when Albert touched the rat, he jumped and fell forward.

The second time he began to whimper.

After two presentations Albert was given a week off.

Session 2 The following week the rat alone was presented. Then three presentations were made with the rat and the loud noise. This was followed with one presentation of just the rat and then two more with the rat and the noise; finally the rat alone was presented.

So far, Albert had had seven presentations of the rat with the noise.

Findings After five paired presentations in session 2, Albert reacted to the rat alone by immediately crying, turning to the left, and crawling quickly away from the rat.

Session 3 To see if the fear was transferred, Albert was brought back 5 days later and presented with some toy blocks to play with. This was a neutral stimulus that could be used to stop the fear response, as Albert liked playing with them. Presentations were then made of the rat followed by a presentation of a rabbit, then a dog, a seal-fur coat, some cotton wool, then Watson's hair and finally a Santa Claus mask. These presentations were interspersed with the blocks being presented to calm Albert down.

Findings After each presentation of the blocks Albert played with them happily, but the other stimuli produced negative responses of crying, moving away from the stimulus, and crawling away. He showed less negativity to the cotton wool.

Session 4 To see how time had affected the response, 5 days later Albert was presented with the rat on its own. Although the response was still there, it was weaker, so it was decided to 'freshen up' the response to the rat and also condition the response to the dog and rabbit, by hitting the steel bar when they were presented. Albert was then taken to a well-lit lecture theatre to see if the response was the same as it was in the small room used so far.

Findings The fear response to the dog, rat and rabbit were pronounced: Albert cried and crawled away from the objects. In the different room the fear reaction was slight. Once the response was 'freshened' again, the fear response to just the stimuli was pronounced. The blocks still produced no fear reaction.

Session 5 One month later Albert was tested with various stimuli; these included the Santa Claus mask, the fur coat, the rat, the rabbit and the dog.

Findings Albert continued to show fear reactions to a varying degree to all of the stimuli, sometimes crying, sometimes crawling away. With the rabbit he seemed to be less frightened and wanted to play with it, although when he touched it he usually showed the fear response to some degree.

Conclusions *Session 2* – after five paired presentations the conditioning of a fear response was evident, so it is possible to condition fear through classical conditioning.

Sessions 3 and 4 – transference of the fear had been made to other similar objects, although it appeared that objects less like the original stimulus, e.g. cotton wool, resulted in less negativity.

Session 5 – time had not removed the fear response.

Albert was taken out of the hospital on the day of session 5, so Watson and Raynor were never able to test their aim of trying to find ways of removing a phobia in the laboratory. We do not know if Albert had a fear of furry animals for the rest of his life. Research by Jones on Little Peter (Jones, 1924) did show how a fear of rabbits could be overcome using a treatment of systematic desensitisation. For this treatment of a noise phobia, see page 119.

Try this …

Make up a cartoon storyboard of Watson and Rayner's research on Little Albert. It does not matter if you cannot draw, use stick figures and add one or two words to explain what is happening in each frame.

Check your understanding

1   What theory did Watson and Raynor support?

2   Identify the conditioned stimulus, unconditioned stimulus, conditioned response and unconditioned response in this study.

3   What is meant by the term 'generalisation' in this study?

2.2 Biological

One of the problems of research is that it often looks at people who have already been diagnosed with a disorder, such as schizophrenia. It is then difficult to identify cause and effect: is it the brain structure that causes schizophrenia or the schizophrenia that causes the malformed brain structure? Even within the biological approach there is conflict, for example the biological approach may explain schizophrenia in terms of genetic tendency (see Gottesman and Shields' study (1976), below), but work with patients who had Parkinson's disease showed the link between dopamine and schizophrenia and led to the dopamine hypothesis. This states that patients with schizophrenia have higher than normal levels of dopamine. The diathesis stress theory is that people are born with an inherited tendency towards schizophrenia but the illness is brought about by stress, often in adolescence or young adulthood.

Key study

Gottesman and Shields, A review of recent adoption twin and family studies of schizophrenia

Aim To review research on genetic transmission of schizophrenia.

Methodology A review of adoption and twin studies into schizophrenia between 1967 and 1976.

Studies reviewed:

◆ three adoption studies

◆ five twin studies.

In total there were 711 participants in the adoption studies. In the twin studies a total of 210 monozygotic (identical) twin pairs and 319 dizygotic (non-identical) twin pairs were studied.

Procedure The incidence of schizophrenia in adopted children and monozygotic twins was extrapolated from the research. This was done by comparing biological parents and siblings and adoptive parents and siblings in the adoption studies. In the twin studies the concordance rates (how often both twins were diagnosed with schizophrenia) for monozygotic and dizygotic twins was compared.

An increased incidence of schizophrenia in biological relatives and higher concordance rates between monozygotic twins would indicate a genetic basis for schizophrenia.

Findings All three adoption studies found an increased incidence of schizophrenia in adopted children with a schizophrenic biological parent, whereas normal children fostered to schizophrenic parents and adoptive parents of schizophrenic children showed little evidence of schizophrenia.

One of the studies by Kety (1975) found that biological siblings of children with schizophrenia showed a much higher percentage of schizophrenia (19.2 per cent) compared with adoptive siblings (6.3 per cent).

All twin studies found a higher concordance rate for schizophrenia in monozygotic twins than dizygotic twins. In Gottesman and Shields' own study (1972) this was 58 per cent in monozygotic twins, meaning that if one twin had schizophrenia then there was a 58 per cent chance the other would have it, compared with a 12 per cent concordance rate for dizygotic twins.

Conclusions There is obviously a significant genetic input into the onset of schizophrenia, but with concordance rates less than 100 per cent there must be some interaction with the environment. There is also some confusion as to whether one or many genes are responsible for predisposing a person to schizophrenia.

Check your understanding

1   Which method did Gottesman and Shields use?

2   How did they use concordance rates in studies?

3   Which of their findings which suggest a genetic link in the transmission of schizophrenia?

2.3 Cognitive

Research by Maher (1974; see page 138) as a cognitive psychologist explaining schizophrenia, suggests that it is perfectly logical to assume that if we cannot hear what someone is saying, they must be whispering, and if they are whispering and do not want us to hear, it must be about us, and so we are sensible to be worried that someone is out to get us! Beck (1967) and Ellis (1991) are the founders of the cognitive approach and have much to say about how faulty thinking can influence our behaviours, and logically, as the next section will show, how rectifying illogical thinking can remove dysfunctional behaviours. The following study (Beck et al., 1974) investigates cognitive distortions in patients with depression.

Key study

Beck et al., Interviews with patients undergoing therapy for depression

Aim To understand cognitive distortions in patients with depression.

Methodology Clinical interviews with patients who were undergoing therapy for depression.

Participants 50 patients diagnosed with depression, 16 men and 34 women, aged 18 to 48 with a median age of 34. Most were judged to be middle or upper class and of at least average intelligence.

Design Independent design as the patients were compared with a group of 31 non-depressed patients undergoing psychotherapy, matched for age, sex, and social position.

Procedure Face-to-face interviews with retrospective reports of patients' thoughts before the session as well as spontaneous reports of thoughts during the session. Some patients kept diaries of their thoughts and brought these to the therapy sessions.

Records were kept of the non-depressed patients' verbalisations to compare with those of the depressed patients.

Findings Certain themes appeared in the depressed patients that did not appear in the non-depressed patients. These were low self-esteem, self-blame, overwhelming responsibilities and desire to escape, anxiety caused by thoughts of personal danger, and paranoia and accusations against other people.

Depressed patients had stereotypical responses to situations, even where inappropriate, for example if a passer-by did not smile at him, one patient would feel inferior. Depressed patients regarded themselves as inferior to others in their social or occupational groups, for example less attractive, less intelligent, less successful as a parent.

Some patients felt themselves unlovable and alone, even when others showed friendship. Self-blame was shown even when this was illogical, for example a mother who blamed herself for not picking a nicer day when it rained on a family picnic.

These distortions tended to be automatic, involuntary, plausible and persistent.

Conclusions Even in mild depression, patients have cognitive distortions that deviate from realistic and logical thinking. These distortions related only to depression and not to other areas.

Check your understanding

1   What was the aim of the study?

2   How did the participants report their cognitions?

3   What common cognitions were found in the depressed patients?

Section summary

◆   The different approaches' assumptions influence their explanations of the causes of dysfunctional behaviour.

◆   The biological explanation is the one most commonly used in our society, as this reflects the emphasis on mental health being a medical problem.

◆   The prescription of anti-depressants, tranquilisers and antipsychotic drugs reflects this view; these are now more often seen as short-term fixes that need to be combined with other 'talking' therapies such as CBT to address the underlying problems.

Take it further

Research other treatments based on these approaches, such as electroconvulsive therapy as a biological treatment for depression. Try to relate them to the assumptions of the approach. Compare their efficacy and usefulness.

3 Treatments of dysfunctional behaviour

Try this ...

Make a list of all the ways you know of helping people with psychiatric disorders or dysfunctional behaviour. Can you identify which psychological approach each one is based on?

The variety of treatments covered in this section will reflect the approaches in the explanations section. Thus it is possible to see the logic behind the treatments.

This section will look at the following approaches:

◆   behavioural

◆   biological

◆   cognitive.

Behavioural

The behavioural perspective says that behaviour is learnt and so has little to do with the individual and more to do with the situation they are in.

Biological

The biological approach – sometimes called the somatic approach – has several methods of treating dysfunctional behaviour. Probably the most common is drug therapy, where chemical imbalances can be reduced by giving drugs. This is used in most disorders, and is often prescribed by doctors rather than psychologists.

Cognitive

Ellis, together with Beck, was one of the founders of the cognitive approach (see pages 120–121), and so his rational emotive therapy (RET) (1991) is soundly based on the cognitive approach to treatment, the assumption that illogical thought processes somehow cause dysfunctional behaviour, and therefore need to be restructured.

3.1 Behavioural

As Watson and Raynor showed (pages 115–116) the learning of phobias appears to be a valid explanation. Little Albert learnt to have a phobia by being presented with two stimuli together, the rat and the loud noise, until his response was fear of the rat alone. Behaviours such as phobias could be *unlearnt* in the same way. By pairing the phobic stimulus with something pleasant or relaxing, the treatment of phobias should be effective, and is known as systematic desensitisation. In terms of classical conditioning the fear response can be replaced by a conditioned response of calm. The stimulus that causes the fear is presented with something that makes the patient feel calm. In Jones's research, Little Peter was given his dinner when presented with the fear object of a rabbit. Eating made him feel good and so he learned to associate the rabbit with feeling good. Eventually the rabbit on its own made him feel good, rather than fearful. Research by McGrath (1990) in the key study below shows how successful the treatment can be for reducing phobias in a case study of a girl with a phobia of loud noises.

Key study

McGrath, Successful treatment of a noise phobia

Aim To treat a girl with specific noise phobias using systematic desensitisation.

Methodology A case study that details the treatment of a noise phobia in one girl.

Participant Lucy, a 9-year-old girl who had a fear of sudden loud noises. These included balloons, party poppers, guns, cars backfiring and fireworks. She had lower than average IQ, and was not depressed, anxious or fearful (tested with psychometric tests), so only had one specific phobia.

Design A single-participant design.

Procedure Lucy was brought to the therapy session, and the programme explained to her and her parents, who gave their consent for further sessions.

At the first session Lucy constructed a hierarchy of feared noises. These included doors banging, cap guns, balloons and unexpected party poppers.

Lucy was taught breathing and imagery to relax, and was told to imagine herself at home on her bed with her toys. She also had a hypothetical 'fear thermometer' to rate her level of fear from 1 to 10. As she was given the stimulus of the loud noise, she paired her feared object (the loud noise) with relaxation, deep breathing and imagining herself at home with her toys. This would naturally lead her to feel calm. She then associated the noise with feeling calm. So after four sessions she had learned to feel calm when the noise was presented. She did not need to imagine herself at home with her toys any more.

Findings At the end of the first session, Lucy was reluctant to let balloons be burst even at the far end of the corridor. When the therapist burst the balloon anyway, Lucy cried and had to be taken away. She was encouraged to breathe deeply and relax.

By the end of the fourth session, Lucy was able to signal a balloon to be burst 10 metres away, with only mild anxiety.

In the fifth session, Lucy held a deflated balloon, then a slightly inflated balloon and eventually was able to allow a small balloon to be burst in the consulting room. At the end of the session Lucy was able to pop the balloons herself.

Party poppers were then introduced over the next three sessions, and Lucy went from not allowing them into the consulting room to being able to pop one if the therapist held it.

Cap guns were then introduced and were used outside, but Lucy was quickly able to agree to one being fired in the consulting room.

By Lucy's tenth and final session, her fear thermometer scores had gone from 7/10 to 3/10 for balloons popping and 9/10 to 3/10 for party poppers; the cap gun had gone from 8/10 to 5/10.

Conclusions It appears that noise phobias in children are amenable to systematic desensitisation. The important factors appear to have been giving Lucy control to say when and where the noises were made, and the use of inhibitors of the fear response which included relaxation and a playful environment.

Check your understanding

1. Which behaviourist theory is this technique based on?

2. What did McGrath ask Lucy to do when the balloons were popped?

3. How many therapy sessions did Lucy have to become less fearful?

3.2 Biological

The research by Karp and Frank (1995) is a review article which looks at research into the effectiveness of drug therapies for depression. Often the success of such therapies will support the biological explanation as to the cause of the disorder. For a more in-depth discussion of depression, see pages 131–136.

see pages 131–136.

Key study

Karp and Frank, Combination therapy and the depressed woman

Aim To compare drug treatment and non-drug treatments for depression.

Methodology A review article of previous research into the effectiveness of single treatments and combined drug and psychotherapeutic treatments of depression.

Participants The research which was reviewed concentrated on women diagnosed with depression.

Design Much of the research used an independent design, with patients having single drug treatment, single psychological treatment, combined treatments and sometimes placebo groups.

Procedure Depression was analysed using a variety of depression inventories, and patients were tested generally prior to treatment, after treatment and in some cases after a period of time as a follow up. Some health practitioner assessments of symptoms were also used by some of the research.

Findings Many studies found that adding psychological treatments to drug therapy did not increase the effectiveness of the drug therapy. Occasionally studies did show less attrition when combination therapies were used. This means that people were more likely to continue with treatment if cognitive therapy was given in addition to drug therapy.

Conclusions Although it would seem logical that two treatments are better than one, the evidence does not show any better outcomes for patients offered combined therapy as opposed to only drug therapy, showing the effectiveness of drug therapy on depression.

Check your understanding

1   What method did Karp and Frank use?

2   How do Karp and Frank conclude that drug therapy is effective for treating depression?

3.3 Cognitive

Based on his cognitive theory, Ellis (1991) identified the ABCs of rational emotive therapy:

◆   the **A**s are the activating events that contribute to someone's psychological disturbance. This might be failing an exam, or being criticised by someone

◆   the **B**s are the beliefs, so if you think you are stupid because you fail an exam, or if you think no one loves you because you are criticised, these beliefs will influence your psychological well-being

◆   the **C**s are the consequences, which are what happen if you have these faulty and illogical beliefs. Failing one exam does not mean you are stupid; however, if you think it does, this will influence the way you think and feel about yourself, however illogical those thoughts and feelings are.

Ellis carried out various studies to show the effectiveness of his therapy. One of the first was in 1957; his clients were a mixed group, diagnosed as neurotic or borderline psychotic, each of whom had remained in treatment for at least ten sessions. Ellis's global rating of 'little or no', 'some distinct', or 'considerable' improvement, made when each case was closed, suggested significantly more favourable results with RET than with other treatments. Nearly half (44 per cent) of the RET cases showed considerable improvement, compared to 18 per cent for analytically oriented therapy and 13 per cent for analysis. However, it might not be suitable for every person or every disorder; patients are individuals and may respond more to one therapy than another. Also of relevance here is Meichenbaum's Stress Inoculation Therapy, a cognitive treatment for stress (see pages 102–104). Ost and Westling's (1995) research (see pages 130–131) is a more controlled study with self-reports and psychometric testing replacing a subjective 'much improved' diagnosis, making it more objective than Ellis's research. The key study by Beck et al. (1978) compares drug therapy (pharmacotherapy) with cognitive therapy and finds that cognitive therapy leads to better treatment of depression than drug therapy.

Key study

Beck et al., Comparing pharmacotherapy and cognitive therapy

Aim To compare the effectiveness of cognitive therapy and drug therapy.

Methodology Controlled experiment with participants allocated to one of two conditions.

Design Independent design with random allocation to cognitive or drug-therapy conditions.

Participants 44 patients diagnosed with moderate to severe depression attending psychiatric outpatients' clinics.

Procedure Patients assessed with three self-reports before treatment using Beck Depression Inventory, Hamilton Rating Scale and Rasking Scale.

For 12 weeks, patients had either a 1-hour cognitive therapy session twice a week or 100 Imipramine capsules, prescribed by visiting the doctor for 20 minutes once a week.

The cognitive therapy sessions were prescribed and controlled, and therapists were observed to ensure reliability.

Findings Both groups showed significant decrease in depression symptoms on all three rating scales. The cognitive treatment group showed significantly greater improvements on self-reports and observer-based ratings, 78.9 per cent compared with 20 per cent of those with drug therapy.

The drop-out rate was 5 per cent in the cognitive therapy group and 32 per cent in the drug treatment group.

Conclusions Cognitive therapy leads to better treatment of depression, shown by fewer symptoms reported and observed, and also better adherence to treatment.

Check your understanding

Make a list of the strengths and weaknesses of each of the treatments.

Take it further

Try to find similarities between the treatments. You might consider what they are trying to achieve with treatment. Is there any kind of responsibility on the part of the patient? Consider how the approach each treatment adopts might limit the effectiveness of the treatment.

Section summary

◆ The treatments of dysfunctional behaviour are not limited to those in this text; there are other approaches beyond the specification, such as humanistic client-centred therapy and psychodynamic therapies. Who can forget Freud's case study of Little Hans (1909) in the AS course?

◆ Within the approaches that have been covered, there are many more treatments, for example there are biological treatments such as electroconvulsive therapy.

◆ Similarly there are many therapeutic techniques based on the assumptions of operant conditioning, such as token economies, and on classical conditioning, such as flooding, in addition to McGrath's systematic desensitisation described on page 119.

U3
2

Disorders

The first part of the specification requires you to look at the different characteristics of three categories of disorders:

◆ affective, e.g. depression, bipolar, cyclothymic disorder

◆ anxiety, e.g. phobias, post-traumatic stress disorders, obsessive-compulsive disorder

◆ psychotic, e.g. schizophrenia, delusional disorder, substance-induced psychotic disorder.

The second and third parts ask you to investigate one disorder from one of these categories, and study in more detail different explanations and treatments for your chosen disorder. This allows you to gain some in-depth knowledge on an area of dysfunctional behaviour that interests you.

This area of the course describes:

◆ explanations and treatments of one anxiety disorder – phobia

◆ explanations and treatments of one affective disorder – depression

◆ explanations and treatments of one psychotic disorder – schizophrenia.

Remember that you need to know the characteristics of all three types of disorder, but the explanations and treatments of only one disorder, such as one affective disorder or one anxiety disorder or one psychotic disorder. You do not have to choose one of the disorders described in this textbook if there is another disorder that you find fascinating.

Themes and perspectives

It is important to remember that no single approach can hold the whole explanation for human behaviour, so a combination of two or even three approaches is sometimes seen as more effective. This means that the debate of reductionism and to some extent determinism can be applied to this topic. The biological and cognitive approaches and the behavioural perspective have assumptions about the causes of human behaviour, including dysfunctional behaviour. These might be the learning associated with the behaviourist perspective or the physical explanation adopted by the biological approach. Cognitive psychology is much more concerned with individuals' thought processes and how these might lead to distorted thinking associated with dysfunctional behaviour. The emphasis of the biological approach on nature and the behaviourist emphasis on nurture make the nature–nurture debate fundamental in discussing dysfunctional behaviour.

Treatment has to be considered ethically. An individual may not want to be treated – they may feel there is nothing wrong with them – and this brings into question society's right to be protected versus the individual's right the to choose their treatment. The other ethical consideration that researchers have to take into account is that if one treatment is shown to be more effective than another, the control group should be offered the effective treatment. Often it is randomly decided who gets the effective treatment, and the other participants have the right to benefit from a proven effective therapy.

Weblinks

Information is available to support people with the disorders discussed in this section (see Contents page).

1 Characteristics of disorders

For the purposes of this specification the distinctions between anxiety, affective and psychotic disorders will be made in a general way, but with an understanding that there is a variety of disorders in each category and individual differences in the way people may display symptoms.

It is important to note that the following criteria are summaries from lengthy diagnostic tools and should in no way be used to try and diagnose anyone. If you have concerns about a person's behaviour, don't try an amateur psychiatric diagnosis, but seek help from someone who is qualified to help, or who can put you in touch with a qualified practitioner.

Anxiety disorders

Anxiety disorders give a continuous feeling of fear and anxiety which is disabling and can impose on daily functioning. They can be triggered by something that may seem trivial to others; they may even be triggered by non-existent threats that nevertheless seem very real to the person. In the UK in 2000 the Office of National Statistics reported that 1 adult in 6 in the UK had a neurotic disorder such as anxiety or depression, which are probably the most common disorders diagnosed in this country, and 1 in 200 had a psychotic disorder such as schizophrenia.

Try this …

Think about a time when you were really worried about something. It might have been your driving test, exams, or a new job. How did you feel just before you began? Can you explain this in terms of the physiological stress reaction?

Anxiety disorders encompass many different disorders, including panic disorder, phobias, post-traumatic stress disorder, and generalised anxiety disorders. The example used here is phobias.

An anxiety disorder – phobia

Phobias essentially have a definite, *persistent* fear of a particular object or situation. This stimulus, for example a dog, snake or bird, will provoke an immediate response, which may be similar to a panic attack. The person may experience physical symptoms such as shortness of breath or palpitations, and will feel intense terror and may begin to lose control. The person with the phobia realises that these fears are irrational, the response far outweighing any realistic consequences of being in the situation. Even this response is not sufficient to be diagnosed with a specific phobic disorder, but if the fear of the object results in a person's everyday life being disrupted, for example taking a long detour to avoid a dog, the disorder may be diagnosed.

DSM-IV classification for specific phobia
(Reprinted with permission from *The Diagnostic and Statistical Manual of Mental Disorders*, Text Revision, Fourth Edition (Copyright 2000). American Psychiatric Association)

- marked and persistent fear that is excessive or unreasonable
- exposure to phobic stimulus provokes immediate anxiety response
- the person recognises the fear as excessive
- the phobic situation is avoided
- the phobia disrupts the person's normal life
- the phobia has lasted more than 6 months in people under 18 years of age.

ICD-10 classification for specific phobia (World Health Organisation 2005)

- the psychological or autonomic symptoms must be primary manifestations of anxiety, and not secondary to other symptoms such as delusion
- the anxiety must be restricted to the presence of the particular phobic object or situation
- the phobic situation is avoided wherever possible.

Affective disorders

We all have different moods; sometimes we are happy and sometimes sad, and these are natural responses to events in our lives. However, you will see that the characteristics of mood or affective disorders are disabling moods. This means that the disorder prevents the individual from leading a normal life, at work, socially or within their family, which would cause them to be diagnosed with depression or bipolar disorder.

Try this …

1   What effect do you think the weather has on your moods? If you wake up and it is a bright sunny day, do you feel better or worse than on a grey rainy day? Does it make no difference?

2   If dysfunctional behaviour is a continuum, what do you think are the characteristics of someone who is abnormally happy or someone who is abnormally sad?

In affective disorders a person's fundamental mood is changed, usually to depression but sometimes to elation (mania). Affective disorders are sometimes known as mood disorders. Bipolar is a fairly well-known disorder where moods fluctuate between manic episodes and depressive episodes, or mixed episodes with features of both. These episodes are normally separated by periods of normality, but some patients experience rapid cycling, where depression and mania rapidly alternate. Bipolar is thought to be severe, but less severe disorders still cause distress, though they are seen as more long-term. Dysthymia is a mood disorder that is not considered to be as severe as major depression, but can be thought of as chronic depression. The symptoms include those of depression, such as poor appetite or overeating, insomnia or hypersomnia, low energy or fatigue, low self-esteem, poor concentration or difficulty making decisions, and feelings of hopelessness, but they must have been present for at least 2 years. Cyclothymia is a milder form of bipolar disorder. Its characteristics are a variation between hypomania and dysthymic mood. Just one experience of hypomania may be enough to diagnose cyclothymic disorder. Hypomania is where a person's mood is persistently elated or irritable, to an extent that prevents normal functioning. It is not the same as the manic episodes in bipolar disorder, as psychotic symptoms are absent.

An affective disorder – depression

Depression is more than just feeling 'down', although it can be seen as a continuum with patients having some or all of the symptoms to a greater or lesser degree. Common symptoms are reduced concentration, lack of self-esteem, pessimism, disturbed sleeping and eating habits, and sometimes ideas of self-harm. A general loss of interest and increased tiredness are the most typical symptoms and patients may complain of 'feeling nothing'. Sometimes, particularly in children, irritability rather than a sad mood is seen.

DSM-IV classification of single-episode depression
(Reprinted with permission from *The Diagnostic and Statistical Manual of Mental Disorders*, Text Revision, Fourth Edition (Copyright 2000). American Psychiatric Association)

Five or more of the following symptoms:

◆ insomnia most nights
◆ fidgeting or lethargy

◆ tiredness
◆ feelings of worthlessness or guilt
◆ less ability to concentrate
◆ recurrent thoughts of death.

The symptoms are not caused by medication, or situations such as recent bereavement, and they are enough to hinder the person from important day-to-day activities.

ICD-10 classification of depression

◆ depressed mood
◆ loss of interest and enjoyment
◆ reduced energy.

Other common symptoms are:

◆ marked tiredness after only slight effort
◆ reduced concentration and attention
◆ reduced self-esteem and self-confidence
◆ ideas of guilt and unworthiness
◆ bleak and pessimistic views of the future
◆ ideas or acts of self-harm or suicide
◆ disturbed sleep
◆ reduced appetite.

Psychotic disorders

Try this …

Get one friend to whisper a long story in your ear and try to tell another friend what you did at the weekend. How difficult is it to maintain logical thought processes while hearing something different?

Psychosis is the general term for disorders that involve a loss of contact with reality. It covers many disorders, which may involve delusions (hallucinations that cause a person to lose their sense of what is really happening in their life). Understandably it can lead to withdrawal from the outside world as the person becomes more confused and disorientated. Psychoses are treatable, mostly using drug therapy, but other therapies have their role to play in helping the patient, which can allow them to continue to lead a normal life. There is evidence that shows a relationship between the increase in psychotic disorders and increase in substance abuse. Research published in the *Lancet* in 2007 reviewed 35 studies into the link between recreational drug use and schizophrenia, and found that any use of cannabis increased the risk of a psychotic disorder (Moore et al., 2007). However, there are many other explanations from the psychological approaches that will be considered later. And of course in psychology we investigate trends in behaviour, not certainties, so while it is true to say that you have an increased likelihood of developing a psychotic disorder if you use recreational drugs, there is no certainty that you will, and likewise, a person can suffer from schizophrenia without ever using drugs. Human behaviour is too complicated to attribute behaviour to one single cause.

Psychotic disorders tend to be characterised by delusions and disorganised speech or behaviour. They include all types of schizophrenia, as well as schizoaffective disorders and brief psychotic disorders. Symptoms tend to be both positive, with behaviours such as distortions in thinking, and negative, where normal behaviours are missing, such as emotional reactions or fluent speech.

A psychotic disorder – schizophrenia

Schizophrenia has positive and negative symptoms. Positive symptoms include delusions, auditory hallucinations (hearing voices) and thought disorder. This is where there is an underlying problem with conscious thought that has an effect on a person's language. Negative symptoms are so named because they are considered to be the loss or absence of normal characteristics such as losing emotional responses, inability to feel pleasure when nice things happen, and a lack of motivation. There is often a disorganised aspect to a person's behaviour, shown in chaotic speech or actions.

***DSM-IV* classification of schizophrenia** (Reprinted with permission from *The Diagnostic and Statistical Manual of Mental Disorders*, Text Revision, Fourth Edition (Copyright 2000). American Psychiatric Association)

Two or more of the following:

- delusions
- hallucinations
- disorganised speech
- disorganised behaviour
- negative symptoms.

Plus:

- social occupational dysfunction
- at least 6 months' duration
- no other explanation can be found, such as medication or developmental disorders.

ICD-10 classification of schizophrenia

- thought echo, thought insertion or withdrawal, and broadcasting
- delusions of control
- hallucinatory voices
- persistent delusions
- persistent hallucinations
- incoherence or irrelevant speech
- catatonic behaviour
- negative symptoms such as marked apathy
- a significant and consistent in the overall quality of some aspects of personal behaviour.

Check your understanding

List as many of the key symptoms of each disorder as you can. Check back to the lists to see how many you got right.

Section summary

- The *DSM* and *ICD* (see pages 110–111) have shown how the characteristics of disorders are identified and categorised, so it is fairly easy to see the characteristics of each type of disorder.

- What is also clear is that there is room for misdiagnosis, as some people may not show all of the characteristics, or may show some to a greater or lesser degree.

- Diagnosis is not simply a checklist of disorders to be ticked against a patient's symptoms.

- There is room for disagreement; biases by cultures or practitioners may unwittingly lead to misdiagnosis or even a diagnosis where there should not be one.

The specification for this section states that exam candidates should know the characteristics of an anxiety disorder, an affective disorder and a psychotic disorder. These have been covered above. The second part of this section allows candidates (or their teachers) to choose one disorder type to study in depth. Again this can be one affective (such as depression), one anxiety (such as phobia) or one psychotic (such as schizophrenia). What follows are the behavioural, biological and cognitive explanations for one anxiety disorder (phobia), one affective disorder (depression) and one psychotic disorder (schizophrenia) and the treatment of the disorders based on the three approaches.

2 Explanations of an anxiety disorder – phobia

2.1 Behavioural explanation

You will have seen from Watson and Raynor's study (pages 115–116) that one behaviourist explanation for phobias is that of classical conditioning. Operant conditioning also provides a possible explanation for the acquisition and reinforcement of a phobic behaviour. If someone is rewarded (reinforced) for showing a phobic reaction, this could perpetuate the behaviour. Imagine that you are a child in bed at night and you hear thunder, you run to your parents' bed where it is warm and comforting. Next time you hear the thunder, what are you going to do? Stay in bed where it is lonely or go to the comfort of your parents' bed? By now you have discovered that you will get lots of cuddles if you are frightened of thunder, and so continue to show this fear every time you hear thunder. This behaviour becomes so entrenched that the fear reaction becomes an automatic response to thunder, and by definition the response is unreasonable. It might also be linked to imitating a role model, and research by Bandura and Rosenthal (1966) found that humans would develop a fear reaction to a buzzer if they witnessed a person showing pain when the buzzer sounded. The research used a stooge or confederate who was an accomplice of the researcher and was pretending to be shocked when the buzzer sounded.

Key study

Watson and Raynor, Conditioned emotional reaction

For full details of this study, see pages 115–116. In summary, the study found that Albert, a boy of 11

months, was conditioned to have a phobia of rats by pairing the rat with a loud noise. This fear was then transferred to other white fluffy objects such as a rabbit and a Santa Claus mask.

Check your understanding

1   Which theory was Watson trying to support?

2   What was Albert's initial reaction to the rat?

3   How did Watson and Raynor condition Albert's fear of the rat?

2.2 Biological explanation

The biological approach also looks at generalised anxiety disorders, but does consider humans' biological preparedness to acquire phobias of some things more readily than others. For example a phobia of snakes is easier to acquire than a phobia of something like grass. This is because we have evolved with a fear of things that could harm us, like snakes, darkness and water, but we do not have an inherited tendency to fear flowers, or houses. A person who had a fear of snakes may have been more likely to avoid dangerous snakes and therefore survive to pass on this fear in their genes, whereas a person with no fear of snakes would be more likely to be bitten, die and so not pass on their genes. This is a simplified evolutionary theory, where behaviours that aid survival tend to evolve over time as people with this behaviour in their genes survive and those without it die out. Ohman et al. (1975) set out to show in their research how it is easier to induce phobias of snakes than of non-threatening items such as faces or houses.

Key study

Ohman et al., Types of phobia and biological predisposition to them

Aim To see if phobias of snakes could be more easily conditioned than phobias of faces or houses, indicating a biological preparedness to develop phobias of certain objects.

Methodology Laboratory experiment, with participants linked to a machine that would present pictures and deliver shocks after some of them. Their fear reaction was measured by skin conductance.

Figure 2.10 A fear of snakes is likely to be genetically inherited

Participants 64 paid volunteers aged 20–30 years. There were 38 females and 26 males and they were all psychology students from the University of Uppsala in Sweden.

Design An independent design with participants being in one of three conditions. Electric shocks were given after presentation of snakes, houses or faces.

Procedure Each participant was wired up to a machine that would measure skin conductance. They were given a shock at a level that they as an individual rated as definitely uncomfortable but not painful. Pictures were presented on coloured slides for 8 seconds and if a shock was going to be given it occurred immediately as the picture was shown. Participants were seated comfortably and told that they would experience a number of shocks and see three different types of pictures: snakes, human faces and houses. The order of the pictures was randomised. Half of the participants received shocks after the snakes, a quarter received shocks after pictures of houses and a quarter received shocks after pictures of human faces.

Findings All participants had a similar measure of skin conductance prior to the unconditioned stimulus (shock) being shown.

Participants shocked after they were shown pictures of snakes had on average 0.062 conductance to the snakes and 0.048 conductance to the houses and faces. The higher the conductance the more they were sweating, which is a physiological response to fear.

The control groups who were shocked after faces or houses showed only 0.037 conductance to their conditioned stimuli (houses or faces) and 0.030 to the neutral stimuli that did not appear with shocks.

NB The unit of measurement was micro mhos, a measure of conductance of electricity.

Conclusion Participants were more likely to show fear reactions to snakes than houses or faces, so this shows a biological preparedness to develop phobias to objects that may cause us danger, such as snakes.

> ### Check your understanding
>
> 1   What were the three conditions in this study?
>
> 2   Which was the object that humans are believed to be biologically programmed to fear?
>
> 3   How did the researchers measure the fear reaction?

2.3 Cognitive explanation

The cognitive approach is less specifically concerned with phobias and more with generalised anxiety disorders. Beck's (1941) study into generalised fears does discuss whether his patients could be seen as suffering from phobias. However, they tend not to meet the *DSM* criteria for phobic reactions, so he considers them as anxiety neuroses. He does acknowledge that fear of heart attacks, of being ignored, or of fainting, could all be considered to be similar to phobias. DiNardo (1998) looks at general anxiety disorder (GAD) and tries to find out if the faulty cognition of 'excessive worry' is linked to anxiety. The cognition is faulty because it is excessive. Being worried about something that is threatening or challenging is perfectly normal, but when the worry becomes out of proportion to the threat, anxiety disorder may be diagnosed.

Key study

DiNardo, Generalised anxiety disorder

Aim To assess whether 'excessive worry' is a symptom of GAD.

Methodology Quasi-experiment covering patients attending one of three clinics in the USA.

Design Independent design of patients with and without diagnoses of GAD, so a quasi-experiment as they were not allocated to groups.

Procedure Patients were interviewed twice to assess reliability using two different structured interviews. Interviews used were the Anxiety Disorders Interview Schedule or the Structured Clinical Interview for *DSM-IV-R*. A five-point rating scale for symptoms such as sweating, difficulty in sleeping and excessive worry was used. The frequency of the symptom 'excessive worry' was analysed and the percentage of the day for which each patient said they displayed this symptom.

Findings Significantly more patients with GAD reported excessive worry than non-patients. More patients without GAD reported no excessive worry. Patients with GAD reported excessive worry for 59.1 per cent of the day compared with 41.7 per cent for non-GAD patients.

Conclusion Excessive worry, which indicates faulty thinking as it is excessive, is found in more GAD patients and its absence can be used to rule out a diagnosis of GAD. Patients with GAD spend more time each day worrying.

Check your understanding

Imagine you are a doctor and you are trying to explain to someone why they might have a phobia. Which explanations would you use? Is there anything you would leave out?

Section summary

- As you can see from the evidence described, there are different approaches to explaining anxiety disorders.

- Each approach has some relevance to our understanding.

- It might be more useful to adopt an eclectic approach and use parts of each of these theories to fully understand phobias.

- There are different explanations for any one disorder, and there are also many other explanations not covered here.

- Psychodynamic or social psychologists may have other explanations.

- Within approaches such as the biological approach there are lots of different genetic, chromosomal, neurochemical, and structural explanations.

- All of the explanations have their strengths and weaknesses, some may be better at explaining some disorders than others.

- It is important to realise that human behaviour, including dysfunctional behaviour, has many causes, some of which we have still to identify.

3 Treatments for an anxiety disorder – phobia

Treatment of disorders is a contentious issue in that different psychologists define treatment differently. Is treatment a cure for the mental illness, or management of symptoms to enable a person to live a relatively normal life? The different approaches will take different views, with biologists trying to manage symptoms through physical measures, behaviourists suggesting re-learning learnt behaviour and thereby curing the symptoms, with no concern as to the cause in the first place, and cognitive behavioural therapists trying to cure by restructuring the patient's thinking.

The way the approach explains a disorder will logically lead to the treatment. Each treatment will have its strengths and weaknesses in terms of effectiveness and appropriateness. The ethical implications of treatments also need to be considered. You can then consider the psychological issues such as reductionism in connection with these treatments, which may highlight some of the limitations of any one approach on its own.

What makes a person 'cured' of a phobia? One patient might say that not suffering from the phobia at all is the only cure, others might say that they have learnt to cope with the reaction and handle situations much better and that this is a cure. Other psychologists might think that counselling may help, or that psychodynamic therapies that uncover unconscious issues are needed. This section will look at the three approaches that have been used throughout this area of the course, and at the evidence used to support their treatments of anxiety disorders.

3.1 Behavioural treatments

Try this …

Using classical conditioning, how would you explain a fear of flying in a person who had had to make a crash landing in a plane?

Can you think of a stimulus that would make a person relax and so could be used to help them re-learn their fearful response to planes?

Behaviourists would suggest that treatment should consist of un-learning behaviours, and in the case of phobias this involves classical conditioning. This can be used to pair two stimuli which together will result in a conditioned response of 'no fear'. One of the problems of this treatment is that the phobic response can be so great that it only strengthens the fear, but generally there is a lot of evidence to suggest that systematic desensitisation works. McGrath's study (see page 119) shows how effective systematic desensitisation can be when used on a girl with a phobia.

Key study

McGrath, Successful treatment of a noise phobia

McGrath's study is detailed on page 119 and shows the effectiveness of using systematic desensitisation as a therapy for treating phobias. This case study showed how a 9-year-old girl who had a noise phobia, ended the therapy able to tolerate and even enjoy the loud noises associated with fireworks and party poppers.

Check your understanding

1   Describe the process of systematic desensitisation as used with Lucy.

2   How did McGrath measure the effectiveness of the therapy?

3.2 Biological treatments

Biological treatments are often the first treatment offered for dysfunctional behaviour. This is mainly because a diagnosis is, more often than not, made by a medical practitioner, and the medical approach would support the use of drug therapy. One of the benefits of psychopharmocotherapy, as drug treatments are known, is the speed of the effect, with some drugs have almost instantaneous results and others taking a couple of weeks to bring about a reduction in symptoms. However, other treatments are now used to supplement the biological therapy and a treatment such as cognitive therapy can bring about a longer-lasting change, and without the side effects which drug therapy may incur. Phobias are less likely to be treated with drugs, but Leibowitz's research (1988) showed how some drugs, in this case phenelzine, did help reduce the symptoms of social phobia, and his use of a placebo group and control group given another drug, showed that the phenelzine was the real cause of the benefits seen in the patients.

Key study

Leibowitz, Treatment of social phobia with phenelzine

Aim To see if the drug phenelzine can help treat patients with social phobia.

Methodology A controlled experiment where patients were allocated to one of three conditions and treated over 8 weeks. They were assessed for social phobia on several tests such as Hamilton Rating Scale for Anxiety and the Liebowitz Social Phobia Scale. The latter had common manifestations of social phobia and patients rated 1–4 for the fear produced and 1–4 for the steps taken to avoid the phobic situation.

Participants 80 patients aged 18–50 years meeting *DSM* criteria for social phobia. They were medically healthy and had not received phenelzine for at least 2 weeks before the trial. Each was assessed to see that there were no other disorders and signed consent forms before the research.

Design An independent design with patients being allocated randomly to one of four groups. One group was treated with phenelzine, and one control group was given a matching placebo. A second treatment group was given atenolol and another placebo group was given a matching placebo.

Procedure Patients were assessed at the beginning, and then given their drug or placebo, with gradual increases in dosage of phenelzine or atenolol in the treatment groups. Each patient was then reassessed using the Hamilton Rating Scale for Anxiety and the Liebowitz Social Phobia Scale. Independent evaluators were used to carry out clinical assessments in a double-blind situation.

Findings After 8 weeks significant differences were noted for the phenelzine groups, with better scores on the tests for anxiety compared with the placebo groups. There was no significant difference between the patients taking atenolol and the placebo.

Conclusions Phenelzine but not atenolol is effective in treating social phobia after 8 weeks of treatment.

Check your understanding

1. Why did Leibowitz use a placebo group?
2. How was the patient's phobic reaction assessed?
3. How long did the study last?

3.3 Cognitive treatments

Key study

Ost and Westling, Treating panic attacks

Cognitive behavioural therapy (CBT) uses the cognitive approach to restructuring cognitions but also has aspects of behaviourism. In Ost and Westling's research (1995), relaxation is taught in order to reduce the panic brought about by faulty interpretation of body symptoms.

Aim To compare cognitive behavioural therapy with applied relaxation as therapies for panic disorder.

Methodology A longitudinal study with patients undergoing therapy for panic disorder.

Participants Thirty-eight patients with *DSM* diagnosis of panic disorder, with or without agoraphobia, recruited through referrals from psychiatrists and newspaper advertisements. Twenty-six females and 12 males, mean age 32.6 years (range 23–45 years), from a variety of occupations and some married, some single and some divorced.

Design Independent designs with patients being randomly assigned to either cognitive therapy or applied relaxation.

Procedure Pre-treatment baseline assessments of panic attacks, using a variety of questionnaires, for example Panic Attack Scale, Agoraphobic Cognitions Questionnaire. Patients recorded in a diary the date and situation for every panic attack. Each patient was then given 12 weeks of treatment of 50–60 minutes, with homework to carry out between appointments.

Applied relaxation was used to identify what caused panic attacks, and then relaxation training started with tension-release of muscles. This was gradually increased so that by session 8 rapid relaxation was used and patents practised their techniques in stressful situations.

Cognitive therapy was first used to identify the misinterpretation of body symptoms and then to generate an alternative cognition in response, so that participants would not feel panic when something happened, but come up with an alternative explanation: for example, my heart racing is not a heart attack but a normal physical reaction to stress and it will slow down in a minute. This was then tested in situations where participants had panic attacks induced and were not allowed to avoid them, so that eventually they had to accept that their restructured thoughts were right.

Patients were then reassessed on the questionnaires. After 1 year a follow-up assessment using the questionnaires was carried out.

Findings Cognitive behavioural therapy showed 74 per cent panic-free patients after the treatment and 89 per cent panic free after 1 year.

Applied relaxation showed 65 per cent panic-free patients after the treatment and 82 per cent panic free after 1 year.

Complications such as generalised anxiety and depression were also reduced to within the normal range after one year.

Conclusions Both cognitive therapy and applied relaxation worked at reducing panic attacks, but it is difficult to rule out some cognitive changes in the applied relaxation group, even though this is not focused on in this research.

Check your understanding

1   Who were the participants in Ost and Westling's research?

2   How were the patients assessed before treatment?

3   How did Ost and Westling gather their data?

4   Which group had the highest drop-out rate?

Section summary

◈   Treating phobic disorders is a complex process. There are many aspects of a person's situation to consider.

◈   Some treatments such as drug treatments might be suggested as they have a far more immediate effect on behaviour, but may be recommended in conjunction with cognitive therapy to ensure that the patient changes their cognitions to prevent the disorder returning.

◈   Each one of these approaches, except perhaps the CBT, adopts a reductionist approach in keeping with their assumptions about behaviour, reducing their explanation down to one factor, and treating that one factor.

◈   While we cannot deny that the treatment of disorders has come a long way since the Middle Ages, it is clear that there is still some way to go to ensure that effective treatment is available for everyone with a disorder.

◈   None of these researchers is claiming a 100 per cent success rate, and so the final treatment regimen must still be left to qualified practitioners to decide the best way to help patients with a mental disorder.

4 Explanations of an affective disorder – depression

4.1 Behavioural explanation

The behavioural explanation would suggest that affective disorders are learnt through operant or classical conditioning. Classical conditioning would suggest that we make associations between events or circumstances and mood change, and this leads to learned behaviour which is then diagnosed as depression. Operant conditioning on the other hand would suggest that a lack of positive reinforcement is directly linked with depression. This is explained by Lewinsohn et al. (1975), who suggest that if people lose the positive reinforcement for living normally, that is, going to work, being at college, they may become depressed. For example, many people ask how you are getting on when you start a new job or new school, or have some other major life event, but then do not ask once the novelty of the situation has worn off. Lack of positive feedback can lead to depression, which makes a person less likely to perform well and so reduce the positive feedback even more. It becomes a vicious circle.

U3

2

Key study

Lewinsohn et al., A behavioural approach to depression

Aim To compare the amount of 'positive reinforcement' received by depressed and non-depressed participants.

Method A longitudinal study over 30 days where participants completed a self-report of pleasant activities on the pleasant events schedule, and a self-rating of depression using the depression adjective checklist. This research operationalises positive reinforcement as taking part in pleasant activities.

Participants Thirty participants who were diagnosed with depression, a disorder other than depression and 'normal' controls.

Design Independent design.

Method A quasi-experiment as the independent variable was naturally occurring and therefore not manipulated by the researchers.

Participants were asked to check their mood daily using the depression adjective checklist which included emotions such as happy, active, blue and lucky. The participants ticked the ones they felt that day. Then they were asked to complete the pleasant activities scale rating 320 activities such as talking about sports, meditating or doing yoga. These were rated twice on a scale of three, once for pleasantness, once for frequency. This was seen as positive reinforcement.

Findings There were significant positive correlations between mood ratings and pleasant activities, with involvement in more pleasant activities being correlated with more positive mood ratings.

There were individual differences, from a correlation of 0 to –0.66, which shows that there is more to depression than reinforcement from pleasant activities.

Conclusion There appears to be a link between reinforcement from pleasant activities and mood, but further research is needed to identify the individual characteristics that make some people more influenced by pleasant activities than others.

> **Check your understanding**
>
> 1   What were the three conditions in this study?
>
> 2   How did patients assess their mood?
>
> 3   What was positively correlated with mood ratings?

4.2 Biological explanation

The biological approach to depression suggests that a genetic disposition towards depression may explain why depression can be found in more than one member of some families. It is of course reductionist to assume that genetics is the only explanation, since family groups may have the same socio-economic problems, which could be linked with depression, or the social learning theory could explain the tendency to copy role models.

Some people experience life events that are enough to trigger depression in people who have no relatives with depression. What we do know is that there is a clear link with neurochemicals and depression, serotonin levels are lower in people diagnosed with depression, but we do not know whether the depression reduces the serotonin or the low serotonin causes depression, or even if there is a third factor, which causes both. Wender et al.'s research (1986) into adopted individuals with affective disorders assumes that a genetic link

between family members will increase the tendency to depression. This study is similar to the study by Oruc et al. (1988) mentioned on the specification.

> **Key study**
>
> Wender et al., Psychiatric disorders in biological and adoptive families
>
> **Aim** To investigate the contribution of genetic and environmental factors in the aetiology of mood disorders.
>
> **Participants** Adoptive and biological relatives of 71 adult adoptees, with a mean age of 43.7, who had a mood disorder, plus 71 adult adoptees with a mean age of 44, who were psychiatrically normal. The adults had been removed from their mother at an early age.
>
> **Methodology** Psychiatric evaluations of the relatives were made by independent blind diagnoses of mental hospital and other official records.
>
> **Results** There was an eight-fold increase in unipolar depression among the biological relatives of the index cases and a 15-fold increase in suicide among the biological relatives of the index cases.
>
> **Conclusions** There is a significant genetic link between unipolar depression and suicide.

> **Check your understanding**
>
> 1   How did Wender et al. gather the data for this study?
>
> 2   What was the increase in unipolar depression amongst biological families?

> **Key term**
>
> index case the documented case of a disease included in a study

4.3 Cognitive explanation

The cognitive approach, again using Beck's theory (1967) would explain depression as a result of faulty thinking. His research (1961) shows the faulty thinking of people with depression and how the cognitive approach explains the acquisition of faulty thinking. What makes this difficult to understand is the fact that the patients, even in the face of irrefutable evidence and experience, still persist in these illogical depressive thoughts. There are often times when we feel that we are hopeless at something, maybe after a bad driving lesson, or a poor mark in an essay, but given that we have had better driving lessons, and better essays, we can think logically that we are not useless. However, with an illness such as depression, this is not the case. Seligman originally looked at how dogs could learn quickly, through classical conditioning, that they could not escape an electric shock to their feet. He then noticed that despite being able to escape the dogs did not bother to try, and if they did escape this did not 'teach' them to escape the next time. He found that his theory of learned helplessness could explain depression in humans.

Key study

Seligman, The learned helplessness model of depression

Summary of theory

The original learned helplessness model of depression was based on animal learning studies. Seligman found that dogs given an electric shock which they could not escape would show learned behaviours 24 hours later. These behaviours included not trying to escape, not following one escape with another and passively enduring the shocks. He concluded that the dogs learned that their responses and the outcomes were not related so did not bother to respond to the shocks by trying to escape. If the outcomes of their behaviour are uncontrollable, dogs will give up trying.

Seligman related this to depression in humans. The core depressive symptom is the expectation that whatever you do, nothing will change. This is learned helplessness. He looked at symptoms of depression and the symptoms of learned helplessness and found several similarities. These included: passivity; lowered aggression; loss of appetite; feelings of helplessness; negative expectations; depletion of chemicals such as catecholamine.

He also found that the causes, uncontrollable negative events, were the same and that successful therapies were the same. These included: electroconvulsive shock therapy and antidepressant drugs. He concluded therefore that depression could be seen as a manifestation of learned helplessness.

Check your understanding

1 What species was Seligman's original research carried out on?

2 What is the core cognition in depression which Seligman says mirrors learned helplessness?

3 What are the similarities between learned helplessness and depression?

Try this ...

Imagine you are a doctor and you are trying to explain to someone why they might have depression. Which explanations would you use? Is there anything you would leave out?

Section summary

◆ As you can see from the evidence described, there are different approaches to explaining affective disorders.

◆ Each approach has some relevance to our understanding.

◆ It might be more useful to adopt an eclectic approach and use parts of each of these theories to fully understand phobias.

◆ There are different explanations for any one disorder, and there are also many other explanations not covered here.

◆ Psychodynamic or social psychologists may have other explanations.

◆ Within approaches such as the biological approach there are a lot of different genetic, chromosomal, neurochemical and structural explanations.

◆ All of the explanations have their strengths and weaknesses, some may be better at explaining some disorders than others.

◆ It is important to realise that human behaviour, including dysfunctional behaviour, has many causes, some of which we have still to identify.

5 Treatments for an affective disorder – depression

Treatment of disorders is a contentious issue in that different psychologists define treatment differently. Is treatment a cure for the mental illness, or management of symptoms to enable a person to live a relatively normal life? The different approaches will take different views, with biologists trying to manage symptoms through physical measures, behaviourists unlearning learned behaviour and thereby curing the symptoms, with no concern as to the cause in the first place, and cognitive behavioural therapists trying to cure by restructuring the patient's thinking. The way the approach explains a disorder will logically lead to the treatment, and each treatment will have its strengths and weaknesses. One might not have a lasting effect on the behavioural change, and also the ethical implications of treatments need to be considered. We can then consider the psychological issues such as reductionism in connection with these treatments, which may highlight some of the limitations of any one approach being used in therapy.

5.1 Behavioural treatments

Behaviourist treatments for depression are based on the assumption that depressed behaviours are learned and therefore can be unlearned. There is some intuitive appeal in this, in that some people may be depressed as they are rewarded for being so by having attention from friends, family and therapists. Expectations of them may be lowered, they may not have to work and so there are compelling reasons to maintain the depressed behaviour. The treatment therefore has to teach patients that they will be reinforced for non-depressive behaviours. Lewinsohn's research (1990) shows how, having been taught skill to reduce depression, adolescents showed some improvement but, more importantly, if their parents had been taught to reinforce the non-depressive behaviours their depression was lowered even further. This shows how behaviourist techniques can enhance the success of cognitive techniques when the two are used in combination.

Aim To evaluate the efficacy of a 'coping with depression' course

Methodology A longitudinal study of adolescents aged 15–18 with depression, who were assessed by interview on several depression measures, such as Beck's Depression Inventory.

Participants Sixty-nine adolescents with diagnoses of depression, recruited via letters and announcements to schools, media and doctors. They were from two areas of Oregon. All treatments such as drug therapy had to be stopped before they could take part; 10 withdrew so data were available for 59.

Design Independent design, as patients were randomly assigned to one of three groups. In Group 1 only the adolescent received the course, in Group 2 the adolescent received the course and the parents enrolled in a separate parents' group, and in Group 3, a control group, patients were told they were on the waiting list.

Procedure Participants were assessed by interviews before the treatment started, when it finished and then 1, 6, 12 and 24 months after the treatment finished.

Participants on the waiting list were told that they were on the waiting list and offered other treatment regimes if they felt they could not wait. They were given the treatment at the end of the study.

Treatment was controlled by having detailed manuals for the therapists, with homework and handouts for participants.

Parents were taught how to reinforce expected positive changes in their depressed children.

The adolescents in the treatment groups had 14, 2-hour sessions over 7 weeks. During this time they were given skills training. This focused on relaxation methods, controlling irrational and negative thoughts, increasing social skills and increasing pleasant events in their life. It was more based on experiential learning, where participants practised the skills during the therapy session. It also developed conflict resolution skills where participants could improve their communication and problem-solving skills.

Findings At the end of the treatment only 52 per cent of Group 2 met the *DSM* criteria for depression, and only 57 per cent of Group 1 were diagnosed with depression. Group 3 showed very little change with 94.7 per cent still meeting depression criteria.

In the follow-up, the participant numbers dropped (attrition) but across all of the follow-up interviews, the treatment groups continued to show less and less depression.

Conclusions This clearly shows the efficacy of the 'coping with depression' course, which reinforces changes in negative behaviour with rewarding pleasant events, and positive parental reinforcement. Although there is an element of cognitive behavioural therapy in the cognition restructuring, the behavioural reinforcement is an integral part of this treatment.

Check your understanding

1 Who were the participants in this study?

2 How were the parents involved?

3 What skills were the adolescents taught?

4 Which group had less depression at the end of the study?

5.2 Biological treatments

Biological treatments are probably the ones most people will think of when talking about treating depression. Antidepressants vary in their action, but all act upon the neurological system of the body, often varying the amount of neurotransmitters, such as serotonin, lack of which is associated with depression. The effectiveness of these can be tested by research, and in Karp and Frank's review article (1995) they look at evidence which has concentrated on the effectiveness of treatment for depression in women. Their findings show how biological drug treatments are often as effective alone as they are when combined with psychological treatments such as cognitive therapy showing the validity of drug therapy.

Key study

Karp and Frank, Combination therapy and the depressed woman

Aim To compare drug treatment and non-drug treatments for depression.

Methodology A review article of previous research into the effectiveness of single treatments and combined drug and psychotherapeutic treatments of depression.

Participants The research which was reviewed concentrated on women diagnosed with depression. There were nine pieces of research, from 1974 to 1992. In total, 529 women took part in the selected studies.

Design Much of the research used an independent design, with patients either having single drug treatments, single psychological treatment, combined treatments and sometimes placebo groups.

Procedure Depression was analysed using a variety of depression inventories, and patients were tested generally prior to treatment, after treatment and in some cases after a period of time as a follow up. Some health practitioner assessments of symptoms were also used in some of the research.

Findings Many studies found that adding psychological treatments to drug therapy did not increase the effectiveness of the drug therapy. Occasionally studies did show less attrition when combination therapies were used. This means that people were more likely to continue with treatment if cognitive therapy was given in addition to drug therapy.

Conclusions Although it would seem logical that two treatments are better than one, the evidence does not show any better outcomes for patients offered combined therapy as opposed to only drug therapy, showing the effectiveness of drug therapy on depression.

Check your understanding

1 Which method did Karp and Frank use?

2 What particular research did they review?

3 What were their findings about the effectiveness of drug therapy in depression?

5.3 Cognitive treatments

Cognitive treatments for depression are based on the theory of faulty cognitions which underlie the cognitive theory of dysfunctional behaviour. The aim of such therapy is to restructure the thoughts of the patient from irrational thinking to rational thinking, which will enable the patient to perceive their world more positively and more accurately and so reduce the depression or hopelessness. Ellis (1991) and Beck (1967) are the two founders of cognitive psychology and Ellis's theory is explained on page 120. Here his research (1957) compares the effectiveness of rational cognitive therapy with psychoanalysis and psychoanalytically orientated therapy.

theory is explained on page 120.

Key study

Ellis, Outcomes of employing three techniques of psychotherapy

Aim To compare the effectiveness of rational therapy, psychoanalysis and psychoanalytically oriented therapy.

Methodology Review of patients' cases from therapists' notes.

Design Independent design with allocation to one of the three conditons having been previously treated using one of the three therapies.

Participants Seventy-eight patients treated with rational analysis matched with 78 patients treated with psychoanalytically oriented psychotherapy. Another group of 16 patients who had been treated with orthodox psychoanalysis.

Procedure The therapeutic outcomes of the three groups of patients were compared.

Findings The group with the highest improvement rate was the rational psychotherapy group, 90 per cent showing a distinct or considerable improvement. In the psychoanalysis-orientated group this improvement was reduced to 63 per cent and in the orthdox psychoanalysis group only 50 per cent showed distinct or considerable improvement.

The details of the cases showed that each client tended to hold several irrational ideas. The most improvement was shown in people who changed most of these irrational beliefs.

Conclusions Rational cognitive therapy leads to better treatment of depression than psychoanalytically based therapies.

Check your understanding

1   What were the three conditions in this study?

2   Who were the participants?

3   Only one therapist's cases were analysed, why might this be a problem?

Section summary

* Treating affective disorders is a complex process. There are many aspects of a person's situation to consider.

* Some treatments such as drug treatments might be suggested as they have a far more immediate effect on behaviour but may be recommended in conjunction with cognitive therapy to ensure that the patient changes their cognitions to prevent the disorder returning.

* Each one of these approaches adopts a reductionist approach in keeping with their assumptions about behaviour reducing their explanation down to one factor, and treating that one factor.

* The treatment of disorders has come a long way but there is still some way to go to ensure that effective treatment is available for everyone with a disorder.

* None of these researchers is claiming a 100 per cent success rate, and so the final treatment regimen must still be left to qualified practitioners to decide the best way to help patients with a mental disorder.

6 Explanations of a psychotic disorder – schizophrenia

6.1 Behavioural explanation

Behaviourism might be considered one of the least effective explanations for psychotic disorders such as schizophrenia. The idea that people might learn to suffer delusions or hallucinations seems ludicrous, but there is evidence that people with schizophrenia can learn less maladaptive behaviours (Paul and Lentz, 1977). Logically, if people can unlearn behaviours, it might be reasonable to suggest that the behaviours were learned in the first place. Liberman's (1982) study is based on the behaviourists' belief that social skills in people are rewarding, thereby fulfilling a need. As they are rewarded by having affiliative needs for love and esteem met, the social skills will be repeated. In patients diagnosed with schizophrenia there is no reinforcement for showing/developing social skills and so their social skills are not maintained. The resulting behaviours could lead to a diagnosis of a psychotic disorder such as schizophrenia.

U3
2

Liberman, Assessment of social skills

Aim To identify social skills psychotic patients may lack.

Methodology Review of methods of assessing social skills and identifying problems psychotic patients may have in behaving appropriately in social situations, which results in a lack of social reinforcers.

Participants Research which looked at patients with psychotic illnesses such as schizophrenia.

Procedure This review article identified key features of social skills analysis in previous research. Methods include role-playing of social skills, behavioural assessment of observable behaviour, and biological data. The skills are monitored in novel situations to see durability.

Findings Individual schizophrenic patients lack appropriate social learning from past experiences. Institutionalisation can lead to loss of social skills. Excessive anxiety impedes social performance. Cognitive deficits may also lead to faulty perception of other people's actions, or the situation leading to inappropriate social behaviours.

Conclusions Schizophrenic patients lack social skills necessary to function normally. This may be due to factors such as institutionalisation, cognitive deficits or anxiety. But lack of social skills leads to lack of positive reinforcers for socially acceptable behaviour, so abnormal behaviour is maintained.

Check your understanding

1   What did Liberman find out about schizophrenic patients?

2   What does he think contributes to the loss of social skills?

3   What does a lack of social skills lead to?

6.2 Biological explanation

Probably the most common explanation for schizophrenia is a biological one. Of course, this might be because it is seen as a medical condition which requires drug therapy and if we are treating it with drugs there must be a biological cause. The biological explanation on its own seems too simplistic, Gottesman and Shields' (1976) review shows a clear link, but with

concordance rates of only 58 per cent at best, it is clear that their conclusion that genetics plays only a part in explaining schizophrenia is true. Many social theories go hand in hand with the genetic disposition, such as the stress diathesis model, which suggests a disposition that becomes apparent when stressed, or the schizophrenogenic mother, which suggests that a particular personality in a parent is linked with the development of schizophrenia (Fromm-Reichmann, 1948).

Gottesman and Shields, A review of recent adoption twin and family studies of schizophrenia

This research is detailed on pages 116–117. To summarise, Gottesman and Shields found that twin studies showed a higher concordance rate for schizophrenia in identical or monozygotic twins than between non-identical or dizygotic twins. The concordance rate in their own study was 58 per cent in identical twins, compared with 12 per cent in non-identical twins. They concluded that genes play a significant role in the onset of schizophrenia, but that there must also be some interaction with the environment.

Check your understanding

1   What type of studies did Gottesman and Shields review?

2   What is the difference between monozygotic twins and dizygotic twins?

3   What does the higher concordance rate of schizophrenia in monozygotic twins indicate?

6.3 Cognitive explanation

It used to be thought that cognitive psychology with its emphasis on logical thinking would have little to contribute to the understanding and treatment of schizophrenia. However, more recently there has been much research that seems to indicate that people with schizophrenia are in fact being quite logical in light of their experiences, and whilst their cognitions or thoughts might seem bizarre to us, there is some logic in their thinking. Maher (1974) proposes that delusional thinking is a result of perceptual disorder and this is outlined below.

Key study

Maher, Delusional thinking and perceptual disorder

Summary of theory

This theory starts with the basic assumption that when we experience anything that is strange to us, we try to find an explanation for it. Instead of assuming that this process is faulty in people with a psychotic disorder such as schizophrenia, the hypothesis of this theory is that the cognitive processes used to try and explain a delusion in people with schizophrenia are exactly the same as those used by those considered normal.

All of us, when we have a logical explanation for something, feel a sense of relief that we have come up with an explanation. Even if we do not like the explanation it is sometimes better to have one. But if we share our explanations with someone and they do not agree with us, we either feel more special than them as we have access to more information than they do, or we may believe they are lying to us to prevent us from finding out the truth. Either way, this might make us feel separate from, or even superior to them.

We all try to identify a cause of our experience, and if there is no obvious external cause then it is logical to assume invisible causes. This might explain why a person with psychosis develops fears of radio waves, aliens or forces such as the devil, as these could be invisible causes of their experiences. Hearing voices, or feeling they are being watched, might lead a person to blame agencies such as MI5 or the Communist Party for any strange event they experience.

Maher stresses the rationality of these thoughts given the intensity of the experiences the person has. A person with schizophrenia would identify a strange event, then decide that they are worthy of having been chosen to experience it and who is the cause of it.

The patient also has to identify why this should happen to them. Here they might look at guilty secrets from the past, or punishment for some minor indiscretion, which to the outsider only emphasises the apparent illogical thoughts. For example, a person who perhaps feels guilty about childhood shoplifting might assume that they are being punished for this. A person who did not have psychosis might ask 'Who would be hunted by aliens for some minor fault?', but this explanation would seem perfectly logical to some people with psychosis. They may have enemies from the past who they believe would logically be 'out to get them'. On the other hand, the person may have unusually high self-esteem based on previous experiences and feel they have been chosen to save the world from a disaster.

In conclusion, the delusional person is actually experiencing distorted perceptual input which demands an explanation. This explanation may seem far fetched to others, but can be seen to be perfectly logical in relation to the patient.

Maher suggests that elderly people can become paranoid and believe people are plotting against them. This could lead to a diagnosis of psychosis. Figure 2.11 summarises his explanation in a flow chart.

Figure 2.11 A patient may believe that people are plotting against them

If sensory input is impaired in some way, then the patient, quite logically, holds beliefs that are based on the distorted information available to the person.

7 Treatments for a psychotic disorder – schizophrenia

Treatment of disorders depends on how different psychologists define treatment. Treatment might be considered a cure for the mental illness, or management of symptoms to enable a person to live a relatively normal life? Different approaches will take different views, with biologists trying to manage symptoms through physical measures, behaviourists encouraging re-learning learned behaviour and thereby curing the symptoms, with no concern as to the cause. Cognitive therapists try to cure by restructuring the patient's thinking. The way the approach explains a disorder will lead to beliefs about the treatment. Each treatment will have its strengths and weaknesses in terms of effectiveness and appropriateness, such as the duration of its effect on the behavioural change; also the ethical implications of treatments need to be considered. You can then consider the psychological issues such as reductionism in connection with these treatments, which may highlight some of the limitations of any one approach on its own.

7.1 Behavioural treatments

The behaviourist approach clearly identifies the acquisition of behaviour as being learned, either through classical conditioning, where a person associates two stimuli and they end up producing the same response, or through operant conditioning, where rewarding behaviour leads to its repetition. In the explanation for psychotic disorders the behaviourist approach might seem to have little to offer. After all, who would want to repeat psychotic behaviour? However, operant conditioning would argue that reinforcement of social behaviour leads to its repetition, and in the following research Paul and Lentz (1977) show how patients with schizophrenia given reinforcement for socially acceptable behaviour reduce psychotic behaviours.

Key study

Paul and Lentz, Using social learning to facilitate release of institutionalised patients with psychotic disorders

Aim To compare the effectiveness of social learning and milieu therapeutic centres with hospital programmes for treating patients with psychotic disorders.

Methodology A longitudinal study over four and a half years, in clinical units which used one of three treatments: social learning, milieu and usual institutionalised therapies. Patients were assessed through observations, interviews, and rating scales prior to the project, at six-month intervals and prior to release, once released they were also assessed at six-month intervals.

Participants Three groups of chronically institutionalised psychotic patients from four state hospitals in Illinois. Initially there were 84 patients. They had all failed to be placed in care facilities in the community, so were deemed unlikely to be released from their usual institution. As patients died or were released they were replaced with patients from hospitals that were not already in the study.

Design An independent design with one group going to a centre to receive social learning therapy, one group having milieu therapy and one remaining in hospital to receive usual therapy.

Procedure Each patient was assigned to one of three groups. The social learning therapy unit was based on the behaviourist assumptions of operant and classical conditioning. The basic features of token economies were used, with emphasis on stimulus response training and material reinforcement. The total treatment time per week was 85.2 per cent of their available free time.

The milieu therapy was based on the therapeutic community concept where patients were expected to focus on the group with group problem solving, group pressure and interactions between community members. The total treatment time per week for this group was 85.2 per cent of their free time.

The hospital condition was varied as patients were in different, same-sex wards spread across the hospital, but generally had less time for meetings and focused activities, more time eating, and much more unstructured time and drug administration. The total formal treatment time per week was 4.9 per cent of their free time.

Findings At every assessment the social learning programme was more effective, measured by the inpatient assessment battery (IAB) which used three psychometric tests to assess social behaviour and level of functioning.

The milieu programme showed some improvement over the hospital programme. By the end of the study 92.5 per cent of patients from the social learning centre were released, 71 per cent from the milieu centre and 48 per cent from the hospital, all with similar functioning levels.

In all, 10.7 per cent of the social learning programme, 7.1 per cent of the milieu programme and 0 per cent of the hospital programme were released to independent living, the rest into community care accommodation.

Conclusions The social learning programme was more effective than either the milieu programme or the traditional hospital programmes, both for patients in the clinics and when they were released. The similar staffing levels used in both clinics makes social learning more cost effective.

Check your understanding

1   What was the difference between the social learning therapy and the milieu therapy?

2   How was the participants' behaviour assessed?

3   Which group had most releases into the community?

7.2 Biological treatments

The biological explanation is probably the most common explanation for psychotic disorders. It reflects the medical treatment most often associated with controlling psychotic illnesses. It assumes that if a biological problem is the cause of schizophrenia then the best form of treatment is biological. The effectiveness of the treatments really supports the biological approach to this disorder, although there is evidence of the success of other treatments. Perhaps the historical view of biology causing schizophrenia and therefore providing the only treatment is out of date and the success of cognitive and behavioural treatments suggests that there is more to the disorder than biological factors. Kane et al.'s research (1982) shows the effectiveness of fluphenazine in treating schizophrenia, adding support to the biological theory of dysfunctional behaviour.

Key study
Kane et al., Fluphenazine vs placebo in patients with schizophrenia

Aim To carry out a one-year, double-blind research study to see the effectiveness of fluphenazine as a treatment for schizophrenia.

Methodology A longitudinal study with patients allocated to one of three groups, two treatment groups and one placebo group. Patients were assessed on whether they had a psychotic episode, that is, a relapse in their remission from schizophrenia.

Participants Twenty-eight patients referred to a New York clinic, who had been diagnosed with schizophrenia, had only had one schizophrenic episode, and had been in remission for at least four weeks during the last year. They had no drug abuse or medical conditions, and signed consent forms.

Design An independent design with patients being randomly allocated to one of three groups, receiving fluphenazine hydrochloride, fluphenazine deaconate or a placebo.

Procedure Patients were randomly assigned and given the drugs or placebo. Patients were removed if they 'dropped out', had toxic side effects to the drug or relapsed. Relapse was defined as a substantial clinical deterioration. Two researchers would decide on the reason for a patient leaving.

Findings Out of 17 patients receiving the placebo, 7 had a relapse by 19 weeks and 7 dropped out by 21 weeks.

Among drug treatment groups there were no relapses and one drop-out by 24 weeks. Toxic effects caused two others to drop out by week 32.

Conclusions These results suggest that patients with one episode of schizophrenia can be successfully treated using fluphenazine hydrochloride or fluphenazine deaconate once they are in remission.

Key terms

milieu therapy a hospital environment designed to enhance patients' social skills and build confidence. The milieu, or 'life space', is a safe environment with social opportunities and immediate feedback from staff

token economies therapies that give rewards ('tokens') for desired behaviours

Check your understanding

1   What is a placebo?

2   How did the relapse and drop-out rates compare between the placebo and experimental groups?

3   What were the specific criteria used in choosing participants?

7.3 Cognitive treatments

The cognitive approach used to be considered of little value in psychotic disorders where the patient loses touch with reality. How could a treatment that relies on logic help a person who has lost all sense of logic? However, more recent studies have shown that the psychotic disorders are merely distortions of a person's perceptions and so could be considered to have a cognitive cause. If a person's perception is distorted so that they hear voices, it should be possible to logically restructure the person's perception to a more normal view. This treatment may of course need to be combined with drug therapy as it may take a while to be effective. Sensky et al.'s research (2000) shows how cognitive therapy can be effective in treating patients with schizophrenia.

Key study

Sensky et al., Cognitive behavioural therapy (CBT) for persistent symptoms in schizophrenia

Aim To compare CBT with non-specific befriending interventions for patients with schizophrenia in effectively reducing positive symptoms of schizophrenia.

Design A randomised controlled design. Patients were allocated to one of two groups:

◆   a cognitive behavioural therapy group

◆   a non-specific befriending control group.

Participants Ninety patients, 57 from clinics in Newcastle, Cleveland and Durham and 33 from London. They had diagnoses of schizophrenia that had not responded to medication and were aged 16–60 years.

Procedure Patients were allocated to one of two groups. Both interventions were delivered by two experienced nurses who received regular supervision.

Cognitive behavioural therapy
A normal routine of CBT was used. This meant initially engaging with patient, examining antecedents of psychotic disorder, developing a normalising rationale (a reason for the behaviour) and treatment of other disorders such as depression.

Specific techniques for positive symptoms of schizophrenia were used, including critical analysis of beliefs about auditory hallucinations. The patients were then helped to change their beliefs, and were taught coping strategies to deal with the voices. Delusions and thought disorders were also addressed using cognitive strategies.

Befriending

The patients had the same time allocation at the same intervals as patients in the CBT condition. The therapists were empathic and non-directive. There was no attempt at therapy, the sessions focused on hobbies, sports and current affairs.

Patients were assessed by blind raters at baseline, after treatment (lasting up to 9 months), and at a 9-month follow-up evaluation. They were assessed on several measures including the Comprehensive Psychiatric Rating Scale, the Scale for Assessment of Negative Symptoms, plus a depression rating scale.

Patients continued to receive routine care throughout the study. The patients received a mean of 19 individual treatment sessions over 9 months.

Results Both interventions resulted in significant reductions in positive and negative symptoms and depression. After treatment there was no significant difference between the two groups. At the 9-month follow-up evaluation, patients who had received cognitive therapy showed greater improvements on all measures. They had improved, whilst the befriending group had lost some of the benefits.

Conclusion Cognitive behavioural therapy is effective in treating negative as well as positive symptoms in schizophrenia that are resistant to standard antipsychotic drugs, with its efficacy sustained over 9 months of follow-up.

Section summary

- Treating psychotic disorders is a complex process. There are many aspects of a person's situation to consider.

- Some treatments such as drug treatments have a far more immediate effect on behaviour, but may need to be used in conjunction with cognitive therapy to ensure that the patient changes their cognitions to prevent the disorder returning.

- Each one of these approaches adopts a reductionist approach, reducing its explanation down to one factor, and treating that one factor.

- The treatment of disorders has come a long way, but there is still some way to go to ensure that effective treatment is available for everyone with a disorder.

- None of these researchers is claiming a 100 per cent success rate, and so the final treatment regimen must still be left to qualified practitioners to decide the best way to help patients with a mental disorder.

Key term

empathic having the ability to identify with and understand someone else's feelings or difficulties

Check your understanding

1   Where did the participants come from in this study?

2   How were they assessed?

3   What were the two conditions?

4   When did the benefits of CBT show?

U3
2

Disorders

142

ExamCafé
Relax, refresh, result!

Relax and prepare

Steve

I need an A grade to get my university place, so I have made revision notes on all of the studies and theories on the spec. I know it will mean a lot of revision for the exam, but I'll have plenty of evidence for the synoptic paper, and lots of evidence to evaluate the research in the health option exam.

Kieran

I colour co-ordinate my revision cards using the dividers in my file. I've put all the cognitive explanations and treatments for disorders on blue cards, the biological ones on green cards and the behaviourist ones on pink cards. That way I can easily see which study goes in each section. This helps if a study appears twice in the specification, as I can see how it links to the other sections.

Natasha

I find psychology really difficult with all the different studies, so I'm making a large revision chart, and as we go through each topic in class I put on the chart which study I will revise for that topic.

Refresh your memory

You could make a revision chart like Natasha's. It could look something like this for each section, or you could put all four sections on an A3 piece of paper. You may find that some of the studies appear twice.

	Stress – causes	Stress – measuring	Stress – management
Research 1	Work – Johansson	Physiological method – Geer and Maisel	Biofeedback – Budzynski
Research 2	Lack of control – Geer and Maisel	Combined method – Johansson	Social support – Waxler Morrison

Get the result!

Example answers

Below is a student response written under exam conditions in answer to the following question:

Outline one explanation of an affective disorder of your choice. (10 marks)

Student answer

Depression is an affective disorder and I am going to write about the behaviourist explanation for depression. The behaviourist explanation would suggest learning of affective disorders, through operant or classical conditioning. Skinner's research on animals led him to devise the theory of operant conditioning. This says that if a person is rewarded for something, then as a consequence of that reward the behaviour is likely to be repeated. If someone is not rewarded for something they may feel depressed and feel that there is no reason to be happy.

Lewinsohn's research showed that people who were not positively reinforced for normal life such as going to work became depressed. This starts a vicious circle as the person then doesn't go to work and so doesn't get any reinforcement, so feels even more depressed. Lewinsohn carried out a longitudinal study where participants completed a self-report of pleasant activities and a self-rating of depression. They used a 3-point scale for pleasantness and frequency. There were correlations between mood ratings and pleasant activities, with more pleasant activities being correlated with more positive mood ratings. So there is a link between reinforcement from doing something pleasant and lack of depression.

Examiner says:

The first paragraph shows a good understanding of classical conditioning and applies it neatly to an appropriate affective disorder. There is a good use of psychological terms.

Using research evidence to support the description is a good idea. The understanding of Lewinsohn's research is evident and reasonably detailed.

A concluding paragraph would have rounded off the answer, clearly linking the theory and the research. This would probably have put the answer in the top band. However this answer is good and would meet the criteria for a strong answer.

Below is a student response written under exam conditions in answer to the following question:

Evaluate explanations of affective disorders. (15 marks)

Student answer

There are many explanations for affective disorders, the behaviourist one mentioned before and also cognitive and biological explanations. These have strengths and weaknesses and can be compared to each other. This essay will evaluate these three explanations.

The behaviourist and the biological explanations opt for different sides of the nature–nurture debate, as behaviourists say that affective disorders are learned and biological disorders say that they are genetic and so innate. The cognitive approach also says it is nurture, as it is the way a person sees their surroundings that makes them depressed.

The behaviourist and biological explanations are similar in that they both adopt a deterministic approach, which means that they say that if something happens then certain behaviour must follow. So if you are not reinforced by pleasant activities then you will be depressed. This doesn't take into account free will. There are some problems with this, as not everyone shows depression, even if there is genetic depression in their family, so there is something called individual differences which would explain why not everyone's behaviour is determined.

Each of the studies is reductionist. The biological explanation is reductionist because it reduces the explanation to something biological like genes. The behaviourist explanation is reductionist because it reduces the explanation to something like environment, and the cognitive approach is reductionism as it reduces it down to cognition.

My final point is that each of the explanations has some evidence to support it. The research for each of them is done on real patients in real therapy sessions, so has high ecological validity, and is controlled. Lewinsohn even had a control group to make sure that it wasn't just the placebo effect. The evidence supports the idea that each explanation has some validity.

This shows that the explanations for affective disorders are many and varied and can be compared to each other.

Sport and Exercise Psychology

Contents

Sport and the individual

Sport performance

Social psychology of sport

Exercise psychology

Full references for the studies can be found in the References section on page 330

Introduction

Sport psychology has existed almost as long as psychology itself, although it was not always formalised as an academic discipline. For example, in 1898, Norman Triplett observed that cyclists performed better when competing against other cyclists than when cycling alone. He tested this observation systematically and so the notion of social facilitation was born.

In Berlin in 1920 the first sport psychology laboratory was founded by Carl Diem at the Deutsche Sporthochschule. The first sport psychology laboratory in the USA was established in 1925 by Coleman Griffith at the University of Illinois, where he offered the world's first course in sport psychology. Griffith was interested in the effects on athletic performance of psychomotor skills, mental awareness, muscular tension and relaxation, and personality. A year later he completed *The Psychology of Coaching* (1926), the first sport psychology book to be published. In Eastern Europe it was apparent that by the 1960s major athletics nations from the Eastern bloc, such as East Germany, regularly employed sport psychologists.

Rainer Martens is seen as the pioneer of more recent developments in modern sports psychology. His publications include development work in connection with tests, measures and inventories, and many of his students have gone on to spread the doctrine of sport psychology.

As professional bodies and academic journals have been devoted to sport psychology, so it has grown. In the UK, the British Association of Sport and Exercise Sciences (BASES) is the professional body for sport and exercise sciences, the application of scientific principles to the promotion, maintenance and enhancement of sport and exercise related behaviours. Sport psychology is relevant to major popular sporting events such as tournaments in football, rugby, cricket and golf as well as the Olympic Games, and is therefore accessible, available, and of interest to all.

What do sport psychologists do?

Maybe when we first consider what a sport psychologist is, we think of the *educational* role. We think of someone conveying the principles of sport and exercise psychology to the athlete to help them enhance their performance in terms of outcome and/or satisfaction. They may help with motivation, or imagery, or controlling aggression, for example.

Knowledge of the principles of sport psychology is of value to all those involved in enhancing the performance of an athlete. This includes the *athlete*, who through self-reflection or application of certain techniques can work on their own improvement. Equally so their *coach*, who can guide, advise, befriend and drive the athlete to greater success and fulfilment. Knowledge of sport psychology can formalise what needs to be done by the coach so that an effective programme can be developed and followed. The athlete or coach may wish to refer to a specialist sports consultant, particularly for the application of tests and measures for diagnosis as well as to help the aggressive or demotivated athlete.

There is also the research function. The body of knowledge within sport psychology must be tested and reviewed systematically, and built upon. So the *researcher*, whether in the laboratory or in the field, is integral to the discipline and application of sport psychology.

Finally, there is the sport psychologist who is concerned with the more clinical aspects of the discipline, such as helping the athlete through mental and emotional difficulties using a wider awareness of the athletic experience. Athletes may come up against difficulties related to their sporting lifestyle. Sometimes it is a function of their personality: what has made them outstanding may also be their downfall. At other times it can be the demands of the sport or the corruption of what has been developed. Clinical sport psychologists may look at 'burnout', which without proper guidance could lead to withdrawal from sport. There is also the use and abuse of performance enhancement, as well as its side effects. Body image, weight gain and loss and aggression are all within the realm of the clinical sport psychologist.

The areas of sport psychology covered in this book are:

- Sport and the individual
- Sports performance
- The social psychology of sport
- Exercise psychology.

Sport and the individual

Morgan (1979) highlighted the credulous–sceptical debate concerning the impact of personality on sporting performance. Sceptics would argue that performance is dependent on environment, training, upbringing and so on, while personality has little impact. Those in the credulous camp would point to certain personality types being more suited to some sports than others, or to some team positions than others, or even some personality types being more likely to become elite athletes. Sport psychologists also appreciate the importance of defining and measuring personality for application to the sporting arena. Similarly, aggression and motivation need to be

identified and channelled appropriately to ameliorate rather than detract from performance.

Sports performance

Arousal is the way the body responds to a variety of situations. However, heightened arousal can get in the way of improving performance and lead to anxiety. Top athletes often refer to self-confidence as the deciding factor in achieving competitive superiority.

Social psychology of sport

Sporting activity involves others, whether as a team, in competition, spectating or organising. A coach aims to help a team gel, an audience affects arousal and so can facilitate or inhibit performance, a leader can drive a team collectively to a goal, or fail to do so.

Exercise psychology

Sport and exercise are linked to physical and mental health, and their relation to cancer, HIV and eating disorders are considered here. It is often reported that exercise can give the athlete a natural high and can impact on mood states. Finally, burnout, body image and drug abuse are considered in this area of study.

Sport and the individual

- The Australian Sports Federation defines sport as 'a human activity capable of achieving a result requiring physical exertion and/or physical skill, which, by its nature and organisation, is competitive and is generally accepted as being a sport'.

- What words/parts of this definition imply individual aspects of sport?

- What words/parts of this definition imply social aspects of sport?

There is a range of individual aspects to sporting achievement and success. Personal growth, development of a skill and pursuit of full potential are just some of them. They are achieved by mastering individual qualities and overcoming personal limitations. We already know that psychological aspects account for the individual component in sporting performance. We need to investigate what their impact is and how our knowledge of them can improve our understanding of this area of sport psychology. This area is divided into three sections:

- personality

- aggression

- motivation.

As well as being affected by physical and social environment, our behaviour is also determined by our disposition. This covers who we are, what traits we have and what characteristics we display; all of this impacts on the people we are and how we behave/perform.

Personality

Personality is a concept. It is relatively enduring yet is dynamic, not static. It is hard to agree on a definition; therefore, there is an issue of *validity*. Cattell (1956) attempted to measure it by identifying commonly agreed factors when assessing personality. His measure, known as Cattell's 16PF (16 Personality Factors), is a recognised tool in sport psychology and has been much used in research and measurement of athletes' personality. However, Cattell himself acknowledges its limitations. Eysenck (1965) postulates a trait theory, linking dimensions of personality with physiological functioning. One dimension goes from extrovert to introvert and the other from stable to neurotic. He later added a third dimension, that of psychoticism.

Where is all this leading? As sport psychologists we must ask ourselves whether knowing about an athlete's personality gives us some insight or predictive value into their performance. Are some personalities more suited to sports than others? Does knowing about an athlete's personality help to determine their suitability to one sport over another? Are some personalities more suited than others to certain positions in team sports?

Try this ...

Using books or the internet, find definitions of sport. What aspects are common to most definitions? Which are individual aspects and which are social aspects?

Try to develop your own definition of sport. Pair up with someone else in your class and defend your definition, or amend it if theirs is better than yours.

Aggression

We must also consider an individual's aggressive nature. Again the question arises of how much is due to disposition and how much is due to learning and environment. Ethologists such as Lorenz may look at animal behaviour and draw links with human aggression, although this raises the question of extrapolation. Others would argue that aggression builds up in all of us. Some people let it out little by little; others have bigger 'blow-ups' from time to time. This releasing of pent-up emotion is known as catharsis, a notion proposed by Freud. It explains why some of the more aggressive competitors are mild-mannered away from the sports field.

extrapolation 'drawing out' or inferring something unknown from something that is known, for example drawing parallels for human behaviour from animal behaviour

catharsis an important term in the psychoanalytic approach. It refers to the process of releasing pent-up psychic energy. This can be in a hostile or channelled way, and may be linked to frustration and aggression

Try this …

1   Make a list of people you consider aggressive in the way they approach their sport. These may be people you know personally, or athletes you know through the media.

2   For each one, consider whether their sporting character is similar to other aspects of their life. Are they quiet and reserved people who use sport as the outlet for their otherwise hidden aggression?

3   In the light of the above, to what extent do you agree with the notion of catharsis?

An alternative to Freud's psychoanalytic approach is the behaviourist approach. Embedded in learning theory (the view that our behaviour is determined by learning responses from our physical and social environment), is Berkowitz's Environmental-Cue Theory. Berkowitz and Geen demonstrate in a number of similar studies that factors in our environment can affect how aggressively we respond. This is a key insight into aggression in sport and how it may be channelled. The outcome is in direct contrast to Freud, who would suggest more aggression to encourage release of pent-up negativity whereas Berkowitz and Geen suggest that a brutalising environment increases aggression. Accordingly, one way in which aggression could best be managed is by reducing aggressive role models in the environment. Social Learning Theory, supported by Bandura's research (1961; 1963; 1965), shows that we imitate what we see and if this is reinforced then that behaviour is likely to be repeated. Aggression is best managed by presenting role models who respond to aggression appropriately and effectively.

Motivation

Motivation is anything that compels us to move in any situation rather than stay still. The physical aspect of motivation deals with everything from the ability to the arousal required to improve. Early psychologists would suggest that drive is also a physical aspect (Hull and Spence, 1951 and 1956). This is combined with a psychological component, such as the desire to improve, or be the best, or avoid failure, or the commitment to spend large amounts of time and money. Achieving success and avoiding failure are the basis of the McClelland-Atkinson model of motivation (1953). Although initially using the highly subjective Thematic Apperception Test, McClelland attempted to quantify the components of motivation and developed a way of measuring it psychometrically. Over the years this model has been found to be rather simplistic, and has therefore been added to and become more complex to use. There are therefore other measures of motivation more commonly used, a good example of which is Gill and Deeter's (1988) Sports Orientation Questionnaire (SOQ), which looks at sports-specific motivation, the motive for success in sport. It has been used to compare athletes and non-athletes as well as male and female athletes. Finally, different techniques that may be used to motivate are considered. Extrinsic motivation, which is concerned with external reinforcement (cups, trophies, praise) is considered, as is intrinsic motivation, where partaking in an activity is its own reward. This has been explored by Deci in a number of pieces of research such as Ryan and Deci's (2000) self-determination theory.

Themes and perspectives

Tests and measures are highlighted in this area of the A2 course. Psychometric testing allows for a clinical and arguably objective means of measuring human characteristics. Validity and reliability issues inevitably arise. In his approach to addressing the validity issue, Cattell takes over 18,000 personality words as his starting point. However, reliability is possibly compromised, as Cattell himself suggests that factors such as mood and motivation may affect the responses given at any one time. Gill and Deeter's paper is largely an account of procedure which justifies reliability and validity. They point specifically to their confidence in the construct validity of the Sports Orientation Questionnaire. Eysenck's theory is also realised with a psychometric approach to measuring personality. Simple yes/no responses and a lie scale reduce reliability problems, but we could question whether his somewhat reductionist view of what constitutes personality diminishes the validity of his approach.

Although McClelland and Atkinson latterly looked at psychometric testing, their earlier measurement of personality was based on the more subjective Thematic Apperception Tests deriving from the psychoanalytic school of thought. Their thoroughness and extensiveness are used in a robust justification of the approach. Continuing the psychoanalytic theme, catharsis is used to explain aggressive behaviour, and benefits from intuitive appeal. If we release our inner traumas, conflicts and anxieties, they will not accumulate ready for an explosion, sport acting as a major outlet for psychic energy. The complete antithesis is the behavioural view, which suggests that immersion in an aggressive world will lead to increased aggression. Sport needs to be an arena for controlled/instrumental aggression. Whereas catharsis, along with a biological approach, supports the idea that aggression is innate, behaviourists would postulate that it is a product of the environment. This is at the heart of the nature–nurture debate. It should be noted that all the studies in this section are from a western perspective, rendering the work rather ethnocentric. Perhaps the title of this section is indicative of the American and Eurocentric bias in psychology generally, or perhaps we are merely more likely to find clearer models of individual features of athletes in individualistic as opposed to collectivist cultures.

1 Personality

A person's personality is their disposition, who they are, how they are, their inborn character as distinct from the influences of their physical and social environment. According to Gross (1994), the relatively stable and enduring aspects are what distinguish an individual from others, or to Hollander (1971) they are what makes an individual unique, namely the sum total of that individual's characteristics. This section will try to establish how best to measure personality, consider precisely what it is and identify various ways it can apply to sport.

1.1 Measures

The difficulties of studying personality, including the difficulties in measuring it, have arguably been most successfully addressed in 1956 by Cattell, whose system for measuring personality is still used today.

Key study

Cattell's 16 personality factors (16PF)

How the measure was developed

In 1936, using dictionaries, Allport and Odbert looked up all personality-related words they could find – about 18,000. They reduced this list to 4500 adjectives which they felt described observable and relatively permanent traits.

In 1956, Cattell analysed the Allport-Odbert list, organising it into 181 clusters. He then asked his subjects to rate people they knew using the adjectives on the list. Using factor analysis Cattell generated 12 factors, then added 4 more that he thought should also be there. This resulted in his 16 personality factors, on which he believed everyone's personality could be assessed.

What's in Cattell's 16PF?

The 16 personality factors are dimensions along which an athlete's personality can be measured and are shown in Table 3.1.

Using Cattell's 16PF

Cattell's 16PF is used to produce a personality profile of an athlete. The test is a commercial one and is copyrighted. Instructions on the standardised procedure, application, data-collection, conversion from raw score to standard score, production of personality profile and interpretation are all available at a price. Its use, however, is enduring, and is reported in many studies such as that by Kroll and Crenshaw (1970), described on pages 156–157.

Key terms

construct validity whether a scale measures the unobservable social construct that it purports to measure. It is therefore measuring something that does not exist in a physical sense (e.g. personality, intelligence)

factor analysis a statistical approach that can be used to analyse interrelationships among a large number of variables and to explain these variables in terms of their common underlying dimensions (factors)

	Trait		Also described as 'from … to …'
A	Warmth	Sociability	reserved, cool *to* easygoing, likes people
B	Reasoning	General ability	concrete-thinking *to* abstract-thinking
C	Emotional stability	Ego strength	easily upset *to* emotionally stable
E	Dominance	Dominance	submissive, accommodating *to* assertive, opinionated
F	Liveliness	Surgency	serious, prudent *to* expressive, enthusiastic
G	Rule consciousness	Conscientiousness	expedient *to* conforming, rule-bound
H	Social boldness	Adventurousness	shy, threat-sensitive *to* socially bold, unafraid
I	Sensitivity	Sensitiveness	tough-minded, rough *to* tender-minded, refined
L	Vigilance	Pretension	trusting, accepting *to* suspicious, sceptical
M	Abstractedness	Bohemianism	down-to-earth, conventional *to* absent-minded, creative
N	Privateness	Shrewdness	forthright, unpretentious, open *to* polished, calculating
O	Apprehension	Insecurity	confident, complacent *to* apprehensive, self-blaming
Q1	Openness to change	Radicalism	conservative, traditional *to* liberal, innovative
Q2	Self-reliance	Self-sufficiency	group-orientated, sociable *to* resourceful, self-directed
Q3	Perfectionism	Willpower	undisiciplined, impulsive *to* controlled, compulsive
Q4	Tension	Tenseness	relaxed, composed, low drive *to* restless, high drive

Table 3.1 Cattell's 16PF (Source: Cattell, 1956)

Check your understanding

Evaluation of Cattell's 16PF:

1   What do the terms in the table below mean?

2   How does each apply to Cattell's 16PF?

The first one has been done for you.

Term	Meaning	Application
Validity	Does it measure what it claims to measure?	The issue is whether the 16 factors chosen by Cattell do accurately reflect what is meant by personality. Should any of the 16 factors not be there? Are there any overlaps or grey areas, or are certain aspects of personality missing?
Reliability		The issue is…
Ethnocentricity		The issue is…
Usefulness		The issue is…
Nature–nurture		The issue is…

Other measures

Eysenck's Personality Questionnaire (EPQ) – another psychometric measure of personality. It includes a series of yes/no questions to identify aspects of personality. Lie-detection questions were included in Eysenck's Lie Scale; this asks questions throughout the questionnaire to identify whether certain questions are answered to show the respondent in a good light. Where these contradict other answers given, they will be scored on the lie scale. This test carries the same advantages (objectivity) and disadvantages (reliablity issues) as other psychometric tests such as Cattell's 16 PF.

Rorschach ink blots – the interpretation of ink-blot images, supposedly giving insight into the hidden personality. This is developed from the psychoanalytic approach. An advantage of this approach is that it targets the underlying behaviour, not just the behaviour that is presented. A disadvantage is that the subjective nature of the interpretations causes them to be unreliable. Further, selectivity of information can lead to bias.

Thematic Apperception Test (TAT) – responses to situations, allowing a psychoanalytic interpretation of what is buried in the unconsious, giving insight into the personality. This carries the same advantages and disadvantages as the ink blots described above.

Minnesota Multiphasic Personality Inventory (MMPI) – arguably the most widely used of personality inventories. A series of yes/no questions originally designed to measure personality traits of clinical conditions. Different versions can be used for psychopathological disorders, adolescents or normal people! As well as the above evaluative points, the fact that this is not designed specifically for sport allows us to question its usefulness.

Although it is important to try to measure personality, it helps considerably to know what is meant by 'personality'. A range of theories try to explain this, ranging from the trait and type to the situational.

Trait theories – both Eysenck and Cattell tried to identify traits that constituted personality.

Social learning theory – encompasses the situation approach and suggests that we learn our personalities from our environment, particularly from significant others.

Psychodynamic theory – developed from Freud's psychoanalytic approach. Suggests that our personalities have different aspects (id, ego and superego) operating on different levels (conscious, pre-conscious and unconscious). In addition, aggression needs a release (catharsis), and this has special application to sport.

Interactionist theories – these link the situation and trait ideas, and debate centres around the role of each and the extent of its influence.

1.2 Theories

Key study
Eysenck's Trait Theory

Eysenck initially talked of two dimensions of personality: extroversion (E) and neuroticism (N). Extroversion is seen as the positive one and deals with how outgoing or self-contained you are:

Extrovert -- Introvert

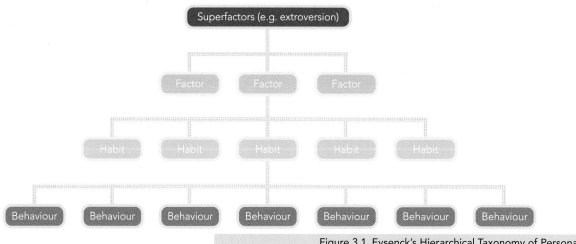

Figure 3.1 Eysenck's Hierarchical Taxonomy of Personality

Neuroticism is seen as the negative trait and deals with how stable or unstable you are:

Neurotic --- Stable

Later, Eysenck added a third dimension: psychoticism (P), which looks at aggression as well as mental instability.

He arrived at these dimensions based on factor analysis, which identifies many possible responses to the question of what might be the constituents of (in this case) personality, and extracts dimensions – factors –

from the mass of information. From this he drew up a hierarchical taxonomy:

Behaviours (e.g. revising for a psychology test) lead to habits

Habits (e.g. preferring to revise in a group) lead to factors

Factors (e.g. sociability) lead to superfactors

Superfactors are the dimensions of extroversion, neuroticism and psychoticism.

Biological basis of Eysenck's Trait Theory

The reticular activating system (RAS) is a part of the brain that monitors arousal levels. An extrovert is someone who is underaroused, so gets bored and seeks stimulation to maintain a good level of activation. They are therefore louder, more outgoing, attention-seeking (stimulation-seeking) individuals who may lack concentration. The opposite is true for introverted personalities.

The autonomic nervous system (ANS) responds to emotion-producing stimuli, including situations that produce stress. Someone who is neurotic will show a rapid and strong response to stressful situations. Neurotic people, therefore, have a low anxiety threshold and may be described as anxious, moody and restless. They tend to experience negative effects (fight-or-flight) in the face of very minor stressors, that is, they are easily upset. The opposite to this is the stable dimension of personality.

Testosterone levels affect psychoticism, accounting for aggression and even psychotic episodes. This dimension was added at a later date.

This allows an assessment of someone's personality by combining where they lie on each continuum (Figure 3.2). From this Eysenck suggested four personality types: Stable-Introverted, Stable-Extrovert, Neurotic-Introvert and Neurotic-Extrovert.

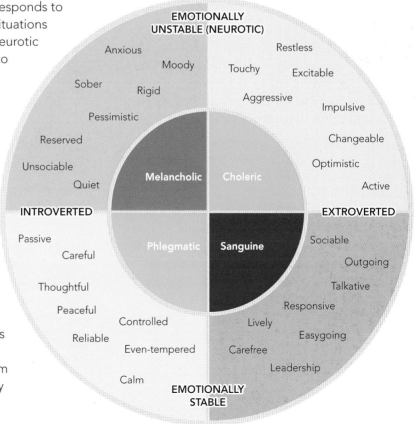

Figure 3.2 Eysenck's Personality Dimensions (Source: Eysenck and Eysenck, 1985)

Check your understanding

1 Think of four people, including yourself, who play sport at various levels. Decide which of Eysenck's four personality types they would be.

2 How objective/subjective is your assessment of these four personalities?

3 How valid is Eysenck's theory as a measure of personality?

Take it further

Hippocrates was an Ancient Greek physician who taught that all illness was brought about by an imbalance in the four humours. Find out more about the four humours.

1.3 Relevance to sport

An example of the relevance of personality theories to sport is addressed in the study by Kroll and Crenshaw (1970), who consider the relationship between personality and sports performance. The question to be asked is whether some personality types are more likely to succeed in sport than others, and whether some personality types are suited to particular sports.

The first part of this question is whether some people are natural born athletes. Are there certain personality types who are likely to make better athletes than others? This is the basis of the credulous-sceptical argument presented by Morgan (1980), which identifies that some sport psychologists will use personality profiles to make predictions about sporting performance, leading to predictions of sporting success. The sceptical camp minimise the value of personality research in making such predictions. It can be said that personality is a predictor of sports performance but not a particularly strong one. According to Cox (2000), personality is one of a number of factors that can contribute to athletic success.

However, Schurr et al. (1977) postulate that athletes are more independent, objective and less anxious than non-athletes. Hardman (1973) finds them to be more intelligent than average. Cooper (1969) describes them as having more self-confidence. It begs the question whether these personality traits produce good athletes or whether sports participation fosters these qualities. Williams and Parkin (1980) compared the personality profiles of hockey players at different levels, using Cattell's 16PF. They found a clear distinction between those competing at club level and international performers, although those performing at national level were not particularly distinct from either group.

Are different personality types suited to different sports? It may be suggested that introverts are better at solo sports such as distance running, whereas extroverts are more suited to high-energy team sports such as rugby. Henry (1941) found body-builders to be preoccupied with masculinity and manliness, although more recent research suggests that this is no longer the case.

Key term

credulous-sceptical argument the debate about the impact of personality on sports performance. The credulous argument is the proposal that athletic performance can be predicted from personality traits. The sceptical argument is the proposal that athletic performance cannot be predicted from personality traits

Key study

Kroll and Crenshaw, Personality profiles in different sports

Kroll and Crenshaw (1970) presented their paper to the International Congress of Sports Psychology, a convention for the contemporary psychology of sport where Kroll was an organiser and keynote speaker.

Aim To compare personality profiles, using Cattell's 16PF, between different sports where the competitors are at established levels of athletic achievement.

In their introduction, Kroll and Crenshaw note that attempts to compare personalities in different sports were relatively sparse and that there was a lack of defined samples for each sport, so it could not be assumed that samples had been truly representative of the sports studied.

Design An independent groups design was used, studying participants from four sports, namely (American) football players, gymnasts, wrestlers and karate participants.

Participants A total of 387 athletes were studied (81 footballers, 141 gymnasts, 94 wrestlers and 71 karate participants). They represented regional or national samples, drawn from a wide area of the middle geographic section of the USA. Their skill and achievement were of excellent to superior calibre.

Apparatus Cattell's 16PF. Several other test instruments to assist and corroborate in measuring aspects of personality.

Procedure Cattell's 16PF was administered to the participants. In addition, other test instruments were administered including the 15-item lie scale of the Minnesota Multiphasic Personality Inventory (MMPI). The athletic quality was controlled by selecting athletes who were described as of excellent to superior calibre. Statistical analysis was employed to determine whether groups of subjects could be distinguished from each other on the basis of the entire personality profile rather than merely considering each component in turn.

Results Significant differences between groups on personality profiles were shown to exist. There were six comparison groups:

1. Football – Wrestling
2. Football – Gymnastics
3. Football – Karate
4. Wrestling – Gymnastics
5. Wrestling – Karate
6. Gymnastics – Karate

There was significant difference between all groups except the football–wrestling group, suggesting that football players' and wrestlers' profiles were similar to each other and significantly different from gymnasts and karate participants, whose profiles were significantly different from each other. The major contributor to the discriminant function can be seen in Table 3.2 (the letters referring to Cattell's 16PF are outlined on page 153).

Conclusion It would seem that Kroll and Crenshaw found significant factors as discriminators between team sports and individual sports, and between certain sports in particular, namely (American) football, gymnastics, wrestling and karate.

Comparison	Major contributor
Football – Wrestling	
Football – Gymnastics	H, C, L, Q_2
Football – Karate	Q_2, H, L, G
Wrestling – Gymnastics	H, B, Q_1, Q_2
Wrestling – Karate	Q_2, Q_4, N, G
Gymnastics – Karate	Q_4, G, F, B

Table 3.2 Analysis for pairs of sports

Check your understanding

Comment on the following in relation to Kroll and Crenshaw's research:

- reliability
- validity
- ethnocentrism
- generalisability to other sports
- usefulness/application to wider populations
- nature/nurture of sports-specific skills.

Section summary

- There are various ways of attempting to measure personality, each with its own issues as well as strengths.
- The trait approach suggests that psychometric testing may prove appropriate and effective. This is exemplified in Cattell's 16 personality factors.
- The same holds true with theories of personality, for example in the approach suggested by Eysenck.
- Kroll and Crenshaw suggest direct application of personality theory to the sporting arena.

2 Aggression

Aggression is defined in many ways in and beyond the sporting arena. Gill (1986) suggests that any definition should include intent (that the act is deliberate), harm (to another living organism) and that it is an action (physical or verbal threat/abuse).

Angry, destructive or reactive aggression is often described as hostile aggression, whereas forceful, legitimate, goal-directed energy is often described as channelled or instrumental aggression. Sometimes, legitimate actions are termed assertive as distinct from aggression, which is unacceptable behaviour in a particular sports setting.

2.1 Instinct theories

Instinct theories are the nature side of the nature–nurture debate. These include physiological

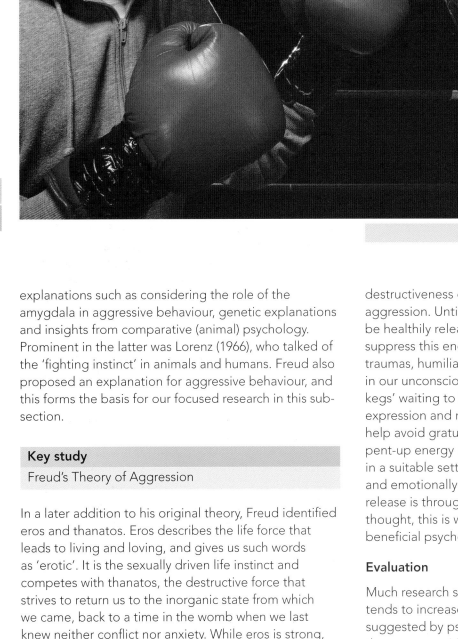

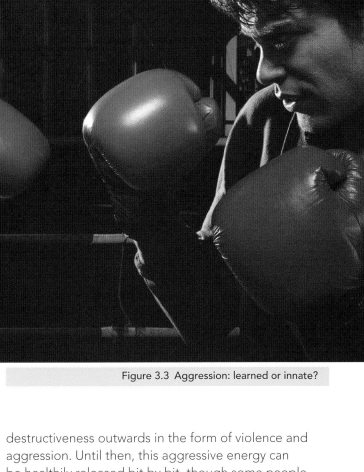

Figure 3.3 Aggression: learned or innate?

explanations such as considering the role of the amygdala in aggressive behaviour, genetic explanations and insights from comparative (animal) psychology. Prominent in the latter was Lorenz (1966), who talked of the 'fighting instinct' in animals and humans. Freud also proposed an explanation for aggressive behaviour, and this forms the basis for our focused research in this sub-section.

Key study

Freud's Theory of Aggression

In a later addition to his original theory, Freud identified eros and thanatos. Eros describes the life force that leads to living and loving, and gives us such words as 'erotic'. It is the sexually driven life instinct and competes with thanatos, the destructive force that strives to return us to the inorganic state from which we came, back to a time in the womb when we last knew neither conflict nor anxiety. While eros is strong, we strive to enjoy life and overcome its trials and conflicts. Thanatos is essentially self-destructive but, if not allowed to give vent to this urge, will turn its

destructiveness outwards in the form of violence and aggression. Until then, this aggressive energy can be healthily released bit by bit, though some people suppress this energy. When this is combined with the traumas, humiliations, conflicts and repressions buried in our unconscious, we find the metaphorical 'powder kegs' waiting to blow. All this energy needs some expression and release: catharsis. Cathartic activity will help avoid gratuitous and indiscriminate violence. If the pent-up energy can be released in a controlled way and in a suitable setting, the individual can remain mentally and emotionally healthy. An ideal setting for cathartic release is through sport. According to psychoanalytic thought, this is why sport is considered to be so beneficial psychologically.

Evaluation

Much research suggests that sport participation tends to increase aggression levels, not reduce it as suggested by psychoanalytic theory (see social learning theory, pages 160–161).

If the catharsis model is correct, competitors from the most aggressive sports should be the most sedentary people, chess players the more violent. This is not the case.

Following on from psychoanalytic theory, cultures with high sports participation should be the most gentle. Cross-cultural studies do not suggest this.

Cross-cultural research shows wide variation with regard to aggression levels, suggesting that social and environmental factors are crucial in determining levels of aggression. These are largely overlooked by the psychoanalytic approach.

> ### Check your understanding
> Explain, with examples, catharsis in a sports setting.

2.2 Social theories

Key study
Berkowitz and Geen, Environmental Cue Theory

Drawing on behavioural psychology, Berkowitz and Geen (1966) suggest that our social and physical environment provides cues that trigger aggressive behaviour. Initially, in situations where arousal is produced, aggression is more likely to occur where there is an aggressive cue. Sport is a situation where heightened arousal is usually evident.

Aim In an ingenious test of aggression, Berkowitz and Geen aimed to test whether filmed violence may serve to elicit aggressive responses, dependent on aggression-evoking cues. They believed that aggressiveness activated by viewing hostility is only in 'low gear'. Other appropriate aggression-evoking cues must be present before the observed violence can lead to a strong aggressive response. Thus a person who sees a brutal fight may not display any detectable aggression until they encounter stimuli having some association with the fight. In the experiment described here, the association with the aggressive scene is the target's name.

Participants 88 male undergraduates at the University of Wisconsin, 72 of whom were volunteers from the introductory psychology course, and earned marks towards their final grade. The remaining 16 participants were recruited from an introductory sociology course several weeks later with no marks offered. These were distributed evenly among the eight treatment groups.

Procedure Variables were arranged so that (1) some participants would be angered, some would not; (2) some would be angered by a person with a name-mediated association, others with no name association; (3) some would view an aggressive scene, others a non-aggressive scene.

1   The participant provided a solution to a problem-solving situation. The confederate would apply mild shocks according to how good they deemed the suggested solution. In the angered condition they applied seven shocks, in the non-angered condition merely one.

2   The participant was met by the experimenter and another supposed participant, actually a confederate. When asked for their names, half the confederates said *Kirk* Anderson and half said *Bob* Anderson.

3   The experimenter then suggested that as a diversion he would show the two men a brief film. Half the participants saw a fight scene from the film *Champion* with actor *Kirk* Douglas (aggressive movie condition). The other half were shown an equally long film of a track race (non-aggressive movie condition).

4   Further in the aggressive movie – Kirk condition, the experimenter casually but pointedly remarked that the first name of the movie protagonist was the same as that of the other person. This was to ensure that a name-mediated connection was established.

Now the confederate was sent to solve a problem and receive shocks, while the naïve participant was to apply shocks for the quality of solution offered. The number and duration of shocks were recorded.

Results A questionnaire asked participants to write down the confederate's name. All 88 men did this correctly. There were several checks on the success of anger induction and a significant distinction between angry and placid participants was found. In comparison with the men getting only one shock, those receiving seven shocks expressed a significantly lower preference for the confederate as a partner in any subsequent experiment.

The paper suggests that there can be little doubt that the seven shocks had made the participants angry. Aggression was measured by the number of shocks administered by the subject. The men displaying the greatest number of aggressive responses were those who had seen the prize fight film after they were provoked and whose fellow participant was named Kirk.

The accomplice's name had apparently caused him to be associated with a violent scene so that he could then elicit strong overt hostility. These participants gave a significantly greater number of shocks than the men in any of the other conditions. The mean number of shocks in each condition is shown in Table 3.3.

The aggression of participants was tested by measuring their willingness to give mild electric shocks to other supposed participants who were actually confederates. Initially they were given either one or seven electric shocks. Those who were given seven shocks responded more aggressively than those who had been given one. Participants were then asked to witness a track race (non-violent) or a prize fight (violent). Those who witnessed the track race responded less aggressively when tested than those who had observed the prize fight. Thirdly, participants who saw the prize fight saw Kirk Douglas as the prize-fighter. When the participant to be shocked was introduced as Bob (Anderson) he received fewer shocks than if he was introduced as Kirk (Anderson).

Berkowitz further went on to identify the 'weapons effect', in which it was suggested that if a weapon of some kind was merely present then this would cue more aggressive behaviour than if one was not. In another of his studies, a badminton racket was incidentally placed in the scene in half the experimental trials, and a rifle in the other half. As above, more shocks were delivered in the weapons condition.

As Berkowitz famously suggests, the finger pulls the trigger but the trigger may also be pulling the finger.

> ### Check your understanding
>
> 1 Explain what is meant by the statement above.
>
> 2 Give a sporting example where this statement could be applied to explain the situation.

2.3 Managing aggression in sport

Key study

Bandura, Social Learning Theory

Based on the studies of Bandura et al. (1961; 1963; 1965) social learning theory is a development from behaviourist thinking, particularly that of operant conditioning and reinforcement. All of us, and young children in particular, observe others' behaviour. We may want to be like that person; therefore, we are likely to imitate some of their behaviour. This is more likely to occur if the person modelling the behaviour is seen to have status. People who have status may include parents, elders, popular friends, someone famous and successful and so on. If the imitated behaviour is then reinforced, it is more likely to occur again and soon the behaviour is learnt and becomes acquired. In the case of aggression in sport, this observe – imitate – reinforce model is often clearly seen. Consider the following examples.

A famous footballer makes a hard and unfair tackle on an opponent. He gets away without a caution. At school the next day one boy says to his friend 'Did you see that tackle yesterday? He's so hard, he's brilliant.' In their next match that friend is more likely to make a hard and unfair tackle on an opponent. If he gets away without a caution and his team-mates give him a lot of positives for being 'hard', then increasingly this aggression becomes part of the boy's behavioural repertoire. Similarly, non-aggressive behaviour can be modelled. Wayne Rooney was advised by his captain, David Beckham, to tie his shoelaces after being provoked rather than lash out at his protagonist. This was highlighted by the commentators and shown on television. A lot of shoelace-tying was observed in UK parks that Sunday! On the positive side therefore, social learning theory can offer a way of avoiding, coping or dealing with aggressive behaviour with the use of positive role models.

As well as imitating observed behaviour, learning can occur through observing the consequences of

Accomplice's name	Aggressive film		Track film	
	Angered	Non-angered	Angered	Non-angered
Kirk	6.09	1.73	4.18	1.54
Bob	4.55	1.45	4.00	1.64

Table 3.3 The number of shocks, on average, administered in each condition

aggressive behaviour. If the consequences observed are favourable, the observer is more likely to adopt that behaviour. This type of learning is known as vicarious reinforcement.

Instinct theories suggest that some people are born aggressive, it is their innate make-up; social learning theory suggests all behaviour is learnt, including aggression. Berkowitz's research suggests the same. By controlling what and who is in someone's environment, we can control how they learn to react to situations.

Take it further

If the behavioural explanations are right, why do we punish people for being too aggressive? It's not their fault, their physical and social environment has made them what they are. Should we not simply set up their environment in such a way that they will learn to react more appropriately? (See Skinner's 1971 book *Beyond Freedom and Dignity*.)

Try this …

Select two people you know personally who play a sport and have a reputation for overly aggressive play. To one, explain about catharsis and agree on cathartic activities, particularly at appropriate times, to help curb their aggressive behaviour. For the other, consider the environment they are exposed to and agree on less exposure to aggressive cues and more exposure to non-aggressive role models. Which method works best at reducing aggression? How did you measure aggression?

Check your understanding

1 Suggest how Environmental Cue Theory might be applied in practice to reduce aggression.

2 Suggest how Social Learning Theory might be applied in practice to reduce aggression.

3 Suggest how psychoanalytic theory might be applied in practice to reduce aggression.

4 Which would you use if you were the coach? Justify your answer.

Section summary

◆ The Freudian psychoanalytic approach to aggression as an innate theory was considered. Freud suggested that we have a destructive instinct. He further suggested that we must release pent-up aggression.

◆ In contrast, Berkowitz's approach was explored as an example of a theory which suggests that aggression is learnt, cues from the environment influencing levels of aggression.

◆ Bandura's Social Learning Theory was reviewed as an approach that may be employed to manage aggression in sport by modelling appropriate behaviour.

3 Motivation

Motivation deals with the drive or stimulation of an organism towards success in completing or taking part in an activity. It is variously described as:

◆ an internal state or condition that activates behaviour and gives it direction

◆ a desire or want that energises and directs goal-oriented behaviour

◆ an influence of needs and desires on the intensity and direction of behaviour.

Franken (1994) provides an additional component:

◆ the arousal, direction, and persistence of behaviour.

Psychology can be criticised for its approach to the study of motivation, traditionally limited to physiological need. Arguably, however, everything we do in life is motivated. From the moment we get up in the morning (or not!), through all our daily activities, to when we go to bed, there is a motive, or motivation, behind everything we do.

To explain this and relate it to the sporting context, we must turn to different approaches. Further, we must be able to identify and attempt to measure motivation. In his theory of motivation, McClelland develops the work of Murray (1938) to suggest that there are three main components to motivation – the need to achieve (nAch), the need to affiliate (nAff) and the need for power (N-Pow).

3.1 Achievement motivation

A number of papers were written by McClelland, Atkinson and others, on work conducted mainly at

Wesleyan University between 1947 and 1953. These were published as a series of articles, but it became clear that an overall picture of achievement motivation was emerging and was brought to focus in a book – *The Achievement Motive* by McClelland et al. (1953).

Until this point motivation had mainly been studied in the realm of bio-psychology, looking at basic physiological motives such as the need for food, water and sex (see Cannon and Washburn, 1912). This was useful in that it identified key aspects of motivation such as need, and the drive to satisfy that need. Hull (1943; 1951) and Spence (1956) introduced more of a behavioural focus, suggesting that the motive was in fact a behaviour which sought to reduce the need. This would result from a deficit state that would energise the organism to seek relief. For example, if hunger was the need, the motive was to seek food in order to reduce the hunger and regain equilibrium.

However, motivation is far more wide-ranging than this and the motivation that applies to the sporting context is scantily addressed by these approaches. We will turn now to the McClelland-Atkinson model of achievement motivation.

Key study

McClelland et al., *The Achievement Motive*

Design Content analysis using Thematic Apperception Test (see procedure below). Much was based on the work of Murray (1938).

Subjects All male. Innumerable imagery responses to Thematic Apperception Tests were analysed, so in fact they were sampling people's thinking, which McClelland describes as an interesting sampling problem.

Procedure Six experimental conditions: relaxed, neutral, achievement orientated, success, failure and success-failure. Each of the different experimental procedures preceded the measure of motivation.

The measure of motivation was content analysis of a group Thematic Apperception Test. Subjects were shown standard pictures and asked to write their own stories based on the following questions.

1 What is happening? Who are the persons?

2 What has led up to this situation? That is, what has happened in the past?

3 What is being thought? What is wanted? By whom?

4 What will happen? What will be done?

The content analysis was pre-tested by noting systematic differences between subjects who had been deprived of food for 1, 4 and 16 hours. Using this and other techniques, a scoring system was devised, using achievement imagery. One chapter of their book carefully considers the measuring instrument, as McClelland et al. call it, and the issues raised, such as reliability of scoring.

People with a high need for achievement (nAch) seek to excel and thus tend to avoid both low-risk and high-risk situations. Predominantly achievement-motivated individuals avoid both low-risk situations (because they are easily attained) and high-risk projects (because they see the outcome as one of chance rather than their own effort). High nAch individuals prefer work that has a moderate probability of success, ideally a 50 per cent chance. Achievement-motivated individuals need regular feedback in order to monitor the progress of their achievements. They prefer either to work alone or with others like themselves.

Ultimately a measure of nAch was developed which the researchers claimed was high in terms of reliability and validity. They found that associations reflected in stories (the answers to the above questions) are significantly influenced by events occurring just before they are sampled. They found this by counting the number of different references to achievement appearing in the stories. Achievement-orienting experiences significantly increase the amount of achievement imagery in written stories, irrespective of background. This was repeated with Navaho children, suggesting that achievement imagery, and hence motivation, may be universal.

Evaluation Ethnocentrism is addressed through cross-cultural research.

There are questions of validity – why should the *number of different references* be added rather than *all references* to achievement? Should some achievement imagery be weighted more heavily than others?

There are questions of reliability – projective tests suffer from being highly subjective. However, use of content analysis with clearly identified criteria improves inter-rater reliability, for example.

Check your understanding

How could you identify the nAch people in a sports team (those driven by the need to achieve), as opposed to the nAF ones (those driven by the need to avoid failure)? Think of a specific example.

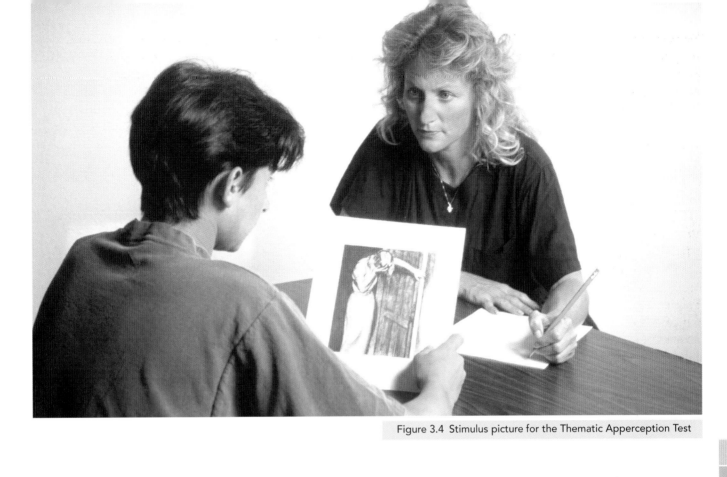

Figure 3.4 Stimulus picture for the Thematic Apperception Test

3.2 Sports-specific achievement motivation

Key study

Gill and Deeter, Sports Orientation Questionnaire

The Sports Orientation Questionnaire (SOQ) was developed (1988) as a multi-dimensional, sports-specific measure of individual differences in sports achievement orientation.

Most sport psychologists consider competitiveness as a sports-specific form of the more general achievement motive. General achievement motivation is widely recognised as the capacity to experience pride in accomplishment or a disposition to strive for success across varied achievement situations and standards. It was Murray (1938) who first discussed achievement motivation, describing it as the desire to accomplish something difficult; to master either physical objects or human beings; to do this rapidly and independently; to overcome obstacles and attain a high standard.

Aim To develop a valid, reliable and useful tool for the measurement of sports-specific achievement motivation.

Sample An initial 32-item version of SOQ was administered to 237 undergraduates enrolled in physical activity skills classes in 1984; 90 per cent of these were taken from the liberal arts faculty so were representative of undergraduates generally. These included competitive (33 males; 64 females) and non-competitive activities (40 males; 100 females). In 1985, data were collected from a second sample of 218 undergraduates, again sampling competitive (77 males; 33 females) and non-competitive skills classes (24 males; 84 females). Finally, a third sample of high-school students were sampled consisting of approximately equal numbers of males and females across grades 9, 10, 11 and 12. Of the 266 students in this sample, 126 (77 males; 49 females) were classified as competitive sport participants and 140 (47 males; 93 females) were classified as non-participants.

Questionnaire Items for SOQ were developed to represent achievement orientation across diverse sport and exercise activities. Specific items were generated by reviewing the achievement and sport competition literature, by consulting with other sport psychologists, and by collecting open-ended responses from diverse samples of sports participants. Throughout, an effort was made to represent diverse approaches to sport achievement, and specifically to include orientation toward individual or personal standards as well as interpersonal competitive standards. These strategies yielded 58 items which were circulated to five raters, all graduate students in an advanced sport psychology seminar, who rated each item on content and clarity. All raters were familiar with the general achievement-motivation literature and related sport psychology work. Only items that were rated as definitely clear and definitely representative of sport achievement orientation by all five raters were retained. The resulting 32 items were put into an inventory. Each item was to be rated on a scale from 'strongly agree' to 'strongly disagree'. The inventory was piloted. No one reported any unclear or ambiguous items or offered any suggestions and the 32-item measure became the initial version for SOQ. The inventory was revised (as discussed in the results section), and the final 25-item SOQ is shown in Table 3.4.

Procedures For both samples of university students, class instructors were contacted prior to the start of classes to obtain permission to administer the questionnaire. On the first day of classes a graduate student attended each class, explained the purpose of the project and administered the 32-item SOQ. Participation was voluntary but all individuals contacted agreed to complete the questionnaires. With the second university sample the same graduate assistants returned to the classes in the middle of the course, after 4 weeks, and readministered the SOQ. A few individuals were absent, had dropped or changed classes, and could not be contacted, but 205 (94 per cent) of the original 218 respondents retook the SOQ and their scores were used for test–retest comparisons.

The authors and another assistant visited the high school and administered the revised 25-item SOQ in a large group setting. Grade 9 students from randomly selected PE classes went to an auditorium during class time. Students from randomly selected homerooms in grades 10, 11 and 12 were called to a large auditorium during their homeroom time. In all cases the senior author introduced everyone, explained the purpose of the project, asked for voluntary cooperation, and distributed and collected the questionnaires with the help of the assistants and some of the high-school teachers. Various analyses were carried out to determine competitiveness, win orientation and goal orientation. These analyses took the form of:

◈ exploratory factor analysis from the main sample

◈ confirmatory and exploratory factor analysis from the other two samples

◈ internal consistency measures and test–retest correlations

◈ SOQ scores were analysed with gender and competitive/non-competitive participation.

Results The results section covers extensive statistical manipulation to evidence the effectiveness of SOQ, and particularly its reliability. For example, reliability was tested with test–retest correlations and found for competitiveness, win and goal orientation correlations of 0.89, 0.82 and 0.73 respectively. Similarly an intra-class test produced correlations of 0.94, 0.90 and 0.84 respectively.

Conclusions Gill and Deeter concluded that:

◈ They had provided evidence showing that SOQ was a reliable and valid measure of sports orientation.

◈ Competitiveness consistently differentiated students from competitive as opposed to non-competitive classes and sports participants from non-participants.

◈ Construct validity was good.

◈ Competitiveness exerts a strong influence on the choice to enter competitive sports situations.

◈ In contrast to competitiveness, win and goal orientation seemed to have less influence on the choice to enter a sport.

◈ Competitive sports participants did tend to score higher on win and goal orientation than non-participants, but unlike with competitiveness, these were neither strong nor consistent.

The data provide good evidence that the SOQ is a stable, reliable and valid measure of sport achievement orientation. This suggests that SOQ can be a valuable measure for the instigation of competitiveness and achievement behaviour in sport and exercise settings.

The SOQ competitiveness score consistently differentiated students in competitive classes from students in non-competitive classes and competitive sport participants from non-participants. These differences provide good construct validity of the sport-specific SOQ, whereas more general achievement and competitive measures have previously failed to make such a distinction.

Competitiveness appears to exert strong influence on the choice to enter competitive sport situations and the group comparisons support this interpretation. The SOQ competitiveness score differentiates students in competitive activities from those in non-competitive activities. In contrast to competitiveness, win and goal orientation seem to have less influence on the choice to enter sport competition situations. Competitiveness was the only important discrimination variable. Apparently highly competitive individuals who enjoy sport competition and strive for sport achievement may also be win-oriented, goal-oriented, or both, but some

	Strongly agree	Slightly agree	Neither agree nor disagree	Slightly disagree	Strongly disagree
1 I am a determined competitor	A	B	C	D	E
2 Winning is important	A	B	C	D	E
3 I am a competitive person	A	B	C	D	E
4 I set goals for myself when I compete	A	B	C	D	E
5 I try my hardest to win	A	B	C	D	E
6 Scoring more points than my opponent is very important to me	A	B	C	D	
7 I look forward to competing	A	B	C	D	E
8 I am most competitive when I try to achieve personal goals	A	B	C	D	E
9 I enjoy competing against others	A	B	C	D	E
10 I hate to lose	A	B	C		E
11 I thrive on competition	A	B		D	E
12 I try hardest when I have a specific goal	A	B	C	D	E
13 My goal is to be the best athlete possible	A	B	C	D	E
14 The only time I am satisfied is when I win	A	B	C	D	E
15 I want to be successful in sports	A	B	C	D	E
16 Performing to the best of my ability is very important to me	A	B	C	D	E
17 I work hard to be successful in sports	A	B	C	D	E
18 Losing upsets me	A	B	C	D	E
19 The best test of my ability is competing against others	A	B	C	D	E
20 Reaching personal performance goals is very important to me	A	B	C	D	E
21 I look forward to the opportunity to test my skills in competition	A	B	C	D	E
22 I have the most fun when I win	A	B	C	D	E
23 I perform my best when I am competing against an opponent	A	B	C	D	E
24 The best way to determine my ability is to set a goal and try to reach it	A	B	C	D	E
25 I want to be the very best every time I compete	A	B	C	D	E

Table 3.4 Sport Orientation Questionnaire (Source: Gill and Deeter, 1988)

highly competitive individuals may be low on either win or goal orientation.

The overall factor stability, reliability and validity evidence suggest that SOQ is a valuable measure for the instigation of competitiveness and achievement behaviour in sport and exercise settings.

Check your understanding

1 Test the SOQ on others in your school/college. How good a measure do you find it to be?

2 Comment on its reliability.

3 Comment on its validity.

3.3 Techniques of motivation

Key study

Deci and Ryan, Self-determination theory (SDT)

This paper was put forward as the culmination of various empirical works in this area (2000). The researchers have thus identified three needs of self-motivation, namely the need for competence (e.g. Harter, 1978), the need for relatedness (e.g. Baumeister and Leary, 1995) and the need for autonomy (e.g. deCharms and Carpenter, 1968; Deci, 1975).

At their best, people are curious, vital and self-motivated. They inspire, show endeavour, extend themselves and strive to learn new skills. Yet it is also apparent that the human spirit can be diminished or crushed. Both children and adults can become apathetic, alienated and irresponsible. How often do people sit passively before a television set, stare blankly from the back of a classroom or wait listlessly for the weekend as they go about their work? This suggests more than mere disposition or biological endowment. Social contexts affect differences in motivation and personal growth, resulting in some people being more self-motivated and energised in some situations than others. Many environmental factors hinder and undermine self-motivation as well as social functioning and well-being. These may thwart the three basic psychological needs identified above. The article identifies outcomes from its review of research into SDT, including intrinsic motivation, and the conditions that facilitate or forestall this type of motivation and the self-regulation of extrinsic motivation.

The nature of motivation

Motivation concerns energy, direction, persistence and equifinality. It is of pre-eminent importance in real-world settings, such as coaching in sport, in that it involves mobilising others to act. The contrast between cases having internal motivation versus external pressure is familiar to us all. The former produces more interest, excitement and confidence manifested as enhanced performance, persistence and creativity (Deci and Ryan, 1991). A major focus of SDT has been to supply a more differentiated approach to motivation. SDT has identified distinct types of motivation, which has consequences for learning, performance, personal experience and well-being.

Intrinsic motivation

Deci and Ryan define intrinsic motivation as the inherent tendency to seek out challenges, to extend and exercise one's capacities, to explore, and to learn. Children at their healthiest are active, inquisitive and curious, even in the absence of extrinsic rewards. However, the maintenance and enhancement of this can be disrupted by non-supportive conditions.

Deci and Ryan (1985) formulated cognitive evaluation theory (CET), which focuses on the effects of reward and feedback on intrinsic motivation. Feelings of competence may enhance intrinsic motivation, particularly when accompanied by a sense of autonomy or internal locus of causality (deCharms and Carpenter, 1968). People must experience their behaviour as self-determined.

Most of the research into the effects of environment on intrinsic motivation focuses on autonomy versus control rather than competence. Extrinsic rewards can undermine intrinsic motivation. Also, not only tangible rewards but also threats, deadlines, directives and imposed goals diminish intrinsic motivation. In contrast, choice, acknowledgement of feelings and opportunities for self-direction were found to enhance intrinsic motivation because they allow a greater feeling of autonomy. Students taught with a more controlling approach not only lose initiative but learn less effectively.

To summarise, the CET framework suggests that social environment can facilitate or forestall intrinsic motivation.

Self-regulation of extrinsic motivation

Much of what appears intrinsic is, strictly speaking, not so. Different motivations reflect the values and regulation of behaviour that has been internalised and integrated. This refers to 'taking in' a value or regulation so that subsequently it will emanate from their sense of self. These are central in childhood socialisation and throughout the lifespan. SDT identifies the process through which non-intrinsically motivated behaviours become self-determined and the ways in which the environment influences these processes. SDT differs in its view of extrinsic motivation in that it can vary in its relative autonomy (Vallerand, 1997). For example, students who do homework because they grasp its value for a chosen career are extrinsically motivated, as are those who do it because their parents compel them to. The first enjoys an element of choice, the latter involves compliance. They vary in their relative autonomy.

Take it further

Give further examples, like that above, from the sporting context. Identify different degrees of self-regulation of extrinsic motivation within the examples you have given.

Conclusions

SDT attempts to explain human activity and passivity, responsibility and indolence. The assumption is that human nature is inclined towards activity and integration but has a vulnerability to the contrary. SDT attempts to identify the conditions that tend to support natural activity or elicit this vulnerability.

Conditions supportive of autonomy and competence facilitated intrinsic motivation, whereas conditions that controlled behaviour and reduced efficacy undermined its expression. So too with non-intrinsically motivated behaviours, where the dramatic power of social contexts to enhance or hinder the integration of social values and responsibility was evident. Autonomy, competence and relatedness were the key needs to foster integration and internalisation. These needs are of great significance to sport psychologists and those charged with motivating others, as is awareness of contexts which thwart satisfaction of these needs. Successful management of these needs will engender commitment, effort and high-quality performance.

Therefore SDT identifies social context to encourage responsiveness to basic psychological needs. Excessive control and lack of connectedness disrupt inherent actualising, resulting in lack of initiative and responsibility. Knowledge concerning the nutrients essential for positive motivation and thus enhancing performance is relevant to all those concerned with cognitive and personality development and those who want to facilitate motivation and commitment. Thus, by attending to the relevance or deprivation of supports for basic psychological needs, sport psychologists are better able to diagnose sources of alienation versus engagement, and enhance human achievement and well-being.

Section summary

◆   Motivation was traditionally considered in a physiological context, in terms of hunger, thirst or sex, for example.

◆   It broadened to a more psychological basis, initially as part of psychoanalytic doctrine and later the congnitive domain. This can be seen in the work of McLelland et al.

◆   The Sport Orientation Questionnaire is an example of an attempt to measure motivation. An insightful paper by Deci and Ryan encourages us to consider principles behind effective motivation.

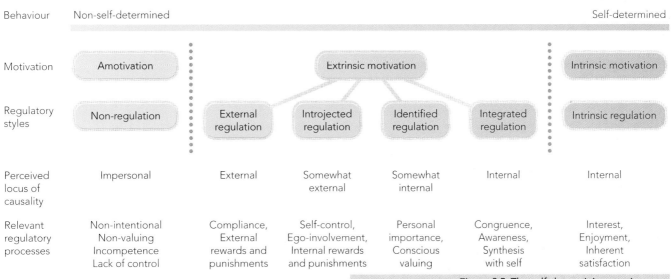

Behaviour	Non-self-determined					Self-determined
Motivation	Amotivation		Extrinsic motivation			Intrinsic motivation
Regulatory styles	Non-regulation	External regulation	Introjected regulation	Identified regulation	Integrated regulation	Intrinsic regulation
Perceived locus of causality	Impersonal	External	Somewhat external	Somewhat internal	Internal	Internal
Relevant regulatory processes	Non-intentional Non-valuing Incompetence Lack of control	Compliance, External rewards and punishments	Self-control, Ego-involvement, Internal rewards and punishments	Personal importance, Conscious valuing	Congruence, Awareness, Synthesis with self	Interest, Enjoyment, Inherent satisfaction

Figure 3.5 The self-determining continuum

Sport performance

Introduction

Successful performance can be achieved by the competitor or team members believing they have performed at the peak of their ability, or even exceeded their expectations in this regard. Successful performance can be achieved by it all coming together on the day, referring to the various components of a performance. Successful performance can be achieved by winning. This section considers what constitutes good performance.

Try this …

Set up a class debate on the above contradiction with the motion 'This house believes that the honour is not in winning but in taking part.' Have speakers to propose, oppose and second the motion, then take questions from the floor. Finally, allow each side to sum up, then take votes from the floor.

Why did the debate go the way it did? Is it a comment on the standard of the debate, the class, the sporting culture in your neighbourhood, county, country?

Was it important who won the debate, or was it the taking part that mattered?

This area will look at the following topics:

- arousal
- anxiety
- self-confidence.

Arousal

All performers, not just athletes, but actors, musicians and people sitting exams, get a sense of anticipation. This arousal is what allows us to prepare for enhanced performance, recognised since Cannon's (1927) notion of 'fight or flight'. It allows us to focus our resources, causing us to be alert and ready for action. Arousal is the subject of our first section in the area of sport performance. It must be noted however, that when we fret, stress or become agitated through too much stimulation at times of impending performance or competition, this has an adverse effect on how we perform. Far from enhancing our ability to function, this anxiety hinders and impedes us in our actions.

Anxiety

As well as physical aspects to performance, there are psychological components that have at least equal impact. At all levels, our expectations of ourselves and our beliefs about our abilities can have a critical impact on our performance.

Self-confidence

Drive theory states that the more we are 'up' for an event, the better we will perform. However, the inverted-u hypothesis suggests that this is true up to a point, known as the optimal point, after which too much 'get up and go' can interfere with performance.

Themes and perspectives

The idea that too much arousal is detrimental to performance derives from a study by Yerkes-Dodson in 1908. This study is about mice learning to choose a black or a white chamber using the negative stimulus of an electric shock, but the meaning and conclusions have drifted over time and the findings are now commonly applied to various kinds of performance. The notion of one response, originally suggested as the 'fight-or-flight' response, was questioned in a paper by Lacey (1967). The work on arousal, by Oxendine (1980), applies the notion of the inverted-u not just to the sporting context generally, but to specific sporting situations.

Too much arousal can lead to anxiety, one aspect of which is measured by Martens' (1977) Sport Competition Anxiety Test. This identifies aspects of anxiety and raises questions of reliability and validity. In a similar vein, the Competitive State Anxiety Inventory-2, developed by Martens et al. 1990, is an attempt to measure the different dimensions of anxiety all in one test (hence the notion of a multi-dimensional test) without compromising reliability or validity. Two British sports psychologists, Fazey and Hardy, challenged the regular inverted-u hypothesis (1988), suggesting that when we are aroused to the point of anxiety, we can suffer a collapse (catastrophe) in performance, and that regaining one's level is much harder to achieve than previously suggested.

Self-confidence in a given situation is known as self-efficacy. This is a concept developed by Bandura (the Bobo doll man), initially looking to help dysfunctional people who were struggling to cope. Again, drift in meaning saw its application to other fields such as sport and business. An acknowledged sports-specific model of self-confidence by Vealey (1986) considers trait and state self-confidence in the sporting arena. Finally, the use of imagery in sport, and particularly to aid self-confidence, is considered.

1 Arousal

1.1 Theories of arousal

Key study

Yerkes and Dodson, The effect of stimulation on rapidity of learning: the 'dancing mice' study

Aim To teach mice to discriminate between black and white using electric shocks, and see which level of shock produced faster learning. This was investigated by varying the strength of an electric shock to see if the strength of shock affects the rapidity with which the mice learn to avoid a black chamber, choosing the white one instead.

Design An independent subjects design – different mice being used in the different conditions of the experiment.

Subjects 40 mice, nearly all aged between 6 and 8 weeks, although one as old as 74 days and one as young as 25 days.

Apparatus As shown in Figure 3.6, the mice would go from their nesting area into the entrance chamber. From here, they could choose to enter a black chamber or a white chamber. The black chamber was rigged up so that if a mouse entered it would receive an electric shock.

Procedure When one of the 40 mice entered the entrance chamber, the experimenter placed a piece of cardboard between it and the route back to the nesting box, and gradually narrowed the space until the mouse made a choice. The white chamber eventually led back to the nesting box. On entering the black chamber, the mouse would receive a shock by the experimenter depressing the circuit switch, at which point it would beat a hasty retreat and renew attempts to choose the right box to enter. The mice were given ten tests every morning. When they got all tests correct on three consecutive days, they were considered to have learnt the task. Mice were tested with weak, medium and strong shocks.

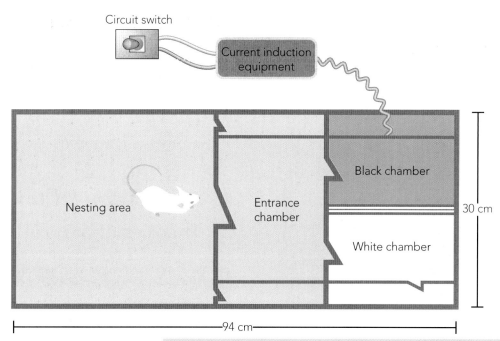

Figure 3.6 Apparatus for the 'dancing mice' study (Source: Yerkes and Dodson, 1908)

Results There were four mice in each condition, two males and two females. Only one of the mice receiving the weak shock acquired the correct habit – it became evident by the twentieth day that the shock was too weak and the experiments discontinued. The results are therefore as shown in Table 3.5.

This can be displayed graphically, giving a u-shaped relationship, as shown in Figure 3.7.

Conclusions

1   With medium stimulation (arousal) it took fewer 'goes' for the mice to acquire the right habit.

2   When the stimulation became too strong the learning took longer.

3   Both weak and strong stimuli result in slow habit formation.

4   The difficulty of the discrimination affects the thresholds at which habit-formation occurs.

If we take Figure 3.7 and understand that the *lower* number of tests represents *better* performance, we could redraw it in relation to arousal and performance as shown in Figure 3.8.

Hence, as arousal increases, so too does performance, up to an optimal point. The more 'hyped up' we are for something, the more we are likely to perform with

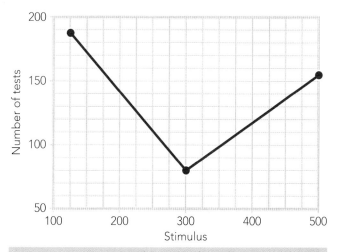

Figure 3.7 The results of the 'dancing mice' study
(Source: Yerkes and Dodson, 1908)

	Mouse 1	Mouse 2	Mouse 3	Mouse 4
Weak	15 volts	20+ volts	20+ volts	20+ volts
Medium	8 volts	9 volts	8 volts	7 volts
Strong	15 volts	13 volts	14 volts	20 volts

Table 3.5 Number of sets of tests received up to the point where errors ceased

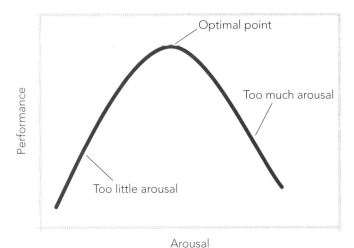

Figure 3.8 The results of the study showing that a lower number of tests represents better performance

energy and belief. But only up to a point: too 'hyped up' will lead to deteriorating performance, maybe mistakes or frustration doing more damage and the increased arousal increasing these negative effects. Thus, too much arousal leads to deterioration of performance; this is known as *anxiety*.

This can be applied to differing skill levels. For example, in tennis a novice player will reach the optimal point much sooner than the more experienced – and thus more competent and assured – player. Hence, they will become anxious sooner and their performance will deteriorate sooner. This will improve as they practise, play and gain experience.

This is further investigated when the optimal level of arousal is applied to different sports (see Oxendine 1980). The optimal point of arousal in golf will be much lower than that for rugby. Hence, the golfer must attempt to keep their arousal under control to be able to perform at peak level, whereas the rugby player must make sure they are 'hyped up'.

Check your understanding

1   Draw an inverted-u graph with performance on the y axis and arousal on the x axis. Show the inverted-u for the novice performer and the inverted-u for the more experienced performer.

2   Draw an inverted-u graph with performance on the y axis and arousal on the x axis. Show the inverted-u for the golfer and the inverted-u for the rugby player.

1.2 Types of arousal

At this point, it is worth noting that we have not considered the different interpretations of the concept of arousal. To some it is a physiological, possibly autonomic response, or it may refer more cognitively to emotional arousal. To others it is activation. Still others link it to energy, drive and motivation. This uncertainty is addressed in the next piece of research (Lacey, 1967).

Key study

Lacey, Somatic response patterning

This paper derives from a conference on psychological stress organised by the US Office of Naval Research and the Psychology Department of York University, Toronto, Canada. Lacey was a speaker at this conference, and his comments moved forward the concept of arousal, then more generally termed 'activation'.

Lacey developed the concept that arousal was not simply one response for all situations, but the evoking of a multiplicity of somatic responses. Lacey comments that the more we gain understanding of somatic functions in a variety of situations, the greater will be our understanding of stress. Individuals experiencing difficulties of an emotional kind or coping with stress will exhibit a wide variety of somatic changes like those shown by an organism preparing for fight or flight. Indeed, the evidence is of completely different forms of arousal – electrocortical, autonomic and behavioural. Each is independent and complex, and different responses are exhibited in different situations. Thus, a measure of one may not necessarily represent a valid index of measurement for another, or for that particular form of stress (arousal).

Lacey finally identifies the key concepts leading to this broadening interpretation:

1   Dissociating somatic and behavioural arousal.

2   Dissociating physiological functions said to be an index of arousal.

3   Patterns of stimulus response, either stimulus-specific or situation stereotypy.

4   Feedback from the cardiovascular system to the brain, this being inhibitory rather than excitatory.

Check your understanding

In what way(s) is Lacey's paper a departure from Cannon's emergency 'fight or flight' response?

Take it further

Complete the table below to illustrate different behaviours in a sports context.

Behaviour	Application to sport
Anger directed outwards	
Anger directed inwards	
Fear	
Responses to auditory stimuli	

1.3 Factors affecting arousal

Yerkes and Dodson's ideas linking arousal (stimulation) and performance (learning) are further developed in the following paper (Oxendine, 1980).

Key study

Oxendine, Emotional arousal and motor performance

Oxendine's paper opens with the observation that people perform best when 'motivated'. Highly excited people can perform feats of unusual strength, speed or endurance. However, there is also contradictory evidence showing that high levels of excitement impede performance of certain tasks. The paper investigates this phenomenon: why motivation may give the same performer an advantage at one time, yet hinder at another.

Emotional arousal is described as those conditions in which one's normal physiological functioning has been intensified.

Oxendine goes on to note that the optimum level of arousal varies (when considering the Yerkes-Dodson inverted-u relationship). Different tasks require different levels of arousal for optimal performance. Further, the level of optimal arousal varies from one person to another. Further still, the optimum level of performance may vary from day to day, even with the same person. However, some generalisations are made: complex tasks are performed better when one's

drive is low, while simple tasks are performed better when one's drive is high. Therefore in a given situation, performance can be hindered by drive which is too high or too low. Drive here is somewhat related to motivation and arousal.

Note that what constitutes 'complex' and 'simple' and what is high drive and low drive remains vague. This means that any performance can be accounted for retrospectively. Thus, the theory lacks predictive value to the sports practitioner and so has limited value.

However, Oxendine suggests extending the inverted-u theory with three generalisations.

◆ First, a high level of arousal is essential for optimal performance in gross motor activities involving strength, endurance and speed.

◆ Second, a high level of arousal interferes with complex skills, fine muscle movements, co-ordination, steadiness and concentration.

◆ Third, a slightly above average level of arousal is preferable to a normal or below level of arousal for all motor tasks.

Fatigue is countered by a surge of adrenalin. Cannon (1929) injected fatigued and rested animals with adrenalin. He reported that these animals had this decrement cut in half within 5 minutes, whereas rested animals did not increase their response time. This shows that adrenalin counters the effects of fatigue.

The message to athletes is that emotionally charged situations do, in fact, elicit significant endurance gains. Although feats of *strength* and *endurance* are often verifiable, Oxendine suggests that situations linking arousal with *speed* are not so accessible to measurement. Clocking frightened people over a measured course is somewhat more problematic. He contends, however, that a child being chased by a bully or a ghost will run faster than the child being told by the PE teacher to run faster!

Oxendine later draws the distinction with complex and fine controlled movements. The golfer, the gymnast or the diver, for example, are particularly susceptible to situations of high arousal and anxiety. Experimental research by Carron (1965) investigating balance, concluded that with tasks of low difficulty, highly aroused subjects were found to be superior, however in tasks of high difficulty, low anxiety subjects proved superior. Stress seemed to be especially detrimental but experience helps to reduce its adverse effects (Bergstrom, 1967). Similar results were found with steadiness. Hussman (1969) states by way of explanation that as emotion increases, functioning intelligence goes down.

What does this all mean for the sports competitor? It means that when looking at the Yerkes-Dodson hypothesis, the optimal point of the inverted-u will be at a different place for different sports. Those requiring complex and fine motor skills will require that competitors maintain a firmer control and lower levels of arousal for peak performance than those competitors of sports requiring gross motor skills with qualities such as strength, speed and endurance.

Finally, Oxendine suggests different levels of arousal required for various sports skills. These are summarised in Table 3.6.

5 – extreme excitation	Rugby tackling and scrum Sprint up to 400m Weight-lifting Sit-ups/push-ups
4	Running long jump Middle/long-distance running Swimming races Judo
3	Basketball Boxing High jump Gymnastics Football (UK)
2	Baseball (pitching and batting) Fencing Tennis Golf (driving)
1 – slight arousal	Archery Bowling Basketball free throw Golf (putting)

Table 3.6 Optimal arousal levels for selected sports skills (Source: Oxendine, 1980)

Check your understanding

1 Oxendine's paper suggests that different sports and different skills require different arousal levels.

2 Use real sporting examples to explain and exemplify this statement.

Section summary

◆ Modern notions of arousal are largely based on Yerkes and Dodson's inverted-u model. This is derived from the 'dancing mice' study. It suggests that to achieve peak performance levels we need enough arousal to drive performance, but not so much as to interfere with peak performance. This produces an optimum level of performance.

◆ Lacey questioned the overarching notion of one type of arousal, and pointed to a number of different possible arousal responses, that is, not 'fight or flight' but 'fight' or 'flight'.

◆ Oxendine developed the idea of the different optimal points on different u-shaped curves to typify different sports skills and, indeed, different sports.

2 Anxiety

Anxiety in sport occurs when the level of arousal exceeds the optimal point and starts to become detrimental. Spielberger (1966) identified two types of anxiety – trait and state. Trait anxiety refers to anxiety as a personality trait, a disposition that contributes to who that person is. State anxiety refers to the state a person is in as a response to a given situation or circumstance. This can be further subdivided into somatic state anxiety and cognitive state anxiety. Somatic state anxiety refers to the physiological state of the person taking them beyond peak performance at a given time; cognitive state anxiety refers to someone's thoughts and feelings (fear, self-doubt) getting the better of them and impeding performance at a given time. How can we measure these two aspects? The next study may help in this regard.

2.1 Trait/state anxiety

Key study

Martens, Sport Competition Anxiety Test (SCAT)

Martens (1977) opens his book on the Sport Competition Anxiety Test with a story about himself as a novice coach taking over a wrestling team. The captain, who was a big name in wrestling at the time, was appearing rather lacklustre. Although he was still winning, he was not showing his usual aggressive, offensive style. He was not worried about his ability or winning personality (trait anxiety) but was becoming distressed and apprehensive as each meeting approached (state anxiety).

However, if seeing a situation as threatening is part of the predisposition of the athlete, then we are talking about that athlete's trait anxiety, known as A-trait. It is this that Martens' Sport Competition Anxiety Test measures. In planning and developing these Sport Competition Anxiety Tests, Martens considered a number of issues:

◆ that a test should be objective rather than projective

◆ that a test seeks to minimise response bias

◆ that there should be an unambiguous procedure

◆ that there should be an easy method for scoring.

The test has 15 items which are self-administered and rated as 'hardly ever', 'sometimes' and 'often'. The scale was originally designed for use with children. Version 1 was administered to 193 male junior high-school children from suburban Chicago schools. They were aged 12–15 years and from mainly white, middle-class families. Many statistical tests were applied to test for reliability and found test-retest reliability to be $r = 0.77$ for all samples, which is well above that recognised as an acceptable level. A number of tests of validity were also applied to deal with content, face, concurrent, predictive, construct, classical, structural and trait validity, amongst others. Martens then reported 11 studies where SCAT was administered to confirm construct validation.

Martens then addresses the administration of his SCAT. In the SCAT there are ten test items: 2, 3, 5, 6, 8, 9, 11, 12, 14, 15. Of these the usual scoring is 1 for 'rarely'; 2 for 'sometimes' and 3 for 'often'. For items 6 and 11 this is scored in reverse. There are five spurious items which are not scored: 1, 4, 7, 10, 13.

	Rarely	Sometimes	Often
1 Competing against others is socially enjoyable			
2 Before I compete I feel uneasy			
3 Before I compete I worry about not performing well			
4 I am a good sportsman when I compete			
5 When I compete, I worry about making mistakes			
6 Before I compete I am calm			
7 Setting a goal is important when competing			
8 Before I compete I get a queasy feeling in my stomach			
9 Just before competing, I notice my heart beats faster than usual			
10 I like to compete in games that demand a lot of physical energy			
11 Before I compete I feel relaxed			
12 Before I compete I feel nervous			
13 Team sports are more exciting than individual sports			
14 I get nervous wanting to start the game			
15 Before I compete I usually get uptight			
Athlete's name			
SCAT score			

Table 3.7 Sport Competition Anxiety Test (SCAT) (Source: Martens, 1977)

Analysis

The score for the response to each question is detailed below. Enter the score for each question in the 'Score' column and then total the column up to provide a SCAT score.

Note that questions 1, 4, 7, 10 and 13 score zero regardless of the response.

Question	Rarely	Sometimes	Often	Score
1	0	0	0	
2	1	2	3	
3	1	2	3	
4	0	0	0	
5	1	2	3	
6	3	2	1	
7	0	0	0	
8	1	2	3	
9	1	2	3	
10	0	0	0	
11	3	2	1	
12	1	2	3	
13	0	0	0	
14	1	2	3	
15	1	2	3	

Total

SCAT score	Analysis
Less than 17	You have a low level of anxiety
17 to 24	You have an average level of anxiety
More than 24	You have a high level of anxiety

Table 3.8 SCAT test analysis (Source: Martens, 1977)

Check your understanding

1. Try the test yourself and then try it on your friends.

2. Try the test on your friends in a non-sporting setting, for example with regard to forthcoming exams.

   ◆ How well does it work for you?

   ◆ How well does it work on your friends?

   ◆ How well does it generalise to non-sporting situations?

3. Comment on why the SCAT 'works' or does not 'work' (reliability/validity/gender bias/subjectivity).

2.2 Multi-dimensional models

Models and measures that incorporate wider dimensions without compromising reliability, validity, objectivity etc. are regularly sought. This 'multi-dimensionality' is the subject of the next study.

Key study

Martens et al., CSAI-2

There is a range of uni-dimensional tests such as the SCAT test on page 174, which is a recognised test of trait anxiety, or Martens' original competitive state anxiety inventory (CSAI) used to measure state anxiety. Spielberger et al.'s distinction of trait and state anxiety (1970) was marked by two parallel tests, namely his trait anxiety inventory (TAI) and his state anxiety inventory (SAI). The research culminated in the recognition of a multi-dimensional theory of anxiety, in relation to the field of sport psychology. This came about through Martens et al.'s (1990) development of the competitive state anxiety inventory-2 (CSAI-2), a multi-dimensional state-anxiety measure specific to sport. Martens et al. (1990) proposed that:

1. Somatic anxiety had an inverted-u shaped relationship with performance.

2. Self-confidence had a positive linear relationship with performance.

3. Cognitive anxiety had a negative linear relationship with performance.

In addition, Martens et al. (1990) utilised a time-to-event paradigm to assist in the demonstration of somatic and cognitive anxiety. They administered their CSAI-2 to a selection of athletes, 48 hours, 24 hours, 2 hours, and 5 minutes before a critical event. They affirmed that the cognitive component stayed stable before the start, but the somatic component began to increase prior to the onset of the event.

Check your understanding

1. What do you understand by trait anxiety?

2. What do you understand by state anxiety?

3. Research, find and draw a diagram showing more than one dimension of anxiety.

Read each statement and then circle the appropriate number to the right of the statement to indicate how you feel right now – at this moment. There are no right or wrong answers. Do not spend too much time on any one statement, but choose the answer which describes your feelings right now.

	Not at all	Somewhat	Moderately so	Very much so
1 I am concerned about this competition	1	2	3	4
2 I feel nervous	1	2	3	4
3 I feel at ease	1	2	3	4
4 I have self-doubts	1	2	3	4
5 I feel jittery	1	2	3	4
6 I feel comfortable	1	2	3	4
7 I am concerned that I may not do as well in this competition as I could	1	2	3	4
8 My body feels tense	1	2	3	4
9 I feel self-confident	1	2	3	4
10 I am concerned about losing	1	2	3	4
11 I feel tense in my stomach	1	2	3	4
12 I feel secure	1	2	3	4
13 I am concerned about choking under pressure	1	2	3	4
14 My body feels relaxed	1	2	3	4
15 I'm confident I can meet the challenge	1	2	3	4

Table 3.9 An extract from the CSAI-2 questionnaire (Source: Martens et al., 1990)

2.3 Models of anxiety

There are various other models of anxiety, from the physiological models to the more psychological models. Many are based on, or develop from, the concept of the inverted-u hypothesis. In a highly considered piece of work, Fazey and Hardy (1988) suggest 'an alternative ending' to the story of the inverted-u relationship.

Key study

Fazey and Hardy, Catastrophe Theory

In considering models of anxiety, it may be that models have been too general or only consider one aspect. Yerkes and Dodson's inverted-u has been used to consider the relationship between arousal and performance, stress and performance, anxiety and performance among others. Where these terms have been used interchangeably, Fazey and Hardy suggest that they need to be clearly differentiated. Whereas Yerkes and Dodson's inverted-u has been used to consider the physiological (somatic) state of arousal, cognitive arousal needs to be considered as well, not only in its own right but also as it interplays with somatic arousal. In the form of anxiety, it can have profound and varied effects. It may be further subdivided into somatic state and cognitive state anxiety.

Possibly the greatest concern Fazey and Hardy express about the inverted-u model is in its application. The model suggests that after the optimal point there is a gradual tailing off in performance. Once an athlete has gone past this point, optimal performance can be regained by tweaking the stress level back down (see Figure 3.9).

In reality however, when a performer goes 'over the top' in a highly stressful situation (somatic) there can be a sudden and dramatic collapse in performance level (see Figure 3.10).

This is often accompanied by a dramatic loss in confidence (cognitive), and far more than a little tweaking is needed to recover confidence and the ensuing performance. Performance will follow a different path (see Figure 3.11). This is termed 'hysteresis'.

This dramatic collapse past the optimal point can be catastrophic, and forms the basis of understanding Fazey and Hardy's Catastrophe Theory. The theory states that:

◆ there are at least two components: cognitive anxiety and physiological arousal

◆ cognitive anxiety is the 'splitting' factor which determines whether the effect of physiological arousal is small and gradual, large and catastrophic, or somewhere between the two

◆ there is a negative relationship between cognitive anxiety and performance under conditions of high anxiety. This is not the case where physiological demand is high but cognitive demand is low.

This begs the question of *how* cognitive anxiety alters the effect of physiological arousal on performance. Parfitt and Hardy (1987) suggest that on simple, well-learned tasks the athlete can control and suppress adverse physiological effects while utilising the beneficial effects. With higher levels of cognitive arousal

Figure 3.9 Regaining optimal performance according to the inverted-u model

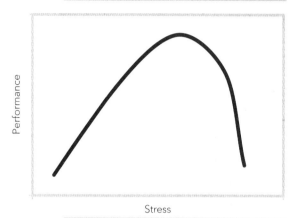

Figure 3.10 Not a gradual decrease in performance, rather a 'catastrophe'

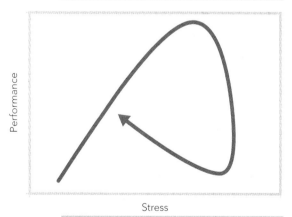

Figure 3.11 Hysteresis: after a catastrophe performance needs to be rebuilt

When cognitive anxiety is low to medium

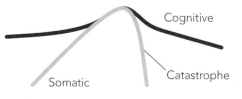
When cognitive anxiety is high

Figure 3.12 Somatic effects of different cognitive anxiety levels

(namely anxiety) this control is disrupted by creating doubt about what is beneficial and what is unhelpful or adverse physiological input. The cognitive overload becomes rapidly and seriously detrimental, fulfilling how we define stress.

Further, whereas physiological arousal is not necessarily detrimental to performance, it will be associated with catastrophic effects when cognitive anxiety is high.

Try this ...

Find an alternative piece of research which explores the relationship between anxiety and performance, both in the sporting context and beyond (e.g. Booth, 1985 looked at the effects of test anxiety on examination performance).

Check your understanding

1   What do you believe to be the relationship between anxiety and performance?

2   Is it an extension of drive theory into an inverted-u, or is it more complex?

3   What is the evidence/reason for your thinking?

4   What are the difficulties in supporting your view?

Section summary

◆   Measurements of the different aspects of anxiety were considered. Spielberger's trait-state distinction and Martens' SCAT test as a measure of trait anxiety were discussed.

◆   A multi-dimensional approach can look at more than one aspect of anxiety, for example Competitive State Anxiety Inventory (CSAI-2).

◆   An alternative explanation to the generally accepted 'going beyond the optimal point' is provided by British sports psychologists Fazey and Hardy. They demonstrated the potentially catastrophic effects of exceeding the optimal level of arousal, and the difficulty of recovering to peak performance.

3 Self-confidence

3.1 Self-efficacy

At the level of elite sport, what is the defining factor that tips the hair's-breadth distinction between success and failure in favour of one athlete over another, or of one team over another? It has been said that confidence is everything. But what is confidence? How can it be identified and measured? How can it be used? The next study addresses these questions.

Key study
Bandura, Self-efficacy

Bandura (1977) developed his theory in an attempt to unify the positions regarding behaviour change. There was a clear shift from the behaviourist view that all behaviour was stimulus-response, reinforcement and association. Bandura believed that this model needed cognitive components such as the individual realising that behaviours have a response that may or may not be desirable. He focused this discussion on the treatment of dysfunctional and defensive behaviour. He took the behavioural model to describe mastery of effective performance, but his main tenet is that it is cognitive processes which explain it. In other words, learning from response consequences is not merely a response which becomes more likely (behavioural) but rather consequences serve to inform participants of what they must do to gain beneficial outcomes, avoid punishing ones and discern which are appropriate (cognitive).

Bandura proposes that where there is fearful and avoidant behaviour, change is sought. It is in this context where *self-efficacy* is assigned a central role for effecting change. It deals with expectations of mastery which affect initiation and persistence of coping behaviour. The strength of people's convictions about their own chances of success will affect whether they even try to cope with given difficult or uncertain situations. So efficacy is about the *person* and whether they think they can execute the *behaviour* necessary to achieve a given *outcome*. This is shown diagrammatically in Figure 3.13.

According to Bandura, efficacy expectations determine how much effort people will put in and how long they are willing to persist to overcome their current circumstance. Whereas Bandura is considering aversive life experiences, this becomes relevant to sport psychology if we consider efficacy as the mechanism

Person ⟶ Efficacy expectations ⟶ Behaviour ⟶ Outcome expectations ⟶ Outcome

Figure 3.13 The distinction between 'efficacy expectation' and 'outcome expectation'

which we use to face the challenge of competitive sports, as we shall see later.

Bandura identifies four sources of efficacy expectations:

- performance accomplishments
- vicarious experience
- verbal persuasion
- emotional arousal.

Let us consider how these sources will help the individual cope with threatening situations they may otherwise seek to avoid. Previous mastery and success will convince them that they can master certain situations again. This source is particularly strong, as repeated success raises mastery expectations such that the odd failure can be absorbed. Indeed, overcoming a failure may strengthen the individual's efficacy to overcome obstacles and challenges. Vicarious experience is observing others being successful and being rewarded; this is a form of modelling and ties in with social learning theory. Suggestions, encouragement, guidance, praise can all help an individual improve their self-efficacy and believe in their ability to overcome feelings of threat. Individuals often judge how stressed and anxious they feel based on their physiological arousal. They will feel more able to cope if they feel this arousal is under control, and unable to cope if they are beset by aversive arousal to a debilitating level.

Sport psychologists have developed the notion of self-efficacy as directly applicable to the sporting arena. Sports self-efficacy has come to refer to expectations of performance from self-confidence and self-belief for a given situation. It is situation-specific self-confidence. Taking the four sources identified above, Bandura's coping efficacy easily lends itself to a sporting context.

Performance accomplishments

Success breeds success. Successful past performance strengthens efficacy. If an individual has had some success, they will believe that they can succeed again. Much success allows the individual to absorb some failure, and even learn and thus improve, from the

experience. Past success is the greatest influence on self-efficacy.

Vicarious experience

'If others can do it, so can I.' Vicarious experience is learning by observing others, and the consequences of their actions. Bandura suggests that seeing others successfully coming through threatening activities, or making unsuccessful attempts without adverse consequences, can generate expectations in observers that they too will improve. Seeing success and the rewards it brings can be appealing and make the observer strive for the same rewards.

Verbal persuasion

Feelings, thoughts and actions can be guided. Words of suggestion and advice can help the performer believe they can achieve more and overcome what has overwhelmed them in the past. Verbal persuasion is often employed due to its availability and ease of use, but its influence is weak compared to the above factors and is more easily extinguished.

Emotional arousal

If we cannot handle the big occasion we may 'freeze' when the occasion arises. We judge our anxiety and vulnerability to stress on our physiological arousal. If this is at a reasonable level and under control, we are more likely to believe we can succeed than when we are consumed with anxiety. Avoiding over-arousal and diminishing anxiety is the final factor in improving self-efficacy.

Check your understanding

Imagine you are coaching a team. Identify a dip in performance that one of your top players is experiencing. Suggest a four-point plan, one for each of the factors described above, to increase their self-efficacy and so reverse their downturn in performance.

3.2 Sport-specific self-confidence

Vealey's research (1986) stands out for inclusion in any course relating to this area of sport psychology. So much other research is borrowed from traditional and other areas of psychology and applied to the sport setting. Vealey's work, however, is sport-specific and derived from within the sporting context itself.

Key study

Vealey, Sport confidence and competitive orientation

Sport confidence was conceptualised into three components:

◈ its trait component (SC-trait)

◈ its state component (SC-state)

◈ a 'competitive orientation' component (to account for the different ways an individual may define *success*).

The relationship between these three can be portrayed as in Figure 3.14, which suggests that for a given situation that is, at the start, objective, an athlete's dispositional level of self-confidence (SC-trait) combines with how competitive they are (competitive orientation). This influences how self-confident they are in that particular circumstance (SC-state) which produces the athlete's behavioural response to the situation leading to their individual outcome, accounting for individual differences to any given situation. This, in turn, has an effect on their overall self-confidence (SC-trait) and

general competitiveness (competitive orientation) which impacts on a future events (SC-state).

Vealey developed inventories to gain measures of SC-trait, competitive orientation and SC-state. She conducted research to validate these measures. This involved five phases of testing.

◈ 666 athletes

◈ high-school, college and adult athletes

◈ athletes tested were basketball players, swimmers and road racers (phase 1); track and field athletes, basketball, baseball, tennis and softball players (phase 2); athletes and members of PE classes with some form of competitive sport (phase 3); high-school and college athletes (phase 4) and 48 elite gymnasts (phase 5). Phase 1 tested internal validity and social desirability influences; phase 2 was a re-test having modified in light of phase 1; phase 3 analysed test–retest reliability; phase 4 tested concurrent validity and phase 5 construct validity.

In conclusion, the model has been seen to be an effective way to conceptualise self-confidence on specific sport situations. The evidence supports the theory as well as the valid operation of the constructs proposed.

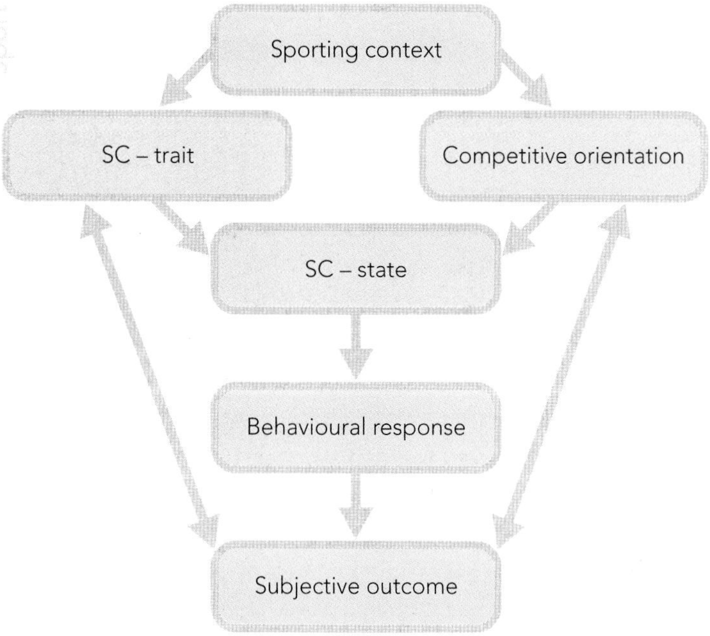

Check your understanding

Which do you consider the most important outcome of sporting performance, satisfaction or success? Justify your answer.

3.3 Imagery

A number of theories attempt to explain why imagery can have such an important impact on performance; psychoneuro-muscular theory facilitates motor skill learning because imagined events innervate the muscles in much the same way as physical practice. Symbolic learning theory suggests that a coding system helps people acquire movement patterns. The imagery develops mental skills such as concentration and confidence. Psychological skill hypothesis prepares and programmes the muscles for actual movement.

Woods (2001) identifies four functions of imagery in sport. These are mental practice, increasing self-confidence, controlling arousal and understanding and retaining information.

Figure 3.14 Vealey's model of sport confidence (Source: Vealey, 1986)

Mental practice

Imagery is a form of covert practice where the athlete creates or re-creates scenarios in the mind, in the absence of real-world experience. At its most effective it will involve all the senses, including visual, auditory, kinaesthetic and mood elements. The brain interprets images literally, and processes the information in much the same way as real stimuli. Although psychologists are not exactly clear how imagery works, it seems likely that the mind–body connection is facilitated via the development of a mental blueprint of performance.

Woods offers six explanations of why mental practice plus physical practice produces better performance levels than physical practice alone.

1   It allows the athlete to try out strategies, run through routines, or as Thierry Henry (Barcelona and French footballer) does, whenever he makes a mistake he immediately re-runs the sequence in his mind but with a desirable ending.

2   It allows private performance practice without anxiety (maybe caused by audience effect).

3   It allows the athlete to suspend time and motion. Shooting a goal in netball can be frozen at various points to perfect technique in stages, then combined into one operation, ready for improved technique when on court.

4   It allows rehearsal and consolidation of newly acquired skills or moves between practices.

5   It encourages focused attention on each part of what is being practised at the athlete's own pace of learning.

6   It further allows the athlete to respond to ongoing performance cues. It would appear that when we imagine activity, there are small muscular reactions of the appropriate muscle or body part.

When athletes have been injured, imagery work has been related to enhanced recovery times. It also allows rehearsal of the acquired skills so that they do not become forgotten or lost.

Increasing self-confidence

A self-confident athlete is one who believes they can successfully execute a skill, and execute it better than an opponent. Imagery helps to achieve goals such as this. In sport, imagery is often used in coaching alongside target-setting. As the athlete sets the target, *visualises* its fulfilment, puts it into practice and is then successful, so their self-belief and hence

their confidence level increase. If you are convinced that you can perform to your optimum and fulfil your goals, you will be confident. Conversely, if you lack confidence, anxiety is created, concentration breaks down and effort is reduced. If you are over-confident you may not prepare thoroughly for competition or may not be fully focused, and so performance can only be sub-optimal.

Controlling arousal

Another function of imagery is its role in techniques of relaxation. There are formally recognised strategies for controlling arousal, such as the tense-relax method or progressive relaxation technique. Many athletes practise yoga as part of their relaxation and preparation for competition. They may visualise anxiety and tension as red, escaping from their body as they breathe out, while visualising calming and refreshing blue being inhaled as they breathe in.

Communicating information

The use of evocative language can make a coach's words so much more readily accessible and inspirational. 'Exploding off the blocks' is a euphemism for getting off to a good start, as 'having a good engine' is a euphemism for stamina. Looking for 'steel' in a challenge may be the most effective way for a coach to inspire his team, rather than a more literal request.

> ### Check your understanding
>
> Think of four examples, one for each of the four functions identified above, where imagery can help the athlete. Describe how each could be used.

Section summary

◆   A form of situation-specific self-confidence is 'self-efficacy'. This involves beliefs about our capability to carry out behaviours to produce given outcomes. Bandura's model of self-efficacy is commonly applied to sports settings by sport psychologists.

◆   Vealey proposed a model of sport-specific self-confidence, which identified the process an individual uses to determine their perception of their ability to be successful in sport.

◆   Related to an athlete's self-confidence is the use of imagery. There are different uses of imagery for different purposes.

Social psychology of sport

Pause for thought

◆ What did Shakespeare mean when he wrote in *As You Like It*:

'All the world's a stage,

And all the men and women merely players'?

Introduction

It is already apparent that social situations cause us to behave differently according to the people involved and the expectations and dynamics of the group. What is less apparent is just how much the social situation impacts on who we are and how we do things, how much the social situation directs and even controls our actions. (Think back to the Milgram study, or Piliavin et al.'s research in the New York subway, in your AS course.)

Try this ...

1 Consider the following situations:

  ◆ a student talking to a teacher in school

  ◆ a son/daughter talking to parents at home

  ◆ someone socialising with a group of friends

  ◆ a person alone with their boyfriend/girlfriend.

2 In what ways do people behave the *same* in each of these situations? (This is to do with a person's *disposition*.)

3 In what ways do people behave *differently* in each of the above social contexts? (This is to do with the *situation*.)

Sport is both a co-operative and a competitive endeavour, and the people in our social environment affect our sporting behaviour because of how we perceive them and think they may judge us.

When we work as part of a team, other people may be involved in leading, coaching, training or otherwise trying to enhance our performance. People may be watching us perform. Even solo athletes compete against others

and in front of judges, scorers and an audience. How we relate to these people, how we perceive them and how we think they perceive us form the area of social psychology in sport. This area will look at:

◆ group cohesion

◆ audience effect

◆ leadership and coaching.

Try this ...

1 Choose any two sporting activities.

2 List all the people who might influence performance and what their roles are.

Group cohesion

What are the indefinable qualities that turn a collection of disparate individuals into that hopefully purposeful, cohesive unit that we call a 'team'? What is the process that brings us to the point where our interactions with the others in the team are settled, where there are some positives between members of the team, a distinct identity exists that defines our team as a unit and there is a shared understanding of purpose, of what the team is trying to achieve? This is what group cohesion is all about, and a model put forward by Tuckman (1965) traces the process of moving from that collection of individuals into what we recognise as a team. We also look at social loafing, whereby the collective scores/performance of a team do not match the total scores/performance of the competitors in the team when performing individually. Swimmers' individual times were quicker than the combined times of the same swimmers when competing in a relay event.

This is evidenced in a study by Latane et al. (1979). It is also important to specify whether the cohesion is about working together to achieve a specified goal or about the degree to which the group generally get on with each other and can work together as a unit. These are known as task cohesion and social cohesion respectively, as identified by Carron (1982).

Audience effect

Performance is often heightened when others are present; this is known as social facilitation. Sometimes, however, performance suffers in the presence of others; this is known as social inhibition. These are commonly attributed to arousal, but why does this arousal come about? Cottrell (1968) suggested it was not merely the presence of others that caused the arousal, but a social anxiety about being judged by the others seeing our performance. This was termed evaluation apprehension. The phenomenon of physiological arousal affecting performance was investigated by Zajonc et al. (1969). They compared the times of cockroaches running alone, against a competitor and in front of a cockroach grandstand on both simple and complex tasks. This supports the physiological account of arousal, but begs the question of extrapolation.

Finally, why is it that in competitive team sports, the team playing 'at home' is considered more likely to be victorious than a team playing 'away'? The home advantage was first systematically examined by Schwartz and Barsky (1977), who considered why between 53 and 64 per cent of home matches are won. A possible explanation is social facilitation, and Schwartz and Barsky put forward a number of reasons why this might be the case.

Leadership and coaching

As well as working together, teams need to be guided towards a common goal. Their aim is essentially two-fold, to achieve team satisfaction and successful performance. Some leaders are appointed and formally recognised, such as the manager, the coach, the captain. Others emerge due to their character and personality as befits the situation. It could be suggested that this is purely due to personality – some people are simply born leaders, others are not. This idea is explored by the Great Man theory, which attempts to identify if successful leaders share certain characteristics. Other models attempt to consider what contingencies are involved in effective leadership. One of these is by Chelladurai (1978), who proposes a dynamic

interrelation between the situation, the leader and the team members. A final aspect of leading a team, united toward the same goal, is through its training, so the role of a coach is crucial to a team's success. With this in mind, the final aspect considered in this section is the use of a coaching behaviour assessment system to develop coach effectiveness training programmes.

Key terms

group cohesion the bond or glue between members of a team

social loafing the reduction in effort made by individuals when performing as part of a team

task cohesion shared commitment among members of a team to achieving a common goal

social cohesion people's belief that getting on with each other will be fundamental to their team

social facilitation process gains in performance caused by the presence of others

social inhibition process losses in performance caused by the presence of others

evaluation apprehension the phenomenon whereby performance will be enhanced or impaired in the presence of persons who can approve or disapprove of the performance

extrapolation 'drawing out' or inferring something unknown from something that is known, for example drawing parallels for human behaviour from observing animal behaviour

Themes and perspectives

The experimental method is highlighted in this section. A main benefit of this method is that it allows control of extraneous variables. This way, having conducted our research, we can be confident that any changes observed can be more reliably attributed to the independent variable. In other words, we can be more confident of cause and effect, and that the changes we witness are not due to other, uncontrolled factors. The experimental method is sometimes criticised for lacking ecological validity (not being applicable to real-world scenarios). While this may be true, it rather misses the point of experimental research. When trying to understand the complexity of human experience we need to tease out individual factors involved. An experiment attempts to isolate factors to gain an insight into one such factor involved in the greater 'whole'.

When we look at Zajonc's cockroaches, we see that physiological arousal does affect performance: even cockroaches, who are bereft of cognitive and social awareness, respond physiologically. We therefore have evidence of a physiological aspect to social facilitation. If we did this in humans only, we would never know if cognitive *or* biological aspects caused the change in performance. In evaluation apprehension, competitors have performed better in front of a blindfolded audience than a non-blindfolded one. Of course, this is not a natural situation, but it successfully isolates the fact of competitors being aware of others' judgements, hence is a strong basis for evaluation apprehension.

Also highlighted in this section is the notion of a meta-analysis. Although secondary data, it allows the researcher to draw out salient points from a wide range of sources. This breadth of data is one of the main benefits of using a meta-analysis. The fact that conclusions can be corroborated from such a wide range of research provides a further advantage of this approach. However, the fact that the researcher is 'picking out' the information that they want, makes the evidence highly subjective.

> ## Key term
>
> meta-analysis a study of studies. It gathers second-hand data but allows a researcher access to a huge variety of samples and procedures which taken together may be more meaningful than a single piece of research

Observations provide the researcher with more ecologically valid material, in other words drawn from a more natural setting and so generalisable to a real-world scenario. Unfortunately, what is gained in ecological validity is lost in control of extraneous variables. Observations can be selective, subjective and biased. However, by combining observations in a broader setting, such as a meta-analysis as described above, reliability of data can be increased.

An alternative is to assess human characteristics numerically. Psychometric testing is particularly useful in an applied setting in that it allows human endeavours to be measured, monitored and compared. Smith et al. (1977) developed a system known as a Coach Behaviour Assessment System (CBAS) and we have seen how this has been utilised to guide coach effectiveness training, as put forward by Smith et al. (1979), among others. It does, however, raise the question of whether human characteristics and behaviours can be reduced to numbers or whether the human element is partially lost.

> ## Try this ...
>
> Now that you have read this introduction, look again at the second 'Try this' on page 182. You should now be able to identify a wider range of people who might affect sporting performance.

1 Group cohesion

1.1 Theories

Earlier we referred to *disposition* (innate characteristics) and *situation* (consisting of both the social and physical environment). Within the social aspect of situational influence we find that a group's dynamic (the ever-changing relationships and interplay between group members) can have considerable impact, particularly on performance. Most commentators assume that groups go through a number of stages of getting to know each other and perform cohesively.

> ### Key study
> #### Tuckman, Developmental sequence in small groups
>
> A think-tank of social psychologists, of which Tuckman was a part, was looking at small group and organisational behaviour at the naval Medical Research Institute, Bethesda, Maryland, USA. Altman had been collecting articles on group development and gave them to Tuckman to see if any patterns emerged. Tuckman (1965) reported identifying four stages: orientation/testing/dependence, conflict, group cohesion, functional role-relatedness. For these he evolved the terms: 'forming,' 'storming,' 'norming,' and 'performing', and proposed his stage theory of group development.
>
> 1   **Forming** – the coming together of the team members. Through testing, members start to become cohesively oriented as they seek acceptance from others, and so come to depend on the group and its hierarchy.
>
> 2   **Storming** – conflict typifies this stage, with banter, posturing, challenging, as group members vie for position in the group hierarchy. The group influence is resisted as individuals seek to affirm who they are, particularly in relation to the others in the group.

3 **Norming** – resistance is overcome as in-group feeling and cohesiveness develop, agreed standards evolve and new roles are adopted. Personal opinions or feelings are intimated and accepted. People find their niche.

4 **Performing** – the final stage in which roles become flexible and functional. Interpersonal structure and group energy become channelled into the task. Conflicts resolve and the structure supports task performance.

In 1977 Tuckman suggested that much literature had identified termination of the group for a range of reasons, from irreconcilable differences to task completion. He proposed that this stage be called 'adjourning'.

Whereas Tuckman originally set out to seek and review the literature on group development, his model has enjoyed expression with practitioners in various applied settings. Sports practitioners seem particularly comfortable with Tuckman's model as a useful and usable explanation into group development and dynamics.

Check your understanding

1 Is the team in Figure 3.15 forming, storming, norming or performing?

2 What may have happened in the other stages leading up to this point?

3 What may happen after this stage?

4 Explain your suggestions.

1.2 Social loafing

How well a team performs collectively is all-important. However, working collectively can amount to a reduction from peak performance by the individuals within the team. Co-ordination difficulties provide a possible explanation; another reason for a team's performance not amounting to the sum of the individuals' ability could be 'social loafing', which is the subject of our next study.

In 1927, Ringelmann conducted a study where some workers were asked to pull on a rope alone or with 1, 2 or 7 others. Their efforts were measured with a strain gauge. The results are shown in Table 3.10.

By the time eight people are pulling together, less than half of the effort per person is achieved compared to pulling alone. This offends the common-sense view of teamwork and working together, as well as psychology which suggests that the presence of others heightens arousal and so should increase performance (at least on familiar, well-learned and/or simple tasks). So the Ringelmann effect poses the question of when and why collective effort is less productive than individual effort, a question addressed by Latane et al. (1979).

Figure 3.15 Forming, storming, norming or performing?

No. of people	1	2	3	8
Total weight pulled	63 kg	117 kg	160 kg	248 kg
Weight pulled per person	63 kg	59 kg	53 kg	31 kg
Individual effort	100%	93%	85%	49%

Table 3.10 The effects of social loafing

Key study

Latane et al., Many hands make light work

Experiment 1

Methodology Latane et al. wanted to replicate Ringelmann's work conceptually. On eight occasions, six undergraduate males studying introductory psychology from Ohio State University were invited to help the experimenters judge how much noise people make in social settings. The participants were asked to judge cheering and applause, and also to judge how loud these seem to those who hear them. The participants were asked to: (1) clap or cheer as loudly as possible for 5 seconds, and (2) judge noises. Both performers and observers were asked to guess how much noise had been produced. After some practice there were 36 trials of yelling and 36 trials of clapping alone, in pairs and in groups of four and six. The order of these trials was counterbalanced. Measures were taken by a General Radio sound-level meter placed at 4m from each performer.

Results The noise produced did not grow in proportion to the number of people. The average sound pressure generated per person decreased with increasing group size ($p<0.001$). Two-person groups performed at only 71 per cent of the sum of their individual capacity, four-person groups at 51 per cent and six-person groups at 40 per cent.

Discussion As in pulling ropes, it appears that when it comes to clapping and shouting many hands do, in fact, make light work. Ringelmann's findings had been replicated using a different task in a different historical epoch and culture. It could be attributed to social loafing; an alternative explanation could be faulty social processes, as Steiner (1972) suggests. He points out that as group size increases, the number of co-ordination links (and thus the possibility of faulty co-ordination) also increases. Experiment 2 tries to resolve these competing explanations.

Experiment 2 – co-ordination loss or reduced effort?

For this part of the study, there were six more groups of six male undergraduate volunteers. The aim was to remove the 'non-reduced effort' factors, so participants were told

the experiment was about sensory feedback rather than judgements of others and of themselves. Participants wore blindfolds and headsets so they could not see or hear the others in their group, and were told the room was soundproofed. Despite these social factors (i.e. co-ordination) being removed (i.e. lost) and despite the fact that in Experiment 1 participants applauded and clapped with all the excitement, embarrassment and conformity that go with such a situation, the two studies produced similar results. This points to the robust nature of the phenomenon of social loafing.

> ### Check your understanding
>
> 1 Test out the social loafing phenomenon in a setting of your choosing.
>
> 2 Why do you think it occurs – reduced effort or co-ordination loss? Explain your reasoning.

1.3 Aspects of cohesion

We have so far considered the process by which a team or group forms and develops, and how a team can suffer in loss of overall performance. However, the real question is how together that group is and how united the team is. Groups are social units and cohesion is the glue that bonds them together. Cohesion is a construct which represents the strength of the social bond within the group. Group cohesion has been explored by Carron, working with others as seen in research such as Carron and Bennett (1977) and Carron and Chelladurai (1981 and 1982).

Key study

Carron, Cohesiveness in sports groups

Carron broke his perceptions of cohesion in sport into four areas:

- the theoretical framework
- application to sport
- implications and limitations
- future directions.

General theoretical perspective

This derives from the work of Festinger et al. (1963), who proposed that cohesion was at least bi-dimensional.

They said that to understand group dynamics and how groups bind together, it was necessary to look at (a) the source of rewards and (b) the means to achieving the rewards. These notions have been developed to be considered as two components, namely social cohesion and task cohesion (as first proposed by Mikalachki in Enoch and McLemore, 1967).

Sports research perspective

While theory acknowledges that there are two dimensions to group cohesiveness, cohesion has been operationally defined as one general dimension. For example, Martens et al.'s sport cohesiveness questionnaire measures seven aspects of cohesiveness, including the degree of friendship or interpersonal attraction among group members, the sense of belonging, and the level of teamwork perceived to be present in the group. This emphasis on social cohesion typifies the measures that are commonly used.

Limitations

As suggested above, issues of validity prevail. By emphasising social cohesion (sometimes referred to as cohesiveness-as-attraction) other factors that induce cohesiveness are overlooked, such as the goals and objectives relating to performance. Second, groups characterised by low levels of mutual attraction and negative affect do not necessarily lead to break-up or even disruption. Third, attraction is not needed for groups to form. Formation can occur because people share similar values or they can see a clear goal-path. Finally, there is no agreed single, general concept of cohesiveness.

Further, measures of cohesion have tended to look at the group as a whole, often with average or aggregated scores. However, the perceptions of individuals within a group have been overlooked. For example, a wide range of scores can average out around the middle, as can a whole set of mediocre responses. The result is the same, but the group dynamic and perception very different. Measures other than the mean, such as modal values, tend to be overlooked.

Future directions

Carron has brought together the various parts of an overarching system for developing cohesiveness in sports teams. This can be represented as shown in Figure 3.16.

> **Check your understanding**
>
> 1 Which is most important, social cohesion or task cohesion?
>
> 2 How much more important is it than the other one?
>
> 3 Are they totally separate or do they overlap? If so, in what way?

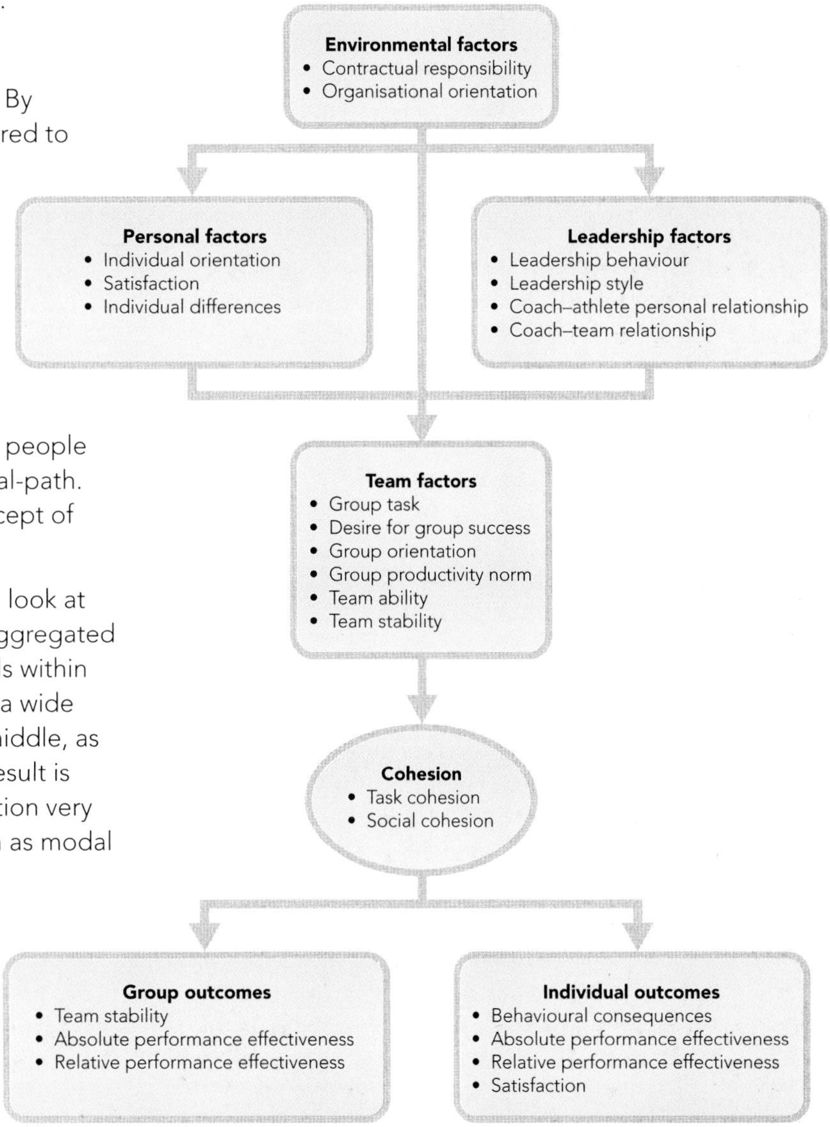

Environmental factors
- Contractual responsibility
- Organisational orientation

Personal factors
- Individual orientation
- Satisfaction
- Individual differences

Leadership factors
- Leadership behaviour
- Leadership style
- Coach–athlete personal relationship
- Coach–team relationship

Team factors
- Group task
- Desire for group success
- Group orientation
- Group productivity norm
- Team ability
- Team stability

Cohesion
- Task cohesion
- Social cohesion

Group outcomes
- Team stability
- Absolute performance effectiveness
- Relative performance effectiveness

Individual outcomes
- Behavioural consequences
- Absolute performance effectiveness
- Relative performance effectiveness
- Satisfaction

Figure 3.16 Carron's system for developing cohesiveness in sports teams (Source: Carron, 1986)

Section summary

◆ Tuckman proposes a catchy mnemonic that traces the development of group functioning.

◆ Social loafing, while not strictly dealing with cohesion, is often considered in this area. Maybe lack of cohesion brings about social loafing.

◆ Latane et al. suggest that social loafing is a phenomenon beyond faulty group processes.

◆ Carron takes a closer look at aspects of cohesion, most notably social cohesion and task cohesion.

2 Audience effect

Audience effect refers to a change in performance brought about by the presence of others. An audience may be passive, as in your family watching you practise at home, or a stadium full of spectators. Alternatively, they may be co-acting, that is, taking part in the activity either competitively or co-operatively.

In 1898, Triplett noticed that cyclists' times were quicker when racing against another cyclist than when riding alone 'against the clock'. This was tested by asking 10-year-old boys to wind as many turns on a fishing reel as they could within a given time. It was found that they could manage more turns when two boys did this in the same room than when the task was undertaken alone. In fact, just the knowledge of other boys doing the task in another room (therefore an unseen, co-acting audience) enhanced performance. However, Allport (1924) found that while the quantity of behaviours may increase, the quality may decrease given certain circumstances. These notions of social facilitation and social inhibition were identified by Dashiell (1930). Research was moved on by Zajonc (1969), whose work is based on drive and arousal. He claims that an audience produces arousal in a performer. This heightens the dominant response. With a simple, familiar or well-learned task, this increase in arousal will heighten performance (explaining social facilitation). With a novel, unfamiliar or complex task, this increase in arousal will impair/diminish performance (explaining social inhibition). Zajonc claims that the *mere presence* of an audience produces the aforementioned arousal and audience effects. Critics have challenged the mere presence concept, suggesting that even a passive audience interacts with the performance, such as clapping, cheering and booing. One such challenge comes from Cottrell et al. (1968), as shown below.

2.1 Theories

Key study

Cottrell et al., The effects of an audience versus the effects of the 'mere presence' of others

Aim Cottrell aimed to show that Zajonc's notion of the mere presence of an audience overlooked the impact from that audience. He therefore set out to compare a task carried out with a blindfolded audience (mere presence) with one carried out with a non-blindfolded audience.

Sample A total of 45 introductory psychology university students performed a pseudo-recognition task; 15 performed the task alone, 15 before an audience of two passive spectators, and 15 before an audience of two who were not spectators and were blindfolded.

Apparatus and materials The stimuli were ten nonsense words – AFWORBU, BIWONJI, CIVADRA, JTEVKANI, LOKANTA, MECBURI, NANSOMA, PARITAF, SARIDIK, and ZABDLON – similar to those used by Zajonc and Sales (1966). The training stimuli were 4 × 6-inch photos of each word. The test stimuli were 2 × 2-inch slides of each word. The slides were presented on a tachistoscope. A stopwatch was used to time the stages of the experiment.

Key terms

dominant response the response that supersedes the other possible responses

tachistoscope a type of projector that shows an image for a specific but adjustable period of time

Procedure Words were practised and pseudo-recognition trials were started. Subjects were told it was a study of how people learn a foreign language, hence the strange words. The number of responses in the pseudo-recognition trials was recorded, giving the dependent variable. There were three conditions of the independent variable. In the *alone condition* the subject was alone in the room during testing. In the *audience condition*, two confederates posing as fellow introductory psychology students arrived in the experimental room early for a supposed colour-perception experiment. They were allowed to watch the present experiment while waiting for theirs and thus became an audience. The *mere presence condition* was the same as the audience condition, except the confederates were asked to put on blindfolds in preparation for their (alleged) forthcoming experiment.

Results and conclusions

As can be seen from Figure 3.17, mere presence and alone produce a similar level of response, but the audience condition stands out as having a significantly greater number of responses. This suggests that mere presence, as Zajonc stated, is not sufficient to affect performance, but that the audience needs to be involved, active or at least alert. The findings otherwise are close to Zajonc's: the presence of an audience increases the individual's general drive.

On the pseudo-recognition trials the presence of an audience enhanced the emission of dominant responses. However, the mere presence of other persons of the same status and in the same physical proximity as the audience did not enhance the emission of dominant responses.

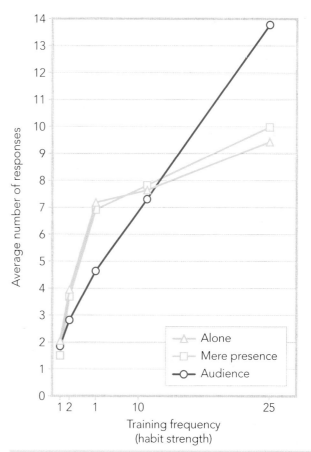

Figure 3.17 Graph to show the level of response in the alone, mere presence and audience conditions (Source: Cottrell et al., 1968)

> **Check your understanding**
>
> How does this study help you to explain sports performance in front of various types of audiences?
>
> In the light of this study, how should an elite athlete train for a big event?

2.2 Studies

Key study

Zajonc et al., Cockroach studies

A year after the previous study, however, Zajonc presented some intriguing evidence in support of his theory. He turned his attention to cockroaches, and the fact that they are repelled by light. Zajonc set up a cockroach run in which he placed a light at one end.

Subjects 72 adult female cockroaches (*Blatta orientalis*).

1   When the light was turned on, the cockroach ran away from the light as quickly as possible. Zajonc timed how long it took to reach the end of the run. He calculated an average of ten trials. This was the alone condition.

2   Next, he placed two cockroaches in the run, and again timed how quickly they ran to the end. He calculated an average of ten trials. This was the co-acting audience condition.

3   Finally, he built a cockroach grandstand. This was Perspex housing with compartments just large enough to fit one cockroach, though not large enough for them to turn around. This was placed by

the side of the run and so formed a non-coacting audience of cockroaches. Again, Zajonc placed a cockroach in the run, and timed how quickly it ran the run, calculating an average of ten trials. This was the non-coacting audience condition.

4   The three conditions above were repeated using a cockroach maze instead of a cockroach run. This was a complex as opposed to a simple task, hence affecting the dominant response.

Findings Taking the lone cockroach in a cockroach run as a benchmark, the cockroaches in front of the grandstand (the non-coacting audience) were faster, while the coacting cockroaches, running against each other, ran the fastest.

Taking the lone cockroach in a cockroach maze as a benchmark, the cockroaches in front of the grandstand (the non-coacting audience) were slower, while the coacting cockroaches, running against each other, ran the slowest.

Conclusions The first thing Zajonc suggests is that the presence of others increases arousal. When a task is simple, familiar or well-learned, this arousal enhances good performance, which is the dominant response in this instance. When a task is novel, complex or unfamiliar, it enhances poor performance, which is the dominant response in this instance. The cockroach run demonstrates the former and the cockroach maze the latter.

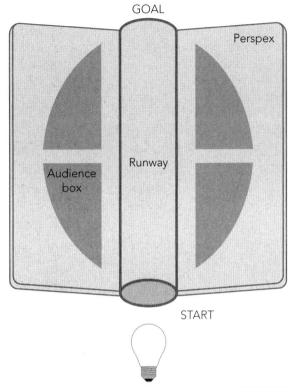

Figure 3.18 Diagram showing layout of 'cockroach run' (Source: Zajonc et al., 1969)

Check your understanding

1 What sporting situations can Zajonc's research be applied to?

2 Can we draw valid and reliable conclusions on the basis of watching cockroaches in a run or maze?

3 Make a case for *and* a case against. What do you think?

2.3 Home advantage

While we may observe an improvement in performance in front of an audience, and the nature of the audience beyond 'mere presence' may be important, we may also observe the phenomenon whereby, to varying degrees, there is an advantage in playing 'at home' in front of your own audience of spectators. Whether or not this observation can be supported by documented evidence and, if so, why this should be, was studied by Schwartz and Barsky (1977), among others. They took their inspiration from the sociologist Durkheim, who talked of a common passion in the midst of an assembly and the invigorating influence of a supportive social congregation. This effect of community support on performance is well recognised in sport and is known as the home advantage.

Key study

Schwartz and Barsky, Home advantage

Method One major source for Schwartz and Barsky included 1880 major league baseball games played in 1971 (see Table 3.11). This represents 97 per cent of all games played in that year in the American and National Leagues. Also recorded were home team outcomes for all 182 games played in 1971 in the professional American and National Football Conferences. The same information was gathered from the 910 games played by 182 college football teams in 1971. The next set of data consists of 542 games played in both divisions of the National Hockey League in the 1971/72 season; this includes 87 per cent of all games played that year. The final source of information consists of 1485 college basketball games played by the Philadelphia area Big 5 teams over a 15-year period (1952–66).

Results Overall, home victories exceed 50 per cent of all games won. The advantage of playing at home differs from one sport to another, as shown in Table 3.11. The home advantage is at its most decisive in the indoor arenas of basketball and ice hockey. It is least decisive in baseball, where the home team won 53 per cent of their home games (compared to 47 per cent of away games). Football teams won 55 per cent of their home games; college football teams 59 per cent. Away from home the corresponding win percentages were 42 and 40 respectively. However, the effect is most pronounced in indoor hockey where, excluding tied games, 64 per cent are won at home and only 36 per cent away from home.

In basketball, the Big 5 win 82 per cent of their games at home. The success at home seems largely attributable to offensive (attacking) play rather than better defensive play. In addition, a hostile crowd can bring about deterioration in the play of the away team rather than improve the performance of the home team, suggesting that an away disadvantage may account for the home advantage. Arousal theory goes a long way to explaining the findings. The home effect is most pronounced when a strong team hosts a weak team; the damage is most pronounced for the away team when the task is difficult, that is, playing away to a strong team. Ironically therefore, successful performance is affected not only by an athlete's skill and abilities but also the number and enthusiasm of their well-wishers.

Conclusions

1   The home advantage is most pronounced in the indoor sports of ice hockey and basketball, least so in the outdoor sports of baseball and football.

2   The major factor in home advantage for all sports is more effective offensive play rather than defensive action.

3   Playing at home or away is as strong a correlate of a team's performance as is the quality of its players.

4   Home advantage is almost totally independent of visitor fatigue and lack of familiarity with the home playing area.

5   Away disadvantage is often as significant an explanation as home advantage. This may be explained by arousal theory.

> #### Check your understanding
>
> Explain point 5 (above). Why might this be the most important explanation of home advantage?

Section summary

◆   As sport psychologists, we need to be aware of the serious effect the presence of an audience may have on performance. Cottrell showed that the effect was caused by more than mere presence; he demonstrated this by showing that a blindfolded audience has less effect on performance than an all-seeing one.

◆   How the presence of others causes physiological arousal was established by Zajonc et al. They did this by looking at the response of cockroaches running alone, in competition and in front of an audience.

◆   Schwartz and Barsky offer some insight into the phenomenon of home advantage.

3 Leadership and coaching

Leadership is where an individual leads or directs the activities or behaviour of a group towards a shared goal. In the sports setting this can be the leadership of an organisation, team or club. This section looks at how leadership comes about and how effective it can be. Coaching involves a very specific type of leadership whereby one person encourages the development of skills in individuals and in a team.

3.1 Trait and type theories

Key study

Stogdill, Great Man theory

An initial question when considering leadership is whether leaders are born or made. The notion that some people are born with the qualities essential to leadership is the trait approach, known as the 'Great Man' theory. Many researchers have suggested and studied this approach to explaining leadership, including Stogdill (1948). His survey was concerned with studies where some

	Sport			
		Football		
	Baseball	Professional	College	Hockey
Home team outcome	1971	1971	1971	1971–72
Win	53 (989)	55 (100)	59 (532)	53 (286)
Lose	47 (891)	41 (74)	40 (367)	30 (163)
Tie		4 (8)	1 (11)	17 (93)
Total	100 (1880)	100 (182)	100 (910)	100 (542)

No. of cases is given in parentheses

Table 3.11 Percentage of games won by the home team in baseball, football and hockey (Source: Schwartz and Barsky, 1977)

attempt has been made to determine the traits and characteristics of leaders. Carrying out what we would now call a meta-analysis, Stogdill scoured psychological literature for research about the trait approach and extracted the relevant data in his quest to find consistency and patterns. The survey lists only those factors which were studied by three or more investigators. Data are obtained from various groups by various methods, giving a broad range of social composition and of different methodologies.

Methodology

1 Observation and time sampling of behaviour in group situations

The behaviour of two or more individuals is observed in situations which permit the emergence of leaders.

2 Choice of associates (voting, naming, ranking, sociometrics)

Members of a group are asked to name the person whom they would prefer as a leader, possibly describing the characteristics which make them a desirable leader.

3 Nomination by qualified observer

Leaders are named by those in a formal position to identify group leaders such as teachers, club leaders or other adult observers.

4 Selection of person occupying position of leadership

Leadership is regarded as synonymous with holding office or any appointed position of responsibility.

5 Analysis of biographical and case history data

Most of these studies were based on the analysis of biographical data.

6 The listing of traits considered essential to leadership

Different groups, such as business executives and members of the professions, were asked to list the traits which they believed essential for leadership.

7 Supplementary aspects

Various measures have been employed to determine the traits associated with leadership. Most frequently used are tests of intelligence and personality but we also find questionnaires, rating scales and interviews.

Results

1 Chronological age

The evidence as to the relation of age to leadership is quite contradictory. Leaders were found to be younger in six studies where chronological age was apparent, and to be older in ten studies, otherwise there was either no difference, or this aspect differed with different situations.

2 Height

The general trend of these studies was to a weak positive relationship, with leaders found to be taller in nine studies and only two studies finding leaders to be shorter. Note, however, Napoleon, Hitler and Mahatma Gandhi.

3 Weight

A weak positive correlation between weight and leadership was suggested, seven studies finding leaders to be heavier and two finding them to be lighter.

4 Physique, energy, health

Whereas some studies suggest that superior physique is a characteristic of leaders, the correlation coefficients regularly fall short of 0.3. This suggests that there is no consistent relationship.

5 Appearance

The evidence suggests a possible relationship between appearance and leadership, with eleven studies finding that leaders present a better appearance.

6 Fluency of speech

This possibly more than any other in Stogdill's review is the feature possessed most consistently by leaders studied. Features such as 'confident in tone of voice' or 'pleasant voice' typified the responses in this section. Even observations such as 'longer duration of verbal excitation' and 'talkativeness' are seen to be correlated to leadership. Further evidence is identified, such as vividness and originality of expression.

7 Intelligence

In general, leaders appear brighter and the average child or student leader surpasses the average group member in intelligence. However, it should be noted that a number of studies indicate that too great a difference militates against leadership.

8 Scholarship and 9 Knowledge

With a high degree of uniformity leaders are found to get better grades than non-leaders and have better knowledge of how to get things done.

10 to 24

Stogdill outlines fifteen more features that may identify leaders in terms of traits. The strength of their relationship to leadership is commented on, as well as the number of studies presenting with each feature.

General discussion and conclusion

Stogdill's research is a good example of many studies that have been conducted into identifying which traits typify the quality of 'leader'. However, there is little consistency to suggest that a leader in one situation will inevitably be a good leader in a different situation. This lack of a consistent set of qualities to identify a good leader in all situations has always rendered the 'Great Man' approach short on credibility.

Check your understanding

1   In pairs, list as many leaders as you can, from a variety of contexts.

2   Try to identify qualities that they seem to have in common.

3   See what qualities other pairs have identified in common with your own.

4   Would it be safe to conclude that you have identified qualities of leadership? Justify your response.

3.2 Contingency theories

An alternative approach is to look at the *style* of leadership. The oft-quoted research by Lewin et al. (1939) looked at 10-year-old boys in a model-making club. Their leaders were autocratic, democratic or laissez-faire. The group with the autocratic leader produced the most, but production declined and conflict ensued when the leader left the room. The group with the democratic leader produced a little less than the autocratic group, but continued productively when the leader was not present. The laissez-faire group experienced low production levels and much more conflict than the other groups. Significantly, however, when the leader and hence the leadership style changed, which it did at 5-weekly intervals, the performance of the group changed in accordance with its new leadership style. An interesting criticism of this study is that it took place in the USA (a democracy), so the boys were brought up and schooled in this regime. The outcome, therefore, may have been a comment on familiarity with a leadership style rather than the effect of the leadership style itself.

Fiedler (1964) suggested that the trait approach alone could never account for leadership, as leadership was *contingent upon* a number of factors. He identified leaders as person-orientated or task-orientated, as measured by how well they got on with their 'least preferred co-worker'. This he correlated with the nature of the task to suggest that simple, well-learned tasks required a task-orientated, autocratic leader, as did difficult, complex or novel tasks. Moderate tasks, however, would benefit from a more democratic, person-orientated leader. And so the notion of a contingency theory of leadership was born. This was effectively applied to the sport setting by Chelladurai (1978). There are clearly contingencies beyond those investigated by the trait approach that need to be borne in mind when considering 'What makes a successful leader?'

Key study

Chelladurai, Multi-dimensional model of leadership

This piece of research is an attempt to identify what these contingencies are and how they interact to explain the question of what makes a good leader in sport. Chelladurai (1978) identifies three possible leader behaviours, as follows.

Prescribed leader behaviour confirms and conforms to the norms and expectations of the organisation in which leadership is being examined. It is the behaviour prescribed by the authority of the institution. The captain of the England cricket team sits on the Board of Selectors, and his role requires him to turn up when the Board meets. The situation determines this behaviour.

Preferred leader behaviour is what the team members would choose their leader to have. It may also mean 'preferred' as in 'preferable', as a team whose confidence was low would need a leader who was praising, encouraging and gave them some self-belief. Therefore the team members' preferences or needs determine this behaviour, although the situation could have an impact as well.

Actual leader behaviour is the tangible behaviour that the leader really displays, irrespective of the prescribed or preferred behaviour. This is determined by the leader's traits and innate characteristics.

Chelladurai suggests that different types of leader behaviour displayed together should be called congruence. He concludes as follows.

◆   When prescribed, actual and preferred leadership are all incongruent then a laissez-faire outcome should ensue.

◆   When prescribed and preferred leadership are congruent but the leader's actual behaviour is incongruent to these, then the removal of the leader is on the cards.

◆   When preferred leadership is congruent with actual leadership but the prescribed leadership behaviour is incongruent, the team will experience satisfaction but performance may suffer.

◆ When prescribed leadership is congruent with actual leadership but the preferred leadership behaviour is incongruent to these, then successful performance is likely but at the expense of team satisfaction.

◆ Only when all three are congruent will ideal performance and satisfaction be promoted.

These points are summarised in Table 3.12.

Prescribed	Actual	Preferred	Laissez-faire
Prescribed + Preferred	Actual		Removal of leader
Actual + Preferred	Prescribed		Team satisfaction
Actual + Prescribed	Preferred		Successful performance
Prescribed + Actual + Preferred			Ideal performance and satisfaction

Table 3.12 Congruence table (Source: Chelladurai, 1978)

> ### Check your understanding
> Describe five scenarios (real or imaginary) which could be explained by the contingencies outlined above.

3.3 Coaching

Coaching involves the transmission of skills for application to the sporting situation, and relies on the coach's ability to effectively impart the knowledge necessary for successful participation.

Key study

Smith et al., Coach effectiveness training

Baseball coaches in a children's league from Seattle, USA engaged in a pre-season training programme. Success was defined as being able to relate effectively rather than solely improve in a win/loss count. The programme was based on previously identified cognitive-behavioural guidelines and measured using the 12-category coaching behaviour assessment system (CBAS) (Smith et al., 1977). The effects of the training programme on coach behaviours and player perceptions, attitudes and self-esteem were assessed. The hypothesis was that differences in attitudes towards trained versus untrained coaches would be most pronounced for children with low self-esteem.

Participants Initially there were 34 Seattle-area male Little League Baseball coaches. They were from three leagues, involved at major level (10- to 12-year-olds) and senior level (13- to 15-year-olds); 18 were assigned to the experimental condition and attended the training session and 16 were assigned to the control (no-treatment) condition, however three were lost due to 'team mergers or changes in residence', leaving 13 in this condition. The mean age of the coaches was about 36 years, with an average of just over 8 years of coaching experience.

The training session
This lasted about 2 hours and was led by the authors. Participants were presented with guidelines developed from previous research. The explicit goals of the guidelines were to increase positive interactions between coach and players, as well as among team-mates, and to reduce fear of failure. The various guidelines were designed to increase the coaches' awareness of their own behaviours and repeatedly focus attention on the guidelines. Behavioural feedback was provided in terms of the 12 behavioural categories in the coaching and behavioural assessment system (CBAS).

The coaches were observed during the first 2 weeks of the season by trained coders, and thorough feedback provided.

Evaluation procedures Coaches from the experimental group and the control group were compared in terms of observed behaviours (observed by 16 undergraduates trained for 4 weeks, by means of the CBAS), players' perceptions, players' attitudes to themselves, the coaches, team-mates and the sport. There was also assessment of self-esteem using an adaptation of Coopersmith's self-esteem inventory (1967). The 12 response categories of the CBAS are shown in Table 3.13.

Results

Comparability of experimental and control coaches

On player-perceived behaviours, there were no significant differences in any of the 12 behaviour categories. A total of 26,412 behaviours were coded during game observations.

Reactive behaviours	Desirable performances	Positive reinforcement
	Mistakes/Errors	Non-reinforcement
		Mistake contingent encouragement
		Mistake contingent technical
Instruction		
		Punishment
		Punitive
		Ignoring mistakes
	Misbehaviours	Keeping control
Spontaneous behaviours	Game-related	General technical instruction
		General encouragement
		Organisation
	Game-irrelevant	General communication

Table 3.13 The 12 response categories of the CBAS

Self-esteem changes

The trainer group increased from 51 to 52.5 on their self-esteem score, whereas the control group fell from 52 to 50.7. The greatest change in attitudes was found amongst those whose self-esteem was low, who appeared most sensitive to variations in the coach's behaviour.

Team records

Mean winning percentage for trained coaches was 54.5 per cent, whereas the control coaches won 44.7 per cent of their games.

Discussion The results of the present study indicate that the experimental training programme exerted a significant and positive influence on coaching behaviours, player-perceived behaviours and children's attitudes to their coaches, team-mates and other aspects of athletics performance. A positive change in self-esteem was also observed in children who played for the trained coaches.

Check your understanding

1   Is it worth having a coach? What evidence would you refer to in support of your answer?

2   Who benefits most from coaching? What positive aspect of change may account for this?

Section summary

◆   Leadership can be seen as a trait that some people have more than others. Alternatively, it can be seen as how well a person can respond and guide others in a given situation. There are different types of leaders and leadership.

◆   Stogdill's research is an example of the trait approach to leadership. He analysed a large sample of leaders to see whether they had any traits in common.

◆   This can be developed into models that take account of the various aspects of leadership, known as contingency models. Chelladurai developed a sport-specific model of sports leadership in which he identified different types of leaders, based on trait, situation and the group/team being led. Successful outcome referred to satisfaction as well as successful performance.

◆   The Coaching Behaviour Assessment System was used to assess a system of coach effectiveness that seemed to indicate a positive influence and a positive change in the athlete, particularly in their self-esteem.

Exercise psychology

Pause for thought

◆ Most of us are aware of the major benefits of exercise and sports participation to our physical health, particularly in regard to the condition of our heart and vascular system. However, there may be other physical health benefits. With a partner, talk about different illnesses and whether physical activity might help them; you may also want to consider factors such as age and sex.

◆ Look at Figure 3.19, and write down as many positive and negative psychological effects as you can of participating in the London Marathon.

Figure 3.19 Is marathon-running good for you?

Introduction

Exercise and sports participation can have a wide range of effects on our physical and psychological well-being. Although we often assume that these effects are positive in terms of our mental and physical states, we should not forget that exercise and sports participation also have some potentially negative effects.

Exercise psychology has been divided into three sections on the specification and considers the following:

- exercise and pathology
- exercise and mental health
- issues in exercise and sport.

Exercise and pathology

Exercise and sports participation may have a variety of effects on diseases and physical disorders. Research has focused on the effect of physical activity on heart disease (including cholesterol and high-density lipoprotein (HDL) levels), cancer, strokes and osteoporosis, as well less the obvious effects on eating disorders and HIV. Some studies have used retrospective exercise histories and then compared these to rates of disease, whilst others have tracked physical activity patterns and related them to disease and mortality rates in longitudinal studies. Another type of study has collected data from a number of studies in a field of research and used the technique of meta-analysis to look for consistent findings in the research.

Exercise and mental health

Engaging in regular physical activity can influence our mental health and general psychological mood. More vigorous exercise may play a role in creating euphoric mood states by stimulating the release of endorphins. In a more general sense, many studies have found a link between exercise and reduced levels of depression and anxiety, and improved mood. These changes have been demonstrated with a wide variety of samples, including psychiatric patents and athletes. Some of the main methodological issues in this area have related to the difficulty of directly investigating the effect of neurochemicals on the brain and the widespread use of questionnaires to measure changes in mental health and mood states.

Issues in exercise and sport

A number of issues in exercise and sport may have stemmed from growing pressures on athletes to produce better performances more often. Athletes may over-train in the belief that more training results in better performance, and this coupled with the possibility of more competition can produce burn-out and withdrawal from sport. These pressures, along with the intrinsically necessary requirement for certain sports to have particular body morphologies, may put athletes at more risk of developing eating disorders. Some athletes may resort to drugs to help improve performance. However, it has been found that the use of placebos in place of performance-enhancing drugs can produce beneficial performance and psychological adaptations. These findings may be useful in highlighting to athletes the potential benefits of using psychological technique rather than chemical enhancements.

Themes and perspectives

A number of potential issues relating to this area of have already been highlighted above. Another important consideration in some studies is the use of control groups for comparison with experimental groups and whether these groups are matched for key variables. The extent to which some studies have external validity, particularly in regard to population validity, may also be noted.

> **Key terms**
>
> mood a longer-lasting emotional reaction to an event or stimuli, which may have a positive or negative dimension
>
> external validity whether the procedures and participants used in a study can be generalised to other settings and populations

1 Exercise and pathology

1.1 Exercise and its relation to cancer

Evidence from a variety of sources has suggested that greater exposure to ovarian hormones such as oestrogen increases the risk of breast cancer (Henderson et al., 1985). Exposure to ovarian hormones comes from the total counts of menstrual cycles during the woman's gynaecological age. The early onset of menstruation typically means more menstrual cycles in a lifetime and a quicker stabilisation of cycles into a regular pattern, also contributing to the total accumulation of menstruations. It has been proposed that any factor which could reduce the number of menstrual cycles in females might also therefore be a means of reducing exposure to ovarian hormones and a way of lowering breast cancer rates (Bernstein et al., 1994). Strenuous exercise could be one such factor that might influence the incidence of breast cancer, as it has a significant impact on menstrual activity during adolescence, reducing the frequency of menstrual cycles (Bernstein et al., 1994).

Key study

Bernstein et al., Physical exercise and reduced risk of cancer in young women

Aim To investigate the potential relationship between different levels of exercise and the risk of breast cancer.

Procedure The design of the study was a case-control study using 545 newly diagnosed breast cancer patients and a matched control group of 545 women without breast cancer. The women were relatively young, aged 40 or below. The case group and the control group were individually matched for variables such as date of birth (within 36 months), race (white) and neighbourhood of residence.

The 545 cancer patients were originally obtained from a group of nearly 1000 potential participants. The remainder were either deemed unsuitable for participation by their own doctors or were unavailable for participation.

Interviews were used to obtain the average number of hours of physical exercise undertaken per week, from their first period to within one year of diagnosis of breast cancer. Bernstein et al. compared the activity levels of the women in the two groups to see if this was a predictor of breast cancer rates.

Results The findings suggested that 1–3 hours of exercise per week could reduce the risk of breast cancer in young women by around 30 per cent. This figure rose to over 50 per cent if the participant had regularly maintained 4 or more hours of physical activity per week.

Conclusions Exercise may be one lifestyle factor that can be relatively easily modified to reduce the risk of breast cancer in younger women.

Key terms

gynaecological age the duration in time throughout which a female has menstrual cycles

case-control study a study comparing participants who have a condition with participants who do not have that condition

self-efficacy the belief that you can meet a challenge or achieve your goals

Check your understanding

Explain how exercise could reduce the risk of breast cancer in young women.

Take it further

Bernstein et al. (1994) used retrospective data about exercise patterns in their study.

What are the potential dangers of using such data?

1.2 Exercise and its relation to HIV

Infection with HIV-1, the subsequent development of AIDS and the terminal nature of the disease causes a great deal of anguish in many HIV patients. Negative mood states and a lowered subjective sense of well-being may play a role in reduced immune system effectiveness. A weakened immune system could be an important factor in any disease, but may be especially pertinent to a disease that involves an infection of the immune system itself. Any intervention that might improve an HIV patient's sense of well-being and mood would no doubt be welcomed for this effect alone, but the fact that it might also contribute to the countering of immune suppression would be especially valuable in the management of this disease. Exercise has been shown to improve mood states (see exercise and mental health, pages 200–204) and regular exercise may be a way to influence the overall sense of well-being of HIV patients (Lox et al., 1995).

Key study

Lox et al., Exercise and psychological well-being in HIV patients

Aim To attempt to positively change the subjective well-being of HIV patients using a 12-week exercise programme.

Procedure The researchers measured pre- and post-programme levels of physical self-efficacy, positive and negative mood, and life satisfaction levels. A total of 33 HIV-1 patients were randomly allocated to an aerobic exercise group, a weight-training group or a stretch/flexibility control group.

Physical self-efficacy was measured using the physical self-efficacy scale (PSES) developed by Ryckman, Robbins, Thornton and Cantrell (1982) which uses a 6-point Likert scale. Physical self-efficacy includes expected physical skills capabilities and the confidence levels displayed when performing skills in front of other people. Mood states and life satisfaction levels were also both measured by established questionnaires.

A demographic questionnaire was used to control for variables such as involvement in counselling/support groups, current relationships and time since notification of infection. Progress on the exercise programme was logged daily on a workout sheet.

Participants engaged in the three conditions for about 45 minutes, three times a week. The stretch/flexibility group were asked to avoid any other forms of exercise activity for the 12-week period of the study.

Results The results found that participants in the aerobic and weight-training conditions reported significantly higher levels of physical self-efficacy, positive mood and life satisfaction than the control group. Physical self-efficacy levels, positive mood and life satisfaction increased for aerobic and weight-training groups between pre- and post-programme measures. This was in contrast to the stretch/flexibility group, which reported a decline in all three measures. Additional findings indicated that the aerobic condition group reported higher levels of life satisfaction than their counterparts in the weight-training condition.

Furthermore, the time since notification of infection modified some of the effects of the training programme, those who had been diagnosed with infection within the last 48 months reported a minor decline in life satisfaction compared to those who had known about their infection for longer than 4 years.

Conclusion These findings suggest that regular physical exercise can have a positive effect on the long-term sense of perceived well-being of terminally-ill HIV-1 patients.

> **Check your understanding**
>
> How might exercise assist HIV-1 patients in their battle against their infection?

> **Take it further**
>
> Why might physical self-efficacy be important to an overall sense of well-being in the above study?
>
> Can you use Bandura's (1982) self-efficacy theory to help your explanation?

1.3 Eating disorders among athletes

Is being an athlete a risk factor for developing an eating disorder? Hausenblas and Carron (1999) identified a number of reasons why this might be so. Western societal norms demand fitness and thinness, and athletes are no less prone to these pressures. In fact, they may be under greater pressure because of the need to be ideally fit for their activity, a pressure that might be enhanced by coaching and support staff. Excessive dieting and exercise may be a regular part of athletic preparation and it is possible that the value of food may be reduced by excessive exercise until eventually weight loss develops into eating disorder. Lastly, Hausenblas and Carron suggested that the very qualities that may make a person a successful athlete (perfectionism and compulsiveness) may also make them vulnerable to eating disorders, since these characteristics are common in eating disorders in general.

Perhaps some athletic activities create more risk of developing eating disorders than others. Hausenblas and Carron (1999) suggested that there are three groups who may be at greater risk: athletes who have strict weight limits for their events, athletes who need to be small or thin for their activity and athletes who need to be thin for aesthetic reasons.

> **Key study**
>
> Hausenblas and Carron, Eating disorders in athletes

Aim The aim was to establish whether athletes were at greater risk of developing an eating disorder than the general population, and whether some athletic activities place certain athletes at greater risk than others. The researchers also investigated gender as an additional risk factor in athletes developing eating disorders. Eating disorders were taken to be anorexia and bulimia.

Procedure The investigation used a meta-analysis of 92 studies to investigate the hypotheses. These studies used three measures of eating disorders. Drive for thinness was assessed as a key behaviour common to both anorexia and bulimia. *DSM–IV* definitions of anorexia and bulimia were used as the other measures.

The analysis covered 58 different sports, grouped into six categories for comparison (aesthetic, endurance, ball game, weight-dependent, power and technical). The analysis also compared gender, age and level of competition against non-athletic control samples.

Results The findings were naturally complex with so many variables. The researcher used a calculation called effect size (ES) to analyse the differences between groups.

The ES for male athletes showed higher levels in athletic males than the control non-athletes in measures of anorexia and bulimia, and for drive for thinness. No differences were found in any measures for males competing at different levels of competition. The highest reported bulimic measures were in aesthetic, weight-dependent and endurance sports.

Interestingly, the ES for females did not show a difference between the drive for thinness in athletes and non-athletes. However, female athletes reported greater levels of anorexia and bulimia measures than female non-athletes. Athletes who competed at high-school levels reported higher levels of bulimic measures than female athletes competing at college level.

Conclusions These results suggest that both male and female athletes have a higher prevalence of eating disorder symptoms than non-athletes and this may be due to the additional demands placed on them by sports.

Check your understanding

1. Give four or more reasons why athletes may be at increased risk of developing eating disorders.

2. Can you explain how the issue of cause and effect might be relevant to this study?

Try this ...

What sort of applications would the studies that you have looked at in this section have in everyday life?

You might want to consider what steps practitioners and other interested parties may wish to take in education, coaching and medicine.

2.1 Theories of exercise and mental health

Key study

Steinberg and Sykes, The endorphin hypothesis

Despite the physical rigours of exercise and sports participation, it is generally held that we may feel better as a result of being physically active and at times we may even experience a sense of 'euphoria'. A number of physiologically and psychologically based theories have been put forward as explanations of this improvement in well-being. One of the most prominent of these is the endorphin hypothesis (Steinberg and Sykes, 1985).

The endorphin hypothesis suggests that vigorous sustained physical activity produces the natural 'pain-killing' substance beta-endorphin in response to the stress placed upon our bodies.

Endorphin is similar chemically to morphine (opiate) and is known to bind to some of the opiate receptor sites in the nervous system. Consequently, it may have a similar action on the body, reducing synaptic activity to control pain and more controversially, triggering addiction-like changes in synaptic plasticity. This could explain why phrases such as 'endorphin high' and 'exercise junkie' may have a scientific basis.

Key terms

aesthetics an emotional reaction to aspects of our environment such as sport, art or nature

synaptic plasticity the ability of nerve cells to join and change the strength of their connection

Endorphin is released into the bloodstream by the pituitary gland and into the brain by the hypothalamus. The problem for researchers has been the inability to directly measure endorphin levels in the human brain in response to strenuous exercise. It is known that endorphins that have been released into the blood do not cross the blood-brain barrier easily (Farrell, 1989), and this has raised doubts over whether endorphins could have an effect on the brain, though their actions may work on areas of the nervous system where endorphins from the blood can reach, such as the spinal cord.

The endorphin hypothesis was derived from research using mice. Christie and Chesher (1982) were able to

Figure 3.20 Endorphins may help us to sustain rigorous physical activity

has been shown to increase BDNF levels in animals, along with serotonin and norepinephrine in a complex web of interactions.

Another physiologically based theory is the hyperthermic model, which suggests the increased temperature associated with exercise and other activities such as saunas or even hot showers have a relaxing effect (Daley, 2002). For example, Horne and Staff (1983) compared the effects of vigorous exercise with passive heating and found similar positive mood effects.

Psychological theories of mental health and exercise suggest that improvements in our mental well-being may be due to improvements in self-esteem or as a result of the power of exercise to distract us from negative thoughts and emotions (Daley, 2002).

> ### Check your understanding
>
> 1   Which type of exercise causes the release of endorphins?
> 2   Why might endorphins lead to a state of euphoria in athletes?
> 3   Explain how someone might become 'addicted' to exercise.

Weblinks

You might like to read more about BDNF or the beneficial effects of exercise on mental health (see Contents page).

show that mice became 'swimming junkies' in response to regular exercise.

Research has also shown that blood plasma levels of beta-endorphins increase with exercise. Mougin et al. (1988) studied Nordic skiers who had increased levels of endorphins after long-distance exercise. Daniel et al. (1992) used aerobic class members; they gave half the sample Naltrexone, which blocks opiate receptor sites, and half a placebo drug. Participants in the placebo group reported significantly better mood states than the Naltrexone group.

Alternative explanations have challenged the endorphin hypothesis. Brain-derived neurotrophic factor (BDNF) has generated a great deal of interest in researchers. BDNF seems to have a role in neurone maintenance and development, and may be linked to mood. Exercise

2.2 Benefits of exercise and mental health

The endorphin hypothesis suggests that we can improve our mood states by exercising, but this explanation may relate more to those engaged in relatively intensive levels of activity. The possible relationship between physical activity and improved mental health in a broader sense has also been widely researched, and the evidence also supports the overall positive effects of exercise (Leith and Taylor, 1990).

Key study

Leith and Taylor, A review of the psychological aspects of exercise

Aim To review a decade of research studies into the effects of exercise on mental health in order to draw out any consistent findings as well as assessing those findings in the context of a critical evaluation of the methodology used in the collection of those data.

Methodology A decade of published studies was reviewed, totalling 81 research projects. The researchers used a computer search to obtain the studies, which were categorised into three groups based on Campbell and Stanley's (1963) system of categorisation (pre-experimental, quasi-experimental and experimental). The purpose of the categorisation was to place each piece of research in the context of its methodology so that the value of its findings could be assessed. Where possible, findings were reported in relation to specific measures of mental health. These included measures such as Profile of Mood States (Morgan, 1979), State-Trait Anxiety Inventory Scale (Spielberger et al., 1971), Cattell's 16 personality factors (Cattell, 1956) and Beck's Depression Inventory (Beck et al., 1961).

The samples were as wide ranging as the studies themselves, and included students, alcoholics, psychiatric patients, children, adults, males, females, special-education classes and teenagers.

Results

Pre-experimental research

The researchers further divided pre-experimental research into one-shot case-studies, one group pre-test/post-test designs and static group comparisons according to Campbell and Stanley (1963). The first of these categories was not represented in this part of the review.

Seven of the nine studies in this category showed significant improvements in the chosen measures of mental health (see Table 3.14 for example findings).

The methodological limitations of these studies were also reported and it was found that only three studies had control groups, which made it difficult to make valid conclusions about causality.

Quasi-experimental research

The researchers placed 46 studies in this methodological category. Nearly all studies used the non-equivalent control group design without random allocation to groups; 36 of the studies showed significant improvements in the particular mental-health measures used. A wider range of mental-health measures were reviewed in this category (see below for examples of measures not previously mentioned).

The principle methodological weaknesses reported with these studies was a lack of matching between experimental and control groups, or an absence of random allocation to groups.

> **Key term**
>
> internal validity whether a study has been affected by biases or errors in the study design

Experimental research

A further 26 studies were reviewed under this category, 13 of which showed significant improvements, with an additional five studies reporting partial improvements in various mental-health measures. The main design used by studies was the pre-test/post-test control group (random allocation of subjects to groups and groups to conditions). This design was reviewed as the least likely to suffer from issues relating to external and internal validity.

Conclusions 70 per cent of studies reported significant improvements in mental health. When the researchers

Study	Variables	Sample	Psychological tests	Finding
Hayden and Allen (1984)	Anxiety and depression	Male and female college students	State-Trait Anxiety Inventory Scale and Beck's Depression Inventory	Significant improvement
Renfrow and Bolton (1979)	Personality	Male adults	Cattell's 16 PF	Significant improvement
Wilson et al. (1980)	Mood	Male adults	Profile of Mood States	Significant improvement
Wilson et al. (1981)	Adult anxiety	Males and females	State-Trait Anxiety Inventory Scale	No significant improvement

Table 3.14 A selection of results from pre-experimental research (Source: adapted from Leith and Taylor, 1990)

Study	Variables	Sample	Psychological tests	Finding
Tucker (1983)	Self-concept	Male college students (weight-lifters)	Tennessee Self-concept Scale (Fitts, 1964)	Significant improvement
Goldfarb et al. (1987)	Affect	Male adults	Multiple Affect Adjective Checklist	No change

Table 3.15 A selection of results from quasi-experimental research (Source: adapted from Leith and Taylor, 1990)

Study	Variables	Sample	Psychological tests	Finding
Marsh and Pearl (1988)	Self-concept	Female children	Self-concept: Scale for Children	No change
Fremont (1984)	Mood	Male and females (depressed)	Unnamed measures	Significant improvement

Table 3.16 A selection of results from experimental research (Source: adapted from Leith and Taylor, 1990)

added the partial improvements to this figure, it rose to 80 per cent. At face value this certainly suggested that exercise had a positive effect on a range of mental-health variables.

However, when the data were analysed by type of design, the findings became less convincing, only 50 per cent of experimental studies reported significant improvements, compared with 78 per cent of studies for the pre-experimental group.

It was also suggested by Leith and Taylor (1990) that it would have been important for more studies to measure other variables such as fitness gains, type and duration of exercise, as these may have a bearing on the overall effectiveness of exercise.

Take it further

- Why is it important to have a control group to establish causality in a study?
- What impact would matching have on the validity of comparisons between exercise and non-exercise control groups?
- Why do review studies have particular significance in reporting the findings of research in a particular area of research interest?

2.3 Mood states

Check your understanding

1 Which type of study was Leith and Taylor's research?

2 What was the aim of this study?

3 Name the three categories used by the researcher to analyse the studies.

4 Give some examples of the variables measured and the related instruments.

5 What do the results suggest about exercise and mental health?

Try this ...

Design a questionnaire that measures positive mood states. You may be able to find a small sample of volunteers who would be willing to complete the questionnaire after doing exercise or sports. You may even be able to make comparisons by conducting pre- and post-exercise measurements.

Remember: any research you conduct should follow the British Psychological Society ethical guidelines. Pay particular attention to the type of questions you ask; they should be non-intrusive.

Weblinks

You can find more about how mood states have been measured (see Contents page). If your school has access, you might like to consult the British Psychological Society ethical guidelines (see Contents page).

Key study

Morgan, Mental-health model

The possibility of using psychological testing to predict the performance of athletes has long been of interest to researchers. In the 1970s, researchers began to investigate the predictive powers of psychological tests for rowers (Morgan and Johnson, 1978), distance runners (Morgan and Pollock, 1977) and wrestlers (Nagle, 1975, cited in Morgan, 1979). Instead of looking for specific traits that might predict performance, they focused on mood. This was mainly measured by the Profile of Mood States (POMS) questionnaire (McNair et al., 1971), which includes the key variables tension, depression, anger, vigour, fatigue and confusion. This was then used to create a profile of the mental health of the athlete. It was then hypothesised that athletes with positive mental health were more likely to be successful.

The mental-health model was tested in a series of studies which involved elite athletes and the selection process for national representative honours. Morgan and Johnson (1978) profiled rowers prior to their involvement in the elite national training camp. The Minnesota Multiphasic Personality Inventory (MMPI) was used to test the rowers; 57 of the 60 rowers consented to be tested, and were told that the results would have no bearing on selection for the final 16 places in the team. No profiles were analysed until the final selections had been made. The researchers predicted that successful rowers would be those who scored high in vigour and extroversion, and low in anxiety, tension depression, anger, fatigue, confusion, neuroticism and conformity.

The results showed that the psychological tests had the capacity to make predictions about athletes even at the elite level: 10 of the final 16 successful rowers and 31 of the 41 unsuccessful rowers were identified by the test. Thus 41 out of 57 predictions were accurate. The successful and unsuccessful elite rowers had opposite profiles following the research prediction.

In another study by Nagle et al. (1975), hopefuls for the 1972 US Olympic wrestling teams were profiled using the POMS. It was again found that psychological tests could predict athletic performance even in the homogeneous environment of an Olympic team training camp.

Successful athletes were higher in vigour and lower in tension, depression, anger, fatigue and confusion than the unsuccessful athletes. The profile for the successful athlete was called the 'iceberg' profile (see Figure 3.21). The results were repeated for the 1976 wrestling team and a similar profile was also found with successful long-distance runners (Morgan and Pollock, 1977).

Check your understanding

1. What are the key features of positive mental health in relation to sports performance?

2. Why was the profile of a successful athlete known as an 'iceberg' profile?

3. Why is it so striking that the profiling could distinguish between elite athletes?

Take it further

- Could mood states be a temporary and changing variable?

- If so, how could they influence the predictive powers of measures such as POMS?

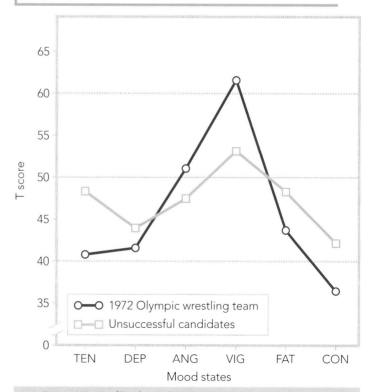

Figure 3.21 Profile of mood states (Source: Morgan, 1979) (Note: A score of 50 represents the mean for a set of data. A score of 60 or 40 indicates that it is one standard deviation above or below the mean.)

3.1 Burnout and withdrawal

The ever-increasing demands placed on many athletes mean that they may have to commit more and more time and energy towards their sport. Athletes may believe they have to train harder to achieve success, assuming that more training is likely to result in better performance. The consequences of this may be burnout and withdrawal. Costhill et al. (1991) investigated training volume in swimming.

Key study

Costill et al., Adaptations to training volume in swimming

Aim To investigate whether different amounts of training in swimming produced measurable differences in performance.

Participants The study used 24 male college swimmers, divided into two matched groups (Long and Short) for stroke, prior training experience and skill.

Procedures The two groups would train together for the first 4 weeks of the study, consisting of one daily session of 1.5 hours. For the next 6 weeks, the Long group trained twice a day for 1.5 hours while the Short group continued with 1.5 hours per day. Both groups trained together for the final 14 weeks of the study, training once a day for 1.5 hours. The Short group averaged 4950 metres per day in comparison to the Long group, who achieved 9435 metres per day. The swimmers all used an interval style of training.

Measurements were taken of a variety of physical performance indicators. These included swimming power, heart-rate, muscle biopsies, blood samples and swimming technique. The swimmers also took part in a number of normally scheduled competitions that were used to assess performance against pre-testing competition achievements.

Swimming power was measured by the CYBEX tethered machine using a maximal effort swim of 365.8 metres. Muscle biopsies measured biochemicals associated with physical performance (phosphofructokinase, phosphorylase and citric synthase). Blood tests measured cortisol, testosterone and lactate levels. Pre-training or base-line levels were taken where appropriate. Psychological measures of mood were also taken as part of this study, but were reported in a separate study by Cox et al. (1991), see below.

Results The results can be seen in Table 3.17.

Conclusions The findings consistently suggest that at the very least, lower levels of training do not disadvantage the athlete in terms of performance improvement, in fact by some measures, athletes actually benefit from a relatively low level of training. There were also some signs of fatigue in the Long group, with increased cortisol and reduced testosterone levels, though these were not chronic.

Check your understanding

1   How can these physiological findings be related to the psychological aspects of burnout?

2   Explain how the population validity of this study might limit the generalisability of the findings to all swimmers.

During the above study by Costill et al. (1991), the Profile of Mood States questionnaire was used to assess the mental-health condition of the two swimming groups over the 24-week training period. The results indicated that there were no significant differences

Test	Short	Long
Swimming power	Improved by 18.4%	Improved by 11.6%
Maximum sprint velocity	Improved by 3.9%	Improved by 3.7%
Swimming technique	Improved by 16.6%	Improved by 15.7%
Competitive performances	Significant improvement from previous session	Significant improvement from previous session
Lactate levels		Significantly higher than the Short group
Cortisol levels	Stable	Significant increase
Testosterone	Declined	Declined

Table 3.17 Summary of results of investigation into different amounts of training in swimming

in the mood states of the Long and Short groups (Cox et al., 1991). The only difference of note was that during the period where the Long group were training twice a day, they reported higher levels of fatigue than the control group who were training once a day. Cox et al. explained these findings in terms of training load. In Morgan et al.'s (1987) original study of training overload in swimmers, mood disturbance occurred in training regimes of between 54,000 and 84,000 metres per week. In this study, training loads never reached this critical threshold, with the Long group reaching a maximum of 50,000 metres per week.

3.2 Body image in sport

We have already seen through the work of Hausenblas and Carron (1999) that athletes may have certain beliefs, attitudes or expectations about their own body shapes in relation to their sport as well as in relation to broader societal influences. These same expectations may also be a factor in determining exercise and sports participation because, as Hart et al. (1989) have suggested, people who do not have a perceived physique appropriate to the exercise situation may be less motivated in participation. The cause of this lack of motivation may be anxiety over their body image and the evaluation of others (Hart et al., 1989).

It is worth noting that body image is about perception and research has found evidence to support the widespread existence of body image distortions in people of normal weight (Hart et al., 1989). For example, Miller et al. (1980) reported that 54 per cent of college graduates were dissatisfied with their body image. Miller et al. (1980) found that 70 per cent of female college students thought they were slightly overweight, compared with 18 per cent of males. Anxiety over the evaluations of others was termed social physique anxiety by Hart et al. (1989) and is a concern about the reactions of others to the exerciser's self-perceptions of their body image. The study below is used in place of Cash (1994) which is given as an example in the OCR specification.

Key terms

body image belief and perceptions about one's own physical appearance

social physique anxiety a person's anxiety over potential evaluations of other people about their physique

expectancy effects a bias in participants who expect a particular outcome from the study

Key study

Hart et al., Measurement of body-image anxiety

Aim To develop a means of measuring social physique anxiety and to test whether those who scored highly on this scale also developed feelings of anxiety about their body image when placed in a fitness evaluation conducted by other people.

Measuring social physique anxiety

The social physique anxiety scale (SPAS) was developed for the study. It consisted of 12 questions, with a 5-point Likert-type rating scale.

The scale was tested using almost 200 men and women against a range of other established questionnaires that measured aspects of anxiety associated with social evaluations which were integrated into the SPAS (construct validity testing).

Sample The subjects were 56 female undergraduate students. Half of these (28) had scored in the top third on the SPAS and the other half had scored in the bottom third. The average age was 18.4 years and women were chosen because they are more likely to be concerned about physical evaluation.

Procedure Each participant was placed in a fitness evaluation situation and then tested on a questionnaire to see how stressed and uncomfortable they were as a result of the evaluation. The results of the two groups were then compared.

Participants were tested individually, weighed and read a standardised instruction which informed them that they were about to be tested. They were told that the test consisted of a 1-minute interview and physical examination both about body fat and muscular tone.

The stress scale was an 11-point Likert scale and the women were also asked to select their body shape from eight body forms.

Results Women in the high social physique anxiety (SPA) group scored significantly higher stress scores, felt less comfortable and recorded more negative thoughts about their body image than the low SPA group. Women in the high SPA group weighed more, were taller and had higher body fat percentages than the low SPA group.

Conclusions The findings provided support for the link between evaluation by other people and anxiety about body image (social physique anxiety), and the most anxious women were at least partially justified in their concerns according to the objectively measured of weight, height and body fat.

	Not at all	Slightly	Moderately	Very	Extremely characteristic
1 I am comfortable with the appearance of my physique/figure					
2 I would never worry about wearing clothes that might make me look too thin or overweight					
3 I wish I was not so uptight about my physique/figure					
4 There are times where I am bothered by thoughts that other people are evaluating my weight or muscular development negatively					
5 When I look in the mirror I feel good about my physique/figure					
6 Unattractive features of my physique/figure make me nervous in certain social settings					
7 In the presence of others, I feel apprehensive about my physique/figure					
8 I am comfortable with how fit my body appears to others					
9 It would make me uncomfortable to know others were evaluating my physique/figure					
10 When it comes to displaying my physique/figure to others, I am a shy person					
11 I usually feel relaxed when it is obvious that others are looking at my physique/figure					
12 When in a bathing suit, I often feel nervous about the shape of my body					

For each item, respondents indicate the degree to which the statement is 'characteristic or true of you'.
These responses are scored from 1 (not at all) to 5 (extremely). The scoring is reversed for Items 1, 2, 5, 8 and 11.
When the score is totalled the closer it is to 60 the higher the social physique anxiety level.

Table 3.18 Social Physique Anxiety Scale (Source: Hart et al., 1989)

Check your understanding

Explain how the evaluations of others might impact on exercise participation and motivations, especially in women.

3.3 Drug abuse in sport

The physical effects of performance-enhancing drugs are well known, but researchers have also been interested in their potential psychological effects. An area of particular interest has been expectancy effects, where performance-enhancing drug-taking may have a placebo-like action on performance. Were this to be demonstrated, such research could have important applications in the education of athletes about alternative psychological methods of performance enhancement, which would be legal (Maganaris et al., 2000).

Key study

Maganaris et al., Psychological expectancy effects using a steroid placebo in strength training

Aim To investigate the potential expectancy effects on strength-training progress of an anabolic steroid placebo.

Sample The study used 11 national level power lifters who had been together in a training group for 2 years running up to the commencement of the study. One of the coaches was a member of the research team and the participants and coaches were well known to each other. All the lifters repeatedly reported that they had never taken any agents banned by their governing body or the International Olympic Committee. This in turn is likely to have made the lifters relatively naïve about the possible benefits of drugs, and as such made them prone to the publicity that is associated with such substances.

Originally, the lifters approached their coaching staff to ask about anabolic steroids (AS) and it was this event that prompted the study.

Procedure Participants were told that the substance they were taking was a new rapid action oral AS. In fact they received a saccharin placebo.

The ethics of the study were considered very carefully, given the fact that real AS use would have prohibited the lifters from competing. The study was justified ethically because the participants expressed a possible intention to take AS and because of the potential important applications of the study to anti-drugs education. The lifters completed a consent form that told them there would be no harmful effects.

Dietary supplements and training schedules were controlled for 14 days prior to the study and were also monitored during the period of the study.

A base-line strength measure was taken at the end of the 14 days, consisting of a 1 repetition maximum lift on bench press (the most a person can bench press once), dead lift and squat.

The first stage of the trials was to give the lifters two tablets of the fast-acting AS five minutes before performing the three-test lift. The athletes were then given two more tablets to use during the coming week.

In the second stage of the study, the lifters were questioned about their training and all recorded an increase in rep count (the maximum number of lifts on one exercise before needing rest), maximum lift and vigour. The sample was then divided into two halves. One half went on to complete the three tests (AS/AS group) while the other half were told about the actual nature of the study (AS/P group). These lifters were given the choice of taking the drug but most did not take up the offer. They were then tested using the three lifts.

A thorough debrief was undertaken for all participants and particular care was given to explaining that their improvements in performance had been totally due to the psychological effects of a saccharin placebo.

Results The results can be seen in Table 3.19.

The AS/AS group showed significant improvements in all three lifts for both trials compared to the base-line recording at the start of the study.

The AS/P group experienced a significant improvement for the first trial only.

Conclusions The results confirmed a significant placebo effect from the perceived use of an anabolic steroid and suggest that expectancy effects are indeed significant, though short-lived once the true nature of the substance was revealed.

The results were so significant at this level that in fact that the majority of lifters moved up to international competition.

Participant no.	Experimental group	Bench press Trial 1	Bench press Trial 2	Deadlift Trial 1	Deadlift Trial 2	Squat Trial 1	Squat Trial 2
1	AS/AS	+10	+10	+10	+12.5	+12.5	+12.5
2	AS/AS	+5	+7.5	+10	+10	+15	+15
3	AS/AS	+10	+7.5	+10	+10	+10	+10
4	AS/AS	+7.5	+10	+10	+10	+12.5	+10
5	AS/AS	+12.5	+12.5	+12.5	+10	+12.5	+10
6	AS/AS	+7.5	+7.5	+12.5	+12.5	+12.5	+12.5
7	AS/P	+12.5	+2.5	+12.5	–2.5	+12.5	+2.5
8	AS/P	+10	+7.5	+10	0	+12.5	0
9	AS/P	+10	–2.5	+10	0	+12.5	+2.5
10	AS/P	+10	+7.5	+12.5	–2.5	+10	–2.5
11	AS/P	+10	+7.5	+12.5	–2.5	+10	–2.5

Table 3.19 Changes from baseline on three competition lifts for participants in strength training (Source: Maganaris et al., 2000)

Section summary

- Research suggests that regular exercise can reduce the risks of breast cancer by as much as 50 per cent (Bernstein et al., 1994).

- HIV patients commonly suffer low levels of psychological well-being. Lox et al. (1995) found that resistance and aerobic exercise could significantly improve patients' sense of well-being.

- Hausenblas and Carron (1999) found that athletes of both sexes were at greater risk of developing eating disorders and that athletes in certain activities were at higher risk than others.

- Vigorous exercise can produce a strong sense of well-being, even euphoria. A popular explanation of this effect has been the endorphin hypothesis, according to which the body's own natural painkiller acts on the nervous system in much the same way as morphine.

- Leith and Taylor (1990) reviewed 81 studies, assessing the mental health impacts of exercise. They found that 70 per cent of studies reported significant improvements in mental health. When the researchers added the partial improvements to this figure, it rose to 80 per cent.

- Research on mental health models and mood states found that successful athletes were found to be higher in vigour and lower in tension, depression, anger, fatigue and confusion than unsuccessful athletes. The profile for the successful athlete was called the 'iceberg' profile.

- It is a commonly held belief that more training will produce improved performance in sports. However, Costill et al. (1991) found that swimmers who trained less performed as well as those who trained more and were superior in some measures of performance.

- In their study on measurement of body image anxiety, the findings of Hart et al. (1989) provided support for the link between evaluation by other people and anxiety about body image (social physique anxiety).

- Maganaris et al. (2000) demonstrated that fake performance-enhancing drugs (placebo) seem to have a positive effect on the performance of weight lifters. This also acted as a demonstration of the potential power of psychological effects on athletic performance.

ExamCafé

Relax, refresh, result!

Relax and prepare

Refresh your memory

Revision checklist: personality in sport

A simple revision aid is to make a checklist summarising the key points of a study and taking four potential issues that you will prepare to evaluate it. Copy and complete the table below.

Explanation/ Study	Self-reports	Nature–nurture	Reductionism	Applications
Cattell's 16PF	Self-reports may create socially desirable answers that threaten the measurements' validity		Reductionist measure of personality in sport	
Theories of personality		Trait theories are nativist (nature) because of their biological basis	Trait theories may be reductionist because they have a biological basis	
Kroll and Crenshaw				Coaches may be able to use research findings in player selection

Get the result!

Example answers

Below is a student response written under exam conditions in answer to the following question:

Outline one social theory of aggression in sport. (10 marks)

Student answer

One social theory of aggression in sport is Berkowitz's Cue Theory, which suggests that aggression in sport is caused by environmental factors. One element of the theory is anger. If an athlete were to become angered in the situation this would make aggression more likely. Furthermore, observing violence by other people in the situation could also make aggression more likely. In this sense, it is a social theory of aggression in sport because of the influence of people on our behaviour. For example, a rugby player would act in a violent way if they had earlier seen two other players fighting or if their opponents had cheated, which would make them angry.

The second part of the theory concerns the effect of cues in the environment. Aggression is much more likely to happen if there are additional aggressive cues in the situation being observed. Berkowitz called this the 'weapons effect' and he argued that anything like a weapon in a situation could act as an aggressive cue and produce aggression.

This could explain aggression in sport because sports equipment might be perceived as a type of weapon. Another example would be fan violence where other fans or athletes witness some supporters wielding weapons or using seats as weapons.

Examiner says:

In the first paragraph the student clearly identifies one social theory and explains why it is considered a social theory rather than another type of explanation of aggression. An example is used to clearly relate a non-sport-specific theory of aggression to sport. In the second paragraph the theory is expanded on and some more interesting examples are used.

This is a good answer.

Below is a student response written under exam conditions in answer to the following question:

Evaluate social theories of aggression in sport. (15 marks)

Student answer

Cue theory has supporting evidence which adds to the credibility of this explanation of aggression in sport. Berkowitz and Geen used the experimental method to investigate whether participants would give greater electric shocks having previously watched either a neutral or a violent film. Participants were further divided into more groups depending on whether they had been angered by 7 electric shocks or 1. The study found that participants who had received 7 shocks were more likely to act in an aggressive way. Those who watched the violent film also acted in an aggressive way. The study design was further developed by adding a rifle into the situation to test the weapons effect. Berkowitz and Geen found that the weapon condition produced greater levels of aggression than a badminton racket in the same situation. These findings suggest that the key parts of the study — anger, observing violence and the weapons effect — are valid causes of aggression.

The cue theory may be limited in its validity to the sports situation because it is a general theory of aggression which was not researched specifically in sport. Environmental processes may be slightly different in sport and the theory may not be so relevant.

This theory is also limited in that it only considers the causes of aggression as environmental. There may be other theories which challenge cue theory and may be a more valid explanation of aggression in sport.

Examiner says:

A good range of evaluative points covered. Cue theory is evaluated in detail, but the candidate really only addresses the need for more than one social theory at the end and there may have been a better way to structure the answer in order to gain more marks. Nonetheless, this is a good answer under exam conditions.

For example, Excitation Transfer Theory argues that aggressive behaviour is caused by arousal in the situation. As arousal increases, extreme behaviours such as aggression are more common. Sport is full of potential sources of arousal, such as crowds and coach behaviour. This may therefore be a more relevant explanation of aggression in sport.

A very different nativist alternative explanation of aggression in sport is Freud's Psychoanalytic Theory. Here aggression is innate, driven by the violent instinct thanatos. Sport actually provided an acceptable outlet for this build-up of aggression in the person. So we would expect to see aggression in sport as humans are aggressive and sport is an outlet or cathartic activity.

Cue theory may be determinist because it was based on behaviourist ideas. It argues that anger, observation of violence and aggressive cues will cause aggression in people. But this ignores cognitive or humanistic factors which may cause individual variations in our response to such influences.

Lastly cue theory may have applications in sport to either increase or decrease aggression where needed. A coach could use anger, violent or peaceful observations and cues to achieve lower or higher levels of aggression.

Another social theory of aggression in sport is Bandura's Social Learning Theory. This also has supporting experimental evidence from Bandura's Bobo doll study, which found clear evidence of observation learning from role models. The study also highlighted the potential importance of social learning for causing aggression in young athletes, because Bandura's study was conducted on children. However, this theory may be of less value in explaining adult aggression in sport.

Psychology of Education

Contents

Studies used in the Psychology of Education option

Teaching and learning

Student participation

The social world of teaching and learning

Enabling learning: dealing with diversity

Full references for the studies can be found in the References section on page 330

Introduction

Psychology and education go very well together. For those who study psychology, educational settings offer a rich environment in which to apply psychological theories and concepts. For those who work in educational settings, psychology can provide a valuable source of knowledge to understand their practice. This option covers four main areas that provide you with an opportunity to apply your psychological knowledge to educational contexts. It is important for us to consider the diversity of both the settings and the individuals within them. The point is also made that the application of psychology to education is not just limited to formal educational settings but also considers the wider learning of individuals. We are, after all, learning throughout our entire lifespan.

Teaching and learning

This area covers some of the main theories that attempt to explain how we acquire knowledge. It also considers the teaching and learning process by looking at a wide range of theoretical perspectives. It acknowledges that teaching and learning are complex processes and that simple explanations are unlikely to explore the wide variety of individual experience.

Three theories of knowledge acquisition are compared, including 'stage' theories such as Piaget's famous four levels. Social construction theories consider learning to be more of a social event than Piaget had considered and finally behaviourist models that regard the external environment as paramount are presented. The diversity of how individuals approach learning is explored and this highlights how we may all have different ways of approaching a learning situation. The final section considers this same point but from the perspective of the teacher and how they may prefer to approach teaching.

Student participation

This area considers how individuals are motivated into action, or even inaction, and the possible sources of

motivation are discussed. There is a focus on how good early experiences may have life-long effects and how emotions may have an impact on learning. Finally, the effect on ability grouping on student motivation is discussed.

Motivation is not as straightforward as many would at first think, the possible explanations for why individuals behave the way they do is open to a wide range of interpretation. This is reflected in the discussion that is based on psychodynamic, humanist and cognitive theories. It is acknowledged that not all students wish to be engaged in educational activities and that ways to improve engagement are varied. For example, the importance of early experiences are discussed as well as the emotional impact of teaching and learning on young people. Many educational settings put students into groups to encourage them to engage with their studies, and the psychological and academic effect of these groups are discussed.

The social world of teaching and learning

Relationships are central to teaching and learning and in this area the interactions between students and teachers are analysed. The importance of moral development and understanding between individuals is emphasised and the types of communication between teachers and learners are considered.

It is argued that an understanding of how we learn can be improved if the social world of teaching and learning is considered. Theories of personality development such as Erikson's psychosocial model and Kohlberg's description of moral development are presented to provide insight into the behaviour of learners. If we are to understand the complex world of learning, we need to have a good understanding of the individuals who are involved in this process. Two further sections take a closer look at the interactions between individuals. The first considers how students interact with each other and this highlights the importance of supportive relationships and the effects of bullying. The final section takes a close look at how students and teachers interact. It discusses how difficult it is to observe these interactions and also shows how complex this process is.

Enabling learning: dealing with diversity

We are all different and therefore have our own individual learning needs, and this area seeks to discuss how each student can be supported to reach their educational potential. It considers those who have additional educational needs and how teaching and learning may be organised to support them. Strategies that enable ethnic minorities and reduce the disparity between the genders are discussed and it is suggested that good educational practice is beneficial to all students.

Dealing with diversity is probably one of the most challenging aspects of educational settings and three main areas are looked at. These include how learners' additional needs can be met and how educational settings can ensure that all cultures represented are able to participate effectively in learning. The final section reviews the age-old distinction that appears to exist between the genders and questions what

the differences may be, why they exist and what, if anything, can be done about them. What this section regularly highlights is that thoughtful and caring relationships between student and teacher are often the basis of enable all students to participate in learning to the best of their ability. It should not be expected that all students will gain 'top marks', but rather that learners who feel good about their learning experience are more likely to be prepared to do their best.

Summary

Educational settings have changed a great deal in recent years and this has had a huge impact on the potential employment opportunities for those who have a psychological understanding of education. Teachers clearly benefit from such knowledge but so too do learning support assistants, learning mentors and school-based counsellors. However, education does not just take place in schools, and psychological knowledge of education can be used in early-years settings, old people's homes, prisons and hospitals. Even if you do not see yourself in any of these types of employment, your studies have not been wasted, for a psychological study of education helps us to understand people, from the very young to the very old, and this after all is the ultimate goal of psychology.

Teaching and learning

Pause for thought

1   We have all been learning all of our lives. So much so that we are quite used to it and often do not notice it happening. The learning we are most aware of is that which takes place in educational settings. Try the following tasks:

   ◆   Describe how you learnt, or think you learnt, to swim or ride a bike.

   ◆   Describe how you learnt to do long division at school.

   ◆   Compare these two examples, discuss how your learning took place and identify what was the same or different in each case.

2   Learners are all different and we should not be surprised that they may like to learn in different ways. Make a list of the things you do to make learning easier. Compare your list with a friend's. Are they the same?

Figure 4.1 The learning environment

3   Teachers are all different and we should not be surprised that they may like to teach in different ways. If you were asked to teach a Year 7 class about the study on conservation by Samuel and Bryant (1983), how would you do this?

Figure 4.2 Different approaches to teaching

Introduction

The process of teaching and learning is extremely complex as there are so many factors to be considered. This part of the course divides teaching and learning into three areas of study and considers:

- theories of knowledge acquisition
- personal approaches to learning
- personal approaches to teaching.

Theories of knowledge acquisition

There are a variety of theories that offer an insight into individuals' intellectual development, and these usually focus on how knowledge is gained. This knowledge could be related to using numbers, spelling, learning to talk or how to tie shoelaces. The theories presented here will offer different views as to how this may take place. Some regard the interaction with the external environment as being most important, others consider that all children go through the same stages of thinking at the same ages, while still others hold that talking with more expert people is the key to learning.

Personal approaches to learning

The diversity of how individuals go about learning is staggering and of continued significance to educationalists. Just as we all have different personalities, it should be no surprise that we have different preferences as to how we learn. What is interesting here is how psychologists can help us understand why these differences may exist and how a knowledge of them can be used to improve the effectiveness of learning.

Personal approaches to teaching

Most approaches to teaching can be traced back to theories of knowledge acquisition. The approaches covered here are examples of these theories applied to educational settings. They discuss how the learning environment could be organised, how the curriculum could be arranged, and the importance of language being used to guide learners' decision-making processes.

Themes and perspectives

Understanding how individuals acquire knowledge, any preferences they may have for how they learn and how teaching is best carried out is extremely complicated. One of the problems researchers have when considering these issues is whether to concentrate on the whole process or just on discrete parts of it. Therefore the issues of reductionism or holism can be discussed in relation to teaching and learning. Another issue that can be developed from theories of teaching and learning is whether they are of any use in education. It would therefore be hoped that any theory that offers some insight has addressed the issue of complexity and that it also has some practical application.

Try this …

Talk to someone you know who is involved in teaching. This does not have to be in school, it could be at a club, sports centre or drama group; it may even be your psychology teacher. Ask them to talk about one lesson plan or learning task and to explain why they organised it as they did.

Weblink

You can read more about schemes of work (see Contents page).

Select a subject area from the Subject list on the left-hand side and follow the links to find a unit of work. What does this tell you about how the author thinks learning takes place?

1 Theories of knowledge acquisition

1.1 Stage theories

Piaget's four stages of cognitive development

The best-known stage theory of knowledge acquisition has to be Piaget's four stages of cognitive development, or what is sometimes also referred to as intellectual development. Before we reflect on these stages it is worth spending a little time considering the process that led Piaget to develop his ideas. He started to write about children's mental processes as early as the 1920s; during this time he worked with Binet on developing intelligence testing. The observations that fascinated Piaget were not only that children of different ages obtained different scores, but also that their reasoning seemed to be different from that of adults.

Piaget became interested in epistemology; he continued his investigation by observing his own children and then by carrying out a series of experiments.

Links to other studies

See the study by Samuel and Bryant (1983) for more details.

Piaget wanted to find out how children understood their external world and logical concepts such as number and quantity. From his findings, he concluded that children already have an understanding of the world in the form of mental representations called schemas. These are different from those of adults, and children are always changing this understanding so that it works in new situations. This is a constructivist theory as children acquire, or construct, knowledge by changing their existing understandings (schemas) to make sense of new experiences. Piaget called this process *accommodation* as children need to adjust their thinking as a result of taking in, or *assimilating*, new information and using this to make sense of the situation they are in by forming new schemas.

Key terms

contructivist theory each individual actively constructs, or builds up, their knowledge from their own experiences

epistemology the study of how we know what we know

Try this ...

Try to recall what you thought happened to the food you ate when you were young. How does this differ from what you think now? How does your 'young schema' for digestion compare to your 'present schema'?

Piaget noticed that the rules by which children constructed their understanding of the world could be organised into four distinct stages.

1   The sensorimotor stage: from birth to about 18 months, children learn via their senses, e.g. *My food is warm and mushy. It makes me happy.*

2   The pre-operational stage: from 18 months to about 7 years, when symbols (such as words) and general rules become important, e.g. *When I say 'Yum Yum' I get a bowl of the warm mushy stuff.* For the child the sound 'Yum Yum' represents the feeling of being hungry and wanting this satisfied by banana custard.

3   The concrete operational stage: between 7 and 12 years, when thought experiments become a possibility but are still limited by the present world and how it is, e.g. *I like this banana custard well enough, but what if I made it thicker and turned it into a cake-type thing?*

4   The formal operational stage: 12 years and above, when thoughts are governed by logical reasoning and cause and effect can be considered, e.g. *OK, I need 1 pint of milk, 3 mashed bananas, 2 spoons of custard powder, 1 cup of flour and an egg. Ah – the perfect banana custard cake.*

These stages have been criticised due to Piaget's methodology (see Samuel and Bryant, 1983) and also the suggestion of their universal application to all children in all cultures. Importantly, Piaget does not acknowledge the complex social aspect of knowledge acquisition, although he does accept that social factors can motivate learning. His theories provide a picture of the child as a lone scientist trying to understand the external world, rather than the socially orientated child that many of us would recognise.

Piaget's original works are old and complex and it is often easier to read more recent reviews of his work in child development texts such as Berk (2000) or van Geert (1998) for the enthusiast.

Bruner's modes of representation

Bruner (1966) proposed that three stages, or modes of representation, are necessary for knowledge acquisition. He differs from Piaget by suggesting that these are not limited to precisely defined age ranges. What Bruner highlights is that children's intellectual development is dependent on moving through these three stages and that these continue to exist throughout the lifespan of an individual. The stages are called representations, as they represent rules that enable the child to understand the world. There are further differences to Piaget's theory, such as:

1. Considering the social world of the child and how this gives rise to different life experiences and therefore the development of a unique set of rules for each child.

2. Recognising that intellectual development is a result of interacting with the world and not limited by biologically determined age stages.

3. Recognising that language facilitates intellectual development, rather than language resulting from increased cognitive development.

The three stages are:

1. The *enactive stage*: this emphasises 'knowing by doing', e.g. the child knows the actions involved in making a see-saw work.

2. The *iconic stage* (up to 6 years): this involves mental imagery that represents larger 'chunks' of knowledge, e.g. the mental image of how the see-saw works can be changed in the mind or, if necessary, represented as a drawing.

3. The *symbolic stage* (approaching adolescence): when the experience of the world can be represented in symbols, such as language, e.g. the see-saw can be described in words or even mathematically.

Bruner's stages are seen by some not to be stages at all, due to their flexible lifelong nature, but the discrete differences between how children (and adults) are thought to deal with new information makes them worthy of inclusion here.

Check your understanding

1. What are the similarities and differences between Piaget's and Bruner's stages?

2. How would Piaget and Bruner explain learning to ride a bike?

1.2 Social construction theories

Vygotsky and the Zone of Proximal Development: an example of a social construction theory

Vygotsky was a Russian psychologist who was developing his theory of how children acquire knowledge at a similar time to Piaget. His ideas were different from Piaget's but were in turn very influential on Bruner. Vygotsky's theories are regarded as socio-cultural, as both society and culture are thought to have an impact on the child's development.

Try this …

When you read this section, try to identify the similarities and differences between Bruner and Piaget's theories and Vygotsky's ideas.

Vygotsky was developing his ideas in Stalin's Russia, so he was influenced by the Marxist doctrine on the importance of the role of individuals in a group. His work was suppressed as he highlighted individual differences, which was an idea that Stalin considered to be anti-Soviet. This had the impact of hiding Vygotsky's work from the West until the early 1960s, when his book *Thought and Language* (1962) was published, interestingly with a forward by Bruner.

The most enduring idea put forward by Vygotsky is that of the Zone of Proximal Development (ZPD), which has become extremely influential in educational thinking in recent years. Vygotskty suggested that the cognitive development – and therefore knowledge acquisition – of individuals was attributed to interaction with others. Importantly, this interaction with others took place in a social world where language was the main means of communication. The language used in any society is a result of historical and cultural influences, and therefore words carry symbolic meanings.

Try this …

Consider the words we use and how different cultures use different words. Why does *tap* represent a tap? Or the word *love* represent a whole host of feelings and experiences? What do Americans call trousers, or taps for that matter!?

What Vygotsky suggested was that as children interacted with the environment, adults or more knowledgeable others used language (words that had symbolic meanings) to help them make sense of their experiences. Consequently the words served to mediate, or sort out and translate, this experience so that the child interacted with the external world not directly but via others. This process is termed 'social construction' as knowledge about the external world has been obtained in a social environment by more knowledgeable others, using words from a language that contains culturally important symbolic meanings. So language carries cultural meanings and this language is used to organise how the young learner thinks.

From this theoretical understanding Vygotsky proposed the notion of the ZPD. The ZPD was defined as a difference in what a child could achieve alone compared to when given help. The example Vygotsky mentioned referred to trying to diagnose what children with additional educational needs could achieve. He thought they were capable of much more than most people assumed, and he also considered that most diagnostic tasks were so dull that the children were not stimulated to try their best. What he found was that by using interesting activities and talking with children to give advice and suggestions when they got stuck, the children achieved much more than expected. Without verbal assistance the children could only show what they *could do*, but with assistance they could show what they were *capable of* and this difference is the ZPD. The larger the ZPD for a child, the easier they would find learning. If the child had a small ZPD this indicated that they would struggle to acquire new knowledge, so the ZPD is an indicator of a child's ability to learn.

Vygotsky's ideas highlight the importance of social interactions and particularly the use of language to enhance cognitive development. These ideas are attractive as they provide an optimistic view of learning in which children are not constrained by age-linked stages and all children can achieve at a higher level with additional help. Vygotsky's work has gone largely unquestioned as he died aged 34 and could not re-work his ideas as Piaget did. We could question whether all adult help is indeed helpful. Also, it sounds easy to make a child 'cleverer' as all it involves is another person providing a few verbal hints, but we know from experience that just being told how to do something does not mean we can do it! Learning could be more complicated than Vygotsky suggests, but we are beguiled by the simplicity of the ZPD.

Check your understanding

1 How does Vygotsky link language to learning?

2 Why is this a socio-cultural theory?

3 Why is cognitive development described as being socially constructed?

1.3 Behaviourist models

Watson and Behaviourism

In the early 1900s J. B. Watson was a leading light in what was then a new branch of psychology known as Behaviourism. The behaviourists rejected the notion that human behaviour could be understood by considering how individuals comprehended their own behaviour. Instead they favoured an approach that emphasised the importance of how the environment had an impact on human behaviour and as such were only interested in studying observable behaviour that was free from the subjective views of the researcher.

Watson was particularly interested in the relationship between an environmental stimulus and a behavioural response, and famously studied this in the case of 'Little Albert'. The study is described in detail on pages 115–116.

Key study
Watson and Raynor, Conditioned emotional reaction

Aim To investigate if a complex human behaviour, such as an emotional response, could be due to classical conditioning.

Design To observe the fear response of an infant to a white rat by presenting an unconditioned stimulus (a loud noise behind his head) whenever the participant reached for a white rat that he had previously shown no fear of.

Participant An infant called Albert who was tested before and after conditioning.

Findings Albert initially showed no fear of the white rat but after conditioning when Albert was shown the rat he showed fear and would not touch it.

Conclusion Complex behaviours such as emotional responses are learned responses to environmental stimuli.

Evaluation Watson claimed he could use conditioning to train any child to become anything from a beggar to a lawyer.

His views are often seen as distasteful, as they reduce complex human behaviour to simplistic ideas of stimulus and response. It can be argued that being a human involves thoughts and feelings, yet Watson ignores these. The experiment only studied one child and his reactions may not necessarily be applied to all children, although this finding has been repeated and it has been argued by Seligman (1972) that a fear of rats may have an evolutionary advantage.

We could add a final comment: it is extremely unethical to scare participants, particularly babies.

Skinner and operant conditioning

Operant conditioning involves voluntary behaviour, unlike the previous example, which can be regarded as classical conditioning as it focuses on a reflex response. Operant behaviour is observed as the normal behaviour of an organism, for example children will normally cry, reach out, smile and ask questions. Skinner investigated this type of behaviour, although usually in rats and pigeons (see Skinner, 1948), by observing what caused these behaviours to increase or decrease in frequency. He found that if the consequence of a behaviour was rewarding then this behaviour would be increased, but if it was punishing it would be reduced. For example, we can train a dog to sit by rewarding it with a biscuit whenever it sits down after being commanded. The dog will normally sit down and operant conditioning (the offering of the reward) increases the frequency of the dog obeying the command to sit down by providing a positive outcome. In this case the response comes before the stimulus, as the dog sits down before getting the reward.

Skinner argues that this process can be applied to human behaviour and the way we learn. He focuses on the use of positive reinforcement, or reward, which can also be the removal of something unpleasant. What he also suggests is that the frequency of a behaviour is more likely to be increased (shaped) by using intermittent rewards. According to Skinner, it

should be possible to encourage children to engage in learning activities by the careful use of rewards, and for humans this can be praise or the satisfaction experienced when a task is completed. Similar evaluative issues as those related to Watson can be applied to Skinner's operant conditioning, but it must be highlighted that he did encourage the use of rewards and not punishment to improve learning behaviour.

Weblinks

You might like to watch a video of Watson conditioning Albert (see Contents page).

You can view useful summaries on conditioning and Skinner's idea (see Contents page).

Check your understanding

1 What is the order of the stimulus and response in the Watson and Skinner experiments?

2 Why did Watson suggest that it was possible for anyone to have any career?

Section summary

- Piaget considers children's learning to be determined by age-dependent stages and that the child is a 'lone scientist' trying to understand the world.

- Bruner suggests stages that are not age-dependent and are used throughout life, and highlights the importance of language.

- Vygotsky places the child's learning in a social world where language is used to develop understanding.

- Watson and Skinner regard learning as the result of conditioned responses to environmental stimuli.

2 Personal approaches to learning

2.1 Variations on learning strategies

The extraordinary diversity of humans often presents difficulties when studying psychology, for it is challenging to use any one theory to understand individuals in a large group. When we consider learning theories this can become even more complicated, due to the many different ways in which learning takes place. Infants are learning from the moment of birth to respond to their carers and their environment; throughout life we all learn how to behave in socially appropriate ways and, of course, we focus much of our attention on formal learning in school. This section is very much focused on how formal learning takes place and the environment where this usually occurs, namely educational settings. Due to the diversity of the human condition and the many types of educational setting, the first issue to be addressed is the variety of ways in which learners approach their own learning.

Recent years have seen an increase in theories that suggest that individuals have a preferred approach to learning and that they will be more successful if the teaching they receive facilitates these preferences. These individual preferences can be regarded as strategies for learning. We all learn in many different situations and use a variety of strategies to help us cope with the demands of the wide range of our learning experiences. Curry (1983) provides a model that may help us to understand the complexity of how each of us engages in learning activities (Figure 4.3); it tries to deal with the observations that individuals appear to use different strategies for learning, but acknowledges that these often contain similar features.

Try this ...

Think about what you do to learn. Do you learn in the same way for all subjects? Do you learn in the same way all the time?

The model shown in Figure 4.3 highlights the point that the way we go about learning could be better understood by considering different levels of psychological activity. The outer, more variable layer corresponds to the many strategies that learners use and the associated instructional preferences. An example of this could be McCarthy's (1990) 4MAT system, which suggests that learners favour asking different questions about how to engage with the learning activity and that this leads to a preferred type of learning task (see Table 4.1).

Rezler and Rezmovic (1981) developed the learning preference inventory (LPI) and suggested that individual strategies for learning may be linked to whether tasks involved abstract or concrete concepts; whether people are working alone or in groups; and whether work is organised by the teacher or the students. What is important about both the 4MAT and LPI examples is that each learner will engage in learning activities using different strategies. These strategies are not fixed and will change to suit the learning environment. As they learn to be learners they select strategies that help them to cope with the demands of the learning situation.

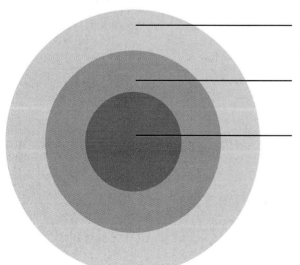

Outer: This represents how each individual would like to engage with the learning activity and is often referred to as an *instructional preference*. This will vary depending on the learning environment.

Middle: This represents how individuals prefer to think about the learning task and involves the intellectual processing of information. This is fairly stable but may change as a result of instructional preference.

Inner: This represents how individuals assimilate and adapt information and is not dependent on what happens in the learning environment.

Figure 4.3 Curry's model of how people approach a learning activity

Preferred question	Type of learner	Preferred learning task/activity
Why?	Imaginative	To develop a meaning or reason for the activity. Needs to take in the experience by speaking, listening and interacting and it needs to be worthwhile
What?	Analytical	Needs to know what to learn and how this can help to develop skills and concepts. Likes to order and name
How?	Common-sense	Active tasks that develop skills and appreciates their usefulness
If?	Dynamic	Opportunity to be creative and adapt the learning to be more relevant to themselves

Table 4.1 The 4MAT system questions

Check your understanding

1 Distinguish between the layers of Curry's model and how they relate to the ways individuals learn.

2 Explain what a learning strategy is.

2.2 Differences in cognitive styles

The outer layer of the model proposed by Curry highlighted the more variable strategies used by learners to cope with learning situations. Once learners are engaged in a learning task, they begin to think about what is involved and to process the more academic information. Curry regards this middle layer as being more stable. At this level of psychological engagement, learning involves considering how the learner will assimilate and use the new knowledge and often this type of information processing is referred to as a *learning style*. Learning styles are considered to be a fairly fixed set of behaviours that are used to approach an educational experience (Bennett, 1990). As such, they differ from the strategies in the previous section since they are linked more to cognitive processes than to activities, and they are less likely to be affected by the learning environment.

One of the most popular learning styles used in recent years is the concept of visual, auditory and kinaesthetic learning (VAK) (Rose, 1985). The idea that individuals have a learning style that reflects a preference towards one particular sensory modality has been developed from what is known as neuro-linguistic programming

(NLP). In NLP it is assumed that information is processed via the senses and that our cognitive processes are affected by the particular sense that is used. It was originally assumed that individuals had preferences towards certain senses and would therefore favour these in a learning situation. Despite the fact that the practitioners of NLP no longer consider this to be the case, VAK is widely used. Many educational settings endeavour to assess their students' VAK learning styles and provide instructional tasks that will support these (see Table 4.2).

Learning style	Learning activity
Visual	Use images, graphs, diagrams, and concept maps
Auditory	Listening to lectures, speeches and talking to others
Kinaesthetic	Involved in physical activity, such as moving, cutting and pasting or the repetition of skills

Table 4.2 The VAK learning styles

Key study

Riding and Raynor, Cognitive styles and learning strategies

In the 1990s Riding and Raynor (1998) began to question the usefulness of learning styles and their application to educational settings. They set out to review the research findings for learning styles and to identify any common features that might highlight how individuals process information.

What they concluded was that many of the existing learning styles had a poor basis in evidence, but also that some features appear to suggest more stable cognitive processes. They concluded that many learning styles are in fact more flexible learning strategies that learners use to cope with learning situations, and that these can be improved or changed. They also found more stable cognitive processes that can be related to the middle layer of Curry's model, where it is assumed that assimilation and adaptation of knowledge occur. Riding and Raynor argued that the idea of *cognitive styles* would be more useful than learning styles, as these are fairly fixed and determine which learning strategies are to be used. They concluded that two dimensions of cognitive style exist and that each operates on a continuum with two opposing preferences:

Dimension 1 Ways of organising information

Either as a *holist* who would, for example, read a poem and understand the general message it contained, or as an *analyst* who would focus on the structures within the poem.

Dimension 2 Ways of representing information

Either as a *verbaliser*, who likes to use words and language, or as an *imager*, who prefers to use visual representations.

It is therefore possible to have four main types of cognitive style (see Table 4.3), each of which will influence the preferred learning strategies. The learning strategies may change, but Riding and Raynor argue that the cognitive styles stay the same.

There is much academic and professional debate over the validity and reliability of learning styles used in educational settings. Platt (2001) claims to find no evidence for NLP theory or the effectiveness of its practice and this casts doubt over the VAK model of

learning. In 2004 Coffield and colleagues reviewed the existing literature on learning styles and concluded that all those in use in educational settings lacked validity and reliability. Although the VAK model was not reviewed, many of the existing styles included the notion of information-processing preferences linked to the senses. The Coffield-led research looked at Riding and Raynor's cognitive styles and found that they had some validity but little reliability, in other words there is some evidence for information-processing being linked to cognitive styles, but this has not yet been replicated enough for the academic community to accept its usefulness.

Try this …

Riding and Raynor suggest that the way we organise information does not change. Consider how you learn: do you prefer the whole picture or are you the sort of person who likes to analyse the fine detail of everything?

Many professionals working with young people will find these conclusions difficult to accept, as they use learning/cognitive styles and find them helpful. It may well be that when teachers engage with learning/cognitive style theory it results in interesting multi-modal lessons that students find enjoyable. This enjoyment can serve to raise self-esteem, develop productive teacher–student relationships and ultimately improve learning. Of course, there is also the possibility of the power of suggestion and simply suggesting to a student (or teacher) that this way of learning will be better may just make it so.

		Ways to organise information	
		Holist	**Analyst**
Ways to represent information	Verbaliser	Holist/verbaliser	Analyst/verbaliser
	Imager	Imager/holist	Imager/analyst

Table 4.3 Cognitive styles

Check your understanding

1. What sort of learning activity would V, A and K learners prefer?

2. If you were a holist/verbaliser, how would you prefer to learn?

3. What are the academic objections to learning/cognitive styles?

4. Why may teachers find learning styles useful?

2.3 Theory of multiple intelligences

This final subsection will discuss Gardner's (1993) theory of multiple intelligences (MI). If we return to Curry's model (Figure 4.3 on page 224) the inner layer is thought to represent stable cognitive processes that are not affected by the external world. Gardner argues that cognitive styles are a result of each individual having a range of different intelligences, of having multiple intelligences. He has identified seven core intelligences, shown in Table 4.4.

These intelligences identified by Gardner were distinguished from fairly limited skills or abilities by having to meet certain criteria. Among these were that the intelligence must be linked to a specialised part of the brain and that there should be some evidence of individuals, such as prodigies, exhibiting unusual talents in this area.

The main contention of MI theory is that educational systems do not reflect the many diverse ways in which children can learn, and concentrate too much on logical and linguistic intelligence. Each child is thought to have different levels of each of the intelligences and as such will have differing cognitive styles that in turn lead to distinct learning preferences or strategies. While the learning strategies are responsive to changes in the educational environment, MIs are fixed. Therefore, to help facilitate learning by reducing the number and variety of strategies a learner must adopt, Gardner proposes that teachers should provide learning opportunities that are more closely linked to the MIs. The sorts of activities that teachers offer children should be those that engage a range of the seven MIs, therefore singing about Shakespeare is as valid as writing an essay on his work.

Try this ...

Think about Table 4.4 and discuss with friends who you think is the most intelligent person. Make a list from most to least intelligent.

Just like learning styles, MI has been readily taken up by educational settings, and many professionals will claim that adopting the principles of MI has improved students' learning. Despite this, the academic community is not so accepting and reports such as that by Waterson (2006) question the evidence base for such an approach. Some professionals criticise MI, as it creates the impression that all children can perform to high educational standards given an appropriate MI-based experience, and this could make it difficult to distinguish academic ability. It may well be that the success of MI is not so much based on the fact that humans have a range of intelligences but, just as with learning styles, it provides an opportunity for exciting lessons and opportunities to develop successful relationships between teachers and students.

U3

4

Check your understanding

1   Why does Gardner say there are multiple intelligences?

2   How may MI theory improve learning?

3   What are the objections to MI?

4   Does it matter if academics and practitioners do not agree?

Intelligence	Area of intelligence	Types of people	Example
Linguistic	Using words, reading, writing and has a high verbal memory	Writers, lawyers, teachers	J.K. Rowling
Logical–mathematical	Numbers, abstract thought, computers	Engineers, doctors	Albert Einstein
Spatial	Good hand-to-eye co-ordination, clear visual memory of places	Sailors, surgeons, painters	Tracy Emin
Musical	Identify notes, pitch, rhythm	Musicians and composers	Robbie Williams
Bodily-kinesthetic	Dexterous, good at movement and balance	Athletes, builders, dancers	David Beckham
Interpersonal	Often extroverts and can empathise with others	Teachers, managers	Nelson Mandela
Intrapersonal	Ability to be introspective, very self-aware of own emotions and goals	Psychologists, writers	Dalai Lama

Table 4.4 Gardner's seven core intelligences

3 Personal approaches to teaching

3.1 Behaviourist use of objectives and monitoring of tasks

Just as individuals approach learning in many ways, there are also many ways in which teachers or educators approach the organisation of the teaching or instructional process. The approaches used can be classified by identifying the main principles. One such classification relates to the use of behaviourist objectives to set up and monitor how and what students learn.

The behaviourist perspective emphasises the importance of observable outcomes and is less interested in what may be happening cognitively or socially within a learning environment. Within this approach it is important for the teacher to be clear what the expected outcomes are and what process they expect the students to go through in order to master them. This focus on students mastering, or showing that they have achieved the expected outcome, is sometimes termed *mastery learning*. Teachers are therefore required to set clear criteria for learning, identifying what the student must do and what the student is expected to have achieved. When teachers do this they are controlling the learning environment carefully, which of course relates to the behaviourist approach, where it is argued that observable behaviour is the result of environmental stimuli.

Try this ...

Who controls your learning? Is it your teacher or you? Discuss whether what the teacher does has any influence on what and how you learn.

In this approach it is necessary to separate educational outcomes from educational processes, and this is not as straightforward as may at first be thought.

◆   An *outcome* is the expected behaviour or level of performance that can be observed at the end of a learning task.

◆   A *process* is the expected behaviour performed during a learning task.

The process and outcome behaviours that are expected by the teacher become specific behavioural objectives as these are activities they anticipate the learner will do. They can therefore be used to monitor the progress of individual students' learning. These behavioural objectives can also be termed *learning* objectives, and within a planned learning task it would be expected that three types of these objectives are used:

1   What the student will do (turn decimals into fractions).

2   What the learning activity is (using a calculator).

3   How success is identified (writing down at least 15 correct answers in response to 20 questions).

The use of learning objectives such as these places a clear focus on outcomes and the need to carefully control the learning environment.

Ausubel (1977) suggested that educators should use *advance organisers* – tools or mental aids to help learners make links between the last lesson and the present learning situation. This can be linked to a behaviourist view of teaching as the teacher organises the learning environment, but the main impact is a cognitive one, as the initial activity helps the learner identify conceptual links in their learning experience. A clearer example of the use of learning objectives is that referred to as 'Bloom's taxonomy'. This was originally formulated in the 1950s but has recently been updated by Bloom's co-author (Krathwohl, 2002). This taxonomy outlined what behaviours should be observable after a learning activity and grouped these into cognitive, affective and psychomotor domains. The most commonly used is the cognitive domain.

Key study
Krathwohl, A revision of Bloom's taxonomy

This study was a review of the original taxonomy and was carried out in the same way by consulting 'measurement specialists' and meeting to agree a consensus on what the different levels of the taxonomy

Term	Description
Remember	Recall information (Did the tortoise or hare win?)
Understand	Construct meaning (What is the hare and tortoise story about?)
Apply	Carry out a procedure (Develop a theory to explain the result)
Analyse	Consider all the parts/factors (Why was the hare lazy? Would you do this?)
Evaluate	Make judgements (Would all hares do this?)
Create	Use the parts/factors to make something new (Write another story about a race between a hedgehog and a badger)

Table 4.5 Bloom's taxonomy – updated

should be. The taxonomy is largely regarded as a measurement tool to identify educational achievement. Table 4.5 summarises the findings; you can see how the cognitive demand increases as you read down the table.

Evaluation This is mainly a theoretical construction and may not reflect the complex nature of teaching and learning situations. If learners always want to start with easier material, this may become quite dull and predictable and reduces the opportunity for more exciting experiences. This is similar to the view that encouraged Vygotsky to develop his theory of the ZPD (see page 221).

The behaviourist approach to teaching seeks to control the learning environment and identifies clear behaviours that it is expected will be observed if learning is successful.

Try this ...

Write a series of questions based on Bloom's taxonomy for a lesson on using the 'i before e' rule.

Check your understanding

1   What is the difference between an outcome and a process?

2   What do behaviourist teachers try to control?

3   Why is Bloom's taxonomy an example of a behaviourist approach?

3.2 Cognitive approaches of discovery learning

This subsection will show how Bruner did not just theorise about how learning may take place, but also considered how best to organise the curriculum. This distinguishes him from Piaget and Vygotsky, both of whom developed theories of learning, although neither suggested how his theory might be put to practical use. Bruner initially outlined his ideas as to how teaching should take place and how the curriculum should be organised in a ground-breaking book called *The Process of Education* (1960). Even though this is a large body of work and nearly 50 years old, it is still a vital and important key study.

Key study
Bruner, *The Process of Education*

Bruner developed the ideas in this book from his existing research into cognition and also as the result of an education conference in 1959. Bruner's great skill is to bring together ideas to form compelling and useful theories, and it was his job to summarise the discussions at the 1959 conference; this task resulted in this book. The two main ideas that will be discussed here are discovery learning and the spiral curriculum.

Discovery learning

Bruner provides evidence from observations of classroom practice that if children are engaged in a task that offers some level of enquiry, they can perform at a much higher level than would usually be expected. He argues that learning is not just about grasping general principles but also involves developing an attitude towards learning and the possibility of solving problems. Simply being told facts about a subject, such as psychology, is not helpful in developing a learning attitude: Bruner recognises the importance of thinking like a psychologist (or mathematician etc.). In order for this to happen, students must use enquiry and *discover* the general principles rather than just being told.

An example is given in relation to a lesson on social and economic geography, where the students are given a map that has physical features but no city names. Their task is to place the right cities in the correct locations. What resulted was a discussion about what resources and transport a city needs and from this an understanding of why cities are located where they are. This task highlights how what could have been an uninspiring task has been converted into an exciting challenge that has resulted in knowledge being gained. Bruner also provides examples of discovery learning in mathematics, but in both cases he acknowledges that this must not be the only way to organise learning. Discovery learning is time-consuming and sometimes it is best to simply tell learners what they should know, especially if there is not a difficult concept to grasp. For example, it would be a waste of time waiting for students to discover how to do long division or research the names of chemical elements.

The spiral curriculum

At the time of writing *The Process of Education*, Bruner was beginning to consider the difficulty of applying Piaget's stages to educational contexts and was questioning the rigidity of the stages (he had yet to formalise his modes of representation theory, see page 220). He did not believe that children's thinking was as restricted to ages as Piaget had proposed, and boldly stated that any subject could be taught to any child of any age. Although this may sound implausible, Bruner added a limitation that makes the idea more acceptable, namely that the teaching needed to be 'intellectually honest' and take account of the learner's capabilities.

The example provided by Bruner refers to teaching literature and science where the subject matter is presented at a level that matches the learners' thinking. The curriculum becomes a spiral because the subjects can be taught year after year, each time adding more information as appropriate to the learners' ability. There is no need therefore for them suddenly to be surprised by being told that all materials are made up from atomic particles!

Evaluation Bruner's ideas are still influential and yet he is self-critical of discovery learning. The spiral curriculum

is a fascinating idea, but ironically the regular teaching of subject areas can also make them appear boring to children.

Try this …

Try to produce a spiral curriculum for understanding teaching and learning for children from Key Stage 1 to Key Stage 3. Think about what to start with – this should be appropriate to children of Key Stage 1 age – and then work up. Simple! Or is it?

Check your understanding

1   Where do Bruner's ideas come from?

2   Explain discovery learning.

3   In the spiral curriculum, why does Bruner state that the intellectual challenge must 'honestly' reflect the learners' ability?

3.3 Social constructivism – cooperative learning and scaffolding

The theory of social constructivism suggests that knowledge is constructed as a result of social interaction (see page 221). This differs from Piaget's view that the individual child constructs their own knowledge as result of interacting with the external world. Cooperative learning builds on the social constructivist idea that we can learn better when interacting and talking with other people. This is typically seen in schools where students are encouraged to work in groups and to share tasks. It is argued that this not only aids learning but also improves self-esteem and has other social advantages. Another common example of social constructivist-influenced teaching is that of scaffolding, which was first reported in the key study below.

Key study
Wood et al., The role of tutoring in problem-solving

Aim To investigate the nature of 'tutoring' – when an expert helps someone less expert or a novice.

Sample 30 children equally divided into 3-, 4- and 5-year-olds and by gender.

Design Participant observation of a construction task. The task involved connecting 21 wooden blocks to make a sturdy pyramid. Tutors were present to offer verbal or 'showing' guidance. The tutor would allow the child to complete as much as possible by themselves and only intervene when the child got stuck.

Findings The tutor's responses were described as 'scaffolding functions' and are shown in Figure 4.4.

Evaluation The researchers found that with scaffolding the children could carry out the task far better than expected. The observations focused on one child at a time and may not reflect a real learning environment. Also, the authors had considered the process of scaffolding before the task, so they may have followed their own self-fulfilling prophecy regarding the findings.

Scaffolding can be seen to be far more complex than many expect it to be. It is a carefully thought-out set of procedures that needs to be considered before the task is started. This differs from Vygotsky's brief description of the ZPD, where he was more inclined to follow the child's lead, as in this example the task is initiated and maintained by the tutor.

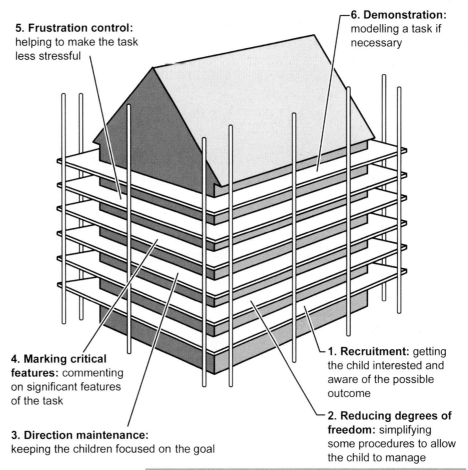

5. Frustration control: helping to make the task less stressful

6. Demonstration: modelling a task if necessary

4. Marking critical features: commenting on significant features of the task

3. Direction maintenance: keeping the children focused on the goal

1. Recruitment: getting the child interested and aware of the possible outcome

2. Reducing degrees of freedom: simplifying some procedures to allow the child to manage

Figure 4.4 The 'scaffolding' of learning

U3

4

Check your understanding

1   What is social constructivism?

2   What are the advantages of cooperative learning?

3   Explain how 'scaffolding' helps learners to learn.

Section summary

◆ Behaviourists focus on identifying learning objectives.

◆ Learning objectives identify what is to be learnt and can be used to monitor learning.

◆ Discovery learning helps learners to think like an expert.

◆ The spiral curriculum allows any subject to be taught to any child.

◆ Cooperative learning can help knowledge acquisition and raise self-esteem.

◆ Scaffolding is a learning relationship between an expert and a novice.

Student participation

Pause for thought

1 Why do we do what we do? If you think about your friends or family members, it will probably be clear that they are not all equally busy. Some people like to fill their lives with all sorts of activities and others seem to be happier doing less.

    ◈ Think of all the activities you are involved in and make a list of what encourages you to engage with them.

    ◈ Think about some of the activities you could be involved in and make a list of the things that prevent you from engaging with them.

    ◈ Can you identify any common themes in a and b that might provide some insight into what motivates you?

2 Think about your life as a learner. Now repeat the process in question 1, but this time focus on when you engaged, or did not engage in *learning*. (Hint: Has all your learning taken place in classrooms?)

3 Compare two subjects, one you are good at and one you struggle with, and try to explain why this is so.

Introduction

This area considers what makes students engage in educational activities. This may not be quite as easy to answer as you may think, as we are all individuals and we all have different reasons for doing what we do. The three following sections are covered to help investigate what may motivate learners:

◈ theories of motivation

◈ encouraging educational engagement

◈ student beliefs and expectations.

Theories of motivation

This section considers whether motivation comes from within individuals (intrinsic) or is dependent on the outcome of our behaviours (extrinsic). Three broad theories are presented to provide a variety of viewpoints. The psychodynamic theories highlight the role of unconscious processes; humanist theories focus on the individual's desire to become a fulfilled person; and finally attribution theories combine cognitive and emotional processes. To understand why there is a wide variation in the ways individuals engage in educational activities, it is useful to have a variety of theoretical insights, as it is unlikely that any one theory can be applied to everyone.

Encouraging educational engagement

This is the 'holy grail' for all educators, for if they could only find the answer their jobs would be much easier! Three interesting but very different insights are provided. One insight highlights the importance of getting a good start to learning in pre-school by engaging in good play activities and how this can be seen to have a significant impact on later educational and social success. Another looks at the popular theme of emotional intelligence (EI) that is present in many schools today and how understanding emotions may make learning easier. Finally the psychological effects of putting learners into ability groups is discussed and seeks to identify whether this helps young people to engage in educational activities.

Student beliefs and expectations

This section focuses on the learner and how they view learning, and not what others may do to them. The learner can often be forgotten in education as adults may focus on what they think they need to do, without taking time to listen to young people. The initial focus centres on how the expectations of learners and educators may differ and what impact this can have on academic success. It can be seen that the children who 'know what to do' engage more in learning behaviours. Learned helplessness addresses the difficult idea that maybe not all children feel like getting involved in learning activities and considers the behaviours that may result from this. Lastly, the effect of improving self-esteem is addressed and questions whether just being made to feel good about learning is enough. The suggestion is made, that if learners are to be encouraged to engage in educational activities, then they need to be able to see their abilities as controllable and therefore changeable.

Themes and perspectives

Understanding why people do things is extremely complex, due to the large number of variables that could account for any particular action. To be able to identify cause and effect in educational settings is difficult, as there are so many potential confounding variables. The lists you made in the 'Pause for thought' section on page 232 will no doubt identify the many reasons (variables) for your level of educational engagement and any one of these could be the root cause of your motivation. Many of the studies also raise interesting ethical issues. For example, if a particular scheme is so successful, then could there be an obligation for the psychologists involved to ensure that all children are exposed to this scheme? How would you feel if you were in one of the comparison groups and found out, 30 years later, that if you had been in another group you could have been earning more and have better job prospects?

Try this ...

Think about a significant learning event in your life; it can be either good or bad and from any period of time. Imagine you are writing your autobiography and this experience is in one of the chapters. Now write about the experience, trying to use at least one side of A4. Read your stories to each other and talk about them and make a note of what you learn about your own learning experience. When you finish studying this area, go back and read your story again. Do you understand it in the same way? If not, what has changed?

1 Theories of motivation

The concept of motivation should be one that most people are aware of. Motivation is a word we use in our everyday language and yet its psychological definition is not as straightforward as it may first seem. It is generally used to explain observed behaviour, so in an odd way we do not see motivation, but instead just the behaviours that result from it. For example, if a student has not completed their homework a teacher may say that they were not motivated enough to engage with the task. Therefore it is the behaviour of not doing the task that is focused on and not the possible causes for this response. The intention of this section will be to discuss what motivation may be and to consider some of the theories that attempt to explain why individuals behave as they do.

Try this ...

Record where the idea of 'motivation' is used and what it means. What do you think motivation is (give examples from sport, drama, school etc.)?

Motivation is something that happens within individuals to make them carry out certain behaviours. It may cause behaviours to change or initiate new ones. Beck (1990) provides a simple but useful definition, which is that motivation 'makes people act the way they do'. It is possible to group the infinite variety of human behaviours into two main groups, those who:

- are motivated by the outcome or consequence, such as learning spellings to do well in a test. We would say that learning the spellings is *extrinsic motivation*. This is because it satisfies the goal-orientated outcome to do well in the test.

- are motivated for their own sake, such as reading a novel. We would say that reading is *intrinsically motivated*. This is because the book has been read just for pleasure and there is no outward goal attached to this behaviour.

The distinction between extrinsic and intrinsic motivation can be useful in helping to organise and make sense of the many theories of motivation, but Claxton (1992) argues that all motivation is intrinsic. His rationale is fascinatingly simple, as he argues that extrinsic motivation will only be effective if the outcome behaviour produces a reward that has meaning to

Figure 4.5 What motivates reading?

very tightly controlled environment, once the rats' intrinsic needs were met the behaviours stopped. Maybe Claxton is right and ultimately all motivation is intrinsic. The following theories concentrate on intrinsic views of motivation.

Try this ...

Consider all the reasons you give for doing/not doing homework. Can you identify which are intrinsic or extrinsic?

Psychodynamic theories

Psychodynamic theories regard unconscious processes as being the ultimate cause of all behaviour. Indeed it is possible to regard the ideas of Freud and his followers as all being theories of motivation. Freud was 67 when he proposed that observed behaviours were the result of the interaction between three structures of the mind called the id, ego and superego (see Freud, 1961). The id is unconscious, pleasure-seeking and is the source of sexual and aggressive instincts; the ego is conscious and attempts to control the demands of the id and superego; finally the superego, which is part conscious and part unconscious, guides moral decisions.

Freud proposed that the ego attempts to reduce the potentially unreasonable demands of the id and superego and achieves this by employing *defence mechanisms*. These are also unconscious and seek to protect our conscious mind from our primitive instincts and overbearing superego. In an educational setting these defence mechanisms may be the cause of certain behaviours (see Table 4.6).

the individual. In the example above, if the student really did not care what score they would get for their test, then they would not revise for it. It could also be argued that they really did want to do well but the task was too hard so they gave up on it. Do not forget that individuals can be motivated to behave in a certain way, or not to behave in a certain way. Whichever way you look at it, what matters is the meaning that the individual brings to the situation and this is intrinsic.

Most theories of motivation tend towards valuing intrinsic factors and the only theories that value mainly extrinsic factors are those related to behaviourism. This is interesting when discussing education, as many settings will use extrinsic rewards as a means of encouraging students to engage with learning or to manage behaviour. What Claxton would argue is that these rewards will have no effect on student behaviour unless they provide something that has meaning for the individual. Even Skinner's rats would stop pressing levers when they were full, which suggests that in this

Motivated behaviour	Defence mechanism	Cause of behaviour
Forgetting unpleasant thoughts, such as homework, French vocabulary, where to go for PE	Repression	Pushing unwanted thoughts/demands into the unconscious
Feeling inadequate at school so bully younger children	Displacement	Redirecting your feelings from a threatening object (the school or a teacher) to a less threatening one (a younger pupil)
Misbehaving in lessons	Projection	Justifying your unpleasant behaviour by claiming that everyone else does this anyway. It is easier to see others as naughty rather than just yourself

Table 4.6 How defences may be used during learning

These psychodynamic theories are quite general and can be applied to many situations; it is also possible to provide many other reasons as to why someone may be a bully. It is because of this generalisation that many people find them unhelpful and prefer explanations whose causality is easier to prove.

One of the fundamentals of psychodynamic theory is the need to reduce the demands of the id and superego; this is often referred to as a *drive reduction* theory. This perception that the mind does not like excessive arousal is also problematic for many educationalists, as many people quite clearly enjoy high levels of arousal and find that they work better under stress. In an educational context this can be seen in many ways, such as leaving your revision until the last minute, choosing subjects that you find really difficult and even getting involved in dangerous activities 'just for the buzz'.

> **Check your understanding**
>
> 1 What is the difference between extrinsic and intrinsic motivation?
>
> 2 Why might it be possible to consider that all motivation is intrinsic?
>
> 3 Give two examples of how defence mechanisms may motivate behaviours at school.
>
> 4 Explain why it is difficult to apply psychodynamic theory to education.

1.2 Humanist 'needs' theories

The most popular 'needs' theory is that of Maslow's (1954) Hierarchy of Needs. Maslow studied 48 people who he considered had fulfilled their potential and referred to as having self-actualised. The people he selected included Einstein, Freud and Roosevelt and from these he used his knowledge as a psychotherapist to identify what characteristics they would have. He believed that all people would have the same needs, that these are inborn and, importantly, that if individuals are going to be able to self-actualise then a whole series of needs must be met before this can happen. What Maslow finally developed was a staged theory where each of these underlying needs had to be met before the next stage could be fulfilled. This is typically conceived as a pyramid with the lowest level representing more biological reflexes and the higher levels representing more complex psychological needs (see Figure 4.6).

The two lower levels are basic needs. If these are not met the individual may struggle to survive. The highest levels are cognitive needs, linked to more psychological functions. Before these can be met, there are needs that are focused on the social, then the self. Maslow argued that the needs from each stage had to be met before it was possible to proceed to higher levels. This suggestion can be criticised as, for example, many people enjoy putting themselves at risk, such as in aggressive games and adrenaline sports, which overrides their safety needs. In relation to education, many students engage in risky behaviours that could lead to expulsion.

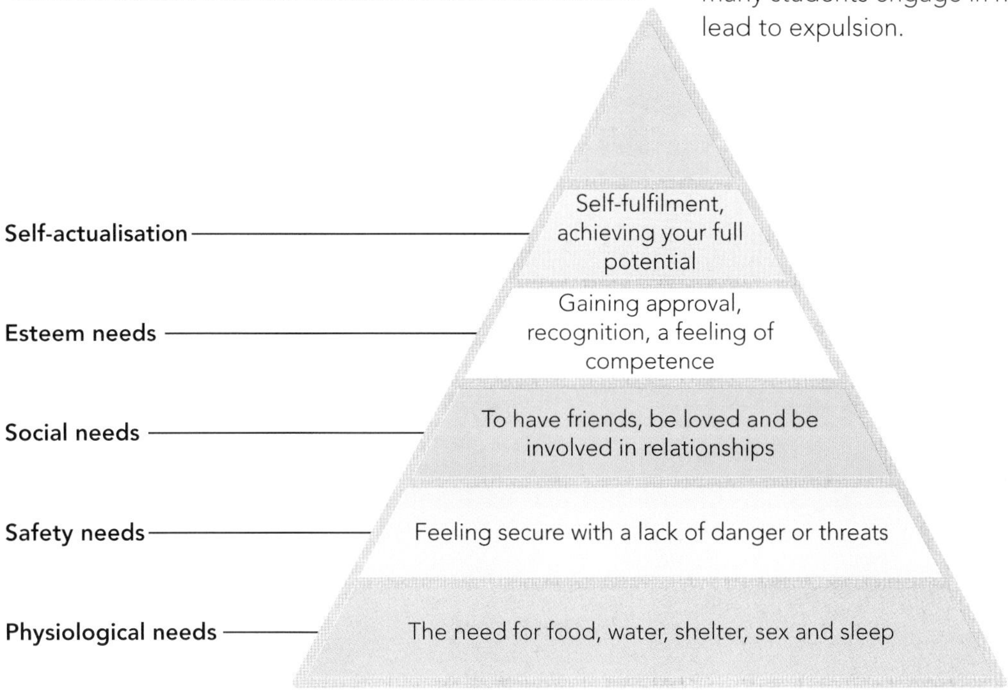

Self-actualisation	Self-fulfilment, achieving your full potential
Esteem needs	Gaining approval, recognition, a feeling of competence
Social needs	To have friends, be loved and be involved in relationships
Safety needs	Feeling secure with a lack of danger or threats
Physiological needs	The need for food, water, shelter, sex and sleep

Figure 4.6 Maslow's Hierarchy of Needs

Maslow's theory is purely based on his assumptions, yet it finds favour in many educational settings and a body of evidence is beginning to develop that may after all support his ideas. It is unlikely that children who are cold and hungry will be in the right frame of mind to access education. Kleinman et al. (1998) provide evidence that children who are hungry are less likely to do well at school. Many educational settings now provide access to breakfast clubs and have policies to reduce bullying. These things, according to Maslow, should support learning as they enable the child's basic needs to be met and provide the motivation to start to 'climb up the pyramid'. This theory is popular and appeals to teachers, who wish to have welcoming classrooms and value the social aspects of learning. However, it is worth adding a word of caution, that focusing on the needs may have the effect of distracting from what is causing them. For example, rather than just providing food, drink, a warm and safe room and encouraging social acceptance of others, it may be more beneficial to consider why these needs are not being met outside the classroom, and then to consider dealing with this problem.

source of motivation. This has become known as attribution theory. One of its main proponents is Weiner, who contends that people use both logical cognitive thoughts and emotions to determine a course of action (Weiner, 2000). This means that the overall attribution, or reason for a behaviour, will depend on the factors that may cause it and how the individual feels about the possible outcome (see Table 4.7). Recently Covington (2000) developed Weiner's theory and added that it would be expected that individuals would come up with attributions that maintained a positive sense of self-worth.

Using Table 4.7 a student could attribute their poor test score due to a lack of ability. This cause is stable, internal and largely uncontrollable. So, to deal with the prospect of many years of failure, students may self-handicap and give up trying in order to protect themselves from disappointment. They are in fact motivated *not to learn*.

If a test score is attributed to effort, this is unstable, internal and controllable; therefore they can do something about it. This means that a student who tries hard and gets a good score would be likely to repeat this effort to maintain the good feeling.

Attribution theory can be seen to be very useful, although it is possible to come up with multiple attributions for the same behaviour (say, failing a test). What is important is not to regard it solely as a cognitive theory but to remember to consider the many different feelings that individuals may have about the situation.

Check your understanding

1   What is the difference between the lower levels of the Hierarchy of Needs compared to the top?

2   Why are Maslow's ideas popular?

3   What may be the problem of focusing on needs?

1.3 Cognitive attribution theory

Psychologists have long recognised that individuals have a tendency to seek to attribute reasons for a particular behaviour, in other words to identify the

Try this …

Think about your own academic attainment. What attributions do you use when you do well and what attributions do you use when things do not go so well?

Cause	Features of the cause		
	Stability	Internal or external	Controllable
Ability	Stable	Internal	Little control
Effort	Unstable	Internal	Controllable
Task difficulty	Stable	External	Little control

Table 4.7 Possible cognitive attributions

Check your understanding

1   What do we call the need to find the cause for a behaviour?

2   What are the three features of possible causes of behaviour?

3   Explain how some students can be motivated not to learn.

Section summary

◆   Motivation makes people behave the way they do.

◆   Psychodynamic theories suggest that motivation is due to unconscious processes.

◆   Maslow proposes that all individuals are motivated to fulfil a 'hierarchy of needs'.

◆   Attribution theories consider that cognition and emotion are both used to identify causes of past behaviour and the likelihood of future behaviour.

2 Encouraging educational engagement

This section will consider a number of factors that can affect the educational engagement of learners. Its focus is more on what is done to the learner rather than what they do themselves.

2.1 The importance of play

Much of the focus on how to motivate students to take part in educational activities typically centres on the apparent disaffection of teenagers. This is a rather short-sighted viewpoint and ignores the many educational experiences that children have had early in their lives. There are many theorists who would argue that learning experiences in the early years are the key to encouraging students to engage in education later in their lives. The focus of this subsection is on the importance of play and how an appropriate use of play can be seen to have long-lasting and significant impact well into later life. There are links here with Maslow's theory of a hierarchy of needs, as the rationale behind the importance of successful play activities can be

Figure 4.7 Learning and playing

related to helping children's needs being met and their self-esteem being raised.

Play needs to be considered as more than children being involved in some sort of time-wasting activity that is not focused on learning, or even simply an opportunity to use up 'excess energy'. When children are playing they are developing and mastering a wide range of skills. They may learn physical-motor skills by manipulating objects, or social skills by taking turns and discussing activities. Piaget made it clear that children's cognitive development could be observed during play as children interacted with their environment. Hutt et al. (1989) make the case that children who are actively engaged in exploring play environments show improved long-term development. One of the most impressive studies to highlight this finding has come from the work of the High/Scope early years settings in the USA. These settings have been studied for over 30 years and provide a compelling case for the importance of play in encouraging educational engagement. The key study below provides a recent update to the many reports written by Weikart, including a number written in 1993 with other colleagues (such as Schweihart and Weikart, 1993).

The High/Scope initiative was developed in the USA in the early 1970s. The goal was to investigate what sort of early-years provision had the best impact on later educational and life experiences. It was found that guided play was the most effective. This is where children had a say in which play activity they wanted to engage with, but at the same time an adult would help the child to organise and explore the play activity. This had the advantage of enabling the adult to introduce more formal learning tasks into the play scenario, such as counting or spelling out words. The other ways that play could be organised were laissez-faire, where children could do whatever they wanted, or formal, where there was no choice about which activity to participate in. Both of these last two groups fared less well in future educational and life events.

Key study
Schweihart, The High/Scope Perry Preschool Study

Aim To compare the effectiveness of child-initiated learning during play with other types of play in pre-school provision.

Design A longitudinal experiment. Children were randomly selected to receive a High/Scope pre-school experience where child-initiated learning during play occurred, or no pre-school programme. The participants were regularly assessed as children and later as adults to measure academic success and life events.

Participants 123 African-American children who were at high risk of failing at school.

Findings At the age of 27 large discrepancies can be seen between the High/Scope and non-programme group (see Table 4.8).

Conclusion These findings provide a forceful case for providing good play experiences in the early years. They indicate advantages to both schooling and social behaviour. The high proportion of African-Americans in the study may make the data subject to cultural bias, but Judd (1998) has produced similar findings for the UK.

Outcome	High/Scope group	Non-programme group
Mean IQ	95	84
School achievement (items passed)	36	28
Mental impairment	15	35
Years in Special Education	16	28
Value placed on schooling	75	62
High school graduation	71	54
Earn more than $2000/month	29	7
Own home	36	13
Arrested more than five times	7	35
Children born out of wedlock	57	83

All scores apart from IQ show the mean score as a percentage.

Figure 4.8 Life outcomes at 27

Watch some pre-school television programmes. Can you identify the opportunities for formal learning within them?

Check your understanding

1   Why is play an important pre-school activity?

2   How should play be organised to increase engagement in educational activities?

3   What may be the impact of not having a good early-years play experience?

2.2 The emotional nature of learning

In the previous section, psychodynamic theories for motivation were discussed and the general principle that was highlighted suggested that in order to reduce anxiety the mind uses a variety of defence mechanisms. These mechanisms are unconscious and may be the cause of behaviours towards learning situations. Recent years have seen an increase in the discussion on the use of and effect of emotions in learning. One of the most popular theories is that of emotional intelligence (EI) (Goleman, 1996), who suggests that EI is more important than IQ in determining academic achievement. Importantly he also suggests that if students were to understand their EI better, their performance at school would improve. Put simply, those who have high EI scores or those who have been taught to use their EI will be more motivated to learn and therefore gain higher levels of academic success. This contrasts with the psychodynamic viewpoint that considers unconscious processes as important, as EI claims that a conscious awareness of emotions should enable students to engage more successfully in educational activities.

EI centres around four main principles.

1   **Perceiving** your own feelings and those of other people.

2   **Integrating** the information gained from your emotions into your thinking.

3   **Understanding** emotions and the knowledge gained from them.

4   **Managing** your emotions by not letting them overwhelm you or by not suppressing them.

Goleman (1996) argues this intelligence is more important than IQ, as there are many people who have considerable intellectual ability but are unable to use it effectively as they cannot cope with the emotional impact of learning. For example, it is always harder to revise for an exam if you are anxious, and exam boards will even take difficult life events into account when marking work. For Goleman the emotions are important as they are an 'internal source of energy that influences external behaviour'. If this energy can be managed by perceiving, integrating and understanding emotions, learning will be more successful.

The idea of EI is attractive as it removes the stigma that many feel about rigid IQ tests, but psychologists must be careful in using such a concept unless it proves to be reliable and valid. This is still uncertain as the theory is comparatively new and there is a debate about whether EI is an ability like IQ or instead a personality trait. Whatever the conclusion, this raises two issues that educators need to address:

◆   Is it possible to teach individuals to use their EI more effectively?

◆   Do those people who have high EI scores really achieve more?

There is evidence that EI, or at least social behaviours that resemble it, can be taught. Feshbach (1998) has shown that social behaviours can be changed if children are given programmes that help them to consider their own emotional experiences and those of others. The results indicate that cooperative behaviour increases and insults and bullying are reduced. Although not linked directly to academic achievement, the changes in the incidences of these behaviours are clearly helpful in an educational setting.

Key study

Petrides et al., The role of trait emotional intelligence in academic performance

Aim To examine the role of EI in academic performance and deviant behaviours.

Design Survey using self-report or psychometric tests to record EI, personality and scholastic achievement. Multi-factor analysis was performed on the data collected.

Participants 650 Year 11 students with a mean age of 16.5. 52 per cent were males and 48 per cent were females.

U3

4

Findings EI did have an effect on educational performance, although it was difficult to identify patterns, particularly between subjects. The clearest data indicated:

◆ that low-IQ students who had high EI scores obtained better academic scores

◆ that students with low EI scores had higher unauthorised absences and showed more antisocial behaviour.

Conclusion The data are unclear but they do indicate that EI has an effect and for the above two populations this is fairly robust. The biggest problem with this investigation and any related to EI is having a reliable understanding as to what EI may be and having a valid and reliable means to measure it.

2.3 The implications of ability grouping

This section has considered the need to focus on the value of good-quality play in pre-school settings and how managing emotions may help students with their learning. This final subsection deals with a practical method that has been employed in a bid to motivate students to achieve to the highest standard. This method is streaming or ability grouping. This may not appear to be a psychology-related topic, but what must not be forgotten is how psychology may be used to argue for certain grouping structures and what psychological effect these may have on teachers and students.

In the UK ability grouping has been subject to government intervention. On a broad spectrum,

secondary education used to be organised into three distinct levels:

◆ secondary modern schools for the lower abilities

◆ grammar schools for the high abilities

◆ technical schools that focused on future employment possibilities for brighter children.

Children were assigned to one of the above schools depending on their performance in a test that became known as the 11+. Most areas of the UK now have comprehensive schools that do not select children by ability. Most European countries are also organised along comprehensive lines.

Sukhnandan and Lee (1998) found that ability grouping had no overall effect on academic performance, but the findings from recent research evidence have consistently found that segregating by ability tends to favour the high achievers ahead of lower achieving students (for example: Boaler, William and Brown, 2000 and Castle, Deniz and Tortora, 2005). A recent report from the DfES (2006) has confirmed these earlier findings.

Key study

DfES Research Report, Pupil grouping strategies and practices at Key Stage 2 and 3

Aim To investigate whether ability group had an impact on the academic attainment of students.

Design This was a case study based on 24 schools (12 primary and 12 secondary) that represented four geographical areas. Data were gathered by using existing attainment scores, interviewing teachers and policy-makers and observation of classroom interactions.

Participants See Table 4.9.

Findings This is a huge report, so the selection of findings offered here is only a summary.

◆ The case study found no evidence that ability grouping raised achievement, although it did confirm the findings from previous research that if there were gains these were for the high-ability groups only.

Observations				Interviews			
Participants	Year 6	Year 7	Year 9	Managers	Teachers	Year 6	Years 7 and 9
Numbers	82	52	31	35	61	88	87

Table 4.9 The distribution of participants

- Key Stage 2 settings that used ability groupings obtained lower results than expected.
- Pupils in low-ability classes made less progress and developed anti-school attitudes.
- Boys and ethnic minorities are over-represented in low-ability groups.
- All classes, whether in sets or not, had pupils with a wide range of abilities.

Conclusion Ability grouping does not appear to raise academic achievement and has a negative impact on the motivation of all but the high-ability students. These findings are extremely reliable as they confirm many previous pieces of research. The validity is also high, as the authors have used a wide range of measures and participants to get a full picture of educational achievement.

There is an assumption that before students are placed into ability groups, academic ability is relatively fixed and the best way to deal with this situation is to provide different learning experiences for different abilities. Consider this in the light of attribution theory and what impact this may have on young people in educational settings. It seems that for many, low self-esteem and low confidence are accompanied by unhelpful negative feelings towards schooling. There are also concerns about the impact of ability grouping on the segregation of social and cultural populations. What the case study highlights is the need for teachers to be clear about the educational rationale for grouping by ability (or of course not) and how this will be effective in meeting the educational needs of each student. All students have a range of abilities, aspirations and motivations and these needs should be met by the educational setting, so it is important that decisions are based on reliable research evidence.

Check your understanding

1 What does ability grouping mean?

2 Why may students be placed in groups of different ability?

3 What are the usual effects on academic achievement when students are placed in ability groups?

Section summary

- Young children learn through play.
- Well planned play in pre-school can have a significant impact on educational and future life experiences.
- Learning can be an emotional experience and students who are more emotionally aware tend to do better.
- Emotional intelligence can have an impact on social behaviours.
- Ability grouping does not have a wide-ranging impact on educational achievement.

3 Student beliefs and expectations

The previous section indicated that academic success is not due purely to cognitive process but can also be impacted by good play opportunities in the early years, or an understanding of emotional processes. This section continues this insight by considering how learners' beliefs and expectations can affect their engagement in appropriate educational behaviours.

3.1 Social roles and academic success

Compared to other everyday experiences, educational settings tend to have very different expectations about the roles of individuals. For example young people are made to stand still in the cold, sit still for long periods of time and even carry out tasks that appear to have no meaning! The expectations can change from class to class and between teachers, and are often different from those at home. This has the effect of leading to a greater likelihood of role confusion and reduces the possibility of 'getting it right'. Doing what teachers expect of you usually means you are a 'good student', whereas 'bad students' are those who fail to behave as expected.

Try this ...

What do you do in school that would seem unusual out of school and vice versa?

The vast majority of young learners are obedient and conform to the expectations placed on them and take on an appropriate role. This is how most of us lead our lives, as people tend to conform in order to fit in and not be left out (see the studies by Milgram, 1963; Piliavin et al., 1969; Reicher and Haslam, 2006). If individuals are unable to conform in educational settings, there is the chance that they will not just be labelled as 'bad students' but also that their academic achievement may be lower than expected. The studies in the previous section by Schweihart (2000) on the High/Scope programme have already provided some insight into the need to guide children's play, as when children are helped to develop appropriate play behaviours, or roles, their future educational and social successes are greatly increased. Therefore the roles that learners adopt can have a significant impact on their future.

Riley (1995) highlighted the importance of understanding the social expectations of becoming a learner at school. She was able to show that if young children entered mainstream schooling being able to identify and label letters and use print, they had an 80 per cent chance of having a reading age by the end of the reception year that matched their chronological age. What was equally important in the findings was that if children had adjusted positively to school and had settled in well to their first year, they were four times more likely to be successful with early reading. Riley was able to show that it is not just a knowledge of letters and words that has an impact on developing reading and literacy, but that those children who quickly adopted the roles that were expected, those who settled in, were more likely to improve. This provides clear evidence that the way children behave influences learning and that it may be necessary for teachers to consider how to help students develop appropriate learning behaviours.

Conforming to expected social roles does not mean that students will always engage with their learning, as for some students it may be more important to be a member of the group that does not engage with learning. Individuals who find learning difficult may find it easier to avoid learning and to become part of a sub-group that does not value it. This group will then view the process of learning in a negative manner and accuse those who do want to learn as being 'creeps' or 'keens'. The need to affiliate with a group can be very powerful and there are real challenges involved in attempting to motivate disaffected learners, as this requires them to reject one group and to attempt to join another. Miller (1997) has reported some success in doing this by using adults who are not part of the school to mentor

individuals. The result was to improve GCSE exam results by about half a grade for each subject. Widmer and Weiss (2000) found that older siblings could encourage younger brothers or sisters to adopt positive behaviours towards schooling. For this to happen, the older sibling needed to be regarded by the younger as a positive role model and for the older sibling to offer support in learning and protect them from bad things happening at school.

> ### Check your understanding
>
> 1   How may schooling cause role confusion?
>
> 2   Why may the way individuals behave have an impact on educational engagement?
>
> 3   Suggest ways to develop appropriate educational behaviours.

3.2   Learned helplessness

The previous subsection dealt with the idea that to become an effective learner there are appropriate ways of behaving, or roles, that make it more likely for learning tasks to be engaged with. This subsection develops from this standpoint and considers the views that the learner may have about their own abilities and in particular why they may not engage with learning activities. It may also be thought of as attempting to understand why individuals appear to be motivated to do nothing.

The original idea of learned helplessness was developed by Seligman (1975) when he proposed that once an animal realised that it had no control on the events and outcomes in its life, it would give up trying to do anything. He showed this by subjecting dogs to electric shocks in cages where there was no escape; after a short while they gave up even attempting to avoid the shocks. When these dogs were later placed in similar cages that had a means of escape, what was significant was that they did not attempt to escape. They had learnt that their behaviour had no effect on their environment and so gave up or had learnt to be helpless. What is important here is that the behaviour learned in one situation was repeated in another different situation. The dogs could have escaped the shock from the second cage but did not attempt to, so the learning to be helpless was seen to be transferred to another situation. Although originally proposed to account for the onset of depression, this theory has been readily applied to education and learning.

The general assumption is that if individuals regularly fail to achieve in an educational setting, they will give up trying, as they have learnt that their actions have no effect. Hiroto and Seligman (1975) attempted to show that learned helplessness could be produced 'by suggestion'.

Key study
Hiroto and Seligman, Generality of learnt helplessness

Aim To investigate whether suggested learned helplessness affects performance across a range of activities.

Design There were three groups and two conditions, see Table 4.10.

The participants were placed in three groups and asked to stop a loud noise using a keypad or to solve a set of anagrams.

Participants 96 undergraduates (51 males, 45 women) who responded to an advert to take part in a noise-pollution study.

Findings Participants in group 1 took longest to work out how to stop the noise and also took longer to solve the anagrams. The participants never actually failed in the noise and anagram conditions but were told they had, or would. This gave them the impression of failure that was later transferred into a different context.

Conclusion Being told you have failed to learn in one context (noise) has induced a failure behaviour that has been transferred into another context (anagrams).

This investigation is more applicable to learning in humans than the original experiments on dogs. The learning contexts are quite limited, however, and do not really reflect all of the interactions that usually accompany a learning task. It may therefore be difficult to generalise these findings to more complex settings.

Check your understanding

1. Is making little attempt on a task the same being unmotivated?

2. Why would animals/people give up trying?

3. Is it important in which context learned helplessness occurs?

3.3 Developing positive self-esteem

There seems to be some common sense in the idea that if learners feel good about themselves then they should be willing to engage in educational activities. Certainly this is at the centre of Maslow's Hierarchy of Needs (see page 235), as once our basic physiological and social needs have been met, then self-esteem needs are the next on the journey to self-actualisation, and Rogers' notion of 'positive regard' (Rogers and Freiberg, 1994). It will be helpful to have an understanding of what self-esteem may be. Self-esteem is a sort of evaluation of ourselves; if we like our characteristics or abilities, we can be said to have high self-esteem (or a low self-esteem, if we do not feel good about ourselves).

Unfortunately the research on the link between self-esteem and academic achievement suggests that self-esteem has little impact. Valentine et al. (2004) reviewed the findings on the relationship between self-belief and academic achievement and found that although positive self-beliefs are related to higher academic achievement, the size of this relationship is small. What does seem to be clear is that students can be made to feel differently about their *abilities*. This depends on the quality of the feedback from teachers and whether it is clear that they care (Canfield, 1990). The difficult job for teachers therefore is not to focus on self-esteem, or trying to make students feel good about themselves, but rather to pay attention to helping them to understand their abilities and skills. What is important

Condition	Group 1	Group 2	Group 3
Loud noise	Asked to stop the noise with a keypad Told they had failed regardless of their success	Asked to stop the noise with a keypad Told they were successful regardless of their success	Just heard the noise
Anagram puzzle	Told it was unsolvable	Told it could be solved	Told nothing

Table 4.10 Table showing groups and conditions

is to be able to focus on what matters for the learners: heaping praise on work that has little or no value to the students will probably be counter-productive. It is also worth considering that just as learned helplessness (see pages 242–243) can be transferred from one context to another, so too can behaviours for achievement. Therefore the child who values and does well at sport, or plays a role in a school play, will feel good about these abilities and this in turn may encourage them to engage in learning activities they may not previously have attempted.

If students are to be motivated to engage in learning by helping them understand their abilities, it is important to help them value their achievements. This process can be regarded as a sort of attribution training, as the goal is to change the way in which students attribute the reasons for success or failure. Dweck has been researching this area for many years and sees the key to motivation as understanding how learners attribute their own ability to their achievements. She argues (Dweck, 2000) that there are two concepts of ability:

- an entity view, which is stable and uncontrollable
- an incremental view, which is unstable and controllable.

These views are held by both teachers and learners and will have an effect on what is expected as a suitable outcome to learning.

The incremental view of ability relates hard work to being clever: the more you try, the cleverer you get. Within this view ability is not threatened by failure, as you can either try harder or adjust the task to achieve success. Typically, tasks will be related to mastering skills and learners will enjoy trying to improve their skills. If the goals are moderately difficult then these can be extremely motivating.

The entity view considers ability to be unchangeable. These learners will set goals that are not demanding in order to ensure success, since failing the task could reduce their self-esteem. The overall effect is to organise learning so that it is not demanding and reduces the chances of failure.

Dweck argues that in order to be motivated, learners need to be able to attribute their successes or failures to their own actions, which means they can do something about them. Having an incremental view of ability is important, as this suggests that students are in control of their achievements. Although the focus is not on self-esteem, this can be increased by using Dweck's ideas of attributional training. What this suggests is that raising learners' self-esteem is not sufficient to improve educational engagement, but that changing the way they think about their own ability will have a positive impact and ultimately raise self-esteem.

Check your understanding

1   Why is self-esteem a difficult concept to apply to education?

2   Is it helpful to make students 'feel good' about themselves?

3   How may different views of ability be helpful in engaging students in educational activities?

Section summary

- Children who can identify their roles as learners will achieve better academic results.

- Mentors can help learners to engage with education.

- Experience of failure in one context can lead to failure in another.

- Positive feedback can have a significant impact on academic achievement.

- Academic success can be increased if learners have an incremental view of ability and can attribute success or failure to their own actions.

The social world of teaching and learning

What do you think about at the end of the year when you take time to reflect on all the things that have happened to you? Do you recall all the wonderful knowledge that your teachers have tried to get you to learn, or are the most memorable moments to do with other events? Many people find that their years in education go by in a blur, and that 10 years after it is all over they no longer remember how to wire a plug, or when 'i' goes before 'e'.

Introduction

The social side of teaching and learning is an important aspect of the learning process, as humans are social animals and generally enjoy the company of others. It would be a sad state of affairs if all our learning took place alone in front of computer screens. Therefore it is vital that psychologists consider the social interactions that take place in educational settings and what effect these may have on educational outcomes. We shall investigate this by considering the following:

◆ personal and social development

◆ student–student social interactions

◆ student–teacher social interactions.

Personal and social development

This section highlights the importance of understanding how individuals in a social environment may develop their personalities. The work of Erikson discusses the idea that as individuals learn from significant life events, the outcome of these can in turn affect the type of personality that may develop. Rogers highlights the individual's need for acceptance and approval and how an understanding of this need can help students to learn. Finally, we will look at Kohlberg's theory of moral development that provides some insight into how individuals make decisions about right or wrong.

Student–student social interactions

There are more students in educational settings than anyone else, so it is vital that we consider how they interact with each other. The case is made for educational settings to think about developing students' abilities to understand how other people may be feeling and to care for each other. Academic achievement can be seen to be related to the quality of friendships and in general students who have strong friendship groups tend to perform better. The opposite can be seen for students who are either bullies or who suffer from bullying. Anti-bullying strategies are reviewed and the effectiveness of breaking the conspiracy of silence is emphasised. Ultimately if students are to do well at school they need to feel safe and respected by their peers and teachers.

Student–teacher social interactions

Learning environments are busy and complex places and investigating what is happening is not an easy process. The Flanders Interactional Analysis technique identifies ten categories of behaviours that may indicate what sort of communication is taking place between teachers and learners. This can be helpful in enabling teachers to review and develop their practice. The impact of teachers' expectations on students' performance is reviewed and stresses how low expectations can lead to poor performance. The final subsection looks in detail at the communications between teachers and learners and concludes that students benefit from positive and cognitively engaging interactions.

Themes and perspectives

Considering the social world of teaching and learning provides the opportunity to reflect on the ecological validity of many studies. Kohlberg, for example, asked children to make decisions about hypothetical situations and advanced his theory of moral development from this. Galton provided evidence on the interactions within a classroom by drawing on two longitudinal studies that involved observations being made every 25 seconds. The studies showing a correlation between friendship and academic success are interesting but this finding may be influenced by many other confounding variables, such as social class.

Try this …

Make a list of the characteristics of teachers who helped your learning to progress. Can you use this to provide guidance for trainee teachers?

1 Personal and social development

When thinking about teaching and learning there is a tendency to focus on cognition and the development of academic knowledge, but educational settings are about far more than just acquiring knowledge. In the section on student motivation a number of theories (from, for example, Maslow, Goleman and Seligman) were discussed that highlighted the importance of how the individual feels about themselves.

This section recognises that individuals also develop an understanding of who they are and what sort of

social roles are appropriate while attending educational settings.

1.1 Developmental stages

Freud's theory of personal development is linked to the idea of negotiating psycho-sexual stages (see his 1909 study of Little Hans) and the development of the id, ego and super-ego. The section on student participation discussed how this theory could be related to an understanding of what may motivate individuals to learn. Many people are uncomfortable using Freud's ideas, due to the lack of empirical evidence and the high level of subjectivity. This subsection will outline the work of Erikson, who originally trained as a psychoanalyst and used these ideas to develop a theory of personality that did not focus on sexuality.

Erikson (1963) originally outlined his understanding in a publication entitled *Childhood and Society*. As the name suggests, his focus was on the child in society and he emphasised the importance of individuals developing an understanding of who they were in relation to their social world. Erikson agreed with Freud (and Piaget) that development took place in stages and that the negotiation of each stage influenced the development of personality. Unlike Freud, however, Erikson regarded the stages as continuing throughout a person's lifespan, arguing that each of his eight stages took place during approximately age-related times and involved learning from experience that could have either a positive or negative outcome. These will be reviewed in relation to educational settings (see Table 4.11).

The final three stages are:

1   Intimacy vs isolation: young adulthood

2   Generativity vs stagnation: middle adulthood

3   Ego integrity vs despair: late adulthood

These do not fit so easily into the majority of educational settings, but are still regarded by Erikson as learning events that need to be negotiated. If adults do this successfully they will understand the importance of close relationships, be able to support future generations as parents or mentors and finally have a sense that 'it has all been worthwhile'.

Erikson's work is important as it regards learning as something that happens all the time throughout the lifespan and not just in classrooms. It is also much more user friendly and more easily applied than Freud's theories, due to the focus on social events rather than sexuality.

Stage	Age	Learning event for the child	Successful outcome	Role of adult
1 Mistrust vs trust	0–18 months	Food and care needs are met	Learns to trust others	To be sensitive to the child's needs
2 Autonomy vs shame	18 months–3 years	Child becomes responsible for 'self-care,' i.e. feeding, using toilet and dressing	Feels confident of own abilities; develops independence	To support but not overly so, as this could have a negative impact on confidence
3 Initiative vs guilt	3–6 years	The child has a desire to initiate activities	Develops a willingness to explore and investigate but can judge when this is appropriate. Is becoming independent	To provide supervision without taking over
4 Industry vs inferiority	6–12 years	Child sees that the 'work' they do is valued by others such as peers, teachers and parents	Shows a desire to do a good job or complete a worthwhile activity	To provide realistic challenges that can be seen to be useful. Use mistakes as a springboard for learning
5 Identity vs role confusion	Adolescence	The individual starts to make clearly thought-out choices that reflect their abilities and beliefs	Develops an understanding of the self that recognises own unique abilities and beliefs. Has an understanding of 'who I am'	To provide opportunities to discuss 'issues'. Avoid criticising the things young people do. Be honest and do not give unrealistic expectations

Table 4.11 The first five of Erikson's stages of personality development and their relation to learning

Try this ...

Table 4.11 describes successful outcomes. What would the unsuccessful outcomes be? Hint: what are the two possible outcomes for each stage (mistrust vs trust)?

Check your understanding

1   How do Erikson and Freud agree and disagree?

2   Where does Erikson see learning taking place?

3   What advice would Erikson give to a pre-school, primary and secondary teacher?

1.2 The need for acceptance and approval

Erikson's theory of staged personality development is focused on the interaction between the individual and society. This subsection will consider a similar premise, though the focus is not on separate stages of development but rather in considering the whole human experience as being important. The focus is therefore on the individual and their understanding of their experiences, but this will be seen to take into account the needs of others. This is a *phenomenological theory*, which is the name given to theories that highlight the importance of understanding the individual's subjective experience.

Rogers originally conceived his ideas of personality development while working as a psychotherapist. The

Figure 4.8 The child's needs being met

central idea behind his theory is that individuals seek the approval and acceptance of others. Rogers (Rogers and Freiberg, 1994) calls this the need for *positive regard*. This can also be seen as a theory of motivation, as Rogers argues that this is what drives our behaviour. His ideas are general ones, but have been applied to psychotherapy as *person-centred psychotherapy* and to education as *student-centred learning*. Despite the fact that the theory focuses on the individual subjective experience, this is understood in relation to the social expectation of others. This may be clearer if some examples are used.

Children are aware of their own needs and desires, for example they know when they are hungry or do not understand the learning task in front of them, as this is their subjective experience. They would like these needs to be met, but this is not always possible as their carers may have other things to do before providing food, or there could be other children who have the same needs. This puts the child in potential conflict with other people, by making unreasonable demands on the carer or by trying to have their needs met ahead of other children. Rogers argues that the child will have to compromise their needs in order to ensure their acceptance and approval by others. To do this they will have to curb their desires or wait their turn. This response is needed if the social world is to function, as in reality it is impossible to meet everyone's individual needs. What is important for children is that adults are able to make them aware that these feelings are not

wrong and that there is a need to respect the feelings of other people.

What Rogers highlights in his people-centred theories is the conflict between what an individual wants and what in reality an individual can get. He describes this as people developing an *ideal self*. This is the person that they would really like to be if all their fantasies and desires could be met. For learners this can be getting all their spellings correct or being able to draw an apple that actually looks like an apple. In educational settings it is the role of adults to help children to deal with this conflict and to ensure that the child is not left with feelings of disapproval. In the example above this would be achieved by making children aware that the fantasy they carry of the ideal self is not wrong. This will help the child to develop useful self-insight that can be used in other situations. If adults make children feel guilty about their ideal-self desires, or even allow them to have all their needs met, this will not facilitate them being able to develop behaviours that will encourage positive regard and will put them in conflict with themselves and others in society.

Try this …

Make a list of all the things you really want to do. Discuss these with a fellow student and imagine what would happen if everyone always did whatever they wanted to do!

Weblink

You might like to read more about Kohlberg's theory of moral development (see Contents page).

Check your understanding

1   What does 'phenomenological' mean?

2   Explain how this person-centred theory is linked to others in society.

3   How can adults help children develop behaviours to encourage positive regard?

1.3 Moral development

To understand the social world of teaching and learning it is essential to have an appreciation of moral development, or how individuals come to an understanding of right and wrong. Both Erikson's and Rogers' theories are based on the notion that there is some level of individual decision-making. For example, if a child is negotiating the 'initiative versus guilt' stage, they will be making judgements as to whether it is right or wrong to start, stop or feel guilty about an activity. For Rogers' person-centred theories the child is trying to decide about the 'rightness' of doing what their ideal self wants alongside the importance of considering other people's needs. These sorts of decisions are complex and often involve abstract ideas of fairness and justice and require individuals to think. This need to think about moral decision-making led Piaget (1965) to develop his own, typically, staged theory of moral development. The essential idea within his theory was that children are initially egocentric, so all moral decisions are based on seeing situations from their own point of view. As their cognition develops they are able to see the viewpoint of others and take this into account. It is only at this stage that Piaget thought children were making moral judgements.

Piaget's ideas have been developed over many years by Kohlberg (for example, 1981). He used stories of hypothetical situations that involved difficult decisions in order to gain insight into the thinking of children and adults. From this he proposed three main levels of moral development:

1   Pre-conventional moral reasoning (2–7 years). This is influenced by the child's own experience of punishment and reward. Right actions tend to be those that have the outcome the child wanted.

2   Conventional moral reasoning (7–11 years). Children try to do what they think will please other people. Rules for right and wrong are absolute and cannot be changed.

3   Post-conventional moral reasoning (12 years and beyond). Right responses are related to socially responsible actions. Wider ideas that involve an individual's conscience relate to universal principles such as justice and human rights.

Try this ...

Have a discussion about which behaviours in your educational setting are regarded as right or wrong. Has this been the case throughout your educational experience?

Kohlberg's ideas are interesting (see pages 16–17) and can be seen to be helpful to teachers in trying to understand the behaviour of young people; they can also provide guidance on how to set rules. Adults should not be surprised if pre-school children do not always do as they are told, as their focus is on their own needs and not the needs of others. Also, the 'tale-telling' of primary-school children matches the stage that suggests that children have an absolute view of right and wrong. Finally, Kohlberg's stages should alert those who work with adolescents to the fact that it is very likely that they will not just accept rules and will feel the need to question authority, especially if the rules conflict with their own consciences.

Kohlberg's ideas have been criticised, but recent evidence (Boom et al., 2001) does suggest that his stages are linked to cognitive development. The ability of young children to make moral decisions was questioned by Wainryb et al. (2005), who found that getting young children to tell their own stories showed them to be capable of higher-level moral decision-making than was previously thought possible. There are questions that can be asked about the validity of Kohlberg's technique in questioning participants about made-up stories, as these do not reflect real situations and could therefore produce answers that do not match real situations. Arnold (2000) showed that the moral responses of participants are different if the situation presented involves helping someone else rather than meeting their own needs. Finally, Gilligan (1982) suggested that Kohlberg's use of only Western males in

U3

4

The social world of teaching and learning

his study gave a biased view of moral decision-making. In general what this highlights is the complex nature of moral decision-making, and as such events are influenced by individuals' own beliefs and also the emotion and context of a real situation.

> ### Check your understanding
>
> 1   Why is there a link between moral decision-making and cognition?
>
> 2   Summarise Piaget's stages of moral development.
>
> 3   Outline Kohlberg's stages of moral development.

Section summary

◆ Understanding personal and social development is helpful in understanding the social world of teaching and learning.

◆ Erikson highlights the importance of social interaction in development.

◆ Erikson's eight stages involve learning from experience.

◆ Rogers considers that people need to feel accepted and approved.

◆ Kohlberg views the moral decision-making process as being a cognitive event.

2   Student–student social interaction

This section looks at how interactions between students can impact on educational settings. The previous section highlighted the need to understand personal and social development and what events may cause these to vary at different ages. It also considered how the desire to be accepted and approved can affect the behaviour of learners and how individuals may make moral decisions. The social world of teaching and learning involves far more interactions between students than it does between students and adults. This in itself justifies the need to pay more attention to these events. Initially moral decision-making and the advantage of developing empathy will be discussed. Then the association between how friendships or bullying can be linked to academic outcomes will be highlighted. Finally, the section looks at strategies to deal with bullying.

2.1 Empathy and morality

Empathy can be regarded as the ability to stand in someone else's shoes and understand how they are feeling. Empathy is an important component in emotional intelligence (Goleman, 1996) and is also closely linked to interpersonal intelligence, which is one of Gardner's (1993) multiple intelligences (see page 227). If we all had the ability to be empathic, the world would be a much easier place to inhabit, as everyone would appreciate and understand how others were feeling. All this may sound utopian, yet there are clearly advantages to be gained if empathy could be encouraged in educational settings.

Empathic individuals will have caring attitudes towards other learners and this could be more useful when considering appropriate responses, or making moral decisions. Kohlberg argued that the highest level of moral decision-making involved using universal principles of right and wrong. This has been challenged by Gilligan (1982) who objected to the Western male bias in Kohlberg's study as women and other cultures were not included. Gilligan proposed that the highest level of moral reasoning would be related to the principles of responsibility and care for all people. Few studies have found any differences in moral reasoning between males and females (for example, Turiel, 1998) so although Kohlberg did not include women, his findings do seem to be applicable

Figure 4.9 Stepping into someone else's shoes

to both genders. What is important about Gilligan's idea is that it questions what it means to be moral. Her focus on care as the highest level does highlight some useful issues. Both men and women value justice and care for others when making moral decisions, but Skoe (1998) claims that women are more care-orientated than men.

This raises a number of issues for educational settings when considering how students behave towards each other. If males and females value justice and care equally, then it is important to encourage students to focus on care – in other words, to develop empathy with others. The problem with focusing on the idea of justice is that this is linked to sets of socially agreed rules that are not always fixed. For example, a common rule is that shouting out in class is wrong, but if there is an emergency and you need to get an adult's attention quickly, it becomes right. Therefore, the moral response of caring for others often overrides rules of social convention. Educators could be advised that young people are more likely to be guided towards appropriate behaviour if the focus is on developing an empathic understanding of the needs of others. Noddings (2005) refers to this as educating for 'response-ability', and she sees the main aim of education to develop caring attitudes towards others.

It must be accepted that developing empathy between students is not an easy task and it should not be assumed that just because an educational setting has a personal, social and emotional education programme, students will be turned into paragons of virtue overnight. If it was this easy there would be no more arguing, bullying, disappointment, poverty, war – and the list could go on. This is not to suggest that nothing can be done, as often small things can make a lot of difference. For example, making children aware of the effect of their actions can help them choose more caring responses in the future:

'Tracy, you have made Mandy very unhappy.'

and help them to consider what it would be like to stand in someone else's shoes:

'David, how would you feel if Martin laughed at your picture?'

Try this …

Have a discussion on whether it is possible to teach someone empathy, or how to care. You may want to discuss whether this really is a suitable job for educational settings.

Check your understanding

1   What other theories can empathy be related to?

2   How did Gilligan change Kohlberg's stages of moral development?

3   Why is empathy important?

2.2 Friendship and academic performance

The previous subsection argued that developing caring relationships between students will provide a more conducive learning environment. Friendships represent one of the closest relationships that young people engage in, and this subsection seeks to highlight the link between friendship and academic performance.

Friendships play an important role in individuals' personal and social development, so it should be no surprise that friendships affect educational performance. Young people who have stable and supportive friendship groups have been regularly found in research to be performing better than students who have fewer friends (Wentzel and Caldwell, 1997). They argue that one reason for this is that less popular students have negative perceptions of themselves and low self-worth. This makes them more susceptible to being unable to cope with the anxieties that can be linked to learning. Popular students have a larger support network that can provide what Hartup (1996) refers to as cognitive and social scaffolding. Here friends are seen as providing access to help in acquiring knowledge and social support to deal with learning anxieties. When students carry out learning tasks with friends they are more willing to take risks and explore activities further than they would be alone. This deeper engagement with an activity may be a reason why learning and friendship appear to be linked. Hartup (1989) also notes that rejected children will be more likely to become adults who have a tendency towards criminal activity and to not complete their studies.

Research by Demetrio et al. (2000) found that teachers used their understanding of the importance of friendship in a number of ways that could serve either their own needs or those of the student. Teachers are well aware of the sensitivity that needs to be applied to organising the transfer of students from primary to secondary school. This is recognised as a potentially stressful but exciting time and care is taken to keep as many friendship groups together as possible. They also point out that the opposite happens too and that this transition can be used as an opportunity to separate friendship groups that are not seen as helpful. The advantages of encouraging students to work with friends are often acknowledged by teachers as a way of maintaining or improving self-esteem or reducing anxiety. Demetrio and colleagues also found that students were sometimes separated from friends to facilitate the development of social skills, or to manage behaviour. This is justified by the positive impact it can be seen to have on students' learning and in contributing the knowledge that being with friends is not always a positive experience.

> **Try this …**
>
> Have you ever been separated from friends at school? Discuss how you felt at the time and if it had an effect on your learning.

Demetrio's research also highlighted students' understanding of the effect that friends have on their learning and that they are capable of making their own decisions as to who they work with. They found that the students knew which friends were helpful and also which friends they were more likely to waste time with. Certainly the older students had found it easier to rationalise the groupings imposed on them by the educational settings and how these might help them to access their learning more effectively. Secondary-school students were seen to be less reliant on friendship groupings and were able to value the support they obtained from friends, even if they were not taught together. Students were aware of the qualities a good friend at school should have. These included being listened to, being able to explain, being tolerant and funny, and working at the same standard.

Check your understanding

1   Why is it important to consider friendship in educational settings?

2   What considerations do teachers make when placing students in groups/schools?

3   List the positive and negative effects of friends on the teaching and learning process.

2.3 Anti-bullying strategies

Bullying comes in many forms and represents the most negative aspect of student–student interactions. All organisations are required to protect individuals from bullying, but it is a sad fact that bullying occurs and going to work or school increases many people's chances of being bullied. Any incidence of bullying will involve a bully and a victim. Olweus (1993) has been one of the most active researchers into bullying and has identified general characteristics for each.

Bullies tend to have experienced:

◆   a lack of love and care in their early life

◆   too much freedom and insufficient boundaries

◆   physical or emotional punishment.

Victims tend to:

◆   be slight or have distinguishing features

◆   have low self-esteem

◆   lack the social skills to know how to respond to bullying.

Many programmes have been developed to help reduce bullying, including the government's 'Don't Suffer in Silence' anti-bullying package (DfES, 2002). The strategies suggested have a number of main themes:

◆   raising awareness of bullying by sending out leaflets or running meetings

◆   incorporating bullying issues into learning programmes

◆   promoting individual intervention with the bullies and victims.

When working with bullies it is suggested that they are made aware of the impact of their actions and how they make their victims feel. This can be difficult, as one reason for bullying can be to get attention from others. It is also possible that victims will feel more isolated if they are provided with special one-to-one help and therefore whole-school approaches are often favoured. These may include opportunities for role-play, where students can practise how to respond to bullying. Typically this involves encouraging victims to be more assertive when approached by bullies. Tatum and Herbert (1992) report that anti-bullying strategies are effective as long as they are carefully applied and the key study below provides an up-to-date example of how a policy of 'telling' can have a significant impact.

In small groups, list all the types of bullying that may take place. Now see if you can design strategies to help potential victims avoid being bullied.

Key study
Smith and Shu, What good schools can do about bullying

Aim To review 10 years of anti-bullying strategies and report on their effectiveness.

Design A questionnaire-based longitudinal survey.

Participants 2308 children (1238 boys, 1070 girls) from 19 schools. 305 were from primary school (year 6). The schools involved came from a larger (440) random sample and represented those who responded in time.

Findings These findings only refer to the effectiveness of taking action on bullying.

Table 4.12 highlights that if the victim tells someone about the bullying, more often than not it is reduced.

- Telling is successful as it breaks the 'culture of silence'.
- Telling family members is the most successful and classmates the least successful.
- The overall amount of bullying had diminished over the 10 years since anti-bullying strategies were introduced.
- Ignoring is a successful strategy if carried out consistently (though not with very aggressive acts).
- Younger children would cry rather than ignore and this is not successful.
- Bystanders offer little help to victims of bullying.
- Teachers can be a powerful source of help.

Conclusion Speaking out is effective and schools need to develop an ethos where children can communicate their concerns. Bystander apathy is a concern but peer-support programmes could be useful in talking about this issue. Personal and social education programmes need to focus on specific types of bullying and not just general issues. For example, aggression, rumour-spreading, the need for acceptance.

Bullying can have a significant negative impact on the social world of teaching and learning. Although it is a complex problem, fairly easily introduced strategies can be effective. Smith and Shu's research (2000) provides encouraging findings and also highlights areas for development. The data are fairly robust as they have been gathered over many years and represent a wide range of participants and school types.

Check your understanding

1. What are the characteristics of bullies/victims?
2. How can bullying be tackled?
3. What does the Smith and Shu study tell us about dealing with bullies?

Section summary

- Caring for others is an important feature of the social world of educational settings.
- Friendships have an effect on educational achievement.
- Students are aware of the qualities of a good friend and how these can be helpful for learning.
- Bullying prevents both the bully and the victim from engaging effectively with learning.
- Breaking the conspiracy of silence is effective in tackling bullying.

	Effectiveness (%) when the victim told their ...		
	teachers	family	classmates
Bullying stopped	27	22	17
Bullying got less	29	34	26
Nothing changed	28	32	47
Bullying got worse	16	13	11

Table 4.12 The effectiveness of 'telling' about bullying

3 Student–teacher interaction

In the previous section the importance of the nature of interactions between students was investigated and it was seen that this can have both positive and negative effects on educational achievement. This section will consider how messages between students and teachers are sent and received.

3.1 Comparison of student–teacher communications

In the social world of teaching and learning, communication mainly takes place from the teacher to the student. What is difficult, as with any communication, is making sure that the listener understands what the speaker says. In an educational setting the teacher or other adult in charge will need to make their wishes clear to large groups of learners. This is different from everyday communications between two individuals who can each give a lot of attention to trying to understand what the other is talking about. In a teaching and learning environment communication involves many more individuals, often more complex ideas are being discussed, and added to this there is anxiety for both the adult and the learner. It is no wonder, then, that in this busy and complex environment messages often get confused. A teacher's greeting into a lesson such as:

'Hurry up and settle down. We've got a lot to get through today.'

may be heard by some of the learners as:

'You lot are so slow. Last time you were here you didn't work hard enough.'

The teacher's intention was not to put the students down but to encourage them to get ready for work.

Equally, from the student's perspective:

'This lesson is really boring.'

can be heard by the teacher as:

'I don't like you or this lesson.'

but the message the student was trying to put across may have been:

'This lesson is difficult and I need more help.'

We have probably all, on many occasions, been in situations where the communication was not quite as clear as it could be. This is more a problem for teachers than for learners, as the teachers are in charge of the learning situation. It must be accepted that teaching is a difficult and challenging and, of course, rewarding job and understanding interactions with students is not easy. Indeed, it can take many years to develop the necessary skills.

The Flanders interactional analysis technique (Flanders, 1970; Wragg, 1999) is a system that can be used to investigate what is communicated in a learning environment. Flanders lists 10 categories that he regards as all the types of communication and the behaviours related to them that take place during the teaching and learning process. The analysis is divided into what teachers and students say and whether this communication is to initiate or respond (see Table 4.13).

The Flanders interactional analysis technique can be used effectively when observing teaching and learning situations. The technique involves the observer making a judgement on what type of communication is taking place every 3 seconds. From the findings it is possible to develop an understanding of the communications between teachers and students and this can then be used to help teachers develop their practice. Merrett and Wheldall (1990) used this technique and reported that teachers use four times as many disapproving comments as approving comments about behaviour. Interestingly they found that this ratio was reversed when they looked at comments made by teachers about academic work. It seems that teachers are more likely to tell pupils off for bad behaviour than for poor academic work.

Try this ...

See if you can have a go at using the Flanders interactional analysis. If you can't do it in a classroom, your teacher may have some videos of lessons that you can use.

Check your understanding

1   Why may messages get confused between the sender and receiver?

2   What are the two main types of communication?

3   Why is it helpful to have ten categories of behaviour to observe?

Communicator	Type of communication	Category
Teacher – talk	Response	**Accepts feelings:** Can accept positive or negative feelings from the learner in a non-threatening manner
	Response	**Praises or encourages:** Often by using 'jokes', nodding or simply saying 'mmm'
	Response	**Accepts or uses students' ideas:** Clarifies, builds or develops suggestions from students
	Questioning	**Asks questions:** Asks questions that it is expected the students can answer
	Initiation	**Lectures:** Provides facts, opinions or even interesting questions
	Initiation	**Gives directions:** Provides directions or commands that students should follow
	Initiation	**Criticises:** Uses statements to change students' behaviour or justify what they (the teacher) are doing
Pupil – talk	Response	**Pupil – Talk response:** A predictable response to the teacher. It does not go beyond what is expected
	Initiation	**Pupil – Talk initiation:** Initiates communication or makes an unpredictable response
	Initiation	**Silence/confusion:** No communication. Silence makes no sense to the observer

Table 4.13 The Flanders interactional analysis categories

3.2 Teacher expectations

The communication between the teacher and the learner is complex and the Flanders interactional analysis technique allows some insight to be gained about the sorts of interactions taking place. This subsection intends to extend this understanding by focusing on the sorts of expectations teachers communicate to their learners.

You may have heard of the idea of a 'self-fulfilling prophecy'. This suggests that the expectation of a particular behaviour causes others to behave as the expectation predicted. A famous study by Rosenthal and Jacobsen (1968) showed that if primary-school teachers are given information that suggests some of the children they teach should do well, then this is in fact what happens. The 'self-fulfilling prophecy'

occurs and the children do better than was expected. Self-fulfilling prophecies are not the only issues associated with teacher expectations. Teachers may hold expectations about learners that are not based on accurate information, or they may have expectations that do not change as the students' ability changes. Kuklinski and Weistein (2001) found that expectations varied for different age groups. The expectations for younger learners often match the self-fulfilling prophecy, whereas for older learners it appears to be harder for teachers to change their expectations despite the students' ability changing.

If teacher expectations had no impact on teaching and learning it would be possible to ignore them, but the Rosenthal and Jacobsen study suggests that this may not be the case. There have been many questions raised about this original study and Raudenbush (1984)

The social world of teaching and learning

concluded that the overall effect, at least on IQ, was very small. More recent research has identified long-lasting consequences of low teacher expectation of learners' abilities. Good and Brophy (2003) reported that when teachers held expectations that were lower than the students' actual abilities, this had the obvious effect of lowering expectations and also exposed students to inadequate teaching. Despite these interactions being complex and difficult to study, it is fair to say that teachers' expectations can have a considerable influence on learners. What is particularly worrying is when these expectations are lower than what students can achieve. This is a complicated area of study and earlier work by Brophy and Good (1974) simply highlights that teacher expectations have an effect on student performance.

Try this …

Can you recall what people said to you when you felt encouraged to do your best at a task, or what was said that really made you want to give up? What sorts of communications could teachers make to raise students' expectations?

Key study

Rubie-Davies et al., Expecting the best for students

Aim To compare teacher expectations and outcomes of student reading performance for ethnic groups within New Zealand.

Design Survey data collected at the start of the school year to record teachers' expectations of their students' reading levels. Data on students' actual achievement.

Participants 540 students (261 were New Zealand European, 88 were Maori, 97 were Pacific Islanders and 94 were Asian), 21 primary-school teachers.

Findings The expectations of the reading level for Maori students were lower than for any other ethnic group. Despite Maori children achieving similar results at the start of the year, by the end of the year these students had made the least progress.

Conclusion Teachers had not adjusted their expectations of Maori students and the effect of this was to limit their performance. Positive self-fulfilling prophecies were operating for the other ethnic groups.

This study provides important evidence on the worrying effects of low expectations. The authors are aware that this effect may not be exclusively linked to ethnicity, as

the students' social status was not taken into account. There is also the possibility of the teachers' ethnicity being a confounding variable.

Although there can be no easy solution, it is worth emphasising the need for teachers to consider how they communicate and to endeavour to present positive expectations of their students. This may be helped by using fewer 'black and white' commands, asking open questions that allow students to develop their ideas and showing concern when students fail to understand tasks.

Check your understanding

1   What is a self-fulfilling prophecy?

2   How do teachers' expectations vary with different aged learners?

3   What are the consequences of low expectations?

3.3 Types of questions and demands used by teachers

This subsection takes into account the two previous discussions that highlighted the difficulty in analysing the interactions in a classroom and also made the case for ensuring that teachers have high expectations of their students. The focus is on a piece of research that has been part of a longitudinal study of classroom processes and will serve to provide more details about interactions between teachers and learners. The research project is known as the Observation Research and Classroom Learning Evaluation (ORACLE), and is similar to the Flanders technique in that a number of categories are identified and then recorded. However, in this case various behaviours were recorded every 25 seconds and this has resulted in some very detailed findings. The research presented here resulted from the original ORACLE (1975–1980) findings and the subsequent repeating of this process between 1996 and 1998. This period is interesting as it spans the pre- and post-National Curriculum years. Detailed research such as this, based in a real school setting, can have a significant effect on teaching and learning. The key study below builds on previous research by Galton et al. (1999) into the interactions within the classroom.

The social world of teaching and learning

Key study
Galton et al., Continuity and progression in science teaching at Key Stages 2 and 3

Aim To investigate the factors that may account for the dip in positive attitude to science. This had already been identified in Key Stage 2 and was now being reported in Key Stage 3.

Design A case study of observations of science teaching in Year 6 (KS2) and Year 7 (KS3). Observations recorded a wide variety of classroom interactions including categories such as questioning, type of teaching activity and statements used by teachers.

Participants Approximately 140 boys and 140 girls.

Findings Year 7 teaching style had changed little between the two ORACLE studies but Year 6 was now very similar to Year 7. This was due to an increased amount of whole-class teaching. In both years whole-class teaching accounted for about 35 per cent of the time.

Year 6 pupils were involved in more group work than Year 7 pupils, but not by much (17 per cent compared to 14 per cent).

There were significant differences in the interaction exchanges between the Years 6 and 7. See Table 4.14.

These results suggest that in Year 7 students are asked fewer questions and that these are closed and often related to supervising behaviour ('Are you sure you want to do that?'). The work for Year 6 students is therefore more enquiry based.

Questions (scores in %)	Year 6	Year 7
Total	21.5	17.9
Open ended	20	8.4
Supervision	9.3	29.6

Table 4.14 Types of questions teachers asked students

The results in Table 4.15 indicate that teachers suggest more ideas and provide more feedback to Year 6 students and the Year 7 teachers spend more time on routine management issues ('Can you put that away?').

Statement made by teacher (in %)	Year 6	Year 7
Total	61	60
Ideas	3% more than Year 7	
Feedback	3% more than Year 7	
Routine	11	15.5

Table 4.15 Types of statements teachers made to students

Figure 4.10 Taking control of your learning

The cognitive demand within lessons for each year was also recorded and it was found that the ratio of questions to statements was the lowest in science compared with the other core subjects. The questions that were asked were of low cognitive demand and provided little opportunity for individual investigation.

It was also found that by June of Year 7 the measures of enjoyment had fallen by 3.5 per cent for the higher achievers and 0.2 per cent for the low achievers. There was also a significant increase in work-avoiding behaviour.

These findings present an overall picture of the experience of science in Year 7 having a low level of cognitive demand and few opportunities for learners to get involved in activities that they have some control over. Also much of the communication from the teachers is focused on order and routine than on learning. This is in contrast to the experience in Year 6.

Conclusion Secondary-school students need to be encouraged to think independently. This could involve teachers providing more opportunities for guided discovery and trying to create a positive learning environment that does not concentrate on management. The work presented in Year 7 needs to be more challenging. Galton concludes that the style of teaching and interacting is more important than subject content if students are to remain motivated when they transfer from Key Stage 2 to 3.

Check your understanding

1 How does Year 6 differ from Year 7 for pupils studying science?

2 What are the methodological issues of recording behaviour every 25 seconds?

3 How could you improve the interaction between teachers and students in Key Stage 3?

Section summary

- Teachers' communications to students are not always understood as intended.

- Identifying categories of behaviour can be a useful technique to observe communication between teachers and students.

- Teachers' expectations can have a significant impact on students' achievement.

- Low expectations are often linked to ineffective teaching strategies.

- There is evidence that secondary-school teachers could offer students more challenge by providing a positive learning environment and spending less time dealing with routine matters.

Figure 4.11 Suddenly it all seems so dull

Enabling learning: dealing with diversity

Pause for thought

◆ Get together in small groups and discuss what it is that can stop you learning.

◆ If you were to move school to Erinsborough High, how would this be different from your experience now and what extra 'needs' do you think you might have?

◆ One of the fascinating features of the human condition is its diversity, and it follows that our different needs can make the way teaching and learning are organised very complicated.

It is no exaggeration to say that every single human being is different. Even identical twins will have different behaviours. These differences between human beings are what make education fascinating and challenging, as no single answer can ever provide a solution to all the possible teaching and learning situations. It is important that we see difference or diversity as a positive attribute and not as a deficit. Diversity brings with it a host of new possibilities and experiences that will encourage creativity and exploration. This area is intended to highlight how diversity can be a positive quality in enabling the learning of all students. The three aspects of diversity that will be addressed are:

◆ additional needs

◆ culture

◆ gender.

Additional needs

This section considers the importance of identifying the learning needs of individual students, particularly those who may need extra support. What is highlighted is that individual tuition or support is remarkably effective and that the strategies used are of benefit to all learners. The issue of gifted and talented students is raised and in particular how educational settings may organise their learning environment. This organisation may match academic achievements, but it may also provide social problems for the learners involved. The final subsection refers to providing intervention and support for learning difficulties that are not present all the time. The debate about how best to teach children to read provides the first focus and asks whether government policy is as straightforward as is suggested. The second focus reflects on how differentiation can be used to provide for the needs of learners.

Culture

The UK has for many years been a multicultural society and the differences between the educational attainments of the ethnic groups that make up this culture are often discussed. The first subsection seeks to identify what differences actually exist and what may be causing achievement to be lower than expected. Recent data would seem to suggest that prior educational success is important, especially fluency in English. Evidence is presented to suggest that strategies that help to raise the achievement of ethnic groups can raise the achievement of all students. The importance of smaller classes and caring relationships is also seen to support the learning of all students. Finally, the significance of role models and positive support is addressed, highlighting the impact of individuals 'other than teachers' on students' learning.

Gender

The first subsection considers the academic success of males and females and attempts to draw attention to the disparity between cognitive ability scores and examination performance. This discussion emphasises how examination success and 'intelligence' may not be as clearly linked as many think. The tendency to want to focus on differences is highlighted again when considering the brain structure of males and females. The brain of the two genders is found to be very similar indeed. The few differences that do exist are discussed and it is suggested that these may be reasons why females have advanced language skills and men are better at visuo-spatial tasks. The final subsection returns to the debate about the differences in academic achievement between the genders and considers what strategies may be employed to make the 'under-achieving' boys do better. It should come as no surprise

Figure 4.12 No two children are the same

by now that the findings suggest that the strategies used to improve boys' educational performance will also improve girls' performance. Good teaching is beneficial to all students.

Themes and perspectives

Many of the topics in this area of the A2 course provide excellent examples of the nature versus nurture debate, and this has extremely important implications in education. If ability or performance at school is thought to be controlled solely by biology then this would suggest that there is little that teachers can do, as individuals will only be as able as their genes allow. If education is seen as a nurturing event, this provides hope, as individuals will be able to improve when given the right support. The nature–nurture debate is never 'won', as it is clear that both have an impact on educational performance. Clearly not all learners will obtain full marks in all tests, but they can all be encouraged to do their best. This area certainly shows that nurturing, or good and caring teaching, can improve the achievements of all learners and that nurturing is effective across the diverse human population.

1 Dealing with additional needs

All learners have needs that must be met if they are to achieve their full potential. Some will have greater difficulty engaging in the learning process than others of their age group. Those whose problems with learning are greater than their peers' are referred to as having special or additional educational needs. This will often lead to the developing of an Individual Education Plan (IEP) whose function is to provide strategies that will help meet the learners' needs. This is an *individual* plan, which highlights the idea that learning can be improved by addressing the needs of the individual. This section will look at some ways in which additional needs are met.

1.1 Individual support

Providing individual support has long been known to improve academic achievement. Bloom (1984) tutored students using mastery learning techniques (see page 228) on a 1:1 basis and in groups of 28 to 32. The results he obtained were not entirely surprising, but the magnitude was. Predictably, he found that students who had received individual tutoring did much better than those who had been taught in groups. Significantly, he found that 1:1 tutoring could move students from the 50th percentile to the 98th percentile.

> ## Key term
>
> percentile is one hundredth of the population; to move from the 50th to the 98th percentile means moving from the middle of the population to being very near the top

Bloom found that the improvement of the students taught in groups was only about half that of the 1:1 students. It may sound as though we have stumbled across the 'holy grail' of teaching and learning, as Bloom has shown that individual tutoring is hugely successful. Unfortunately it is also hugely expensive and almost certainly impossible as it would require every learner to have their own individual tutor! The rationale for providing IEPs is based on sound evidence and many learners with additional needs do have individual adult support such as that provided by Teaching Assistants or Learning Mentors. We shall consider the type of support offered next.

Lewis and Norwich (2004) reviewed the teaching strategies used for pupils with moderate, severe, profound and multiple learning difficulties (they did not include learners who had sensory or motor difficulties) and other pupils. Their overall conclusion suggested that successful teaching strategies were the same for all learners, whether they had additional needs or not. This is important when considering the issue of inclusion, as it implies not only that *all* learners can be taught together (included) but all learners can *participate* together in the learning process. Being present in a classroom does not necessarily mean that the learner is engaged – they have to be able to access and use the teaching provided.

What is interesting about Lewis and Norwich's (2004) findings is that they do not suggest that teachers do the same thing in the same way for all learners, but that the general approaches to teaching and learning need only minor 'adjustments' to accommodate most learners. They suggest that teaching strategies need to differ along a continuum and that certain areas require highlighting in order to meet the individual needs of those who have learning difficulties. Among their proposals are:

- provide more opportunities to use knowledge in more than one context
- use more examples to help students to learn concepts
- provide more time to solve problems
- ensure students have successfully mastered one stage before moving to the next
- encourage students to think about their own learning strategies
- regular focused assessment.

These findings are encouraging as they indicate that all learners benefit from thoughtful teaching, and certainly pupils with learning difficulties can be included in classrooms as the teacher can use the same strategies. The list shown above does not ask teachers to do anything different, only to modify what they already do.

Weblink

You may like to follow a personalised learning link on the internet (see Contents page).

U3
4

> ## Check your understanding
>
> 1. What did Bloom (1984) find out?
> 2. Explain the difference between inclusion and participation.
> 3. What do Lewis and Norwich mean by considering teaching strategies to be a continuum?

1.2 Provision for gifted and talented students

The previous subsection considered the additional needs of learners with learning difficulties. This subsection will investigate those learners who have exceptional abilities, and although this may suggest that they find learning easier, being gifted and talented may provide its own unique additional needs. The impact of putting more able students into different teaching groups or even schools was discussed on page 240, where it was concluded that most students, apart from the brighter ones, do not benefit from ability groupings (see Sukhnandan and Lee, 1998). Gifted and talented pupils will often, though not always, be in the brighter groups.

The provision for exceptional students in the UK is an extremely recent event, with all schools from 2006 being required to identify their gifted and talented learners. These students have always existed and there are many reasons for the sudden interest in them. The government is increasingly interested in the academic achievements of young people, and by identifying this group it is possible that national school achievements could be raised even higher.

Weblink

You might find it interesting to look at the school and college achievement and attainment tables (see Contents page).

Until now bright students have always been assumed to be able to cope with learning; it seemed more important to 'help' the lower-ability learners.

A fundamental problem when considering gifted individuals is how they can be identified and essentially what are these 'gifts and talents'. The DfES (2002) regards gifted students as those who have a particular ability in one or more statutory subjects and talented students as those who have abilities or skills in art, music or performing arts. Those who are considered to have exceptional abilities are usually thought to be in the top 5 per cent of the population. Holahan and Sears (1995) report on a large longitudinal study of individuals who were identified in the early 1920s as having IQs in the top 1 per cent. In general they describe the group as being early walkers and talkers who tend to be physically strong, emotionally stable and have low levels of delinquency.

Despite the above list of positive attributes, there are problems in being gifted and talented, and just being labelled as such can cause persecution (Freeman, 1997). The children can often find themselves isolated from their peers as their more advanced language and adult interests can be the cause of ridicule. There are significant problems in joining the appropriate social group, as their peers can regard them as aloof, but if they join older age groups they can still appear out of place. These problems are also realised in

educational settings and provide a challenge for teachers to meet their additional needs. If the needs of gifted and talented pupils are not met, they are more likely to become bored and unmotivated and may misbehave.

A common strategy to deal with the individual needs of exceptional students is to accelerate their progression through school. This means putting them into teaching groups with older pupils who are doing more advanced work. This may create social problems as the student will not be able to interact with their peers, but it is also acknowledged that they prefer the company of older children. A compromise may be to allow acceleration in certain subjects but to keep the gifted and talented student with their peer group for non-academic subjects. The previous subsection suggested modifying existing teaching strategies for those with learning difficulties, and this principle can also be applied here. Lessons need to include more demanding tasks with challenges that are motivating, and encourage higher-level and more creative thinking.

Check your understanding

1 What are the general characteristics of gifted and talented individuals?

2 What problems may be caused by being gifted and talented?

3 How can teachers meet the individual needs of gifted and talented students?

1.3 Provision of remedial support

The previous subsections considered the additional educational needs of individuals and in particular how these can be met for those who have learning difficulties and those with exceptional abilities. In these two examples the additional need can be regarded as an ongoing characteristic of the individual's life. This section will look at additional needs that may not occur all the time, and this is likely to include all learners at some stage of their learning journey. The areas highlighted will be learning to read and differentiation. Learning to read has become another main feature of government policy, but even without this intervention it is clearly vital for all learners. Differentiation refers to how an educational experience can be changed to match students' abilities.

Reading

One of the fundamental outcomes of any educational system is to enable individuals to read. The issues surrounding how children learn to read and what can be done about those who are slow at picking up this elusive skill have been a major focus of government policy for many years. The government-commissioned Rose report (2006) has recommended that all schools adopt the 'synthetic phonics' system to teach reading. This involves children first being taught the individual sounds of each letter in the alphabet and then using these to understand how words are made up from them. For example, once the sounds d, o, g have been learnt, when the child says the word 'dog' they will be able to break it down into the three sounds that made it. Whether this method is very successful is still in debate and Wyse and Styles's (2007) review of 30 years of research suggests that synthetic phonics does not have a very strong research base. So the understanding of how children learn to read is still unclear. What is in less doubt though are the useful intervention strategies for helping children whose reading age has fallen well below their chronological age.

The 'Reading Recovery' programme was first developed by Clay (1985) and has regularly been shown (see US Department of Education, 2007) to be effective in meeting the additional needs of slow-developing readers. The programme has similar origins to Bloom's 1:1 tutoring, where children who have been identified as making limited progress with reading are provided with regular 1:1 or small-group support. This support lasts for about 30 minutes each day and for up to 20 weeks, and is most effective when problems are identified early on. During the Reading Recovery sessions children use multi-sensory techniques to make them aware of the sounds of letters and words and use these with adult support to read and comprehend stories. The main focus is to develop the child's problem-solving ability when trying to use words. Despite its success its use is not widespread and this is no doubt related to the cost of 1:1 tuition.

Differentiation

At some stage most individuals will encounter problems with their learning. A general approach that is intended to meet the additional needs of all learners is that of differentiation. The intention is to provide a different learning experience to meet the needs of all individuals.

This approach concentrates on modifying the learning experience to ensure that all learners can participate in the learning event. Differentiation can be carried out in a number of ways:

- Providing different learning venues, these can be schools or classrooms that offer different experiences.
- Starting at different academic levels.
- Having different expectations of the learning outcome.
- Providing a variety of tasks for the same learning event.
- Encouraging the student to use their preferred learning strategy.

All learners are individuals and it is unlikely that any one learning experience will suit them for their whole educational experience, so variety is important. Also, no matter how successful a learner is, they will no doubt have many experiences when they find learning challenging. At some stage everyone has additional needs.

Check your understanding

1   What are 'synthetic phonics'?

2   Why is Reading Recovery so successful?

3   Describe how you could differentiate a psychology lesson.

Section summary

- Successful teaching strategies are effective for all learners.
- Gifted learners can be recognised from an early age and being 'gifted' can lead to many social problems.
- The 'Reading Recovery' programme is very successful in developing reading ability.
- All learners have additional needs at some stage of their learning, and successful differentiation can alleviate these.

2 Enabling ethnic minority groups

2.1 Engagement and achievement of ethnic groups

The previous subsection considered a diverse group of individuals with additional educational needs. This subsection will focus on how culture may affect the educational engagement and achievement of ethnic groups. Ethnic groups are identified by the common cultural features they share, and within the UK the tendency is to focus on immigrant communities from Europe, Africa and Asia. It is worth pointing out at this early stage that nearly all ethnic groups will include individuals (or their parents, grandparents…) who have been born in the UK. Just as data on educational performance are analysed in terms of gender and social class, so they are also analysed in terms of ethnic groups. The recent findings on the educational attainment of ethnic groups (DfES, 2006) found that:

- At the Foundation Stage White Other (non UK); Bangladeshi, Black Caribbean, Black African and Black Other pupils consistently perform below average.

- The consistent high achievers across all key stages are the Indian, Chinese, Irish, White and Asian pupils.

- The consistent lower achievers are the Gypsy/ Roma, Traveller of Irish heritage, Black, Pakistani and Bangladeshi pupils.

- When variables such as prior achievement were controlled for, most ethnic groups are found to make more progress than similar White British pupils.

- Asian pupils have the most positive attitudes towards school, whereas Mixed Heritage pupils have the least positive attitudes.

Findings such as these are often hotly debated and Hammersley (2001) questions the use of such data and suggests that they should be used as part of

Figure 4.13 What factors influence these children's achievement in school?

a debate on how educational achievement can be measured. He highlights the need to question how and why the data were gathered and also to consider the many other variables that could be the cause of such findings. For example, previous work by Davies and Brember (1992) found that both Asian and African-Caribbean children adjusted to their early-years setting better than white children. What is interesting here is to consider why this difference occurs. Is it due, for example, to the setting, parenting, or language ability? Strand and Demie (2005) looked in more detail at the relationship between language and educational achievement.

Strand and Demie, English language acquisition and educational attainment at the end of primary school

Aim To investigate the impact of fluency in English on educational attainment after controlling for age, gender, special educational needs (SEN) and entitlement to free school meals (FSM – this is an indicator for family disadvantage).

Design To compare four stages of fluency in English with a variety of pupil 'background' measures.

Stages of fluency:

1   New to English

2   Becoming familiar with English

3   Become a confident user of English

4   Fully fluent in English

Pupil background measures:

◆   age

◆   gender

◆   SEN

◆   FSM

◆   ethnic group

◆   time spent in Key Stage 2 school

◆   prior attainment.

Results

◆   There is a strong association between the stages of fluency and Key Stage 2 test scores.

◆   Pupils who are not fully fluent (stages 1–3) do less well in English than English-only speakers (this association is less clear in maths and science).

◆   Fully fluent pupils exceed the performance of English-only speakers on all tests.

◆   The poor attainment related to low fluency scores remains even after the pupils' background measures have been controlled for.

◆   Less fluent speakers (stages 1–2) make less progress than English-only speakers, but fully fluent speakers make more progress than expected.

Conclusion Educational attainment is not clearly linked to ethnic groups or other pupil measures, but there is a strong relationship between the stages of fluency in English and achievement. The authors recommend the need to carry out an early assessment of pupils' fluency in English; it would then be possible, with the appropriate training and support, to meet their needs.

Check your understanding

1   What are the ethnic differences in educational attainment?

2   What are the problems with measuring educational attainment?

3   Why is fluency in English a useful measurement?

2.2 Culture and grouping

Learners are put into groups within educational settings for a wide range of reasons. They can be organised by age, ability, subject or gender group and each of these will have a rationale linked to improving the educational experience. When students are organised into age groups, this is usually to make the delivery of an age-related curriculum more efficient. Gender groups have in the past been set up to enable different subjects to be covered and more recently to address the issues related to the achievement of boys and girls. Student grouping can also be organised to respond to the needs of different cultures within a teaching and learning environment. This subsection will look at how grouping may be organised to improve the achievement of ethnic groups and also how they may influence social phenomena such as discrimination.

The earlier findings of Strand and Demie (2005) suggested that fluency in English was a more important consideration than ethnicity. Although this view is not discounted, it is worth noting that if ethnic groups are taken into account there is evidence to suggest that this can have a positive effect on achievement. Ladson-Billings (1995) looked at the characteristics of excellent teachers in African-American schools and from this suggested how other schools may adapt to maximise the success of ethnic groups. She suggested that schools need teachers to consider three principles:

1   Students need to experience academic success.

2   Teaching and learning should develop and continue to use culturally relevant ideas and skills.

3   Students need to be encouraged to challenge the 'social norms' that maintain social inequalities.

The suggestion is that if these are the characteristics of excellent teachers, then if other colleagues adopt these they too will become excellent and their students will in turn perform to a higher level. This may indeed be possible, but it provides a simplistic view of how to change educational expectations. We can question the likely effectiveness of trying to take on principles that are shown by other teachers, as just because someone can carry these out does not mean that they communicate the same message.

Too easily there is an assumption that ethnic groups are less successful in education, and Strand and Demie (2005) certainly show this not to be the case. There are outstanding and poorly performing students in all ethnic groups and it is fair to assume, as we did in the subsection on additional needs, that good educational practice has a positive effect on all learners. One regular suggestion to improve the performance of learners is to have smaller teaching groups. Nye, Hedges and Konstantopoulos (2004) report on the effect of teaching ethnic groups in small classes for the first 4 years of education. Although these were not hugely different from regular classes, 13–17 students compared to 22–26, they found that there were educational benefits that lasted for 5 subsequent years. Their focus was mainly on reading and maths, and they found that the largest positive effect was on reading, which is similar to the findings of Stand and Demie (2005), and it is possible to suggest that the smaller classes gave the teacher more time to concentrate on helping students with language difficulties.

Classrooms are not just about academic achievement, as they provide opportunities for social interactions that may not form part of an individual's everyday life. Aronson et al. (1978) attempted to reduce the discrimination experienced between ethnic groups by organising tasks that were to be completed by mixed ethnic groups. The overall task was broken down so that each child had a responsibility, but collaboration

was required if the task was to be completed. This has been seen to be successful in reducing discrimination in the short term, but the results are not long-lasting. Authors such as Forrester (2005) highlight the need to develop caring relationships within classrooms if students are to consider the needs of others on a more consistent basis.

Check your understanding

1   Why may ethnicity be used to group students?

2   What considerations can teachers make to engage ethnic groups with learning?

3   How may small class size help the learning of ethnic groups?

2.3 Role models and positive support

It has been seen in the previous subsections that the achievement of ethnic groups can be improved by applying the principles observed in excellent teachers and by considering the language needs of learners. This subsection develops the idea of providing support that is not centred on the teaching and learning process and will focus on the importance of providing positive messages and suitable role models.

The DfES (2006) report on Ethnicity and Education discusses the findings of Aiming High: The African Caribbean Achievement Project. The Aiming High project endeavoured to raise the aspirations of African-Caribbean students by encouraging schools to develop whole-school approaches. This may have involved enhancing the students' outlook by taking them on trips to libraries, universities, or museums. The school may have brought in consultants or run projects emphasising the options that may be available after leaving school. What they found was that when schools were committed to this positive approach and made clear to students the wide variety of possibilities available to them, the students and their parents became more positive. Although this sounds simple and probably like common sense, it is surprising that many educational settings have been seen to provide a limited outlook for their students. Indeed this is also one of the findings of the report, as they still found settings that did not provide such a positive outlook for students. They also identified the largest barrier to achievement as unfair and inconsistent behaviour management that penalised African-Caribbean students. Providing positive support is vital. Mac an Ghaill (1988) found that one factor preventing higher achievement was negative peer pressure and criticism. What these findings seem to suggest is that one of the causes for the lower achievement of some ethnic groups could be the lack of aspiration provided by schools and the fear of ridicule from peers.

Paradoxically, despite being very busy places, schools can be lonely for individual learners and some students may find it hard to voice their opinions and have a say. Much research has shown the value of providing positive role models and like the Aiming High project these people are able to show others what may be possible. There is certainly a fear in education that the influence of negative role models can become too powerful and that students will prefer to make wrong or inappropriate choices. Klein (1996) reports the appeal of such projects, while Demie et al. (2006) reviewed the achievement of African Heritage students and identified the good practice that led to them being successful. Unsurprisingly their findings regularly refer to the importance of role models. Teachers are seen as positive role models, especially in the early years, if they encourage good language and writing skills, and later on in school are regarded highly if they are prepared to put themselves out to help a student. They also found that black or African teachers who encouraged and helped celebrate cultural diversity were viewed positively by students.

Positive role models did not only come from within the teaching profession, as many African-Caribbean students had been given positions of responsibility such as being school prefects. This enabled them to be seen publicly as individuals who were capable of holding responsible positions. Interestingly they also identified the importance of positive role models from within the family, particularly for fathers to provide their sons with guidance and prevent them from developing 'the wrong attitude'. The overall impact of Demie et al.'s (2006) findings is to highlight the importance of 'other' people on educational achievement and also to show that improvement in learning is not always related to classroom activities.

Check your understanding

1   What can schools do to raise aspirations?

2   How can students be role models?

3   Why may families be important in raising students' educational achievement?

Section summary

- Educational attainment can be linked to fluency in English.

- The identification of differences in educational achievement between ethnic groups is complex and measurement of achievement needs careful evaluation.

- Small classes in the early years can produce benefits that last for up to 5 years.

- Lack of aspiration can have a significant effect on achievement.

- Positive role models that represent the teaching profession or local community can have a positive impact on educational engagement.

3 Enabling genders

This section looks at the evidence about the differences between the academic achievement of boys and girls. It will consider what these differences are and what factors may be influencing these findings. There will be a discussion on the possible influence of brain development on educational achievement and whether we can use terms such as 'male and female brains'. The final subsection will consider various strategies that may be used to encourage the educational engagement of both boys and girls.

3.1 Gender differences in educational achievement

There can be little doubt that one of the major educational debates in recent years has been concerned with the differences in academic success between boys and girls. A major feature of this debate is that boys are underachieving and girls are doing particularly well. A recent report by the DfES (2007) provides a wide range of findings on gender and education (Table 4.16) from the beginning to the end of compulsory school, and offers a more up-to-date summary than the earlier report by Arnot et al. (1998).

These findings may indicate that girls are doing better than boys because they are more intelligent or have higher cognitive abilities. We discussed on page 227 that intelligence may be made up from many differing abilities, but when mean IQ scores are compared there is very little difference between the genders

Phase	Gender difference
Pre-school	Girls had better communication, social and cognitive skills and were more likely to wave goodbye. Girls were more likely to be read to. Boys improved their understanding of number more than use of literacy. There were no significant developmental differences
Foundation Stage to Key Stage 3	Girls do better in English. Girls are slightly better at maths. The differences for science are very small
Key Stage 4/GCSE	Girls achieving 5+ A–Cs have outperformed boys since 1988, they have been 10 percentage points ahead since 1995 (in 2006, boys 54% and girls 64%) Girls do better in humanities, arts and languages by 10 percentage points. There is a small (less than 5%) advantage for girls in maths and science
A Level	Girls out-perform boys in most subjects but the gap is less than 3 percentage points. Interestingly, boys do better at home economics

Table 4.16 The DfES (2007) findings on gender and education

(Strand et al., 2006). Some tests find that females score higher and others that males are the highest achievers, but in all cases the largest difference found in IQ score is around 2.2 points, which is so small as to be negligible. Strand et al. (2006) analysed the cognitive ability test scores for over 320,000 11- to 12-year-olds. These tests measure verbal, non-verbal and quantitative reasoning. They found that there was very little difference between males and females for any of these tests (see Table 4.17).

These differences are small and are unlikely to have any effect on the overall academic achievement of males or females. One significant difference that Strand et al. did find was that the scores of males showed greater variance than females, with boys being over-represented in the highest and lowest scores. So boys are not seen to be low achievers but rather are more likely to obtain 'extreme' academic scores. Strand et al. (2006) suggest that 'something other' than ability must be responsible for the differential success in examinations. The difficulty of course is to identify what this 'something other' may be.

The differences in achievement between boys and girls are not as straightforward as was possibly first thought, as girls are not just cleverer than boys. It is also important not to focus on the apparent under-achievement of boys at the expense of supporting the learning of girls. All learners need to be encouraged to fulfil their potential and we should not discriminate between the high or low achievers. What is important is that we do not think that getting a high score is simply 'doing well', as the individual may be able to do better. Alternatively, getting a low score does not necessarily mean not having 'done well'; as this could have been the best the individual was capable of.

Try this ...

What do you think might be included in the term 'something other' in this case?

Check your understanding

1. How do the achievements of boys and girls change during their time at school?

2. In what subject areas do girls obtain better results than boys?

3. How do the cognitive abilities of boys and girls compare?

Cognitive ability test (mean scores)	Males	Females
Verbal		2.2 points higher
Non-verbal		0.3 points higher
Quantitative reasoning	0.7 higher	

Table 4.17 Cognitive ability score

3.2 Differences in brain structure

One clear point has to be made early on regarding the differences in men's and women's brain structure, and that is that there are far more similarities than differences between male and female brains. However, we are interested in the differences, and they are often used (amongst many other observations) to explain the differences in educational performance. The debate will essentially be about nature versus nurture. Are we as we are because of our biology, or do other events during our development provide possible explanations?

Solms and Turnbull (2002) emphasise the incredible similarity between the male and female brain and then summarise the few differences that have been reliably recorded. The most obvious difference is the average size of the brain, with men having larger brains than women. This is not just an effect of men being larger than females: the male brain is larger in proportion to the rest of the body than the female brain. As the brain is vital to learning, and staying alive for that matter, it would seem logical to assume that a larger brain would be linked to increased intelligence, or learning capacity. Compelling though this might sound, the relationship between intelligence and brain size is fundamentally flawed. It would suggest that small men are less bright than big men; men will have higher scores for cognitive tests than women; cultures with smaller individuals will be less able than those with larger individuals. This is simply not the case, so the link between brain size and intelligence can be dismissed.

The next most reliable difference between male and female brains is to do with the corpus callosum, the bundle of nerve fibres that connects the left and right hemispheres of the brain. The corpus callosum is proportionally larger in females than males. The significance of this anatomical difference is that females have a more efficient link between the two hemispheres. You will be aware that different areas of the brain are responsible for various functions and that each hemisphere has different 'responsibilities'. There are two main advantages that women may gain from having greater connections between the left and right hemispheres.

The first can be associated with females' consistent ability to score highly in verbal cognitive tasks and to regularly out-perform males in language-based examinations. The more extensive connections between the two hemispheres enable more rapid links to be made and therefore words, images, thoughts and speech can be more effectively combined. It should also be noted that females tend to develop language skills sooner than males and are generally more verbal. Personality tests reveal females to be more empathic and aware of non-verbal social cues, and this again may be related to the increased connections between

the two hemispheres. This allows links to be more readily made and possibly enables many alternative viewpoints to be held at one time. The conflicting argument is the case for men. Solms and Turnbull (2002) argue that men have fewer connections between each hemisphere and as a result will find it easier to focus on one area or issue. As a result this may account for men's higher abilities with visuo-spatial tasks.

These findings may provide some insight into the learning preferences of males and females, for example men prefer more structured logical tasks, while females may prefer more complex language-based activities. What they do not provide is a rationale for the difference in academic performance between the two genders. Strand et al. (2006) suggested that 'some other' factor must account for the differences in educational performance; it is unlikely from the recent discussion that brain differences could be this other factor. In fact, child development texts (for example Bee, 2000) regularly highlight that there are few differences between the behaviour of boys and girls in early life. Therefore any differences that appear later must be linked to nurturing, as the biological bases for differences, such as the brain, do not show enough variation to explain the difference in educational performance between the genders. A suggestion that can be put forward is that gender differences in educational achievement may be more likely to be linked to how we approach and organise the learning environment.

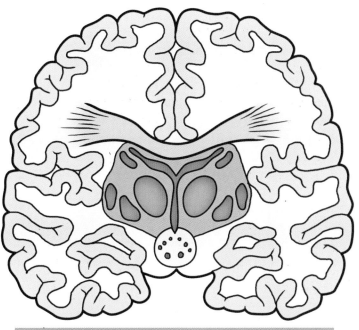

Figure 4.14 A section through the brain showing the corpus callosum (shaded yellow)

3.3 Strategies for enabling the learning of boys and girls

Raising the levels of academic achievement has been a major government focus for many years, and as indicated in the subsection on gender differences, there has been a particular interest in the apparent under-achievement of boys. Younger and Warrington (2005) undertook a major piece of research for the DfES to investigate which strategies were most successful for raising the achievement of boys and essentially found that good ways of teaching were effective for both boys and girls.

Key study

Younger and Warrington, Raising boys' achievement

(Note: this is an exceptionally long research report of 163 pages, therefore only selected areas are discussed here.)

Aim To identify the core strategies in schools that were successful in raising levels of achievement among boys. To transfer these strategies to other schools and monitor their effectiveness.

Design The researchers identified schools that had been successful in raising the achievement of boys over a period of 5 years. They selected eight primary and eight secondary schools that would be referred to as the 'originator school'. The research team identified the successful strategies in the originator school and attempted to transfer these to two 'partner schools' during the 4-year project. The project employed a wide range of methods that were not all used in all settings but were used to allow evidence to be obtained in an appropriate manner from each school. The methods used included:

◆   Focus-group interviews with boys (and girls)

◆   Individual semi-structured interviews with boys (and girls)

◆   Semi-structured interviews with teachers

◆   Visual methods such as allowing primary school children to take photographs

◆   Classroom observations

◆   Questionnaires to staff, students and parents

◆   Attitude surveys

◆   Analysis of pupils' writing.

Findings (on strategies only) The main finding should not be surprising to those who have been reading these sections on education, as Younger and Warrington found that strategies that raised boys' achievement were also likely to raise girls' achievement.

The successful strategies for raising achievement were identified within four main approaches.

Pedagogic approaches (teaching literacy in primary schools only):

◆   Using interactive classroom activities that were both short and focused as well as sustained ongoing activities.

◆   Using speaking and listening to support writing.

◆   Teachers being creative.

◆   An integrated use of ICT to support the production of high-quality work by enabling drafts and amending to be used.

Individual approaches:

◆   Setting realistic and challenging targets based on expectations and not just historical data.

◆   Support provided by credible mentors who can mediate and negotiate for 'their' pupil.

Socio-cultural approaches:

◆   These are particularly linked to the disruptive behaviour of boys, as such behaviour can be seen to have a significant effect on large groups of pupils.

◆   Developing initiatives (often via Citizenship) to encourage team-building.

◆   Involving disengaged boys to take leading roles in creative arts projects, such as drama, dance and poetry.

◆   Encouraging paired reading to raise self-esteem.

◆   Using key leaders or key 'befrienders' who are seen by the pupils as credible, to establish a rapport with disengaged pupils.

◆   Having staff who are committed to creating opportunities to give pupils space to articulate their feelings and emotions.

Whole-school approaches – Single-sex classrooms:

There was no conclusive evidence that putting boys and girls into separate teaching groups had any impact on attainment. In some cases this only served to produce 'sink groups' of badly behaved boys. In others, it reduced the variety of teaching and learning activities as the teachers perceived the group as all having similar needs.

Conclusion The overall conclusion is that good teaching and learning practices (pedagogy) are beneficial to all learners. This does of course raise the issue that if both boys and girls improve, then the gap between the genders is maintained! What must be questioned is whether we find this worrying. Is it the gap in achievement between boys and girls that is of concern? Or is it that boys are not scoring as highly as girls? It could be that boys are achieving to the best of their ability and that girls are in fact better at learning. As the biological differences in brain structure are small, it can be concluded that other social or nurturing factors may be responsible for the differences in achievement. Jones and Myhill (2004) suggest that we are caught up in seeing boys' behaviour as troublesome and therefore they are expected to underachieve; whereas girls are seen as compliant and in turn are expected to be successful. This of course raises the difficult question of whether it is our perception of boys and girls that ultimately influences their academic achievement.

Check your understanding

1. Outline what schools could do to improve the performance of boys.

2. Explain why the research methodology is valid and reliable.

3. What may the 'other factor' be that is responsible for the differences in educational achievement between the genders?

Section summary

◆ These are gender differences in educational achievement in all phases of schooling.

◆ IQ and cognitive ability differences between the genders do not show significant differences.

◆ There are more similarities than differences between the structures of male and female brains.

◆ Females have a larger corpus callosum, which may account for differences in educational attainment.

◆ Boys are often seen as troublesome and less likely to succeed at school.

Enabling learning: dealing with diversity

ExamCafé
Relax, refresh, result!

Relax and prepare

Student tips

Freddie

I like to get together with a group of friends. It's best if there are at least three of us. We decide on an area to revise and then we pick a section and divide it up so at least one person becomes an expert for each subsection. So, if we were going to revise 'student–student social interactions' from the 'social world of teaching and learning' section, then the groups might look like this:

Sub-section	Expert(s)
Empathy and moral development	Poppy and James
Friendship/bullying and academic success	Gemma and Thomas
Anti-bullying strategies	Joyti and Wayne

Experts then tell us about their subsection and we can ask them questions. It's funny how people find different information to talk about and you learn much more than you would by yourself.

Kylie

I find it harder working with other people because I get distracted. I have a big piece of paper in my room and in the middle I have written the names of the four areas of study for one of my chosen options. As I start to revise, I stick 'post-it' notes with questions I need to answer over the appropriate area. When I have answered them, by asking friends or my teacher, I move them to the outside of the poster. It is good to see how quickly the big pile in the middle gets moved to the outside and it makes me more confident that I am learning the right material.

Joyti

I like to work with the 'experts group' but I don't always think of questions or the right things to say when we're together. So I like to send messages to the group after we have met. These might be questions or something that I could have said earlier. I use MSN as I can write more and there is always a record of what we've discussed.

Refresh your memory

It can be helpful to identify research that can be used in more than one area. This does not mean you have to revise less material, but rather that you are sure how you can use ideas in different contexts. For example: behaviourism and cognitive theories can be used to explain knowledge acquisition and motivation; the theories of Rogers and Maslow can be applied to understanding the social relationship of teaching and learning and motivation; and research that highlights good teaching can often be applied to a variety of contexts.

Revision checklist: approaches to teaching

It is important to be able to evaluate research or theories. One feature of this is to be able to identify strengths and weaknesses; these can be quite wide-ranging but will often be linked to the debates set out from page 298. Copy and complete the table below. There is no one right answer and it would be helpful to compare your table to some of your friends'.

Research/Theory	Strength	Weakness
Behaviourist	The identification of learning objectives is useful for teachers as it helps them to focus the lesson and to avoid trying to deliver too much information	
Cognitive		It is too simplistic to consider discovery learning to be the solution to teaching in a variety of contexts. The profession must guard against reductionist solutions to a complex situation
Social constructionist		

Below is a student response written under exam conditions in answer to the following question:

Describe the differences in educational achievement that relate to gender. (10 marks)

Student answer

The difference in educational achievement between boys and girls has been a major focus for government policy in recent years. This is clear even in my school, where we now have Year 7 and 8 students sitting in boy/girl order and some exam classes are only taught to boys or girls. In 2006 Strand carried out some research on the cognitive ability and IQ scores of over 300,000 Year 7 boys and girls and what he found was that the differences between boys' and girls' mean IQ scores were so small that they could be ignored. He also found out that the cognitive ability scores between boys and girls were very similar, although he did notice that boys' scores were more likely to be very high or very low. The girls' scores did not vary as much as the boys'. Strand thought it was not possible to explain differences in academic achievement by suggesting that boys and girls had different levels of intelligence.

A recent government report has tried to summarise the differences in educational achievement between boys and girls throughout all the years in education. They found that there are differences between boys and girls, which is interesting because Strand did not find many. Girls do slightly better than boys at A level, but this is not by much. In Key Stage 4, girls have been doing better than boys for many years and have got more A* to C's than boys for over 10 years; in 2006 there was a 10% gap. Girls do better in humanities and also in maths and science, but not by as much. Girls are much better at English in Key Stage 3 than boys and slightly better at maths, and this is the same during most of primary school. Before children go to school, girls seem to have better communication skills and were more likely to be read to, but there was not a big difference in their developmental scores. It seems that there are differences between boys and girls when their educational achievement is compared, but not when their cognitive abilities are compared.

Examiner says:

This is a competent answer and covers most of the main findings, but it could benefit from a little more detail.

The first paragraph provides a good summary of the findings from Strand et al. (2006) but what would really help would be if this included some data so that there could be a numerical comparison of cognitive test and IQ scores. It would also be useful to discuss the different areas of the cognitive ability tests, as these highlight some of the differences between the genders.

The second paragraph also provides a good summary. It could also benefit from some more data so that the exact nature of the differences could be more accurately discussed. It might have been helpful to present the findings in terms of subjects rather than ages, for example, how the differences in maths scores change throughout the school years.

You may find it helpful to use the word 'gender' more so there are fewer times when you write 'girls and boys'.

Below is a student response written under exam conditions in answer to the following question.

How does the nature–nurture debate help explain the gender differences in educational achievement? (15 marks)

Student answer

The educational achievement of boys and girls is interesting because Strand (2006) found that there was not a lot of difference between the IQ and cognitive ability scores of boys and girls. If these scores are the same we would expect boys and girls to have similar scores for their educational achievement, but we do not find this. The DfES report found that there were differences between the achievement of boys and girls, particularly in Key Stage 4. This is an interesting problem for psychologists and Strand thought there must be something other than IQ or cognitive ability that was making these differences happen. IQ and cognitive abilities can be thought of as part of the nature argument, as these are the abilities that people are born with.

Some other research that highlights the nature part of this argument is to do with the brain structure of boys and girls. What has been found out is that the brains of boys and girls have more similarities than differences. There are some differences and the size of the brain is one of them, but if this made you more intelligent then bigger people who have bigger brains should be cleverer and this just is not true. But women do have a larger corpus callosum that joins the two brain hemispheres together than men. This could be an important difference as it means that women can make links between the two hemispheres better than men and in particular this may explain why women are better at communication and verbal tasks than men. Because their brains can make more rapid connections, it may also be why they are often more empathic than men. So there are some nature differences between the brains of men and women, but their intelligence and cognitive ability scores are very similar.

If there are lots of nature similarities between boys and girls, maybe there are nurture reasons for different educational achievement. Psychologists have noticed that boys and girls behave in similar ways when they are very young but this changes as they get older, so maybe it is something to do with how we bring children up. Some research by Younger and Warrington on how to improve the achievement of boys found that whatever strategies were successful for boys were also successful for girls. This suggests that the way we go about teaching is very important and this is a nurture argument. Some other researchers also suggested that we have begun to think about boys and girls as being very different in school and so we treat them differently, they said that many teachers think boys are troublesome and so they treat them as though they are naughty. The nurture argument may explain why boys and girls have different levels of educational success.

This is a difficult problem and it is probably partly nature and partly nurture, but I do think that teachers may be treating boys differently from girls because they think they are more likely to be naughty. This is why my school has boys and girls sitting side by side as it is meant to make the boys behave, but I think this is unfair because the girls have to put up with the boys' behaviour. It is better when we have different rooms. Maybe if the teachers knew about Younger and Warrington's research we would all do better.

Approaches and Research Methods in Psychology

Contents

Introduction

This unit provides you with the opportunity to think more widely about psychology and in particular how or why we 'do psychology'. Psychology is an extremely broad discipline and it is important that the strengths and weaknesses of this breadth are recognised. The following sections will discuss how psychologists carry out research and the decisions they need to make if this process is to be valid and reliable. We will discuss the different approaches to psychology and how these can provide alternative viewpoints and also consider some of the debates and issues that have concentrated the minds of psychologists for many years. Ultimately we hope to show how good quality, well thought out and carefully designed research provides findings that can be usefully applied to human interactions.

Research methods: the design of a practical project

This section of the specification highlights the need to understand how psychologists design and carry out psychological investigations. The work you covered during the AS course should provide you with a good foundation to continue your understanding of the research process; it is important to recognise all of your learning in psychology and not just to focus on A2 material. Although the examination will not require you to carry out an investigation, it is hoped that your school or college will give you plenty of opportunities to design, carry out and evaluate small-scale psychological research projects. It is easier to understand this section by doing rather than by reading about what someone else has done. This after all is how all the theorists you have studied discovered the 'facts' that have been the basis of this psychology course. There is no reason why you should not be able to become part of this tradition as you engage in your own psychological research.

The examination will be designed to test your understanding of the whole research process, from formulating a research question to suggesting future work or alternative designs. Each of the subsections that follow will help you with this, but it is worth noting that there is often no single 'correct' answer, as what is expected is for you to have an understanding of the psychological research process. The examination will contain a short scenario that will provide a focus for research questions. Typically you will be asked to suggest a research question and an operationalised hypothesis. You will then be expected to propose a suitable design and to provide the details of a procedure that could be replicated. Within this process you should be able to discuss how you would handle the data, and the strengths and weaknesses of your research project. Finally it is expected that you will suggest how the project might be improved.

Research methodology

This subsection will concentrate on:

- selecting a research question and framing an operationalised hypothesis
- justifying the research design and choosing suitable techniques
- considering how to provide a clear procedure
- discussing how to collect and analyse data.

Much of the above has been covered in the AS course and will only be dealt with briefly on pages 279–282. (The section on Practical investigations in the AS book/CD has more information.) The additional information required for the A2 course will be covered from page 283.

Selecting a research question

The exam paper will provide you with a short scenario that is suitable for psychological investigation. Your task is to choose a research question; this is something that you would like to find out about as a result of reading the scenario. It is important here that you do not provide research questions that are too vague or too broad. Simply stating that you want to know how to improve memory, for example, is too vague to develop into a hypothesis. A research question should provide some idea of what you are going to study and why. Don't forget that you need to be able to design a practical project based on your research question, and finding out how to improve memory is a lifetime's work! You need to have a question that is focused and has an achievable outcome. For example, a more appropriate research question could be based on investigating whether children of different ages recall numbers or words better.

Try this ...

Think back to the research questions that were investigated in the key studies. Draw up a summary table of one key study from each option. In one column, write the name of the study and in the other write the research question that was being addressed.

Framing an operationalised hypothesis

Your hypothesis should lead directly from the research question and is a statement that can be tested. The function of the hypothesis is to provide the researcher with a clear statement that can be accepted or rejected as a result of carrying out the research. In a simple way this is how 'things get found out'. The following key terms are examples of types of hypothesis, which may make this clear.

Key terms

research hypothesis this develops from the research question, such as 'The ability to recall numbers and words is dependent on age'. It is a general prediction as to what is expected

experimental (operationalised) hypothesis this is so called because it should clearly state what is going to be measured, for example, 'Young children are better at recalling words than numbers.' This statement is more precise and could be measured as the researcher could identify which age group to investigate and measure how many words or numbers they can recall

null hypothesis this is used when statistical tests are included in the research design. It is a statement of 'no difference' that the statistical test will prove or disprove, for example, 'There will be no difference in the ability of different age groups to recall numbers or words.' If this statement is rejected, it suggests a correlation between age and the ability to recall numbers or words

Finally, it is worth remembering that hypotheses can be one- or two-tailed.

- One-tailed hypothesis: this has a direction, such as 'Younger children are better at recalling words than …'.
- Two-tailed hypothesis: this has no direction, such as 'Different age groups have different abilities to recall words'.

Try this ...

Review the key studies in the table you drew up above, and identify the hypotheses. If you cannot find them, what would you have written?

Research design

Once an operational hypothesis has been provided, the research process can be designed. Many of the decisions taken here will depend on the researcher's own preferred way of working, as not all psychological researchers think in the same way. When you design your research you need to be able to justify why you have selected a particular design, as this will show that you are a thoughtful psychologist.

One of the first features to consider is whether to use qualitative or quantitative methods.

> **Key terms**
>
> quantitative methods involve counting or giving numerical values to what is being measured; these can be argued as being objective measures that may be available for statistical analysis
>
> qualitative methods focus on the subjective views of the participants and involve recording thoughts and feelings

Try this …

Identify two examples each of qualitative or quantitative research methods among the key studies. In each case what was the advantage of using this type of research? How would the study be different if it had been carried out using the other type of method?

The researcher also needs to decide whether the research process is going to be longitudinal or snapshot. Longitudinal research may last for months or even years – see, for example, Schweihart (2006) whose research has been following participants since pre-school – and provide findings over the lifespan, whereas snapshot research only provides insight for a particular time.

Try this …

◆ Which of the key studies have been carried out over long periods of time? What has been the advantage of this? Hint: You may find it helpful to have a look at the Cambridge Study in Delinquent Development. What do you notice about the retention success of this study?

◆ Strand et al. (2006) analysed the cognitive scores for 11- to 12-year-olds. These scores were obtained from 'one off' tests. Do you think this is an accurate way to measure the cognitive ability of an individual?

As a researcher you must also consider how the participants are going to be organised within your research design. Typically there are three main ways to do this and, as before, you must be clear as to the justification for your choice.

1 Independent measures – when different participants are used in different conditions.

2 Repeated measures – when the same participants are used in two or more conditions.

3 Matched pairs – as independent measures but the participants have been matched according to the variable that is being investigated, for example Bandura et al. (1961).

Research design	Condition	
	1	**2**
Independent measures	Participant A	Participant B
Repeated measures	Participant A	Participant A
Matched pairs	Participant A (matched for an experimental variable, i.e. age or IQ)	Participant B (matched for an experimental variable, i.e. age or IQ)

Table 5.1 Research design

Technique	How the research is carried out
Laboratory experiment	Precise controlled manipulation of the independent variable in a lab setting
Field experiment	As above but in a natural setting
Self-report	Participants record their own thoughts and feelings
Questionnaire	Written open or closed responses to researcher's questions
Observation	Observations can be in natural settings or in controlled environments. The participants may also be involved
Case study	Detailed study that involves the collection of a wide variety of data on an individual or small group

Table 5.2 Research techniques

Research methods: the design of a practical project

Finally, the selection of research technique must be justified. This technique is how the research process will actually be carried out.

This list is by no means exhaustive and serves to remind you of the possible techniques available.

Try this ...

- Look at the DfES (2006) research on pupil grouping strategies; this is a case study. Compare this to the observations of Wood, Bruner and Ross (1976). Why do you think the researchers used these techniques?

- Can you find examples in the key studies of each of the techniques in Table 5.2? In each case, can you think of another way to carry out this research?

Samples and sampling

Once a hypothesis has been set up and a research procedure developed, the research can only take place if there are participants available to be involved. The selection of participants is another careful consideration for the researcher, and you must be able to justify how you intend to recruit individuals to take part in your research. As all the research data will be based on the participants, their selection could have an enormous impact on the findings.

Try this ...

Look at adverts on television or in magazines that suggest people have a preference for their product. Can you identify how the researchers obtained the sample of people? Do you think the sample is sufficient to persuade you to buy the product?

It is not feasible to test all people in a population, as this number is so vast. Nor is it feasible to test all the people you would like to target. For example, if there was an investigation on the correlation between autism and the MMR vaccine, the ideal situation would be to test all children who had either the MMR vaccine or autism. The size of this target population is so huge that the investigation would become too cumbersome (and expensive). Therefore psychologists need to be able to select a sample from the group they are interested in that is representative of this population. To prevent bias, various sampling methods can be used.

Sampling method	Sampling procedure
Random	Identifying the entire target population and then selecting from this total group. It is important that each member of the group has an equal opportunity to be selected
Opportunity	Involving those participants who are in the target group that the researchers first meet
Self selected	Using volunteers recruited through adverts
Snowball	Allowing one participant to lead the researcher to the next participant

Table 5.3 Sampling methods and procedures

Try this ...

- Review the key studies and try to identify how the samples were chosen. Can you identify any preferences in how the researchers in particular options select their samples?

- For each of the sampling methods in Table 5.3, suggest the title of a research project that would be best suited to this type of sampling.

- Can you identify any research in the AS or A2 course where the sampling method has been a weakness?

U4

1

Research methods: the design of a practical project

Ethics

The previous pages have concentrated on how to design a psychological investigation and even though sampling has been discussed, little has been said about the participants. The study of psychology is intended to help us understand the human condition and to do so often requires willing human participants. Yet the process of taking part, and indeed the findings, can be uncomfortable. It is the responsibility of the researcher to ensure that participants are not subjected to any physical or psychological harm.

Try this ...

♦ Put the key studies in order, starting with the ones you would least wish to take part in. How would you change the studies at the top of your list to make them more acceptable? Are your changes ethical ones?

♦ Get into small groups where each member has to select a key study to present to the others. This individual needs to support the ethical stance taken in their chosen research. The rest of the group must attempt to identify any ethical weaknesses and challenge the presenter to justify the research design.

All research must be ethical and in recent years researchers have only been allowed to carry out their research once their design has received ethical approval from a committee. (All university and research establishments have ethics committees and follow guidelines such as those set by the British Psychological Society (BPS).)

Weblink

If your school has access, you can look at the BPS ethical guidelines (see Contents page).

There are a number of features that all researchers must be aware of to ensure that their research will not break ethical guidelines, and it is your role as a student to ensure that you do not design unethical research projects. The following features are required to meet the ethical guidelines before research can commence.

1 Informed consent: participants must agree verbally or in writing to take part; young children are unable to do this, so their carers will be asked on their behalf.

2 Assent: young children must be asked if they wish to continue participating.

3 Deception: participants must not be deceived about the nature of the research.

4 Risk/stress: the research process must not expose the participants to stress.

5 Withdrawal: participants must be allowed to withdraw at any time.

6 Confidentiality: participants should not be identifiable in any research material.

7 De-brief: participants must be de-briefed as soon as possible, to make them aware of the real reason for the research and to provide an opportunity to talk about any issues that may have arisen.

Try this ...

♦ Discuss the difficulty of not deceiving participants. What would happen if the researcher provided the participant with too much information?

♦ Make a list of all the sorts of stress a participant may feel during the research process.

♦ The Reading Recovery programme (page 263) has been very successful in improving reading skills. How would you feel if you were a participant in this research process but in a matched pairs group that was not part of the programme?

Materials used in the research process

To be successful a research project needs to be designed so that the research question and operationalised hypothesis can be investigated. If this project provides interesting findings, the author may want to publish their findings in order that other colleagues may be aware of their work. Before these reports are published it is usual for them to be 'peer reviewed'. This means that other psychologists will read and evaluate the report before it is published. One important feature of this process is that sufficient information is provided that would enable the research to be replicated. The design and techniques chosen will provide much of the information necessary for replication, but this will only be possible if the details of the materials that were used are made known. Bandura et al. (1961) provided the details of the toys available to the children and Samuel and Bryant (1983) provided the exact questions they asked, which would enable other researchers to replicate these investigations.

The materials used within the research process are closely linked to the findings. We can question whether Watson and Raynor (1920) would have obtained the same results if they had exposed Little Albert to a frightening image instead of a clashing sound. The image might have frightened an older child but might not have elicited fear in Albert. What was important was that the materials used for the stimulus would frighten Albert. The materials used include not only those that the participant has access to but also those used by the researcher. For example, when investigating the social interactions in the classroom, one technique is to use the Flanders interactional analysis (see page 254). The findings from any studies using this procedure are dependent on the categories used on the FIA recording sheets and therefore it is essential that these materials are clearly identified within the research report.

Controlling variables

Most research is carefully planned to control variables. The operationalised hypothesis will indicate what is to be measured and what the likely effect of the investigation will be. The decision on the design and techniques used will also be an attempt to ensure that no other factors influence the findings. This is in reality a difficult issue. If we consider the hypothesis that younger children can recall words better than older children, the design of the research needs to ensure that it is only the age of the children (independent variable) that will have an impact on the number of words (dependent variable) they can recall. In reality the recall of words may also be influenced by many other factors, such as time of day, how the child feels, conditions at home, the words that are chosen and even the manner of the researcher. These other extraneous variables are what the research design hopes to eliminate.

Try this …

What is the disadvantage of controlling all these extra variables? (Hint: ecological validity.) Is it possible to control the research process so much that extraneous variables are removed?

Researchers commonly try to control variables by using standardised procedures. If these are clearly recorded, future researchers will be able to follow the same procedure and theoretically obtain the same results. One of the expectations for your examination is that you are able to describe a research procedure such that other people could carry out your research design. It is hoped that if this is the case some important extraneous variable can be eliminated. Other examples of extraneous variables are the following.

- Experimenter bias: different researchers might carry out the research process in slightly different ways, which may favour the experimenter favouring a certain research outcome.

- Demand characteristics: different procedures will have a different effect on the participants, who may respond according to what they feel is expected of them.

Try this …

- Make a list of all the materials you have used during the A2 course for your small-scale research projects. Divide these into two groups: those used by the researcher and those used by the participant. Consider what the effect on the findings might have been if the materials used by the participant were slightly different.

- The study by Pennington and Hastie (1988) involved a mock trial. How did they use the materials in the research process to design a realistic scenario? Do you think this was effective? How could you have improved this?

◆ Situational bias: different procedures or situations will have a different effect on the participants and by using standardised procedures it is hoped that all participants have the same experiences. The procedure should be sufficiently detailed to enable similar conditions to be set up by other researchers.

Counterbalancing

On page 280 we mentioned a research design known as repeated measures. If this design is used it means that each participant will take part in two or more conditions. The advantage of this is that the sample size can be smaller than if each participant was to be tested in each condition. The disadvantage is that there could be an 'order effect'. This is an extraneous variable where the order in which the participant performs tasks could have an effect on the findings. For example, if you wanted to find out whether young children can recall words or numbers better by using a repeated measures design, the order of the procedure would be as follows.

1   Test for recall of words.

2   Test for recall of numbers.

It may be that the first task has given the participants an opportunity to practise their memory skills and by the time they carry out the second task they are better at recalling. This is not an effect of the independent variable, but the order of the procedure. To avoid this, counterbalancing is used; this involves splitting the sample so that there is an equal chance of any condition being first or last. This can be complicated for more than two conditions, but for the example above counterbalancing would be as in Table 5.4.

Group A	Group B
1 Test for recall of words	1 Test for recall of numbers
2 Test for recall of numbers	2 Test for recall of words

Table 5.4 Order of procedure

Try this …

◆ Can you find an example of counterbalancing in any of the AS or A2 studies? Can you find examples of where counterbalancing might have been helpful? (Hint: look back at the Pennington and Hastie (1988) key study. Can you identify how they have counterbalanced the presentation of evidence?)

◆ Design a procedure for counterbalancing when there are two independent variables. Now try this for three or more independent variables. Note how much more complicated this becomes as the number of conditions is increased.

Try this …

Loftus et al. (1987) collected a comprehensive range of data. How has the collecting and recording of these data enabled the researchers to validate their findings?

Writing a research methodology

The key to success in writing a research methodology is to ensure that you provide sufficient detail for someone else to replicate exactly what you did. It is also important that the procedure you suggest is suitable for the research question you are investigating.

Use Table 5.5 to help you write a good research methodology. You do not have to carry out everything in order, as each investigation is slightly different, but you should attempt to cover all of the areas. The two blank columns are for you to complete, for example you must be able to justify why you have chosen a certain design or technique. This is what the examiners will expect, as it shows not only that you can design a psychology research project but that you know *why* you are doing what you plan to do. The checklist should remind you to cover each of the steps.

Try this ...

If you can, find the original sources of any studies from the AS or A2 course and read their procedures. Could you exactly replicate the research processes? If these studies are not readily available, carry out the same task using your own small-scale projects.

Step	Points to think about	Justification	Checklist √ or ×
Decide on a research question	The area of study and what you wish to achieve must be clear.		
State your hypotheses	The operationalised hypothesis must identify what you are going to measure.		
Choose the method	Qualitative or quantitative? You must decide if you want rich data (qualitative) or precise data (quantitative).		
Duration of research	Longitudinal or snapshot?		

(continued overleaf)

Step	Points to think about	Justification	Checklist √ or ×
Choose the research design	Independent measure, repeated measures or matched pairs.		
Choose the technique	Self-report, observation, questionnaires etc.		
Sampling	How do you plan to recruit your participants?		
Controlling variables	How will you control the independent variable(s) and reduce the effect of extraneous variables?		
Measuring variables	How will the dependent variable be measured?		
Ethical considerations	Has consent/assent been obtained? Are there any possible risks or stresses?		
Procedure	The full details of what you did. You must include the order of events, numbers of participants and full details of the materials used. It is helpful to provide this information in step-by-step order.		

Table 5.5 Writing checklist

Data analysis

If the research methodology has been successful, the researcher should have data that they can use to help them answer the research question and apply to the hypotheses developed from this. In the A2 exam you will be expected to be able to provide the justification for a method of data analysis and to interpret and describe your findings.

- Qualitative data: these may have been obtained from techniques such as interviews, observations and questionnaires. They are not number based and are usually a record of people's subjective views. They can also involve the collection of visual material. The analysis of this sort of data can be complicated and it is usual to deal with it in two main ways.

  - Categorising: where the researcher attempts to identify similar themes in the responses of the participants.

  - Selection: where the researcher chooses certain comments or observations to highlight an issue they wish to discuss.

- Quantitative data: quantitative research involves the collection of numerical data but surprisingly numbers are not as straightforward as most people first imagine. There are different ways of using numbers to measure variables and these can give the numbers different meanings. These different meanings are referred to as 'levels of measurement' and there are four of these levels, the three most likely to be encountered by A-Level students are explained in Table 5.6.

Weblink

You might like to read an account that promotes qualitative research in psychology (see Contents page).

Try this ...

1. Briefly review the key studies. How many of them are entirely based on qualitative data, or are a mix of qualitative and quantitative data? Do you think psychologists favour a certain type of data?

2. Look at the key study by Wood et al. (1976). Do you think they could have developed this idea using quantitative measurements?

Level	Explanation	Example	Usefulness
Nominal	Data are placed in categories	Counting the numbers of boys and girls playing on 'sit-on toys'	This provides little information; we simply know how many children play with a certain toy
Ordinal	Data are placed in an order	Finding the most popular toy by asking children to rank their favourite toys in order (e.g. first to fifth)	This does not provide much information as the reason for the choices is not known. Also the gap between each ranking is unclear
Interval data	A precise measurement, often using a scale	Measuring how much time boys spend on 'sit-on toys'	This will give an accurate measure of how much time was actually spent on the toys, but it still may not tell us why

Table 5.6 Levels of measurement

Copy out and complete the table below to survey what sort of levels of measurement have been used in the key studies. (Hint: start with the study by Loftus et al. (1987).)

Key study	Nominal level data	Ordinal level data	Interval level data

Having an understanding of the levels of measurement is important, not just because of the issues raised in Table 5.6, but significantly because this knowledge can be used to make decisions on the presentation of data and their analysis.

The presentation of data

Nominal and ordinal data can be analysed by using descriptive statistics. Descriptive statistics do what they say: they describe the data that have been collected. This will be seen to be very different from inferential statistics, which are considered below. The function of descriptive statistics is to highlight any patterns or relationships that may exist within the data. Most of the techniques to do this have been covered in the AS course, but the following can serve as a reminder. Complete Table 5.7 to highlight how each method can be useful.

Inferential statistics

Descriptive statistics are related to describing data and identifying patterns or relationships. Inferential statistics are used to enable researchers to make inferences or deductions from their findings and these inferences are linked to the operational hypothesis and the null hypothesis. Inferential statistics are only recommended for use on interval data as these are the most robust and reliable. You may remember from Table 5.6 that nominal and ordinal data are not precise measurements and some would argue that they are not even true quantitative measurements.

There is no requirement in the examination for you to carry out an inferential statistical test, but you will be asked to explain the findings from such a test. It is recommended that you gain experience in carrying out inferential statistical tests during your A2 course, as this

will help you make sense of the process and understand why it is important. There are examples of how to carry out statistical analysis in the Appendix and you should attempt some of these before reading on.

What do inferential statistics tell us?

Inferential statistics are used to discover the probability that a result has occurred by chance. This is important in order to determine whether the findings from an investigation have happened because of the conditions set up in the investigation, or are a chance event, that is, they might have happened anyway, regardless of how the variables were controlled.

To understand this let us first consider the idea of probability. Probability tells us how likely it is for something to happen. A probability of 1 (which can be written as 100 per cent) means that an event will definitely take place. The lower the probability gets, the less likely it is for an event to happen, for example I could argue that there is a probability of 1 that I will represent my town at any sporting discipline. There could also be a probability of 0.01 (1 per cent) that I will represent my country in a sporting discipline. What this means is that there will be an opportunity to represent my town in a sporting discipline, but there is only a slight chance that I could represent my country. In fact there is a 1 in 100 chance. The end product of carrying out inferential statistical analysis will be a value for the probability of something happening and is usually written as a decimal between 1 and 0 (for example, 0.5, 0.25, 0.1). The probability can also be expressed as a percentage between 100 per cent and 0 per cent. For example, 0.75 (or 75 per cent) is a high probability of something happening, so that if it occurs it is unlikely to be due to chance, and 0.01 (or 10 per cent) is a low probability: if this occurs it may well be due to chance.

How is this probability value used?

To understand this, we must remind ourselves about the null and operationalised hypotheses.

- The null hypothesis states that there will be no difference between the conditions investigated, for example, 'There will be no difference in the ability of children of different ages to recall words or numbers.'

- The operationalised hypothesis states that there is a measurable effect between the conditions, for example, 'Young children will be better at recalling words than numbers.'

Analysis method	Description of what analysis method shows	Key study that uses this method	Advantage or disadvantage of this method
Calculation of measurement of central tendency	(Hint: mean, median and mode)		
Tables of data	(Hint: just the numbers/categories)		
Bar charts	(Hint: visual alternative to tables of data)		
Histograms	(Hint: as above but with continuous data)		
Scattergrams	(Hint: for showing relationships)		
Pie charts	(Hint: helpful for showing proportions)		

Table 5.7 Evaluation of descriptive statistics

Try this ...

Copy and complete Table 5.7.

Inferential statistical analysis focuses on the null hypothesis. It does this because it is a precise statement, 'There will be no difference.' The operationalised hypothesis is less precise as it simply indicates that age has an effect on recalling words or numbers. True quantitative data work best when applied to precise hypotheses. At the end of an inferential statistical analysis there will be a probability value for the null hypothesis. A 0.05 (or 5 per cent) level of probability is usually referred to as having statistical significance.

Statistical significance is the term used for a probability at which the null hypothesis can be rejected and the operationalised hypothesis accepted. The following is the reason.

A 0.05 (5 per cent) probability means there is a 1 in 20 chance of something happening.

This level of chance is applied to the null hypothesis.

This means that there is a 1 in 20 chance of there being no difference in the conditions being investigated.

This level of probability is very low, so the null hypothesis is unlikely to happen and it can be rejected.

If the null hypothesis is unlikely to happen then the operationalised hypothesis can be accepted.

If the statistical analysis produces a probability of less than 0.01 (written as $p < 0.01$) then there is even more reason to reject the null hypothesis. To summarise: if there is only a low probability (0.05 or 5 per cent or 1 in 20 or less) of the null hypothesis being correct (that is, there is no difference in the condition being investigated), the operationalised hypothesis can be accepted as correct. You need to be able to explain this for the examination, so make sure that you understand this statement.

At this point we need to add a word of warning.

Accepting or rejecting the null hypothesis is not always as straightforward as it sounds. There are two main types of possible errors that may result from the research design. These are explained in Table 5.8.

Try this ...

If a statistical test produced an answer of $p < 0.01$, how would you explain this in words and which hypothesis would you accept?

Repeat this for $p < 0.05$.

Type of error	Description	Reason	Solution
Type 1	Accepting the operationalised hypothesis despite the possibility of this being due to chance	Poor research design. Using a level of significance that is too lenient	Use a more stringent significance level (0.01 instead of 0.05)
Type 2	Retaining the null hypothesis despite the possibility of the operationalised hypothesis being correct	Poor research design. Using too stringent significance levels	Use less stringent significance levels (0.05 instead of 0.01)

Table 5.8 Types of error

Evaluation of methodology

The ability to evaluate research methodology is a strong feature of this examination and one of the best ways to practise this is to make sure you have designed, carried out and evaluated your own small-scale studies. It will be difficult if you only try to do this theoretically from the studies contained within the AS and A2 course, as it is often only from experience that it is possible to identify strengths and weaknesses. Consider the repeated measures design, for example. This may sound comparatively easy on paper, but when you try to carry it out the complexities and difficulties become more obvious. Your AS experience should have given you a good foundation for successfully evaluating studies and the A2 course builds on this and places a particular focus on the process of the research methodology.

Discuss in small groups the problems that forensic psychologists face when carrying out research. For

example, it is not ethical to carry out research in the courtroom. So how do researchers deal with this problem?

The study by Petrides et al. (2004) on the link between emotional intelligence and IQ has to deal with a number of variables that may also account for IQ. How do the researchers control for these variables?

Try this ...

Copy and complete Table 5.9. Try to find a key study that provides you with an example of each of the features listed. Do not forget that not all key studies will have examples of each research feature. Each of the features that can be evaluated has been covered in this section, so go back and re-read them if necessary.

Feature of research methodology	Guidance on evaluation	Key study and option area example taken from	Strengths and weaknesses
Research question	Is it clear what the researchers wish to achieve?		
Hypotheses	Are these linked to the research question and is the measurement of variables made clear?		
Qualitative or quantitative method	Is this the most suitable method to answer the research question?		
Research design: use of independent measures; repeated measures or matched pairs	Does this facilitate the reliable collection of data?		
Research techniques: self-report, observations, experiment etc.	Does this facilitate the valid collection of data?		
Control of variables	How have the researchers attempted to control the IV and reduce the effect of extraneous variables?		
Sampling	Is the target population fully represented? Is the target population appropriate?		
Ethical considerations	Is there any chance of risk or stress?		
Ecological validity	Can these findings be related to everyday life? This may be related to how realistic the research process was.		

U4

1

Research methods: the design of a practical project

Table 5.9 Evaluation of methodologies

Approaches, perspectives, methods, issues and debates

This section of the specification requires students to consider all aspects of the AS and A2 course, not just the methodological issues raised in the previous section. This provides the opportunity to have wider debates about psychology and to use all the knowledge you have gained during your studies. One of the interesting things about studying psychology is that it is the study of people, and so we learn more about ourselves as we learn more about others!

Try this …

Discuss the following in small groups.

- What is the most surprising piece of knowledge you have gained during this course?
- Has studying psychology changed the way you 'see the world'?
- If you were to become a psychologist, what would you most want to research?
- What is the most useful thing psychology has taught you?

The examination will expect you to have a wide-ranging knowledge of how psychology is understood, researched and ultimately how it can be of use in everyday life. This is not as straightforward as it sounds, as people have very different views on what psychology is and how it should be studied. What is important for the examination is that you are able to appreciate the views of others and to consider all the alternative viewpoints.

Try this …

Take a straw poll in your group to find out which areas of the specification people preferred. You may find that your colleagues (and you) have tendencies towards certain areas and this may reflect how you think about psychology.

The reason for the rather long title to this section is that it reflects all the alternative ways of thinking about and doing psychology. The following pages will highlight the approaches, perspectives, methods, issues and debates that you need to understand for the examination. It does not mean that we think about these areas on discrete occasions but rather that we should always have these in mind. This sounds difficult at first, but the AS course has already prepared you well for this.

The examination questions will follow a similar format and expect you to be able to do the following:

- outline an approach, perspective, method, issue or debate
- describe two pieces of research that highlight an approach, perspective, method, issue or debate
- discuss the strengths and limitations of an approach, perspective, method, issue or debate
- discuss how one approach, perspective, method, issue or debate compares with another
- discuss the usefulness of the psychology you have covered in the question.

How the approaches, perspectives, methods, issues and debates all fit together

Approaches

The approaches in this syllabus reflect the areas in which psychological research is carried out, and these were the areas covered in the AS course.

- Cognitive: considers mental processes.
- Developmental: focuses on changes over the lifespan.
- Physiological: focuses on the biological basis of behaviour.
- Social: studies the interaction between individuals.
- Individual differences: highlights the diversity of human behaviour.

Perspectives

The two perspectives in the syllabus are the behaviourist and psychodynamic perspectives. Many people may also call these approaches, but in this context they are used to represent to extremes of thinking about the human condition.

◈ Behaviourist: learned stimulus/response relationships provide the explanation for human behaviour.

◈ Psychodynamic: human behaviour is driven by unconscious processes.

If these are considered as perspectives they provide two very diverse ways of considering how humans function. Behaviourism focuses on interacting with the external environment, while psychodynamic theories concentrate on internal processes.

Methods

These have been covered in the previous section and reflect the many different ways in which psychologists go about 'doing psychology', such as observations, case studies, etc.

Issues

Again this has been mainly dealt with in the previous section and focuses on the sorts of issues that psychologists must consider when planning research, such as ethics, qualitative versus quantitative approaches.

Debates

These are the more wide-ranging discussions that psychologists must get involved in to appreciate the problems that need to be addressed when researching human behaviour.

Debate	Discussion
Determinism vs free will	Do humans have a free choice to behave as they wish, or is their behaviour determined for them?
Reductionism vs holism	Should psychologists study and understand the whole person or concentrate on the smallest unit that is responsible for behaviour?
Nature vs nurture	Which has more impact on our development, our genes or our environment?
Ethnocentrism	Is psychological research based too heavily on certain ethnic groups?
Psychology as a science	Is psychology a science and should it follow the 'rules' of science?
Individual vs situational explanations	What makes people do what they do: themselves, or the situation they are in?
The usefulness of psychological research	Can psychology be applied to our everyday lives?

Table 5.10 Debates in psychology

Strengths and limitations of the approaches and perspectives

Approach or perspective	Summary	Strengths	Limitations
Physiological	Studies the biological basis of human behaviour. This may involve discovering localised functions in the brain. This can be done by working with brain-damaged patients but more recently involves neuro-imaging techniques. Often focuses on the chemical basis for human behaviour, e.g. serotonin and depression. May also consider the genetic basis for behaviour.	Has provided a large body of evidence about the locations and chemical basis of behaviour. Clinicians are now able to treat mental disorders with chemicals or by surgery.	Can be regarded as reductionist and therefore does not take into account the whole person. Findings may not show cause and effect: are serotonin levels a cause or effect of depresssion?
Cognitive	This regards mental processes to be important and these are internal, not external, events. What is studied are the processes that come between an external stimulus and the behavioural response. Research is often experimental or linked to developing models of how the mind may work. Recent work is influenced by neuro-imaging.	This is a useful area of study and cognitive psychologists work in a wide range of fields: developmental, social and clinical. The experimental basis provides rigorous findings.	Research is often not ecologically valid. Can be reductionist as it tries to turn complex processes into simple models. It is heavily influenced by computer analogies that provide logical models of the mind, but the mind may not be logical.
Individual differences	This approach recognises that the human condition is extremely diverse and questions the need to provide generalisations about behaviour. Studies are often focused on gender, cultural diversity, personality and pathological behaviour. Research uses a wide variety of methodologies.	Recognises the diverse nature of human behaviour and does not focus on a mythical 'average' individual. Evidence comes from many different sources. Very useful with ready application to everyday life.	Could be following a dream. We are all unique individuals, so ultimately maybe only individuals should be studied. It can highlight differences rather than celebrating diversity.
Developmental	An approach to understanding the human condition that covers the whole lifespan. Researchers use a wide range of methods and techniques. The focus is on how behaviours are initiated and then develop. Typical areas of study include: learning to be social; emotional and moral development; how thinking develops and how children learn to communicate.	This approach considers the whole lifespan and therefore behaviours are seen in context. There is a large and varied body of evidence that has provided interesting insights.	Often focuses on the development of the child to the detriment of adolescents or adults. Wide-ranging research can produce conflicting viewpoints. Often dominated by old 'classic' research.

Approach or perspective	Summary	Strengths	Limitations
Social	Social approaches are concerned with how the individual relates to others. A wide range of research methods and techniques are used to study social interactions. Typically this area focuses on how individuals behave in groups and how these may influence decision-making.	The research is often clearly related to real-life situations. The context of social psychology research makes the findings interesting to many people. A wide range of evidence has been obtained.	Dangerous to make wide-ranging generalisations across all social groups. It can reduce the importance of the individual. Has been dominated by old 'classic' studies.
Behaviourist	This is limited to observable behaviour only. The research is focused on objective experimental techniques. It proposes that all human behaviour is the result of interactions with the external world. Behaviours that obtain a reward will become more common and behaviours that receive negative feedback will be reduced. Understanding the external stimulus and the response is crucial.	Evidence is based on rigorous scientific technique. Stimulus responsive theory has been successfully applied to a wide range of behaviours. Recent behavioural modification techniques have been very successful.	Theory is too simplistic for complex human behaviour. Heavily reliant on animal-based research. The importance of the environment ignores the role of biology. Based on observable behaviour only and does not consider internal processes.
Psychodynamic	Considers that human behaviour is the result of unconscious processes. These are developed during early childhood experiences and are responsible for forming 'models of the mind'. These models will form the basis of behaviours later in life. Many of the theories are related to personality and emotional development.	An influential theoretical base that has had a huge effect on psychological thinking. Basic psychodynamic ideas are part of our everyday vocabulary (ego, defences, extrovert). Theories are used to support many successful therapeutic interventions.	Highly subjective and hard to prove scientifically. Many of the ideas are just that – ideas – and are hard to disprove. The research base is often small, sometimes one or two individuals. Early theories may not be relevant now.

U4

1

Approaches, perspectives, methods, issues and debates

Table 5.11 Summary of the strengths and weaknesses of psychological approaches and perspectives

Try this ...

Copy and complete Table 5.12. In each of the boxes, select one key study or theory from the psychology options you are studying and summarise the strengths and weaknesses for this perspective.

Perspective	Option			
	Forensic psychology	**Health and clinical psychology**	**Psychology of sport and exercise**	**Psychology of education**
Behaviourist	Study	Study	Study	Study
	Strengths	Strengths	Strengths	Strengths
	Weaknesses	Weaknesses	Weaknesses	Weaknesses
Psychodynamic	Study	Study	Study	Study
	Strengths	Strengths	Strengths	Strengths
	Weaknesses	Weaknesses	Weaknesses	Weaknesses

U4

1

Approaches, perspectives, methods, issues and debates

Table 5.12 Strengths and weaknesses of studies for different options and perspectives

Copy and complete Table 5.13. In each of the boxes, select one key study or theory from the psychology options you are studying and summarise the strengths and weaknesses for this approach.

Approach	Option			
	Forensic psychology	**Health and clinical psychology**	**Psychology of sport and exercise**	**Psychology of education**
Physiological	Study Strengths Weaknesses	Study Strengths Weaknesses	Study Strengths Weaknesses	Study Strengths Weaknesses
Cognitive	Study Strengths Weaknesses	Study Strengths Weaknesses	Study Strengths Weaknesses	Study Strengths Weaknesses
Individual differences	Study Strengths Weaknesses	Study Strengths Weaknesses	Study Strengths Weaknesses	Study Strengths Weaknesses
Developmental	Study Strengths Weaknesses	Study Strengths Weaknesses	Study Strengths Weaknesses	Study Strengths Weaknesses
Social	Study Strengths Weaknesses	Study Strengths Weaknesses	Study Strengths Weaknesses	Study Strengths Weaknesses

Table 5.13 Strengths and weaknesses of studies for different options and approaches

U4

1

Approaches, perspectives, methods, issues and debates

Debate: determinism and free will

Determinism

Determinism is the principle that all human behaviour results from either internal or external causes. Therefore the role of psychologists is to study human behaviour and to find out these causes, as once they are known it would be possible to explain present behaviour and predict future behaviour. Behaviourists would argue that all behaviour results from interactions with the external world and the possibility of punishment or reward. Psychodynamic theorists suggest that unconscious processes are the cause of human behaviour. Both of these theories are heavily deterministic, as they suggest that all behaviours have an identifiable cause.

Try this ...

Consider these questions:

◆ Is it possible to predict and control human behaviour?

◆ Can determinism be disproved?

Take it further

If behaviour is determined, how should we deal with those people who are regarded as antisocial. Think about criminals, bullies, liars and cheats. Should we punish them or try to alter their behaviour?

Free will

Free will suggests that human behaviours can be chosen at will. This means that we actively decide what we wish to do. The behaviourists would argue that this 'choice' is in fact a response that has been learned from interacting with the external environment. Psychodynamic theorists would suggest that these 'decisions' are just responses to internal unconscious processes. Believers in free will would argue that behaviour does not have a cause and all individuals are free to make choices about their behaviour. The idea of free will is compelling, as most people like to think they have choices rather than being victims of unconscious processes or the external conditions they find themselves in. This idea does provide a problem for psychologists: if free will does exist, what is the point of studying psychology?! The theorists who most closely adhere to principles of free will are humanists such as Maslow and Rogers (see pages 235 and 247).

Try this ...

◆ Think about any simple and obvious behaviour (say, deciding to play a computer game) and discuss whether this is a free-will decision or whether other processes have determined your actions.

◆ In small groups, discuss whether humans have free will and if so, how should we deal with misbehaviour?

◆ Can you think of an occasion when you would prefer to believe that your actions were determined rather than due to your own free will?

Take it further

Psychodynamic theory is deterministic, yet during the therapeutic process individuals are encouraged to become aware of their unconscious processes. If they do, do you think this now means they have free will?

After discussion of five of the debates you will find a page of synoptic questions to think about.

Psychodynamic theories are used in both education and sport. In the sport option they were applied to an understanding of aggressive behaviour and the role sport may play in helping individuals to handle their aggression, while in education psychodynamic theories were used to suggest mechanisms for motivating behaviours to learn. Do you feel that these theories help you make sense of aggression or motivation?

Is aggressive behaviour something that individuals can control, or are they victims of unconscious processes?

Do psychodynamic theories suggest that the unwilling student has the ability or desire to change their behaviour?

How do you think most people view criminal behaviour? As something individuals choose to do, or something they are 'pre-programmed' to do?

The Great Man theory in sport suggests that some people may be born with the right characteristics to become a leader. Do you think that some individuals are born with the potential to become 'great men'? If the 'Great Man' theory is true, what is the point of leadership training?

Consider McGrath's systematic desensitisation in the Health and Clinical Psychology option. Does this offer a free-will or deterministic explanation for disorders?

Raine (2002) provided evidence that certain brain activities can be related to criminal behaviour. If criminal behaviour can be seen to be determined by brain activity, how may this affect how society deals with criminals?

Consider each of the psychology options. Discuss in small groups whether these options tend to have a deterministic or free-will view of human behaviour.

Approaches, perspectives, methods, issues and debates

Synoptic questions

Debate: reductionism and holism

Reductionism

Reductionism argues that all psychological phenomena can be reduced to their simpler constituent parts and the ultimate goal of research is to identify what these smallest parts may be. Reductionist theories tend to support deterministic viewpoints as human behaviour is seen to be due to a single factor and once this is known it can be used to explain and predict all human behaviour. The logical endpoint of reductionism would be particle physics, as complex behaviours can be broken down into processes of the mind and these can be reduced to neurological activity in the brain; this is due to the chemicals found within the brain and particle physics can be used to help us understand how these chemicals work (Zohar and Marshall, 2000).

Try this ...

- Do you think reductionism is a useful way to explain complex human behaviour? Give reasons for your answer.

- Discuss with a group of friends whether reductionist ideas could account for creative activities.

Holism

Holism is often referred to as Gestalt psychology. It argues that behaviours cannot be understood in terms of the components that make them up. This is commonly described as 'the whole being greater than the sum of its parts'. What this suggests for psychologists is that humans are capable of much more than would be expected from the chemicals, neurones, brain structures and models of the mind. The social psychology approach would favour this view, as one of the regular findings is that the behaviour of individuals is influenced by others. A holistic view of human behaviour would argue that the complexity of this behaviour is so great that a reductionist understanding is not capable of considering even very simple human behaviours. If we were to consider the behaviourist idea of learning by relating external stimuli to responses and the reinforcement that these receive, it could be argued that there is far more to take into account than this simple interaction.

Try this ...

- Holistic arguments can often fail to identify any single cause for human behaviour. What are the advantages or disadvantages of this?

- Discuss in small groups all the possible causes for someone committing a crime. Do you think any one of these would be sufficient to motivate someone towards crime? If not, how many and which ones are needed to 'make' someone behave like this?

- Can you think of any occasions when working as a team was more effective than giving each person a separate task? Does this come close to understanding the idea of holism?

Approaches, perspectives, methods, issues and debates

Galton (2002) set out to identify the factors that may be responsible for the change in attitude that has led to a fall in the number of students wanting to study science. He was attempting to identify a number of factors in the very complex world of the classroom.

Consider ways in which it might be possible to identify individual factors that may have an impact in the classroom.

If Galton's research did not attempt to identify discrete factors, do you think there would have been any point to it?

Clinical psychologists can make diagnoses using the *ICD* or the *DSM-IV*. Discuss whether these provide a reductionist or holistic approach to diagnoses.

Canter and Heritage (1990) attempted to identify whether there were similar behaviour patterns in similar offences. This suggests that they considered it possible to link particular behaviours to certain offences. How useful do you think this approach is?

If behaviour patterns are found to be linked to criminal behaviour, do you think that these may cause such behaviour? How do you account for detectives using 'gut instinct'? Does this involve them using reductionist or holistic understandings of people's behaviour?

Reductionist viewpoints are used to explain behaviours in sport. Eysenck argued that personality could be reduced to a number of identifiable traits that had a biological basis and that our personalities were a combination of these.

Personality is by definition very individual! Do you feel that researchers such as Eysenck are right when they consider it possible to identify such traits? Do you have personality traits that you can see in other people? If other people are different from you, can you identify the traits that cause this difference?

Approaches, perspectives, methods, issues and debates

Synoptic questions

Debate: nature and nurture

Nature

The 'nature' view of psychology is a determinist one, as it suggests that all behaviour is determined by hereditary factors. These hereditary factors are the genetic make-up that individuals are born with, and all possible behaviours can be said to be present from the moment of conception. Our genes are thought to provide the blueprint for all behaviours; some of these will be present at birth, for example the rooting reflex in babies, whereas others are thought to be on a 'pre-programmed' schedule and will emerge as the individual matures. The development of language could be an example of this as children seem to be predisposed to make sounds and understand grammar. This does not happen from birth, but language skills develop rapidly after a certain period of time. When language does develop, it seems to follow the same sequence in all children, which suggests that an inbuilt genetic mechanism is responsible.

Try this …

How many behaviours can you think of that follow a similar developmental sequence? Now try the opposite, how many behaviours can you think of that do not follow a clear development sequence? What do your answers make you think about the nature debate?

Take it further

Extreme nature theories are not very common in psychology. Review the key studies in the AS and A2 courses and try to identify those that have a nature viewpoint, or at least a tendency towards this view. (Hint: the biologically-based theories may have a more nature-focused approach.)

Nurture

The nurture debate is also a determinist stance, as it proposes that all human behaviour is the result of interactions with the environment. Behaviourist theories are nurture theories as they argue that behaviour is shaped by interactions with the environment. Within this debate the individual is regarded as being born as an empty vessel just waiting to be filled up by the experiences they gain from environmental interactions. There can be no limit to what individuals achieve, as this is due to the quality of the external influences and not their genes. This view was popular in the early 1900s, as it provides an optimistic view that anyone can achieve anything as they are not constrained by their inherited capacities. The quality of the environment is crucial.

Try this …

Discuss in small groups if you have had any experiences where being in the right environment has enabled you to develop or learn a new skill.

Take it further

Very few people would now regard either the nature or nurture view as helpful in understanding behaviour. Most psychologists would argue that behaviours result from an interaction between nature and nurture. Look at the theories within each of the A2 option areas. Is it possible to decide whether these have nature or nurture tendencies?

Consider a key study or theory from each option you are studying and try to decide how much this study is based on a nature or nurture view of the world. If you think the study is based only on nature views, score it as 100 per cent nature; if it takes both nature and nurture into account, score it as 50/50 and so on. Is this an easy task? What does this tell you about the nature–nurture debate? Try to work in small groups so you can cover most of the key studies or theories.

Two studies in the education option indicate the importance of nurture. Schwiehart (2000) provides evidence of the positive impact of good pre-school experiences and Younger and Warrington (2005) highlight that all children can benefit from good teaching.

Education theories often emphasise the importance of nurture. Why do you think this may be?

In the Schweihart study, why do you think that good early experiences had the effect they did?

The origins of criminal behaviour are often studied in forensic psychology. Brunner et al. (1993) attempted to discover whether criminal behaviour can be related to genetic disorders and Yochelson and Samenow (1973) also researched the origins of criminal behaviour and how this may be changed. Compare these two studies and discuss in small groups what may cause criminal behaviour and what, if anything, can be done to prevent it.

Kroll and Crenshaw (1970) investigated the link between personality profiles and the uptake of different sporting activities. Think about the friends you know who are involved in sporting activities. Have they taken up these sports because of their personality type, or has the sport had an effect on their personality?

The explanations for mental-health disorders provided by Gottesman and Shields (1976) and Watson and Raynor (1920) are an example of the nature–nurture debate. Which study supports which debate and what insight does each provide?

Synoptic questions

Debate: ethnocentrism

The debate on ethnocentrism is slightly different from those previously raised, as the main focus is the research process and not the broader debates surrounding psychology. Ethnocentrism refers to the possibility of a bias in research towards one ethnic group. If this bias becomes established, the values of this group can become the accepted ones and those who do not share these can be regarded as different. Difference or diversity is not a problem unless this is seen to place others in groups that are regarded as not normal. The essential problem with ethnocentric research is that it provides the views of one dominant ethnic group to the detriment of others.

Try this …

Review the research covered in this course and draw up a table showing research based on European or American groups, compared with research focused on other cultures. What does this tell you about the research base for psychology?

The task above has no doubt highlighted the fact that most of the research we read has a western bias, i.e. it is focused on European or American research reports. Therefore most of the texts we read only reflect this viewpoint. A number of international texts do exist (see Eysenck, 2004) but these are in the minority. This may have the effect of making 'western values' more influential than they should be. These are difficult debates to have, especially as we are so used to our value system that it is difficult to see it as being unrepresentative, or indeed wrong.

Take it further

This is a difficult and sensitive debate to have, but consider the following hypothetical situation. Research in the USA has shown that reading is best taught using a mixture of supported reading, books with action pictures and computer software that 'sounds out' words. Can these findings now be 'rolled out' all over the world? Does the West have an inflated value of the importance of reading? Do these findings mean that those people with access to books, computers and the time and knowledge to take part in supported reading will always read better? Is reading really important to all people?

Try this …

Most psychological research is carried out in the USA or Europe on undergraduates. Can you think of ways to carry out research with a wider representation of ethnic groups?

Ethnocentrism in research can be counteracted either by designing the research process to take other ethnic groups into account, or by focusing on an ethnic group to highlight how they maybe misrepresented in research findings. For example, the key study by Rubie-Davies et al. (2006) highlights how Maori and Polynesian students are affected by teacher expectations. This is the focus of their findings, rather than how teacher expectations affect the other students, although they clearly would have had an effect.

The reading abilities of the students in this study changed over the year. How do you think the differing abilities of the children might have been explained before this research took place? Discuss how it could be argued that this piece of research is biased towards the Maori and Polynesian children. Does this affect the quality of the research?

Can you think of any other pieces of research that may contain bias towards ethnic groups? Try to avoid the obvious evaluative issue that most research is carried out with white, middle-class participants. Consider, for example, Gudjohnsson and Bownes (1992) where they compare responses for English and Northern Irish participants.

In the forensic option Eberhardt et al. (2006) indicate how ethnicity can have an impact on the judgements made when sentencing criminals. What they suggest is that when decisions are made individuals are influenced by ethnicity, even though they may not be consciously aware of this bias.

The sport option discusses Tuckman's theory of forming, storming, norming and performing. Do you think this represents all cultures, or could this be a feature of the American way of life?

The Mental Health Act Commission's Count Me In Census (2005) identified that in certain cultures, men are significantly overrepresented in the mental health system. For example, they found that rates of admission of both genders from the White British and Indian groups were lower than average, whereas the admission rates for people from the Black and White/Black Mixed groups, had rates of up to three or more times higher than average. Discuss why these differences have been found. Are they part of the research process or do they reflect wider psychological issues?

Approaches perspectives, methods, issues and debates

Synoptic questions

Debate: is psychology a science?

This may sound like a strange discussion to be having, and you could be asking why we should worry whether psychology is a science or not. Psychology is a relatively new subject discipline and it has often struggled to be taken as seriously as subjects such as biology, chemistry and physics. If psychology was to be regarded as a science then it could have a higher status. The discussion is not just related to influencing how others may view the subject, but also helps us to think about what psychology is and how psychology should be done. Science is not an arbitrary word given to a group of subjects. The word 'science' is used to group a whole range of subjects that share features about how they explain the world and how this can be investigated. In general the scientific approach can be said to have the following features in common.

- Objectivity: science subjects should be free from subjective (personal) views and should attempt to report things as they are, not how people feel they should be.

- Falsifiability: theories should be able to be disproved, as without this anybody could say anything. If a theory can be disproved it clearly does not work and alternatively if a theory can be proved it does work.

- Replicability: this has been a feature of the section on research methods. Only the findings from methods that can be replicated by others are accepted, as it would be unwise to accept findings if no one is quite sure how they were obtained.

Try this …

Discuss in small groups if you can recall occasions when your friends thought that the knowledge you had gained from psychology was obvious. Did you feel as though you could stand up for these findings more effectively if they had come from scientific-style studies? (Hint: compare Freudian models of the mind to Piaget's stages of development.)

Objectivity is an interesting feature for psychologists as psychology is the study of human behaviour … being studied by humans. Human beings have feelings and beliefs and these are likely to reflect how we see the world. There is also the problem that psychologists can assume that all people experience the world in the same way, particularly when they attempt to generalise findings.

Take it further

Discuss whether it is possible to carry out objective research on subjective experiences. You will need to question if a scientific way of thinking is suitable to investigate the experiences of individuals.

Falsifiablity is also not as straightforward as first thought. There are many theories that are used that have either been disproved or are not falsifiable and yet the psychological community (and others) still find them helpful. Learning style theories are still used despite recent research disproving these, and Maslow's Hierarchy of Needs cannot be disproved. Yet such theories still have a useful role to play in opening up debate into our understanding of the human condition.

Try this …

Try to think of an outrageous disprovable theory that despite its non-scientific status will support a good debate. For example, the mind has four parts that handle different operations: number, words, food and sport.

Replicability: it is easier to repeat the findings of simple, more reductionist, investigations as these have fewer variables. But of course, having fewer variables makes the situation being researched less ecologically valid.

Take it further

Do you think that it is possible to set up investigations that are replicable and can take into account the complexity of the human condition?

Zajonc et al. (1969) applied their findings from cockroaches in runs to sporting performance in humans. If you read back over the key study you will find that it has a lot of the features expected of a piece of scientific research. Despite this being a scientific investigation, is it acceptable to use this evidence to explain human behaviour? Would it have been acceptable to have carried out the investigation on humans rather than cockroaches?

Wheatley (2007) reports on the effectiveness of acupuncture in helping to beat drug addiction. The findings seem to suggest that there is a positive effect, and yet acupuncture itself has little support from the scientific community. Is it possible to have a scientific finding from a technique that itself lacks empirical support? If an intervention seems to have a positive effect, does it need to be scientifically verified?

Kohlberg's famous investigation into moral development used hypothetical scenarios. Do you think that his approach was sufficiently scientific? What are the sorts of issues related to using this technique that could have an impact on the validity of these findings?

In the education option, Smith and Schu (2000) investigated bullying and the strategies used to avoid bullying. They asked children to describe their experiences and used these as the basis of their findings. Is it possible to obtain objective responses in research such as this? Discuss whether the responses need to be objective to be acceptable to the researchers.

Discuss in small groups whether psychological research needs to be scientific. What are the advantages and disadvantages of psychology being seen as a science?

Synoptic questions

Debate: individual or situational explanations

Individual explanations of human behaviour are those that are centred on the person, whereas situational explanations focus on the situation that the individual is in. Situational or individual explanations are often used in educational settings, as they can provide a useful focus for helping to improve students' engagement with learning. If a student regularly underachieves in a subject area there could be two broad reasons for this.

1 Individual: the student has little ability in this area.

2 Situational: the method of teaching does not suit the student.

Just as there was no single answer to the determinism–free-will or nature–nurture debates, so there will be few examples of behaviour that are best explained using just individual or situational explanations.

Take it further

Discuss what you think the implications would be if human behaviour could only be explained in individual or situational terms. (Hint: If individual explanations are used, what may this suggest about the social responsibilities of others?)

Try this ...

◆ Copy the line below, then go back over the approaches and perspectives and place each one where you think it fits best on the line.

←--→

Mainly individual   Mixture of individual/situational   Mainly situational

◆ Select an issue from each option you have studied, for example the difference between the educational achievement of boys and girls. Make two lists of possible reasons for this, one for individual explanations and the other for situational explanations.

◆ Consider the issue you have just made the two lists for. Write out two research methodologies to do further study in this area; make one of these focus on possible individual explanations and the other on situational explanations. How would the two methodologies affect your research design and the ethical considerations you need to consider?

Consider the following broad themes within each of the psychology options.

♦ Why do certain individuals develop criminal behaviour?

♦ Why do some people have healthy lifestyles?

♦ Why are some sports teams unable to cope with losing?

♦ Why are some students reluctant to learn?

Try this ...

Each of these themes can be discussed within an individual or situational perspective. Copy and complete the table below to summarise your findings.

Theme	Individual explanation	Situational explanation
Developing criminal behaviour		
Having a healthy lifestyle		
Coping with losing		
Reluctance to learn		

Use the following studies as starting points:

♦ Berkowitz (1969) who investigated whether the sporting situation aroused violence.

♦ Gudjohnsson and Mackeith (1990) on why some individuals give false confessions.

♦ Lewis and Norwich (2004) who suggested that successful teaching strategies were the same for all learners, whether they had additional needs or not.

♦ Geer and Maisel (1973): is lack of control over life events situational or dispositional?

ExamCafé

Relax, refresh, result!

Student tips

Jo

I get confused with all the terminology in research methods, so I really need to master what all the key words mean. I'm going to write definitions and key terms on separate cards and then pair them up until I get really confident that I know them.

Alice

I need to think about how my research design choices would have to change with different scenarios. I could look at the examples in the textbook and pull out all the different methods that researchers have used and consider whether they could have been done any differently. I could also look on the British Psychological Society website and register for the research digest and get ideas from there.

Stephen

I find it hard to remember all the types of data and the different statistical tests, so I am going to create a table or a flow chart that will let me practise all the decisions for different tests.

Revision checklist: research methods

One of the most useful things you can do to prepare for this exam is to be rock solid in your knowledge of the advantages and disadvantages of different methods and designs. Creating a summary table like this could help you to improve your grasp of all the details.

Method/design	Advantages	Disadvantages	Most likely use
Laboratory experiment	• Lots of control of extraneous variables, which allows just the IV to act on the participant. • This in turn means that it is possible to assert that you have found a cause of a behaviour. • It also makes it possible for other researchers to replicate and then verify findings.	• All this control makes the set-up unlike the complex reality of everyday life. This means that the the behaviour shown and measured could just be an outcome of this paticular situation and the same thing would not be seen outside the laboratory (low ecological validity). • Also, people become unusually compliant and willing to please in an experiment (demand characteristics).	Any behaviour that can be measured in a strictly controlled setting.
Field experiment	Participants may not realise they are part of an experiment and so will behave as they normally do.		
Quasi-experiment			Any research that takes account of a naturally occuring variable such as gender differences.

THINGS TO
REMEMBER
1.
2.

Get the result!

Example answers

In the Research Methods paper you will be given a scenario and asked to design a way of investigating it, for example:

It is often reported today that people do not get enough sleep. This raises some interesting questions such as:

◆ Do males need more sleep than females?

◆ Does diet affect the content of dreams?

◆ Do people sleep better after exercise?

You are required to design a practical project to investigate **one** of the above questions. It must be an experiment with two conditions.

A series of questions will then follow, such as:

1. State the null hypothesis for your investigation.   [3 marks]

2. Outline how **one** extraneous variable will be controlled in your investigation.   [3 marks]

3. Describe in detail the procedure for your investigation, including how you would measure the dependent variable and examples of the materials you would use.

   (Marks are awarded for how feasible it would be to replicate the investigation.)   [13+6 marks]

4. Name the statistical test you would use to analyse your data and justify why you would use this test.   [3 marks]

Example answers

Below is a student response to these questions, written under exam conditions.

Examiner says:

This is a clear statement of no difference and it has both the independent and dependent variable

Student answer

1 There will be no significant difference in the length of time participants spend asleep after 30 minutes of running or 30 minutes of sitting watching television.

2 One variable I would need to control is how much caffeine or alcohol intake there had been during the day as both these products affect sleep patterns.

Examiner says:

The candidate has not said **how** the variable would be controlled. For full marks the candidate needs to say something like 'I would therefore ask my participants not to drink either substance in the twenty-four hours before the study takes place and to drink water instead.'

3   My investigation would be a laboratory experiment with a matched pairs design. Participants would be matched for fitness, age and gender, in order to reduce participant variables.

The independent variable in this investigation would be whether the participants exercised for 30 minutes before going to sleep or whether they sat and watched TV. The dependent variable is the amount of sleep the participants got.

The participants would be split into groups using the criteria of the matched pairs design and putting one of each pair into each group. One group would be timed for 30 minutes running on a treadmill (at an appropriate level and speed for their own fitness) and the second group would sit and watch TV for 30 minutes. To control for the effect any particular TV watching might have, the people on the treadmill would watch the same programmes while running.

In the night the participants would be attached to an EEG machine that would measure their brainwaves so that I could reliably assess how much sleep they had.

4   The statistical test I would use to analyse my data would be the Wilcoxon signed ranks test, as the quantitative data that I would gain are ordinal and my study consists of a matched pairs design.

Examiner says:

This could be more exact. The test is correct, but if the data collected represent time spent on a particular level of brainwave activity, it is likely that they are in fact interval level data (hours/minutes/seconds), so the answer should say 'at least ordinal data'. It would also be more correct to say as well that the experiment was investigating the difference between two conditions and therefore requires a test of difference rather than that it was 'a matched pairs design'.

Examiner says:

Marks are allocated for the independent variable, controls, type of sample and how it was selected, the allocation to the groups, the description of the test, examples of materials, the conditions (including location and time of day) and the scoring of any test. For any seven of these or similar points, you get one mark for the point outlined and one mark for elaboration or clarity that allows accurate replication.

So in this answer, marks would have been gained for the independent variable, the test, the controls, when it would happen and the materials that would be used. What is missing is detail about the type of sample and how it was selected and where the experiment would be carried out.

The design was appropriate, pragmatic and ethical. However, more is needed for quality of design, because without knowing how the sample was selected or any details such as number of participants, it would be impossible to replicate the experiment.

Appendix: statistics

Analysis of data: inferential statistics

Inferential statistics are used to measure the probability that the results obtained during the research process were due to chance. If the level of chance is known then it will be possible to make an intelligent guess (or inference) as to which hypothesis is likely to provide the best explanation for the findings. For more details on probability and inference, read page 288.

The end result of an inferential statistics calculation is a probability value which is reported as a decimal or percentage. When statistical calculations are carried out, the result that has the most significance is a probability of 0.05 or 5 per cent. This means that there is a probability of 1 in 20 that the results have occurred due to chance. This is sufficiently unlikely for researchers to reject the null hypothesis and accept that there is a causal link between the variables being investigated.

For example, if research had been carried out to find out if drinking water helps children to obtain better scores for maths and the statistical test had provided a probability of 0.05 (reported as $p < 0.05$), this would mean that there is a 1 in 20 chance that the null hypothesis (that drinking water will have no impact on scores for maths) is correct. It is therefore very unlikely that there is no effect and so the null hypothesis is rejected. Therefore there is a high probability that drinking water will affect scores for maths. This does not prove the case but infers that there is a link between drinking water and scoring well in maths, as do not forget there is a 5 per cent chance that the null hypothesis could be correct.

Researchers regard $p < 0.05$ as being a *significant level*, as any score equal to or less than this suggests that the null hypothesis can be rejected. This is the most significant number for researchers using inferential statistical tests and it will enable them to pronounce their findings as being 'statistically significant'.

Try this …

Listen carefully to the news or look at newspaper articles. If the reporter uses a phrase like 'there has been a significant increase in gun crime', try to find out if this is a *statistically significant* finding. If it is, how may this affect how people respond to the news?

The next pages will consider how the statistical tests are carried out and how the value for p is obtained. Each test is designed to find an *observed value* that is used with tables of data that contain *critical values* that are in turn used to find the p values. This may sound confusing, but the following sections will make this clear.

There are many types of statistical test as there are different levels of measurement and different research designs. Table 6.1 shows how the statistical tests are linked to levels of measurement and research design.

Research design	Levels of measurement		
	Nominal	**Ordinal**	**Interval**
Independent measures	Chi-square test (test for association)	Mann-Whitney *U* test (test for difference).	
Repeated measures	Sign test (test for difference)	Wilcoxon matched pairs signed ranks test (test for difference)	
Matched pairs		Spearman rank correlation test (test for correlation)	

Table 6.1 Statistical tests

314

Key terms

association an association shows a link between the two variables that is not consistent along the range of data

correlation a correlation occurs when the relationship between the two variables is consistent along the range of data

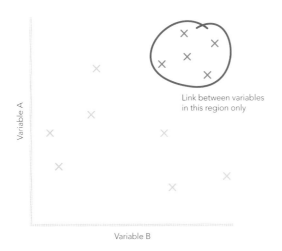

Link between variables in this region only

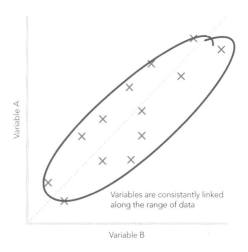

Variables are consistantly linked along the range of data

It is vital that the correct statistical test is used, as each has been designed to take the research design and level of measurement into account. There are many statistical tests, so don't be alarmed if you read research that has used a test you don't recognise.

Try this …

- Look back at three or four of the key studies. In each case, can you suggest which statistical test would have been most suited to the research design?

- Design five pieces of small-scale research so that each one uses one of the tests shown above (you do not have to carry these out).

Take it further

Discuss how you think researchers plan their research. Do you think they decide how to analyse the data before or after they carry out their research? Do you think it will make any difference to the research process if decisions on data analysis are made before or after starting to carry out research?

Using inferential statistics: the Chi-square test (χ^2)

Why use the Chi-square test?

This test is used when the hypothesis predicts an association between variables.

Example

Alternative hypothesis: primary school children respond more positively to extrinsic rewards than secondary school students.

Null hypothesis: there is no association between school stage and response to extrinsic rewards.

Try this ...

Is this a one- or two-tailed hypothesis?

This test can only be used with data that are:

- independent: each participant can only have one score that will be represented in one cell (see below)
- nominal: when data are allocated in categories to provide frequencies.

The Chi-square test will compare the numbers that actually occur in each category (the observed frequency) with the numbers that would be expected in each category (the expected frequency).

How to carry out the Chi-square test.

Step 1: draw a contingency table to arrange the observed data into cells (Table 6.2).

Response to extrinsic reward	School stage		Totals
	Primary	Secondary	
Positive	Cell A 45	Cell B 15	60
Negative	Cell C 5	Cell D 35	40
Totals	50	50	100

Table 6.2 Data for Chi-square test

These are the observed values (O).

Step 2: calculate the expected frequencies (E) for each cell using the following formula:

$$E = \frac{\text{total of row} \times \text{total of column}}{\text{overall total}}$$

The next steps can be summarised as in Table 6.3.

Step 6

The total of $(E - O)^2/E$ is the value for $\chi^2 = 37 \cdot 50$. This is the *observed value*.

Step 7: calculate the degrees of freedom (df) (this is a measure of how much choice there is within the investigation and therefore how much the observations may vary)

$$df = (\text{number of rows} - 1) \times (\text{number of columns} - 1)$$

For this example this is

$$df = (2 - 1) \times (2 - 1) = 1$$

Step 8: find the p value by using the correct table of data. To use this table you must know the degrees of freedom, whether the hypothesis is one- or two-tailed and of course your calculated observed value.

Cell	Step 2	Step 3	Step 4	Step 5
	E	$E - O$	$(E - O)^2$	$\dfrac{(E - O)^2}{E}$
A	$\dfrac{60 \times 50}{100} = 30$	$30 - 45 = -15$	$-15^2 = 225$	$\dfrac{225}{30} = 7 \cdot 5$
B	$\dfrac{60 \times 50}{100} = 30$	$30 - 15 = 15$	$15^2 = 225$	$\dfrac{225}{30} = 7 \cdot 5$
C	$\dfrac{40 \times 50}{100} = 20$	$20 - 5 = 15$	$15^2 = 225$	$\dfrac{225}{20} = 11 \cdot 25$
D	$\dfrac{40 \times 50}{100} = 20$	$20 - 35 = -15$	$-15^2 = 225$	$\dfrac{225}{20} = 11 \cdot 25$

Table 6.3 Chi-square calculations

Step 9: look up the critical value in Table 6.4. For a one-tailed test with 1 *df* the critical value for χ^2 at the 5 per cent level ($p \leq 0.05$) = 2.71. ($\leq$ is used to mean 'is equal to or less than'.) The observed value (χ^2) must be higher than or equal to the critical value for significance to be shown. The calculated observed value (37.5) is higher than the critical value in the table, therefore we can reject the null hypothesis and accept the alternative hypothesis that there is an association between response to extrinsic reward and school stage.

a   One-tailed test

Degree of freedom	Level of significance		
	0.1	0.05	0.01
1	1.64	2.71	5.41

b   Two-tailed test

Degree of freedom	Level of significance		
	0.1	0.05	0.01
1	2.71	3.84	6.64

Table 6.4 Critical values for χ^2

Try this …

* The same investigation was carried out in a different country and obtained the results below. Complete the calculation to decide whether the null hypothesis is accepted or rejected.

Response to extrinsic reward	School stage		Totals
	Primary	Secondary	
Positive	Cell A 47	Cell B 23	
Negative	Cell C 9	Cell D 19	
Totals			

The example given above is for a simple 2 × 2 contingency table.

* Can you design a piece of research that would have a 3 × 2 contingency table? What would your null and alternative hypotheses be?

* Consider the following hypotheses and the data collected. Carry out the chi-square calculation and decide whether the null hypothesis is rejected or accepted.

Alternative hypothesis: choice of car colour is associated with speeding fines.

Null hypothesis: there will be no association between car colour and speeding fines.

Car colour	Speeding fines		Totals
	Yes	No	
Red	Cell A 10	Cell B 32	
White	Cell C 5	Cell D 27	
Black	Cell E 12	Cell F 17	
Totals			

Using inferential statistics: the Mann-Whitney *U* test

Why use the Mann-Whitney *U* test?

This test is used when the hypothesis predicts a difference between two variables.

Example

Alternative hypothesis: Students who drink water during an exam will do better than those who do not.

Null hypothesis: Drinking water will have no effect on exam performance.

> **Try this …**
>
> Is this a one- or two-tailed hypothesis?

This test can only be used with data that are:

- independent: each participant can only have one score in one condition

- ordinal or interval: when data can be put in order or have precise intervals (i.e. temperature or time in seconds).

The Mann-Whitney *U* test will compare the number of scores in each condition or sample and identify whether one sample exceeds the other. For, example, if there are two teams of ten athletes running a race, the Mann-Whitney *U* statistic will identify whether the overall performance of the two teams is different.

How to carry out the Mann-Whitney *U* test

Step 1: record the data in a table with a column for each condition (Table 6.5)

Step 2: each score needs to be allocated points. This is done by comparing each score with those in the other group. 1 point is allocated for each higher score and 0.5 for an equal score. So 63 scores 3 because there are 3 higher scores in the other group (64, 86 and 97) and 40 scores 7 as there are 7 higher scores in the other group.

Step 3: calculate the total number of points for each condition.

Step 4: the observed value for *U* is the lowest total number of points. In this case 30.

Step 5: to find the critical value, you need to know:

- the numbers in each group (*N1* and *N2*). In this case *N1* = 10 and *N2* = 8

- if the hypothesis is one- or two-tailed. This hypothesis is one-tailed as it has a direction.

Participant (*N1*)	Step 1 — Exam score when drinking water	Step 2 — Points allocated	Participant (*N2*)	Step 1 — Exam score when not drinking water	Step 2 — Points allocated
1	63	3	1	19	9
2	40	7	2	43	6
3	47	6	3	64	2
4	25	7	4	86	0
5	74	2	5	53	4
6	40	7	6	97	0
7	61	3	7	48	5
8	82	2	8	58	4
9	51	5			
10	12	8			
Step 3	Total	50			30

Table 6.5 Mann-Whitney points allocation

Appendix statistics

Step 6: for significance at the 5 per cent level ($p \leq 0.05$) the observed value of U must be equal to or less than the critical value. The calculated observed value of $U = 30$. This is greater than the critical value (20) and therefore the null hypothesis is accepted, indicating that drinking water during an exam will be unlikely to improve exam scores.

a One-tailed test at 0.005

N2 \ N1	1	2	3	4	5	6	7	8	9	10	11	12	13
1	–	–	–	–	–	–	–	–	–	–	–	–	–
2	–	–	–	–	0	0	0	1	1	1	1	2	2
3	–	–	0	0	1	2	2	3	3	4	5	5	6
4	–	–	0	1	2	3	4	5	6	7	8	9	10
5	–	0	1	2	4	5	6	8	9	11	12	13	15
6	–	0	2	3	5	7	8	10	12	14	16	17	19
7	–	0	2	4	6	8	11	13	15	17	19	21	24
8	–	1	3	5	8	10	13	15	18	20	23	26	28
9	–	1	3	6	9	12	15	18	21	24	27	30	33
10	–	1	4	7	11	14	17	20	24	27	31	34	37
11	–	1	5	8	12	16	19	23	27	31	34	38	42
12	–	2	5	9	13	17	21	26	30	34	38	42	47
13	–	2	6	10	15	19	24	28	33	37	42	47	57

The critical value in the table = 20.

b Two-tailed test at 0.005

N2 \ N1	1	2	3	4	5	6	7	8	9	10
1	–	–	–	–	–	–	–	–	–	–
2	–	–	–	–	–	–	–	0	0	0
3	–	–	–	–	0	1	1	2	2	3
4	–	–	–	0	1	2	3	4	4	5
5	–	–	0	1	2	3	5	6	7	8
6	–	–	1	2	3	5	6	8	10	11
7	–	–	1	3	5	6	8	10	12	14
8	–	0	2	4	6	8	10	13	15	17
9	–	0	2	4	7	10	12	15	17	20
10	–	0	3	5	8	11	14	17	20	23

Table 6.6 Critical values for U

Try this …

Carry out a Mann-Whitney U test on the data provided on the following hypotheses (Table 6.7):

Alternative hypothesis: The percentage of country music CDs in the music collections of science and art students will differ.

Null hypothesis: There will be no difference in the percentage of country music CDs in the music collections of science or art students.

	1	2	3	4	5	6	7	8	9	10	11	12
Science students	5	10	8	2	2	15	7	2	16	12	6	4
Art students	4	2	4	10	8	2	8	9	2	18	24	6

Table 6.7 Percentage of country music CDs

Using inferential statistics: the sign test (s)

Why use the sign test?

This test is used when the hypothesis predicts a difference between two variables.

Example

Alternative hypothesis: Pupils of similar academic ability who like their teacher will rate their enjoyment of lessons higher than pupils who do not like their teacher.

Null hypothesis: Liking or not liking a teacher will make no difference in enjoyment of lessons.

Try this ...

Is this a one- or two-tailed hypothesis?

This test can only be used with data that are:

- related: when scores from one condition are compared with scores from another
- matched pairs: when participants in each group are paired for specific abilities
- nominal: when data can be put into separate categories.

The sign test compares the direction of the differences within the data. For example, are the pupils in each group more or less likely to enjoy their lessons? This may make more sense with the following example.

How to carry out the sign test (s)

Step 1: record the data and allocate a sign, positive, negative or no change, that reflects the change between each condition (Table 6.8). You need to make sure you are consistent about giving a positive or negative sign. For the table below a positive sign is given if the rating for lesson enjoyment is higher for those pupils who like their teacher.

Step 2: add up the number of signs. In this case there are 6 positive signs, 2 zeros and no negative signs.

Step 3: the observed value (s) is the value for the least frequent sign. This is 0.

Step 4: ignore any 0 signs and calculate the group size (N). This will be $8 - 2 = 6$.

Matched pair	Rating for enjoyment of lesson (5 is high)		Sign allocated
	Pupils who like the teacher	Pupils who do not like the teacher	
1	4	2	+
2	3	1	+
3	4	3	+
4	5	5	0
5	3	2	+
6	5	3	+
7	2	2	0
8	4	2	+

Table 6.8 Sign test sign allocation

Step 5: identify the critical value from Table 6.9. The critical value at the 5 per cent ($p \leq 0.05$) level for $N = 6$ with a one-tailed test is 0. The observed value of s must be equal to or lower than the critical value for the results to be considered significant.

Step 6: as the observed value (O) is equal to the critical value (O) the null hypothesis can be rejected and we can accept that liking your teacher has a significant effect on the enjoyment of lessons.

a   One-tailed test

N	Level of significance	
	0.05	0.01
5	0	–
6	0	–

b   Two-tailed test

N	Level of significance	
	0.05	0.01
9	1	0
10	1	0
11	1	0

Table 6.9 Critical values for *s*

Try this ...

Carry out a sign test on the data in Table 6.10 to see if the following null hypothesis can be rejected or accepted.

Alternative hypothesis: Custodial sentences or community service for young offenders will have a different effect on the likelihood of rescinding.

Null hypothesis: Custodial sentences or community service will not have a different effect on rescinding.

Participant	Likelihood of rescinding (10 is very likely)		Allocation of sign
	After a custodial sentence	After community service	
1	3	0	
2	1	1	
3	0	0	
4	3	3	
5	2	1	
6	7	2	
7	1	1	
8	3	1	
9	1	2	
10	2	1	

Table 6.10 Sample data

Using inferential statistics: the Wilcoxon Matched Pairs Signed Ranks test (T)

Why use the Wilcoxon Matched Pairs Signed Ranks test?

This test is used when the hypothesis predicts a difference between two variables.

Example

Alternative hypothesis: Footballers will be less likely to commit a foul in the game after they have been booked.

Null hypothesis: Being booked will have no impact on the number of fouls a footballer will commit.

Try this …

Is this a one- or two-tailed hypothesis?

This test can only be used with data that are:

- matched pairs: when participants in each group are paired for specific abilities
- related: when the pairs of scores are from the same person
- ordinal or interval: when data can be put in order or have precise intervals (i.e. temperature or time in seconds).

The Wilcoxon Matched Pairs Signed Rank test will compare the scores in two conditions by analysing the differences. If the difference is always in the same direction, for example fewer fouls after being booked, then an effect can be identified. The Wilcoxon test will compare all the differences and calculate the overall effect of the conditions.

How to carry out the Wilcoxon test

Step 1: record the data and calculate the differences (Table 6.11).

Step 2: rank the differences ignoring the sign. For numbers that are the same, use the mean rank that would have been given (−3 occurs three times and occupies the ranks 4, 5 and 6. Therefore all the −3s have the rank of 5). Omit any zero scores.

Participants	Number of fouls per game before being booked	Number of fouls per game after being booked	Difference (Step 1)	Rank of differences Step (2)
1	5	1	−4	7
2	3	0	−3	5
3	4	2	−2	2.5
4	7	1	−6	8
5	12	3	−9	9
6	2	0	−2	2.5
7	1	2	+1	1
8	5	2	−3	5
9	8	5	−3	5
10	2	2	0	

Table 6.11 Wilcoxon rank of difference

Step 3: calculate the value of the positive and negative ranks. In this case positive ranks = 1 and negative ranks = 11. The observed value for T is the sum of the least frequent ranks. So $T = 1$.

Step 4: find the critical value of T. The group size must be used in Table 6.12 and if a difference of zero has been recorded this must be omitted. The group size (N) is therefore 9. The hypothesis is one-tailed as it has a direction. The critical value at the 5 per cent ($p \leq 0.05$) level for $N = 9$ and a one-tailed test is 8. For significance the observed value must be equal to or less than the critical value.

Step 5: the observed value (1) is less than the critical value (8) and therefore the null hypothesis can be rejected and the alternative hypothesis accepted.

a One-tailed test

N	Level of significance	
	0.05	0.01
8	5	1
9	8	3
10	11	5

b Two-tailed test

N	Level of significance	
	0.05	0.01
9	5	8
10	8	11
11	10	13

Table 6.12 Critical values for T

Try this ...

Use the data in Table 6.13 to calculate whether the following null hypothesis can be rejected or accepted.

Alternative hypothesis: The number of visits to the dentist while in secondary school will be different for students with high or low IQs.

Null hypothesis: IQ will have no effect on the number of visits to the dentist during secondary school.

	1	2	3	4	5	6	7	8	9	
High IQ	8	9	7	10	9	7	7	8	6	
Low IQ	4	8	8	7	3	5	10	8	4	

Table 6.13 Number of visits to the dentist during secondary school for pairs matched for IQ

Using inferential statistics: Spearman Rank Correlation test (r)

Why use the Spearman Rank Correlation test?

This test is used when the hypothesis predicts a correlation between two variables.

Example

Alternative hypothesis: There is a correlation between IQ and annual salary.

Null hypothesis: There is no correlation between IQ and annual salary.

Try this ...

Is this a one- or two-tailed hypothesis?

This test can only be used with data that are:

- related: the sets of data must be from the same person or condition
- ordinal or interval: when data can be put in order or have precise intervals (i.e. temperature or time in seconds).

The Spearman Rank Correlation test compares the ranks of each score; if the scores are correlated, then high and low ranks should match. If someone is ranked high (or low) in both conditions there is a positive correlation, but if they are ranked high in one condition and not the other then the correlation is negative.

How to carry out the Spearman Rank Correlation test

Step 1: record the data.

Step 2: rank each set of data independently.

Step 3: work out the differences between the ranks.

Step 4: calculate the square of these differences.

See Table 6.14.

Participant	IQ (Step 1)	Annual salary (£) (Step 1)	IQ rank (Step 2)	Annual salary rank (Step 2)	Difference (of steps) (Step 3)	d^2 (Step 4)
1	120	110,000	11	11	0	0
2	76	14,000	1	2	−1	1
3	102	35,000	7	8	−1	1
4	111	52,000	9	10	−1	1
5	82	12,000	2	1	+1	1
6	115	24,000	10	5	+5	25
7	98	21,000	5·5	4	+1·5	2·25
8	98	40,000	5·5	9	−3·5	12·25
9	93	30,000	4	7	−3	9
10	107	28,000	8	6	+2	4
11	89	17,000	3	3	0	0

[N = 11]

Table 6.14 Spearman rank of difference

Step 5: calculate the sum of the squared differences.

$$\sum d^2 = 56.5.$$

Step 6: calculate the observed value of r.

$$r = 1 - \frac{(6\sum d^2)}{N(N^2 - 1)}$$

$$= 1 - \frac{(6 \times 56.50)}{11(11^2 - 1)}$$

$$= 1 - \frac{(339)}{(1320)}$$

$$= 1 - 0.26$$

$$= 0.74$$

The observed value in this case = 0.74.

Step 7: calculate the critical value for r at the 5 per cent ($p \leq 0.05$) level. For a two-tailed hypothesis (one that has no direction) with a group size (N) of 11 the critical value is 0.618.

Step 8: for the results to be significant at the 5 per cent ($p \leq 0.05$) level the calculated observed value (0.74) must be equal to or greater than the critical value (0.618). This is the case and therefore we can reject the null hypothesis and accept the alternative hypothesis and conclude that there is a positive correlation between annual salary and IQ.

a   One-tailed test

N	Level of significance	
	0.05	0.01
7	0.714	0.893
8	0.643	0.833

b   Two-tailed test

N	Level of significance	
	0.05	0.01
10	0.648	0.794
11	0.618	0.755
12	0.587	0.727

Table 6.15 Critical values for r

Try this …

Carry out a Spearman Rank Correlation test to see if the data in Table 6.16 support the null hypothesis.

Alternative hypothesis: There is a positive correlation between the hours spent training and the number of races an athlete wins.

Null hypothesis: There is no correlation between the hours spent training and the number of races won by an athlete.

	Participants						
	1	2	3	4	5	6	7
Hours spent training	8	4	16	22	10	15	20
Number of races won	2	1	4	7	0	1	12

Table 6.16 Sample data

Glossary

ad hoc (literally 'to this') refers to something created to do a particular job in a particular context, in this case the interviews concerned

adversarial where two sides argue the case in front of the judge and jury

aesthetics an emotional reaction to aspects of our environment such as sport, art or nature

aetiology the cause or origin of a disease or disorder as determined by medical diagnosis

antecedent something that happens or exists before something else

asymptomatic not showing any indications of a disease or other medical condition

attributions explanations an individual gives for another person's behaviour

biometric data data about people that are recorded and kept; they include biological features such as fingerprints, iris scans and DNA samples

body image belief and perceptions about one's own physical appearance

calibrated a machine is set so that the individual's baseline behaviour is the starting point. A person's heart rate at rest will become the baseline, which may differ from another person's heart rate and so their calibrated baseline

case-control study a study comparing participants who have a condition with participants who do not have that condition

catharsis an important term in the psychoanalytic approach. It refers to the process of releasing pent-up psychic energy. This can be in a hostile or channelled way, and may be linked to frustration and aggression

classical conditioning when a natural stimulus (e.g. food) is paired with a neutral stimulus (e.g. a bell) sufficiently often to cause the neutral stimulus to elicit the natural response (e.g. salivating)

constructivist theory each individual actively constructs, or builds up, their knowledge from their own experiences

construct validity whether a scale measures the unobservable social construct that it purports to measure. It is therefore measuring something that does not exist in a physical sense (e.g. personality, intelligence)

content analysis examination of a collection of data from an already existing source such as government statistics. It does not involve collecting data at first hand and is therefore dependent for accuracy on the original source being reliable

cost–benefits analysis a process by which decisions are made. The benefits of a given situation are taken into account and then the costs associated with taking that action are subtracted

credence credibility or authority

credibility deflation where a child witness is seen as fragile and unreliable because of the use of a shield

credibility inflation where a child's testimony is enhanced because they are protected from negative effects of trauma

credulous-sceptical argument the debate about the impact of personality on sports performance. The credulous argument is the proposal that athletic performance can be predicted from personality traits. The sceptical argument is the proposal that athletic performance cannot be predicted from personality traits

criteria of life success a set of nine criteria that are used to judge whether someone has succesfully turned away from crime. They include: no drug use in the last 5 years, no self-reported offence (of six specified) in the last 5 years, satisfactory mental health and no convictions in the last 5 years

cue anything that will jog our memory and help us to recall something; it could be a taste, a smell, a sound or an image

demographic variables population characteristics such as age, income, sex, occupation, education, family size

determinism accepting that behaviour is driven by outside or inside forces that are not under our conscious control or free will. Under this philosophy our behaviour is the result of a chain of consequences

dichotomy a mutually exclusive division into two (here used to place crimes in two distinct categories)

dispositional explanation an explanation of behaviour where blame is placed on the personality or traits of the individual rather than looking for an explanation in their environment, which would be a situational explanation

dizygotic twins non-identical twins

dominant response the response that supersedes the other possible responses

double-blind study a study in which neither the participants nor the know who belongs to the experimental group and who to the control group until all the data have been recorded

dysfunctional unable to function emotionally or as a social unit

empathic having the ability to identify with and understand someone else's feelings or difficulties

enhanced thinking skills (ETS) this is similar to reasoning and rehabilitation and is available in 78 establishments; there are 20 sessions in a programme

epistemology the study of how we know what we know

evaluation apprehension the phenomenon whereby performance will be enhanced or impaired in the presence of persons who can approve or disapprove of the performance

expectancy effects a bias in participants who expect a particular outcome from the study

extraneous variable a factor that is not the independent variable but might influence the dependent variable

extrapolation 'drawing out' or inferring something unknown from something that is known, for example drawing parallels for human behaviour from observing animal behaviour

external validity whether the procedures and participants used in a study can be generalised to other settings and populations

facial morphing taking several 'original' versions of a face and merging them together by using points mapped onto the face electronically. Each successive merging of the face makes it blander and eventually after 16 faces have been morphed there is a very stereotypical image, which oddly most people then find more attractive than any of the original images

factor analysis a statistical approach that can be used to analyse interrelationships among a large number of variables and to explain these variables in terms of their common underlying dimensions (factors)

galvanic skin response (GSR) the electrical current conducted by the skin, which varies according to moisture on the skin. Anxiety causes sweating and so increases the moisture on the skin and its conductance

group cohesion the bond or glue between members of a team

gynaecological age the duration in time throughout which a female has menstrual cycles

haemoglobin a substance in red blood cells that carries oxygen

hostile aggression aggression that is an uncontrolled reaction to a person or stimulus, such as road rage

hypochondriasis an excessive preoccupation with one's own health

icon (religious) a picture of a saint or religious figure

immune system the body's recognition of cells that are not its own, such as illness-inducing bacteria, and its response to fight them

index case the documented case of a disease included in a study

individualist a society where the emphasis is on the individual and people are not interested in the collective interests of the society

inquisitorial where a judge calls their own witnesses and counsel and reaches a judgement independently

instrumental aggression aggression that is a means to an end, for example an aggressive tackle to gain the ball in a rugby game

intergenerational transmission the occurrence of (criminal) behaviour through successive generations of the same family

intergroup between one group and another

internal validity whether a study has been affected by biases or errors in the study design

interpersonal between one person and another

intrapersonal within oneself

McNaghten rules rules establised by the House of Lords following a case in which the defendants, Daniel McNaghten, had shot and killed the private secretary of the prime minister, but was found to have been of unsound mind at the time

meta-analysis a study of studies. It gathers second-hand data but allows a researcher access to a huge variety of samples and procedures which taken together may be more meaningful than a single piece of research

milieu therapy a hospital environment designed to enhance patients' social skills and build confidence. The milieu, or 'life space', is a safe environment with social opportunities and immediate feedback from staff

mock jury a jury made up of a sample of participants who are shown a video or transcript of a court case and have to come to a verdict in a laboratory situation

modus operandi ('way of working') the method used by a criminal while committing a crime, which is often distinctive to that criminal. It is sometimes associated with a 'signature' such as collecting a souvenir from the attack

monozygotic twins identical twins

mood a longer-lasting emotional reaction to an event or stimuli, which may have a positive or negative dimension

nucleotide one of the structural components, or building blocks, of DNA and RNA. A nucleotide consists of a base (one of four chemicals: adenine, thymine, guanine, and cytosine) plus a molecule of sugar and one of phosphoric acid

pathology the study and diagnosis of disease by looking at blood and tissue samples under a microscope

percentile is one hundredth of the population; to move from the 50th to the 98th percentile means moving from the middle of the population to being very near the top.

PET scans use radioactivity to show and record glucose metabolism in the active part of the brain. Glucose is mixed with a radioactive tracer and injected into the person, who then completes a task while being scanned. The brain needs the glucose for its activity and draws it to the active area which then shows as red/yellow

placebo something that is inactive, but is given to people who believe it may contain an active substance

plea of diminished responsbility the excuse that a criminal's behaviour was the outcome of a loss of sanity, even if this was a temporary state caused by extreme emotions

phenotype the observable traits or characteristics of an organism, for example hair colour, weight, or the presence or absence of a disease

point mutation a single point mutation occurs when a single nucleotide is replaced with a different one, in this case on the X chromosome

proactive interference when something that you learned earlier interferes with your memory of the present, e.g. your old phone number interferes with

your new one and confuses you. This effect is strongest if the two memories are similar

probation order a general term given to a whole range of different punishment and treatment options which could include unpaid work, attendance on a treatment programme, a curfew, an exclusion, a residence requirement, electronic monitoring (tags) and any combination of the above. The offender has to meet the terms of the order administered by the probation officer or face a stiffer penalty

prospective a study that starts with participants and follows them to find out which behaviours they show in the future

protective factors those factors that will prevent criminal behaviour

quasi-experiment an experiment where the independent variable is naturally occurring

reconstructive memory when we recall something, it does not happen literally like a tape recorder; using a schema we fit together likely events to make a story, some of which may be highly accurate and some very inaccurate

reductionism an approach that reduces a complex phenomenon such as human behaviour to the simplest explanation possible. Often this means looking for a biological basis for behaviour. The advantage of a reductionist approach is that it can give a greater understanding of something by revealing evidence for a cause of behaviour. The disadvantage is that humans and their environments are so complex that the reductionist explanation falls short of giving the whole explanation of the behaviour

regimen a routine such as a daily routine for taking medication

response bias the tendency of a respondent to answer in the way they think the questioner wants them to

retrospective a study that asks participants to recall their behaviours in the past

risk there could be two ways of looking at the definition of risk, there are high-risk category A prisoners who are kept under high security, and then there are prisoners who are at high risk of re-offending – these are the prisoners referred to here

risk factors those factors that make it more likely that criminal behaviour will occur

schema a mental structure containing information that we hold about something which in turn connects to other schemas, creating a representation of the world or what we call 'knowledge'

self-efficacy the confidence in one's abilities to execute actions or behaviours necessary to attain a given outcome

serotonin a neurotransmitter that is believed to play an important role in the regulation of anger and aggression: lower than normal levels can lead to depression. It is sometimes called the 'feel-good' chemical

shadow jury a jury made up of participants who sit in a courtroom watching events unfold and then discuss the case as a jury with the researchers observing them. In this way they are exposed to the same witnesses, emotions, etc. of the real courtroom, without the ethical difficulties of secrecy being broken

smallest-space analysis a way of interpreting data based on the assumption that the behaviour we are interested in (in this case murder) is being tested if the relationship between every variable and every other variable is examined. A computer program does these correlations and then presents the results as an image. The correlations are also ranked in terms of their importance and the closer the two variables appear, the better the 'fit' between them

social cohesion people's belief that getting on with each other will be fundamental to their team

social facilitation process gains in performance caused by the presence of others

social inhibition process losses in performance caused by the presence of others

social loafing the reduction in effort made by individuals when performing as part of a team

social physique anxiety a person's anxiety over potential evaluations of other people about their physique

stress a state of perceived incongruity between stimulus demands and behavioural output capacity

stressor anything that causes stress

synaptic plasticity the ability of nerve cells to join and change the strength of their connection

system variable variable that affects the accuracy of a witness by the delays it creates and the way statements are taken and given to the police and courts

tachistoscope a type of projector that shows an image for a specific but adjustable period of time

task cohesion shared commitment among members of a team to achieving a common goal

token economies therapies that give rewards ('tokens') for desired behaviours

unconditioned stimulus a stimulus that elicits an innate response, e.g. food elicits salivation

unstructured interviews interviews that do not follow a predetermined set of questions and instead are free-flowing, with one question leading from the previous answer

voire dire translates as 'to give a true verdict'. In the USA, when a potential juror is being questioned about their fitness to serve as a juror, they must respond truthfully to the questions from the defence barrister

References

Abbott, W.F. and Batt, J. (1999) *A Handbook of Jury Research*. Philadelphia: Ali-Aba

Allen, D., Kanner, J.C., Coyne, C.S. and Lazarus, R.S. (1981) 'Comparison of two modes of stress measurement: daily hassles and uplifts versus major life events.' *Journal of Behavioural Medicine*, 4(1)

Allport, F.H. (1924) *Social Psychology*. Boston: Houghton Mifflin

Allport, G.W. and Odbert, H.S. (1936) 'Trait names: a psycho-lexical study.' *Psychological Monographs*, 47(211)

Arnold, M.L. (2000) 'Stage, sequence and sequels: changing conceptions of morality, post-Kohlberg.' *Educational Psychology Review*, 12, 365–383

Arnot, M., Gray, J., James, M., Rudduck, J. and Duveen, G. (1998) *Recent Research on Gender and Educational Performance*. London: HMSO

Aronson, E., Blaney, N., Stephen, C., Sikes, J. and Snapp, M. (1978) *The Jigsaw Classroom*. Beverly Hill, CA: Sage Publications

Asch, S.E. (1946) 'Forming impressions of personality.' *Journal of Abnormal and Social Psychology*, 4, 258–90

Asch, S.E. (1955) 'Opinions and social pressure.' *Scientific American*, 193(5), 31–35

Ausubel, D.P. (1977) 'The facilitation of meaningful verbal learning in the classroom.' *Journal of Educational Psychology*, 12, 162–178

Azjen, I. (1988) *Attitudes, Personality, and Behaviour*. Bristol: Open University Press

Azjen, I. and Fishbein, M. (1980) *Understanding Attitudes and Predicting Social Behaviour*. Englewood Cliffs, NJ: Prentice Hall

Baldus, D.C., Woodworth, G., Zuckerman, D., Weiner, N.A. and Broffitt, B. (1998) 'Racial discrimination and the death penalty in the post-Furman era: an empirical and legal overview, with recent findings from Philadelphia.' *Cornell Law Review*, 83, 1638–1770.

Bandura, A. (1977) 'Self-efficacy: toward a unifying theory of behavioural change.' *Psychological Review*, 84, 191–215

Bandura, A. (1982) 'Self-efficacy mechanism in human agency.' *American Psychologist*, 37, 122–147

Bandura, A. and Adams, N.E. (1977) 'Analysis of self-efficacy theory of behavioural change.' *Cognitive Therapy & Research*, 1(4), 287–310

Bandura, A. and Rosenthal, T.L. (1966) 'Vicarious classical conditioning as a function of arousal level.' *Journal of Personality and Social Psychology*, 3, 54–62

Bandura, A., Ross, D. and Ross, S.A. (1961) 'Transmission of aggression through imitation of aggressive models.' *Journal of Abnormal and Social Psychology*, 63, 575–582

Bandura, A., Ross, D. and Ross, S.A. (1963) 'Imitation of film-mediated aggressive models.' *Journal of Abnormal and Social Psychology*, 1, 589–595

Banyard, P. (2002) *Psychology in Practice*. London: Hodder Education

Baumeister, R.F. and Leary, M.R. (1995) 'The need to belong: desire for interpersonal attachments as a fundamental human motivation.' *Psychological Bulletin*, 117, 497–529

Beck, A.T. (1961) 'A systematic investigation into depression.' *Comprehensive Psychiatry*, 2, 162–170

Beck, A.T. (1967) *Depression: Clinical Experimental and Theoretical Aspects*. New York: Harper & Row

Beck, A.T., Laude, R. and Bonhert, M. (1974) 'Ideational components of anxiety neurosis.' *Archives of General Psychiatry*, 31, 139–172

Beck, A.T., Rush, A.J., Kovacs, M. and Hollon, S.D. (1978) 'Must pharmacotherapy fail for cognitive therapy to succeed?' *Cognitive Therapy and Research*, 2(2), 199–206

Beck, A.T., Ward, C.H., Mendelson, M. et al. (1961) 'An inventory for measuring depression.' *Archives of General Psychiatry*, 4, 53–63

Beck, R.C. (1990) *Motivation Theories and Principles*. Englewood Cliffs, NJ: Prentice-Hall

Becker, M.H., Radius, S.M. and Rosenstock, I.M. (1978) 'Compliance with a medical regimen for asthma: a test of the health belief model.' *Public Health Reports*, 93, 268–277

Bee, H. (2000) *The Developing Child*. Needham Heights, MA: Allyn & Bacon

Bennett, C.I. (1990) *Comprehensive Multicultural Education, Theory and Practice*. Boston: Allyn & Bacon

Benson, J. and Britten, N. (2002) 'Patients' decisions about whether or not to take antihypertensive drugs: qualitative study.' *British Medical Journal*, 325, 873

Bergstrom, B. (1967) 'Complex psycho-motor performance during different levels of experimentally induced stress in pilots.' In L. Levy (ed.) *Emotional Stress*. New York: American Elsevier

Berk, L. (2002) *Child Development*. Boston: Allyn & Bacon

Berkowitz, L. and Geen, R. (1966) 'Film violence and the cue properties of available targets.' *Journal of Personality and Social Psychology*, 3(5), 525–530

Bernstein, L., Henderson, B.E., Hanisch, R., Sullivan-Halley, J. and Ross, R.K. (1994) 'Physical exercise and reduced risk of breast cancer in young women'. *Journal of the National Cancer Institute*, 86(18), 1403–1408

Blakemore, S-J. and Choudhury, S. (2006) 'Development of the adolescent brain: implications for executive function and social cognition.' *Journal of Child Psychiatry and Psychology*, 47(3–4), 296–312

Bloom, B. (1984) 'The 2 sigma approach: the search for methods of group instruction as effective as one to one tutoring.' *Educational Researcher*, June/July, 4–16

Blumer, D. (2002) 'The illness of Vincent van Gogh.' *American Journal of Psychiatry*, 159, 519–526, American Psychiatric Association

Boaler, J., William, D. and Brown, M. (2000) 'Students' experiences of ability grouping – disaffection, polarisation, and construction of failure.' *British Educational Research Journal*, 26(5), 631–648

Boom, J., Brugman, D. and van der Heijden, P.G. (2001) 'Hierarchical structure of moral stages assessed by sorting task.' *Child Development*, 72, 535–548

Booth, P.I. (1985) 'A geometric interpretation of the effects of anxiety on test performance.' *The Mathematical Intelligence*, 7, 56-63

Brehm, J.W. (1966) *A Theory of Psychological Reactance*. New York: Academic Press

Brophy, J. and Good, T. (1974) *Teacher–Student Relationships*. New York: Holt, Rinehart & Winston

Broverman, I.K., Broverman, D.M., Clarkson, F.E., Rosenkrantz, T.S. and Vogle, S.R. (1970) 'Sex-role stereotypes and clinical judgments of mental health.' *Journal of Consulting and Clinical Psychology*, 36(1), 1–7

Brown, I.D. and Groeger, J.A. (1988) 'Risk perception and decision taking during the transition between novice and experienced driver status.' *Ergonomics*, 31, 585–597

Bruce, V. (1988) *Recognising Faces*. Hove and London: Lawrence Erlbaum Associates

Bruner, J.S. (1960) *The Process of Education*. Cambridge: Harvard University Press

Bruner, J.S. (1966) *Toward a Theory of Instruction*. New York: W.W. Norton

Brunner, H.G., Nelen, H., Breakefield, X.O., Ropers, H.H. and Van Oost, B.A. (1993) 'Abnormal behaviour associated with a point mutation in the structural gene for monamine oxidase A.' *Science*, 262(S133), 578–580

Budzynski et al. (1970) 'Feedback-induced muscle relaxation applied to tension headache.' *Journal of Behaviour Therapy and Experimental Psychology*, 1, 205–211

Bulpitt, C.J. and Fletcher, A.E. (1988) 'Importance of well-being to hypertensive patients.' *American Journal of Medicine*, 84(1B), 40–46

Campbell, D.T. and Stanley, J.C. (1963) *Experimental and Quasi-Experimental Designs for Research*. Chicago: Rand McNally

Canfield, J. (1990) 'Improving students' self-esteem.' *Educational Leadership*, 48(1), 48–50

Cann, J. (2006) 'Cognitive skills programmes: impact on reducing reconviction on a sample of female offenders.' *Home Office Findings* 276. London: Home Office

Cannon, W.B. and Washburn, A.L. (1912) 'An explanation of hunger.' *American Journal of Physiology*, 29, 441–454

Cannon, W.B. (1927) 'The James-Lange theory of emotion: a critical examination and an alternative.' *American Journal of Psychology*, 39, 106–124

Cannon W.B. (1929) *Bodily Changes in Pain, Hunger, Fear and Rage*. New York: Appleton-Century-Crofts

Canter D. (1995) *Criminal Shadow: Inside the Mind of a Serial Killer*. London: Harper Collins

Canter, D. Alison, L.J., Alison, E. and Wentink, N. (2004) 'The organised/disorganised typology of serial murder myth or model?' *Psychology, Public Policy and the Law*, 10(3), 293–320

Canter, D. and Heritage, R. (1990) 'A multivariate model of sexual offence behaviour: developments in offender profiling.' *Journal of Forensic Psychiatry*, 1, 185–212

Carron, A.V. (1965) 'Complex motor skill performance under conditions of externally induced stress.' MA thesis, University of Alberta

Carron, A.V. (1982) 'Cohesiveness in sports groups: interpretations and considerations.' *Journal of Sports Psychology*, 4, 123–138

Carron, A.V. and Bennett, B.B. (1977) 'Compatibility in the coach–athlete dyad.' *Research Quarterly*, 48, 671–679

Carron, A.V. and Chelladurai, P. (1981) 'Cohesion as a factor in sport performance.' *International Review of Sport Sociology*, 16, 21–41

Castellow, W.A., Wuensch, K.L. and Moore, C.H. (1990) 'Effects of physical attractiveness of the plaintiff and defendant in sexual harassment judgements.' *Journal of Social Behaviour and Personality*, 5, 547–562

Castle, S., Deniz, C.B., and Tortora, M. (2005) 'Flexible grouping and student learning in a high-needs school.' *Education and Urban Society*, 37, 139–150

Cattell, R.B. (1946) *The Description and Measurement of Personality*. New York: Harcourt, Brace & World

Cattell, R.B. (1956) 'Validation and intensification of the Sixteen Personality Factor Questionnaire.' *Journal of Clinical Psychology*, 12, 205–214

Cattell, R.B. (1965) *The Scientific Analysis of Personality*. Harmondsworth: Penguin Books

Chadda, R.K. and Ahuja, N. (1990) 'Dhat syndrome. a sex neurosis of the Indian subcontinent.' Department of Psychiatry, University College of Medical Sciences, Delhi, India

Chelladurai, P. (1978) 'A multidimensional model of leadership.' Unpublished doctoral dissertation, University of Waterloo, Waterloo, Ontario

Christiansen, K.O. (1977) 'A preliminary study of criminality among twins'. In S.A. Mednick and K.O. Christiansen (eds) *Biosocial Bases of Criminal Behaviour*. New York: Gardiner Press

Christie, M.J. and Chesher, G.B. (1982) 'Physical dependence on physiologically released endogenous opiates.' *Life Science*, 30, 1173–1177

Chung, K.F. and Naya, I. (2000) 'Compliance with an oral asthma medication: a pilot study using an electronic monitoring device.' *Respiratory Medicine*, 94(9), 852–858

Claxton, G. (1992) *Live and Learn*. Milton Keynes: Open University Press

Clay, M. (1985) *The Early Detection of Reading Difficulties*. London: Heinemann

Coffield, F., Moseley, D., Hall, E., Ecclestone, K. (2004) *Learning Styles and Pedagogy in Post-16 Learning. A Systematic and Critical Review*. London: Learning and Skills Research Centre

Comer, R.J. (1998) *Abnormal Psychology*. New York: W.H. Freeman

Cooper, L. (1969) 'Athletics, activity and personality: A review of the literature.' *Research Quarterly*, 40, 17–22

Costill, D.L., Thomas, R., Robergs, R.A., Pascoe, D., Lambert, C., Barr, S. and Fink, W.J. (1991) 'Adaptations to swimming training: influence of training volume.' *Medicine and Science in Sport and Exercise*, 23(3), 371–377

Coté, T.R., Sacks, J.J., Kresnow, M., Lambert-Huber, D.A., Schmidt, E.R., Dannenberg, A.L. and Lipsitz, C.M. (1992) 'Bicycle helmet use among Maryland children: effect of legislation and education.' *Pediatrics*, 89(6), 1216–1220

Cottrell, N.B., Wack, D.L., Sekerak, G.J. and Rittle, R.H. (1968) 'Social facilitation of dominant responses by presence of others.' *Journal of Personality and Social Psychology*, 9, 245–50

Covington, M.V. (2000) 'Goal theory, motivation, and school achievement: an integrative review.' *Annual Review of Psychology*, 171

Cowpe, C. (1989) 'Chip-pan fire prevention 1976–1988.' In C. Channer, *Television Advertising Case Histories*, 2nd series. London: Cassell

Cox, R.H. (2002) *Sport Psychology: Concepts and Applications* (5th edition). New York: McGraw-Hill

Cox, R.H., Costill, D., Robergs, R., Thomas, R. and Bate, T. (1991) 'Effects of training overload on mood states of collegiate swimmers.' *Korean Journal of Sports Science*, 1(1), 83–93

Crace, J. (2004) 'Two brains.' *Guardian*, Tuesday 2 November

Curb, J.D., Borhani, N.O., Blaszkowski, T.P., Zimbaldi, N., Fotiu, S. and Williams, W. (1985) 'Long-term surveillance for adverse effects of antihypertensive drugs.' *Journal of the American Medical Association*, 253(22)

Curry, L. (1983) 'An Organisation of Learning Styles Theory and Constructs.' Paper presented at the Annual Meeting of the American Educational Research Association, Montreal, Quebec

Cutler, B.L., Penrod, S.D. and Dexter, H.R. (1989) 'The eyewitness, the expert psychologist and the jury.' *Law and Human Behaviour*, 13(3)

Daley, A.J. (2002) 'Exercise therapy and mental health in clinical populations: is exercise therapy a worthwhile intervention?' *Advances in Psychiatric Treatment*, 8, 262–270

Daly, M. and Wilson, M. (2001) 'Risk-taking, intrasexual competition, and homicide.' *Nebraska Symposium on Motivation*, 47, 1–36

Daniel, M., Martin, A.D. and Carter, J. (1992) 'Opiate receptor blockade by naltrexone and mood state after acute physical activity.' *British Journal of Sports Medicine*, 26, 111–115

Dannenberg, A.L. (1993) 'Bicycle helmet laws and educational campaigns: an evaluation of strategies to increase children's helmet use.' *American Journal of Public Health*, 83(5), 667–674

Dashiell, J. F. (1935) 'Experimental studies of the influence of social situations on the behavior of individual human adults.' In C. Murchison (ed.) *A Handbook of Social Psychology*. Worcester, Mass.: Clark University Press

Davies, G.M., Shepherd, J.W. and Ellis, H. (1978) 'Remembering faces: acknowledging our limitations.' *Journal of Forensic Science*, 18, 19–24

Davies, J. and Brember, L. (1992) 'The ethnic composition of nursery classes and its effect on children's adjustment to nursery.' *Educational Psychology*. 12(1), 25–33

Davis, D. and Leo, R.A. (2006) 'Strategies for preventing false confessions and their consequences.' In M. Kebbell and G. Davies (eds) *Practical Psychology for Forensic Investigations and Prosecutions*. New York: John Wiley, pp.121–149

deCharms, R.C. and Carpenter, V. (1968) 'Measuring motivation in culturally disadvantaged school children.' *Journal of Experimental Education*, 37, 31–41

Deci, E.L. (1975) *Intrinsic Motivation*. New York: Plenum Press

Deci, E.L. and Ryan, R.M. (1985) *Intrinsic Motivation and Self-determination in Human Behaviour*. New York: Plenum

Deci, E.L. and Ryan, R.M. (1991) 'A motivational approach to self: integration in personality.' In R.A. Dienstbier (ed.) Nebraska Symposium on Motivation 1991: Vol. 38. *Perspectives on Motivation: Current Theory and Research in* Motivation. Lincoln NE: University of Nebraska Press, pp.237–288

Demetrio, H., Goalen, P. and Rudduck, J. (2000) 'Academic performance, transfer, transition and friendship: listening to the student voice.' *International Journal of Educational* Research, 33(4), 425–441

Demie, F., Mclean, C. and Lewis, K. (2006) *The Achievement of African Heritage Pupils: Good Practice in Lambeth Schools*. Lambeth Research and Statistics Unit. Available at http://www.lambeth. gov.uk/NR/rdonlyres/26AFDBCD-B1DE-45BB-85D8-2A3ADB11F4C1/0/African_MASTER5_verA.pdf

Department for Education and Skills (2002) *Bullying: Don't Suffer in Silence: An Anti-Bullying Pack for Schools*. Nottingham: DfES

DfES (2002) *Guidance on Teaching Gifted and Talented Pupils*. Available at http:www.nc.uk.net/gt/

DfES (2006) *Ethnicity and Education: The Evidence on Minority Ethnic Pupils aged 5–16*. (Research Topic Paper: 2006 edition) Available at http://publications. teachernet.gov.uk/eOrderingDownload/DFES-0208-2006.pdf

DfES (2007) *Gender and Education: The Evidence on Pupils in England* (Research Topic Paper: 2007 edition) Available at http://www.dfes.gov.uk/research/data/uploadfiles/RTP01-07.pdf

DfES Research Report 796 (2006) *Pupil Grouping Strategies and Practices at Key Stage 2 and 3: A Case Study of 24 Schools in England*. The University of Brighton

Di Nardo, P.A. (1998) 'Generalized anxiety disorder.' In T.A. Widiger, A.J. Frances, H.A. Pincus, R. Ross, M.B. First and W.W. Davis (eds) *DSM-IV Sourcebook*, Vol. 4. Washington, DC: American Psychiatric Association

Dion, K.K., Berscheid, E. and Walster, E. (1972) 'What is beautiful is good.' *Journal of Personality and Social Psychology*, 24, 285–290

Dooley, E. (1990) 'Unnatural deaths in prison.' *British Journal of Criminology*, 30(2)

Douglas J.E., Burgess, A.W., Burgess, A.G. and Ressler, K. (1992) *The Crime Classification Manual*. New York: Lexington Books

DSM-IV-TR: Diagnostic and Statistical Manual of Mental Disorders, 4th edition (2000). Washington, DC: American Psychiatric Association

Dweck, C.S. (2000) *Self-theories: Their Role in Motivation, Personality and Development*. Philadelphia: Routeledge Press

Eberhardt, J.L., Davies, P.G., Purdie-Vaughns, V.J., and Johnson S.L. (2006) '"Looking deathworthy" – perceived stereotypicality of black defendants predicts capital sentencing outcomes.' *Psychological Science*, 17(5), 383–386

Elder, S.H. (2004) 'Effectiveness of mass media campaigns for reducing drinking and driving and alcohol-involved crashes: a systematic review.' *American Journal of Preventive Medicine*, 27(1), 57–65

Ellis, A. (1957) 'Outcome of employing three techniques of psychotherapy.' *Journal of Clinical Psychology*, 13, 334–350

Ellis, A. (1991) 'The revised ABCs of rational emotive therapy.' *Journal of Rational-emotive and Cognitive-behavioural Therapy*, 9, 139–172

Enoch, J.R. and McLemore, S.D. (1967) 'On the meaning of group cohesion.' *Southwestern Social Science Quarterly*, 48, 174–182

Erikson, E.H. (1963) *Childhood and Society* (2nd edition). New York: Norton

Eysenck, H.J. (1965) *Fact and Fiction in Psychology.* Harmondsworth: Penguin

Eysenck, H.J. (1985) *Personality and Individual Differences: A Natural Science Approach.* New York: Plenum

Eysenck, M. (2004) *Psychology: An International Perspective.* London: Psychology Press

Falshaw, L., Friendship, C., Travers, R., Nugent, F. (2003) 'Searching for "What Works": an evaluation of cognitive skills programmes.' *Home Office Findings* 206. London: Home Office

Farrell, P.A. (1989) 'Lack of exercise on peripheral encephalin entry into whole brain of rats.' *Medicine and Science in Sports and Exercise*, 21, S35

Farrington, D.P. (1994) *Cambridge Study in Delinquent Development [Great Britain], 1961–1981* (2nd ICPSR edn). Ann Arbor, MI: Inter-university Consortium for Political and Social Research

Farrington, D.P., Coid, J., Harnett, L., Jolliffe, D., Sateriou, N., Turner, R. and West, D.J. (2006) 'Criminal careers and life success: new findings from the Cambridge study in Delinquent Development.' *Home Office Findings* 281

Fazey, J. and Hardy, L. (1988) 'The inverted-U hypothesis: a catastrophe for sport psychology.' *British Association for Sports Sciences Monograph* No. 1. Leeds: National Coaching Foundation

Feshbach, N. (1998) 'Aggression in the schools: toward reducing ethnic conflict and enhancing ethnic understanding.' In P. Trickett and C. Schellenbach (eds) *Violence Against Children in the Family and the Community.* Washington DC: American Psychological Association

Festinger, L. and Carlsmith, J.M. (1959) 'Cognitive consequences of forced compliance.' *Journal of Abnormal and Social Psychology*, 58, 203–210

Fiedler, F.E. (1967) *A Theory of Leadership Effectiveness.* New York: McGraw-Hill

Fisher, R.P., Geiselman, R.E. and Amador, M. (1989) 'Field test of the cognitive interview: enhancing the recollection of the actual victims and witnesses of crime.' *Journal of Applied Psychology*, 74(5), 722–727

Flanders, N. (1970) *Analysing Teacher Behaviour.* Reading, MA: Addison Wesley

Ford, M.R. and Widiger, T.A. (1989) 'Sex bias in the diagnosis of histrionic and antisocial personality disorders.' *Journal of Consulting and Clinical Psychology*, 57, 301–305

Forrester, G. (2005) 'All in a day's work: primary teachers "performing" and "caring".' *Gender and Education*, 17(1), 271–287

Franken, R.E., Hill, R. and Kierstead, J. (1994) 'Sport interest as predicted by the personality measures of competitiveness, mastery, instrumentality, expressivity, and sensation seeking.' *Personality and Individual Differences*, 17(4), 467–476

Freeman, J. (1997) *Educating the Very Able.* London: OFSTED

Fremont, J. (1984) 'The separate and combined effects of cognitive-based counselling and aerobic exercise for the treatment of mild and moderate depression.' *Dissertation Abstracts International*, 44, 2413A

Freud, S. (1953–74) *The Standard Edition of the Complete Psychological Works* (24 vols) trans. and ed. J. Strachey with A. Freud, assisted by A. Strachey and A. Tyson. London: Hogarth

Freud, S. (1901) 'The psychopathology of everyday life.' *The Standard Edition of the Complete Psychological Works of Sigmund Freud.* Vol. 6, vii–296. London: Hogarth

Freud, S. (1909) 'Analysis of a phobia in a five-year-old boy.' *The Standard Edition of the Complete Psychological Works of Sigmund Freud.* Vol. 10, 3–149. London: Hogarth

Freud, S. (1920) 'Beyond the pleasure principle.' *The Standard Edition of the Complete Psychological Works of Sigmund Freud.* Vol. 18, 7–64. London: Hogarth

Freud, S. (1961) 'The ego and the id.' *The Standard Edition of the Complete Psychological Works of Sigmund Freud.* Vol. 19. London: Hogarth

Friendship C., Blud, L., Erikson, M. and Travers, R. (2002) 'An evaluation of cognitive behavioural treatment for prisoners.' *Home Office Findings* 161. London: Home Office

Fromm-Reichmann, F. (1948) 'Notes on the development of treatment of schizophrenics by psychoanalytic psychotherapy.' *Psychiatry*, 11, 263–273

Frowd, C., Bruce, V., McIntyre, A. and Hancock, P. (2007) 'The relative importance of external and internal features of facial composites.' *British Journal of Psychology*, 98, 61–77

Gallichan, C. (2002) Available at http://www.fau.org.uk/gallichan_review.pdf

Galton, M. (2002) 'Continuity and progression in science teaching at Key Stages 2 and 3.' *Cambridge Journal of Education*, 32(2), 249–265

Galton, M., Hargreaves, L., Comber, C., Wall, D. and Pell, A. (1999) *Inside the Primary Classroom: 20 Years On.* London: Routledge

Gardner, H. (1993) *Multiple Intelligences: The Theory in Practice.* New York: Basic Books

Gates, S., Smith, L.A., Foxcroft, D.R. (2006) 'Auricular acupuncture for cocaine dependence.' *Cochrane Database of Systematic Reviews 2006*, Issue 1

Geer, J. and Maisel, E. (1972) 'Evaluating the effects of the prediction-control confound.' *Journal of Personality and Social Psychology*, 23(3), 314–319

Gill, D.L. (1986) *Psychological Dynamics of Sport.* Champaign, IL: Human Kinetics Publishers

Gill, D.L. and Deeter, T.E. (1988) 'Development of the Sport Orientation Questionnaire.' *Research Quarterly for Exercise and Sport*, 59(3), 196–202

Gilligan, C. (1982) *In a Different Voice: Psychological Theory and Women's Development.* Cambridge, MA: Harvard University Press

Gillis, C.A. and Nafekh, M. (2005) 'The impact of community-based employment on offender reintegration.' *The Forum for Corrections*, 17(1), 10–15

Glanzer, M. and Cunitz, A.R. (1966) 'Two storage mechanisms in free recall.' *Journal of Verbal Learning and Verbal Behaviour*, 6, 928–935

Goldfarb, A.H., Hatfield, B.D., Storzo, G.A. and Flynn, M.G. (1987) 'Serum B endorphin levels during a graded exercise test to exhaustion.' *Medicine and Science in Sports and Exercise*, 19, 78–82

Goleman, D. (1996) *Emotional Intelligence.* London: Bloomsbury

Good, T.L. and Brophy, J. (2003) *Looking in Classrooms.* Boston: Allyn & Bacon

Gottesman, I.I. and Shields, J. (1976) 'A critical review of recent adoption twin and family studies of schizophrenia.' *Schizophrenia Bulletin*, 1, 360–401

Gross, R. (1994) *Psychology: The Science of Mind and Behaviour* (2nd edition). London: Hodder & Stoughton

Gudjohnsson, G.H. and Bownes, I. (2002) 'The attribution of blame and type of crime committed: data for Northern Ireland.' *Journal of Forensic Psychiatry*, 2(3), 337–341

Gudjohnsson, G.H. and Mackeith, J.A.C. (1990) 'A proven case of false confession: psychological aspects of the coerced compliant type.' *Medicine, Science and the Law*, 30, 329–335

Hammersley, M. (2001) 'Interpreting achievement gaps: some comments on a dispute.' *British Journal of Educational Studies*, 49(3), 285–298

Hammond, D., Fong, G.T.P., McDonald, W., Cameron, R. and Brown, K.S. (2003) 'Impact of the graphic Canadian warning labels on adult smoking behaviour.' *Tobacco Control*, 12(4), 391–395

Haney, C. (2006) 'Testifying for prison reform.' Available at http://www.prisoncommission.org/film.asp

Haney, C. (2006) *Reforming Punishment: Psychological Limits to the Pains of Imprisonment.* Washington, DC: American Psychological Association

Haney, C. and Zimbardo, P. (1998) 'The past and future of U.S. prison policy, twenty-five years after the Stanford Prison Experiment.' *American Psychologist*, 53(7), 709–727

Haney, C., Banks, W.C., and Zimbardo, P.G. (1973) 'Study of prisoners and guards in a simulated prison.' *Naval Research Reviews*, 9, 1–17. Washington, DC: Office of Naval Research

Hardman, K. (1973) 'A dual approach to the study of personality and performance in sport.' In H.T.A. Whiting, K. Hardman, L.B. Hendry and M.G. Jones (eds) *Personality and Performance in Physical Education and Sport.* London: Kimpton

Harlow, J.M. (1848) 'Passage of an iron rod through the head.' *Boston Medical and Surgical* Journal, 39, 389–393 (republished in *Journal of Neuropsychiatry and Clinical Neuroscience*, 11, 281–283)

Hart, E.A., Leary, M.R. and Rejeski, W.J. (1989) 'The measurement of social physique anxiety.' *Journal of Sport & Exercise Psychology*, 11, 94–104

Harter, S. (1978) 'Effectance motivation reconsidered: towards a developmental model.' *Human Development*, 21, 34–64

Hartup, W.W. (1989) 'Social relationships and their developmental significance.' *American Psychologist*, 44, 120–126

Hartup, W.W. (1996) 'Cooperation, close relationships, and cognitive development.' In W.M. Bukowski, A.F. Newcomb and W.W. Hartup (eds) *The Company They Keep: Friendships in Childhood and Adolescence.* Cambridge: Cambridge University Press

Hastie, R., Penrod, S.D. and Pennington, N. (1983) *Inside the Jury.* Cambridge, Mass.: Harvard University Press

Hausenblas, H.A. and Carron A.V. (1999) 'Eating disorder indices and athletes: an integration.' *Journal of Sports & Exercise Psychology*, 21, 230–258

Hayden, R.M. and Allen, C.J. (1984) 'Relationships between aerobic exercise, anxiety, and depression: convergent validation by knowledgeable informants.' *Journal of Sports Medicine*, 24, 69–74

Hazelwood, R. and Douglas, J. (1980) 'The Lust Murderer.' *FBI Law Enforcement Bulletin*, 49(4), 18–22

Health and Safety Executive (2006) Available at http://www.hse.gov.uk/statistics/overall/hssh0506.pdf

Health and Safety Executive (2007) Available at http://www.hse.gov.uk/costs/ill_health_costs/ill_health_costs_intro.asp

Henderson, B.E., Ross, R.K., Judd, H.L. et al. (1985) 'Do regular ovulatory cycles increase breast cancer risk?' *Cancer*, 56, 1206–1208

Henry, F.M. (1941) 'Personality differences in athletes, physical education, and aviation students.' *Psychological Bulletin*, 38, 745

Hill, G. (2001) *A Level Psychology Through Diagrams*. Oxford: Oxford University Press

Hiroto, D. and Seligman, M. (1975) 'Generality of learnt helplessness in man.' *Journal of Personality and Social Psychology*, 31, 311–327

Holahan, C. and Sears, R. (1995) *The Gifted Group in Later Maturity*. Standford, CA: Standford University Press

Hollander, E.P. (1971) *Principles and Methods of Social Psychology* (2nd edition). New York: Oxford University Press

Holmes, T.H. and Rahe, R.H. (1967) 'The Social Readjustment Rating Scale.' *Journal of Psychosomatic Research*, 11, 213–218

Horne, J.A. and Staff, C.H. (1983) 'Exercise and sleep: body heating effects.' *Sleep*, 6, 36–46

Howard League for Penal Reform (2007) Available from http://www.howardleague.org/

Hull, C.L. (1943) *Principles of Behavior*. New York: Appleton-Century-Crofts

Hull, C.L. (1951) *Essentials of Behavior*. New Haven, CT: Yale University Press

Hussman, B.F. (1969) *Sport and Personality Dynamics*. Durham, N.C.: NCPEAM Proceedings

Hutt, S.J., Tyler, C., Hutt, C. and Christopherson, H. (1989) *Play Exploration and Learning*. London: Routledge

Inbau, F., Reid, J. and Buckley, J. (1986) *Criminal Interrogation and Confessions* (3rd edition). Baltimore: Williams & Wilkins

Inbau, F.E. and Reid, J.E. (1962) *Criminal Interrogation and Confessions*. Baltimore: Williams & Wilkins

Ireland, J. (2000) 'Do anger management courses work?' *Forensic Updates*, 63, 12–16

Jahoda, M. (1958) *Current Concepts of Positive Mental Health*. New York: Basic Books

James, W.H., Woodruff, A.B. and Werner, W. (1965) 'Effect of internal and external control upon changes in smoking behavior.' *Journal of Consulting Psychology*, 29, 184–186

Janis, I. and Feshbeck, S. (1953) 'Effects of fear arousal.' *Journal of Abnormal and Social Psychology*, 48, 78–92

Johansson, G. et al. (1978) 'Social psychological and neuroendocrine stress reactions in highly mechanised work.' *Ergonomics*, 21(8), 583–599

Jones, M.C. (1924) 'A laboratory study of fear: the case of Peter.' *Pedagogical Seminary*, 31, 308–315

Jones, S. and Myhill, D. (2004) 'Troublesome boys and compliant girls: gender identity and perceptions of achievement and underachievement.' *British Journal of Sociology of Education*, 25(5), 547–561

Judd, J. (1998) 'Earlier start to lessons leaves British children behind.' *Independent* 28 January, p.13

Kane, J., Rifkin, A., Quitkin, F., Devdutt, N. and Ramos-Lorenzi, J. (1982) 'Fluphenazine vs placebo in patients with remitted, acute first-episode schizophrenia.' *Archives of General Psychiatry*, 39, 70–3

Kanner, A.D., Coyne, J., Schaefer, C. and Lazarus, R. (1981) 'Comparison of two modes of stress measurement.' *Journal of Behavioural Medicine*, 4(1)

Karp, J. and Frank, E. (1995) 'Combination therapy and the depressed woman.' *Depression*, 3, 91–98

Kassin, S.M. and Wrightsman, L.S. (eds) (1985) *The Psychology of Evidence and Trial Procedure*. London: Sage, pp.67–94

Kendell, R. (1975) *The Role of Diagnosis in Psychiatry*. Oxford: Blackwell

Kety, S. (1975) 'Progress toward an understanding of the biological subtraes of schizophrenia.' In R.R. Fieve et al., *Genetic Research in Psychiatry*. Baltimore: Johns Hopkins University Press, pp.15–26

Klein, R. (1996) 'A steering hand away from trouble.' *Times Educational Supplement*, 12 January, p.5

Kleinman, R., Murphy, J., Little, M., Pagano, M., Wehler, C., Regal, K. and Jellinek, M. (1998) 'Hunger in children in the United States: potential behavioural and emotional correlates.' *Paediatrics*, 101, e3

Kohlberg, L. (1963) 'The development of children's orientations towards a moral order: Sequence in the development of moral thought.' *Human Development*, 6, 11–13

Kohlberg, L. (1978) Revisions in the theory and practice of moral development. *Directions for Child Development*, 2, 83–8

Kohlberg, L. (1981) *The Philosophy of Moral Development*. New York: Harper & Row

Krathwohl, D.R. (2002) A revision of Bloom's Taxonomy: an overview. *Theory into Practice*, 41(4), 212–218

Kroll, W. and Crenshaw, W. (1970) 'Multivariate personality profile analysis of four athletic groups.' In G. Kenyon (ed.) *Contemporary Psychology of Sport*. Chicago, IL: Chicago Athletic Institute, pp.97–106

Kuklinski, M.R. and Weistein, R.S. (2001) 'Classroom and development differences in a path model of teacher expectancy effects.' *Child Development*, 72, 1554–1578

Lacey, J.J. (1967) 'Somatic response patterning and stress: Some revisions of activation theory.' In M.H. Appley and R. Trumbell (eds) *Psychological Stress: Issues in Research*. New York: Appleton-Century-Crofts

Ladson-Billings, G. (1995) 'But that is just good teaching: the case for culturally relevant pedagogy.' *Theory into Practice*, 34, 161–165

Latane, B. et al. (1979) 'Many hands make light work: the causes and consequences of social loafing.' *Journal of Personality and Social Psychology*, 37, 822–832

Leibowitz, M.R. et al. (1988) 'Pharmacotherapy of social phobia: an interim report of a placebo-controlled comparison of phenelzine and atenolol.' *Journal of Clinical Psychiatry*, 49, 252–258

Leith, L.M. and Taylor, A.H. (1990) 'Psychological aspects of exercise: a decade literature review.' *Journal of Sport Behaviour*, 13, 219–239

Lewin, K., Lippitt, R. and White, R.K. (1939) 'Patterns of aggressive behaviour in experimentally created "social climates".' *Journal of Social Psychology*, 10, 271–299

Lewinsohn, P., Clark, G., Hops, H. and Andres, J. (1990) 'Cognitive behavioural treatments for depressed adolescents.' *Behaviour Therapy*, 21, 385–401

Lewis, A. and Norwich, B.(2004) *Special Teaching for Special Children: Pedagogies of Inclusion (Inclusive Education)*. Maidenhead: Open University Press

Ley, P. et al. (1973) 'A method for increasing patients' recall of information presented by doctors.' *Psychological Medicine*, 3(2), 217–220

Liberman, R.P. (1982) 'Assessment of social skills.' *Schizophrenia Bulletin*, 8(1), 82–84

Loftus, E.F. and Palmer, J.C. (1974) 'Reconstruction of automobile destruction: an example of the interaction between language and memory.' *Journal of Verbal Learning and Verbal Behaviour*, 13, 585–589

Loftus, E.F. and Palmer, J.C. (1974) *Reconstruction of Automobile Destruction: An Example of the Interaction between Language and Memory* (2nd edition). Oxford: Oxford University Press, pp.585–589

Loftus, E.F., Loftus, G.R., and Messo, J. (1987) 'Some facts about weapon focus.' *Journal of Law and Human Behaviour*, 11(1)

Lombroso, C. (1876) *L'Uomo Delinquente*. Milan: Hoepli

Lorenz, K.Z. (1966) *On Aggression*. London: Methuen

Lox, C.L., McAuley, E. and Tucker, R.S. (1995) 'Exercise as an intervention for enhancing subjective well-being in an HIV–1 population.' *Journal of Sport and Exercise Psychology*, 17, 345–362

Lustman, P. et al. (2000) 'Fluoxetine for depression in diabetes: a randomized double-blind placebo controlled trial.' *Diabetes Care*, 23(5), 618–623

Mac an Ghaill, M. (1988) *Young, Gifted and Black: Student Teacher Relations in the Schooling of Black Youth*. Milton Keynes: Open University

Maganaris, C.N., Collins, D. and Sharp, M. (2000) 'Expectancy effect and strength training: do steroids make a difference?' *The Sports Psychologist*, 14, 272–278

Maher, B.A. (1974) 'Delusional thinking and perceptual disorder.' *Journal of Individual* Psychology, 30(1), 98–113

Mair, G. and May, C. (1997) 'Offenders on Probation.' Home Office Research study 167. London: Home Office

Mann, S., Vrij, A. and Bull, R. (2004) 'Detecting true lies: police officers' ability to detect suspects' lies.' *Journal of Applied Psychology*, 89(1), 137–149

Marsh, H.W. and Pearl, N.D. (1988) 'Competitive and co-operative physical fitness training programs for girls: effects on physical fitness and multidimensional self-concepts.' *Journal of Sports and Exercise Psychology*, 10, 390–470

Martens, R. (1977) *Sport Competition Anxiety Test*. Champaign, IL: Human Kinetics

Martens, R., Burton, D., Vealey, R., Bump, L. and Smith, D. (1990) 'The development of the Competitive State Anxiety Inventory-2 (CSAI-2).' In R. Martens, R.S. Vealey and D. Burton (eds) *Competitive Anxiety in Sport*. Champaign, IL: Human Kinetics, pp.117–190

Maslow, A.H. (1954) *Motivation and Personality*. New York: Harper

McCarthy, B. (1990) 'Using the 4MAT system to bring learning styles to schools.' *Educational Leadership*, 48(2), 31–37

McClelland, D.C., Atkinson, J.W., Clark, R.A. and Lowell, E.L. (1953) *The Achievement Motive*. Princeton: Van Nostrand

McGrath, T., Tsui, E., Humphries, S. and Yule, W. (1990) 'Successful treatment of a noise phobia in a nine-year-old girl with systematic desensitisation in vivo.' *Educational Psychology*, 10(1), 79–83

McGuire, J. (2000) 'An introduction to theory and research: cognitive-behavioural approaches.' HM Inspectorate of Probation Report. London: Home Office

McNair, D.M., Lorr, M. and Droppleman, L.F. (1971) *Manual for the Profile of Mood States*. San Diego, CA: Educational and Industrial Testing Services

Medical Research Council Working Party on Mild to Moderate Hypertension (1981) 'Adverse reactions to bendrofluazide and propranolol for the treatment of mild hypertension.' *Lancet*, 2, 539–543

Meichenbaum, D. (1972) 'Cognitive modification of test-anxious college students.' *Journal of Consulting and Clinical Psychology*, 39, 370–380

Mental Health Act Commission (2005) Count Me In Census available at http://www.mhac.org.uk/census2006/docs/FINAL_web_pdf_censusreport_5th_1-0.pdf

Merrett, F. and Wheldall, K. (1990) *Positive Teaching in the Primary School*. London: Paul Chapman

Milgram, S. (1974) *Obedience to Authority: An Experimental View*. London: Harper Collins

Miller, A. (1997) *Business and Community Mentoring in Schools*. Research Report no. 43. London: Department for Education and Employment

Miller, T.M., Linke, J.G. and Linke, R.A. (1980) 'Survey of body image, weight and diet of college students.' *Journal of American Dietetic Association*, 77, 561–566

Moore, T., Zammit, S., Lingford-Hughes, A., Barnes, T., Jones, P., Burke, M. and Lewis, G. (2007) 'Cannabis use and risk of psychotic or affective mental health outcomes: a systematic review.' *Lancet*; 370, 319–328

Morgan, W.P. (1979) 'Prediction of performance in athletics.' In P. Klavora and J.V. Daniel (eds) *Coach, Athlete and the Sport Psychologist*. Toronto: University of Toronto, pp.173–186

Morgan W. (1980) 'Sport personology: the credulous-skeptical argument in perspective.' In W.F. Straub (ed.) *Sport Psychology: An Analysis of Athletic Behaviour* (2nd edition). Ithaca, NY: Mouvement Publications, pp.330–339

Morgan, W.P. and Johnson, R.W. (1978) 'Personality correlates of successful and unsuccessful oarsmen.' *International Journal of Sports Psychology*, 11, 38–49

Morgan, W.P. and Pollock, M.C. (1977) 'Psychological characterization of the elite distance runner.' *Annals of the New York Academy of Sciences*, 301, 382–405

Morgan, W.P., Brown, D.R., Raglin, J.S., O'Connor, P.J. and Ellickson, K.S. (1987) 'Psychological of overtraining and staleness.' *British Journal of Sports Medicine*, 21, 107–114

Moscovici, S. (1985) 'Social influence and conformity.' In G. Lindzey and E. Aronson (eds) *Handbook of Social Psychology* (3rd edition). New York: Random House

Mougin, C., Henriet, M.T., Baulay, A., Haton, D., Berthelay, S. and Gaillard, R.G. (1988) 'Plasma levels of beta-endorphin and gonadotrophins in male athletes after an international nordic ski race.' *European Journal of Applied Physiology*, 57(4), 425–429

Murdoch, B.B. (1962) 'The serial position effect of free recall.' *Journal of Experimental Psychology*, 64, 482–428

Murray, H.A. (1938) *Explorations in Personality*. New York: Oxford University Press

Nagle, F.J., Morgan, W.P., Hellickson, R.O., Serfass, R.C. and Alexander, J.P. (1975) 'Spotting success traits in Olympic contenders.' *Physician Sportsmed*, 3, 31–34

Nemeth, C. and Wachtler, J. (1974) 'Creating the perceptions of consistency and confidence: a necessary condition for minority influence.' *Sociometry*, 37, 529–540

NICE (2007) Available at http://www.nice.org.uk/nicemedia/pdf/CG23publicinfoamended.pdf

Noddings, N. (2005) *Happiness and Education*. Cambridge: Cambridge University Press

Nye, B., Hedges, L.V. and Konstantopoulos, S. (2004) 'Do minorities experience lasting benefits from small classes?' *Journal of Educational* Research, 98(2), 94–100

Office for National Statistics (2000) Available at http://www.statistics.gov.uk/cci/nugget.asp?id=1333

Ohman, A., Erixon, G. and Lofberg, I. (1975) 'Phobias and preparedness.' *Journal of Abnormal Psychology*, 84

Olweus, D. (1993) *Bullying at School*. Oxford: Blackwell

Oruc, L., Ceric, I. and Loga, S. (1998) 'Genetics of mood disorders – an overview. Part one.' *Medical Archives*, 52(2), 107–112

Ost, L.G. and Westling, B.E. (1995) 'Applied relaxation vs cognitive behaviour therapy in the treatment of panic disorder.' *Behaviour Research and Therapy*, 33, 145–158

Oxendine, J.B. (1980) 'Emotional arousal and motor performance.' *Quest*, 13, 23–30

Parfitt, C.G. and Hardy, L. (1987) 'Further evidence for the differential effects of competitive anxiety upon a number of cognitive and motor sub-components.' *Journal of Sports Science*, 5, 62–72

Paul, G.L. and Lentz, R.J (1977) *Psychosocial Treatment of Chronic Mental Patients*. Cambridge, Mass.: Harvard University Press

Pennington, N. and Hastie, R. (1988) 'Explanation-based decision making: effects of memory structure on judgement.' *Journal of Experimental Psychology, Learning and Memory and Cognition*, 14(3), 521–533

Penrod, S. and Cutler, B. (1995) 'Witness confidence and witness accuracy: assessing their forensic relation.' *Psychology, Public Policy and Law*, 1(4), 817–845

Peterson, C. and Seligman, M.E.P. (1985) 'The learned helplessness model of depression: Current status of theory and research.' In E.E. Beckman and W.R. Leber (eds) *Handbook of Depression: Treatment, Assessment and Research*. Homewood, IL: Dorsey, pp.914–939

Petrides, K.V., Frederickson, N. and Furnham, A. (2004) 'The role of trait emotional intelligence in academic performance and deviant behaviour at school.' *Personality and Individual Differences*, 36, 277–293

Piacentini, M., Meeusen, R., Buyse, L., De Schutter, G., and De Meirleir, K., (1986) 'Hormonal responses during prolonged exercise are influenced by a selective DA/NA reuptake inhibitor.' *British Journal of Sports Medicine*, 38(2), 129–133

Piaget, J. (1932) *The Moral Judgment of the Child*. London: Kegan Paul, Trench, Trubner

Pickel, K.L. (1995) 'Inducing jurors to disregard inadmissible evidence: a legal explanation does not help.' *Law and Human Behaviour*, 19(4)

Piliavin, I.M., Rodin, J.A. and Piliavin, J. (1969) 'Good Samaritanism: an underground phenomenon?' *Journal of Personality and Social Psychology*, 13, 289–299

Platt, G. (2001) 'NLP – Neuro-Linguistic Programming or No Longer Plausible.' *Training Journal*, May, 10–15

Pokorak, J.J. (1998) 'Probing the capital prosecutor's perspective: race of the discretionary actors', *Cornell Law Review*, 83(6), 1811–1120.

Prentice, D.A., and Miller, D.T. (eds.) (1990) *Cultural Divides. Understanding and Overcoming Group Conflict*. New York: Russell Sage Foundation

Price W.H., Strong, J.A., Whatmore, P.B. and McClemont, W.F. (1966) 'Criminal patients with XYY sex-chromosome complement.' *Lancet*, 1(7437), 565–566

Prison Reform Trust (2007) Available at http://www.prisonreformtrust.org.uk/

Public Library of Science (2008) Available at http://www.plos.org/cms/node/335 or

Raine, A. (2002) 'The role of prefrontal deficits, low autonomic arousal and early health factors in the development of antisocial and aggressive behaviour in children.' *Journal of Child Psychology and Psychiatry*, 43(4), 417–434

Raudenbush, S. (1984) 'Magnitude of teacher expectancy effects on pupils' IQ as a function of the credibility of expectancy induction: A synthesis of findings from 18 experiments.' *Journal of Educational Psychology*, 6, 85–97

Reicher, S.D. and Haslam, S.A. (2006) 'Rethinking the psychology of tyranny: The BBC Prison Study.' *British Journal of Social Psychology*, 45, 1–40

Renfrow, N.E. and Bolton, B. (1979) 'Personality characteristics associated with aerobic exercise in adult males.' *Journal of Personality Assessment*, 43, 261–266

Rezler, A.G. and Rezmovic, V. (1981) 'The Learning Inventory.' *Journal of Allied Health*, 10(1), 28–34

Riding, R.J. and Raynor, S.G. (1998) *Cognitive Styles and Learning Strategies: Understanding Style Differences in Learning and Behaviour*. London: David Fulton

Riley, J. (1995) 'The relationship between adjustment to school and success in reading by the end of the reception year.' *Early Child Development and Care*, 114, 25–38

Rogers, C.R. (1997) *Carl Rogers on Personal Power*. New York: Delacorte Press

Rogers, C.R. and Freiberg, H.J. (1994) *Freedom to Learn*. Columbus, OH: Merrill/Macmillan

Rose, C. (1985) *Accelerated Learning*. New York: Dell

Rose, J. (2006) *Independent Review of the Teaching of Early Reading*. Available at http://www.standards.dfes.gov.uk/phonics/report.pdf

Rosenhan, D.L. (1973) 'On being sane in insane places.' *Science*, 179(70), 250–258

Rosenhan, D.L. and Seligman, M.E.P. (1995) *Abnormal Psychology* (3rd edition). New York: Norton

Rosenstock, I. (1974) 'Historical origins of the Health Belief Model.' *Health Education Monographs*, 2(4)

Rosenthal, R. and Jacobsen, L. (1968) *Pygmalion in the Classroom*. New York: Holt, Rinehart & Winston

Ross, D., Hopkins, S., Hanson, E., Lindsay, R.C.L., Hazen, K. and Eslinger T. (1994) 'The impact of protective shields and videotape testimony on conviction rates in a simulated trial of child sexual abuse.' *Law and Human Behaviour*, 18(5)

Rotter, J. (1966) 'Generalized expectancies for internal versus external control of reinforcement.' *Psychological Monographs*, 80(1)

Rotter, J.B. (1966) 'Generalised expectancies for internal versus external control of reinforcement.' *Psychological Monographs*, 30(1), 1–26

Royal Society for the Prevention of Accidents (2007) Available at http://www.rospa.com/roadsafety/advice/driving/info/drinking_and_driving_policy_paper_2007.pdf

Rubie-Davies, C., Hattie, J. and Hamilton, R. (2006) 'Expecting the best for students: teacher expectations and academic outcomes.' *British Journal of Educational Psychology*, 76(3), 429–444

Ryan, R.M. and Deci, E.L. (2000) 'Self-determination theory and the facilitation of intrinsic motivation, social development, and well-being.' *American Psychologist*, 55, 68–78

Ryckman, R.M., Robbins, M.A., Thornton, B. and Cantrell, P. (1982) 'Development and validation of a Physical Self-Efficacy Scale.' *Journal of Personality and Social Psychology*, 42, 891–900

Samuel, J. and Bryant, P. (1983) 'Asking only one question in the conservation experiment.' *Journal of Child Psychology*, 22(2), 315–318

Schurr, K.T., Ashley, M.A. and Joy, K.L. (1977) 'A multivariate analysis of male athlete characteristics: sport type and success.' *Multivariate Experimental Clinical Research*, 3, 53–68

Schwartz, B. and Barsky, S.F. (1977) 'The Home Advantage.' *Social Forces*, 55, 641–661

Schweihart, L. (2000) 'The High/Scope Perry Preschool Study: a case study in random assignment.' *Evaluation and Research in Education*, 14(3), 136–147

Schweihart, L. and Weikart, D. (1993) *Significant Benefits: The High/Scope Perry Preschool Study through Age 27*. Ypsilanti, MI: High/Scope Press

Scottish Government (2007) Available at http://www.scotland.gov.uk/Publications/2007/08/03114725/5

Seligman, M.E.P. (1975) *Helplessness: On Depression, Development and Death*. San Francisco: W.H. Freeman

Seligman, M.E.P. (1972) 'Phobias and preparedness.' In M.E.P. Seligman and J.L. Hager (eds) *Biological Boundaries of Learning*. New York: Appleton-Century-Crofts

Selye, H. (1936) 'A syndrome produced by diverse noxious agents.' *Nature*, 138, 32

Sensky, T., Turkington, D., Kingdon, D. et al. (2000) 'A randomized controlled trial of cognitive–behavioural therapy for persistent symptoms in schizophrenia resistant to medication.' *Archives of General Psychiatry*, 57, 165–172

Sherman, L.W. and Strang, H. (2007) *Restorative Justice – the Evidence*. London: Smith Institute

Simons, L.A., Levis, G. and Simons, J. (1996) 'Apparent discontinuation rates in patients prescribed lipid-lowering drugs.' *Medical Journal of Australia*, 164, 208–211

Sinha, P., Balas, B., Ostrovsky, Y. and Russell, R. (2006) 'Face recognition by humans: nineteen results all computer vision researchers should know about.' *Proceedings of the* IEEE, 94(11)

Skinner, B.F. (1938) *The Behavior of Organisms*. New York: Appleton-Century-Crofts

Skinner, B.F. (1948) 'Superstition in the pigeon.' *Journal of Experimental Psychology*, 38, 168–172

Skinner, B.F. (1971) *Beyond Freedom and Dignity*. New York: Knopf

Sklar, L.S. and Anisman, H. (1981) 'Stress and cancer.' *Psychological Bulletin*, 3, 369–406

Skoe, E.E.A. (1998) 'The ethic of care: issues in moral development.' In Skoe, E.E.A. and von der Lippe, A.L. (eds) *Personality Development in Adolescence*. London: Routledge

Smith, B. et al. (2002) 'Impacts from repeated mass media campaigns to promote sun protection in Australia.' *Health Promotion International*, 17(1), 51–60

Smith, P.K. and Shu, S. (2000) 'What good schools can do about bullying: findings from a survey in English schools after a decade of research and action.' *Childhood*, 7, 193–212

Smith, R.E., Smoll, F.L. and Curtis, B. (1979) 'Coach effectiveness training: a cognitive-behavioral approach to enhancing relationship skills in youth sports coaches.' *Journal of Sports Psychology*, 1, 59–75

Smith, R.E., Smoll, F.L. and Hunt, E. (1977) 'A system for the behavioural assessment of athletic coaches.' *Research Quarterly for Exercise and Sport*, 48(2), 401–407

Solms, M. and Turnbull, O. (2002) *The Brain and the Inner World: An Introduction to the Neuroscience of Subjective Experience*. New York: Other Press

Sowell, E.R., Thompson, P.M., Holmes, C.J., Jernigan, T.L and Toga, A.W. (1999) 'In vivo evidence for post-adolescent brain maturation in frontal and striatal regions.' *Nature Neuroscience*, 2(10), 859–861

Spence, K.W. (1956) *Behavior Theory and Conditioning*. New Haven, CT: Yale University Press

Spielberger, C.D. (1966) *Anxiety and Behavior*. New York: Academic Press

Spielberger, C.D., Gorsuch, R.L. and Lushene, R.E. (1970) *Manual for the State-Trait Anxiety Inventory*. Palo Alto, CA: Consulting Psychologists Press

Steinberg, H. and Sykes, E.A. (1985) 'Introduction to symposium on endorphins and behavioural processes: a review of literature on endorphins and exercise.' *Pharmacology Biochemistry and Behaviour*, 23, 857–862

Steiner, I.D. (1972) *Group Processes and Productivity*. New York: Academic Press

Stogdill, R.M. (1948) 'Personal factors associated with leadership: survey of literature.' *Journal of Psychology*, 25, 35–71

Strand, S. and Demie, F. (2005) 'English language acquisition and the educational attainment at the end of primary school.' *Educational Studies* 13(3), 275–291

Strand, S., Deary, I.J. and Smith, P. (2006) 'Sex differences in cognitive abilities test scores: a UK national picture.' *British Journal of Educational Psychology*, 76, 463–480

Strecher, V.J., and Rosenstock, I.M. (1997) 'The Health Belief Model.' In K. Glanz, F.M. Lewis and B.K. Rimer (eds) *Health Behavior and Health Education: Theory, Research, and Practice*. San Francisco: Jossey-Bass

Sukhnandan, L. and Lee, B. (1998) *Streaming, Setting and Grouping by Ability*, Slough: NFER

Sutherland, E.H. (1934) *Principles of Criminology*. Chicago: Lippincott

Szasz, T. (1973) *The Second Sin*, New York: Doubleday

Tatum, D. and Herbert, G. (1992) *Bullying: A Positive Response* (2nd edition). Cardiff: Cardiff Institute of Higher Education

Thornton, D. and Reid, R.L. (1982) 'Moral reasoning and types of criminal offence.' *British Journal of Social Psychology*, 21, 231–238

Triplett, N. (1897) 'The dynamogenic factors in pacemaking and competition.' *American Journal of Psychology*, 9, 507–533

Tucker, L. (1983) 'Effects of weight-training on self-concept: a profile of those influenced most.' *Research Quarterly for Exercise & Sport*, 54, 389–397

Tuckman, B.W. (1965) 'Developmental sequences in small groups.' *Psychological Bulletin*, 63, 384–389

Turiel, E. (1998) 'The development of morality.' In W. Damon (series ed.) and N. Eisenberg (vol. ed.) *Handbook of Child Psychology* (5th edition). New York: Wiley

United States Department of Education (2007) *What Works Intervention Report: Reading Recovery*. Available at: http://ies.ed.gov/ncee/wwc/pdf/WWC_Reading_Recovery_031907.pdf

Valentine, J.C., DuBois, D.L. and Cooper, H. (2004) 'The relations between self-beliefs and academic achievement: a systematic review.' *Educational Psychologist*, 39, 111–133

Vallerand, R.J. (1997) 'Towards a hierarchical model of intrinsic and extrinsic motivation.' In M.P. Zanna (ed.) *Advances in Experimental and Social Psychology*, Vol. 29. New York: Academic Press, pp.271–360

Van Geert, P. (1998) 'A dynamic systems model of basic developmental mechanisms: Piaget, Vygotsky and beyond.' *Psychological* Review, 105, 634–677

Vealey, R.S. (1986) 'Conceptualization of sport-confidence and competitive orientation: preliminary investigation and instrument development.' *Journal of Sport Psychology*, 8, 221–246

Vygotsky, L.S. (1962) *Thought and Language*. Cambridge, Mass.: MIT Press

Wainryb, C., Brehl, B.A., and Matwin, S. (2005) 'Being hurt and hurting others: children's narrative accounts and moral judgements of their own interpersonal conflicts.' *Monographs of the Society for Research in Child Development* Serial No. 281, Vol. 70(3)

Walters, G.D. (1992) 'A meta-analysis of the gene-crime relationship.' *Criminology*, 30(4), 595–614

Waterson, L. (2006) 'Inadequate evidence for multiple intelligences, Mozart Effect, and Emotional Intelligence theories.' *Educational Psychologis*, 41(4), 247–255.

Watson, J.B. and Raynor, R. (1920) 'Conditioned emotional reaction.' *Journal of Experimental Psychology*, 3, 1–14

Watt, P. et al. (2003) 'Funhaler Spacer – improving adherence without compromising delivery.' *Archive of Disease in Childhood*, 88(7), 579–582

Waxler-Morrison, N. et al. (1993) 'Effects of social relationship on survival of women with breast cancer.' *Social Science and Medicine*, 33(2), 177–183

Weiner, B. (2000) 'Intrapersonal and interpersonal theories of motivation from an attributional perspective.' *Educational Psychology Review*, 12(1), 1

Wender, P.H., Kety, S.S., Rosenthal, D., Schulsinger, F., Ortmann, J. and Lunde, I. (1986) 'Psychiatric disorders in the biological and adoptive families of adopted individuals with affective disorders.' *Archives of General Psychiatry*, 43(10)

Wentzel, K.R. and Caldwell, K. (1997) 'Friendships, peer acceptance and group membership: Relations to academic achievement in middle school.' *Child Development* 68, 1198–1209

Wheatley, M. (2007) 'Needles help beat drug addiction.' HM Prison Service and Cambridge University Institute of Criminology. Available at www.hmprisonservice.gov.uk/prison information/prisonservicemagazine/

Whelan, S. and Culver, J. (1997) 'Teaching young people how to say No.' *Education and Health*, 15(3), 43–46

Widmer, E.D. and Weiss, C.C. (2000) 'Do older siblings make a difference? The effects of older sibling support and older sibling adjustment on the adjustment of socially disadvantaged adolescents.' *Journal of Research on Adolescence*, 10(1), 1–27

Wikström, P-O. (2003) Findings from the Peterborough Youth Study available at http://www.scopic.ac.uk/documents/Peterborougharticle_000.pdf

Williams, L.R.T. and Parkin, W.A. (1980) 'Personality profiles of three hockey groups.' *International Journal of Sport Psychology*, 11, 113–120

Wilson, V.E., Berger, B.G. and Bird, E.I. (1981) 'Effects of running and of an exercise class on anxiety.' *Perceptual and Motor Skills*, 53, 472–474

Wilson, V.E., Morley, N.C. and Bird, E.I. (1980) 'Mood profiles of marathon runners, joggers and non-exercisers.' *Perceptual and Motor Skills*, 50, 117–118

Wolf, D. and Montgomery, D. (1977) 'Effects of inadmissible evidence and judicial admonishment.' *Journal of Applied Social Psychology*, 53, 14–29

Wood, D., Bruner, J.S. and Ross, G. (1976) 'The role of tutoring in problem-solving.' *Journal of Child Psychology and Psychiatry and Allied Disciplines*, 17, 89–100

Woods, B. (2001) *Psychology in Practice: Sport.* London: Hodder & Stoughton, pp.119–120

World Health Organization (2005) *The ICD-10 Classification of Mental and Behavioural Disorders: Clinical Descriptions and Diagnostic Guidelines: ICD-10.* Geneva: World Health Organization

Wragg, E.C. (1999) *Introduction to Classroom Observation.* London: Routledge

Wyse, D. and Styles, M. (2007) 'Synthetic phonics and the teaching of reading: the debate surrounding England's Rose Report.' *Literacy*, 41(1), 35–42

Yerkes, R.M. and Dodson, J.D. (1908) 'The relationship of strength of stimulus to rapidity of habit formation.' *Journal of Comparative Neurology and Psychology*, 18, 459–482

Yochelson, S. and Samenow, S. (1976) *The Criminal Personality.* New York: Jason Aronson

Younger, M. and Warrington, M. with Gray, J., Rudduck, J., McLellan, R., Bearne, E., Kershner, R. and Bricheno, P. (2005) *Raising Boys' Achievement.* RR 636, Department for Education and Skills

Zajonc, R.B. (1965) 'Social facilitation.' *Science*, 149, 269–274

Zajonc, R.B. and Sales, S.M. (1966) 'Social facilitation of dominant and subordinate responses.' *Journal of Experimental Social Psychology*, 2, 160–168

Zajonc, R.B., Heingartner, A. and Herman, E.M. (1969) 'Social enhancement and impairment of performance in the cockroach.' *Journal of Personality and Social Psychology*, 13, 83–92

Zigler, E. and Phillips, L. (1961) 'Psychiatric diagnosis and symptomology.' *Journal of Abnormal Psychology*, 63, 69–75

Zohar, D. and Marshall, I. (2000) *SQ: Spiritual Intelligence, The Ultimate Intelligence.* London: Bloomsbury

Zubin, J. and Spring, B. (1977) 'Vulnerability: a new view of schizophrenia.' *Journal of Abnormal Psychology*, 86, 103–126

Index

Your Exam Café CD-ROM

In the back of this book you will find an Exam Café CD-ROM. This CD contains advice on study skills, interactive questions to test your knowledge and many more useful features. Load it onto your computer to take a closer look.

Among the files on the CD are editable Microsoft Word documents for you to alter and print off if you wish.

Minimum system requirements:
- Windows 2000, XP Pro or Vista
- Internet Explorer 6 or Firefox 2.0
- Flash Player 8 or higher plug-in
- Pentium III 900 MHZ with 256 Mb RAM

To run your Exam Café CD, insert it into the CD drive of your computer. It should start automatically; if not, please go to My Computer (Computer on Vista), click on the CD drive and double-click on 'start.html'.

If you have difficulties running the CD, or if your copy is not there, please contact the helpdesk number given below.

Software support
For further software support between the hours of 8.30am and 5.00pm (Mon–Fri), please contact:
Tel: 01865 888108
Fax: 01865 314091
Email: software.enquiries@pearson.com